מימיני מיכאל

Essays on Yom Kippur and *Teshuvah*

Michael Scharf
Publication Trust
Yeshiva University Press

מגיד
MAGGID

Rabbi Michael Rosensweig

Mimini Mikhael

מימיני מיכאל

Essays on Yom Kippur and Teshuvah

EDITED BY

Rabbi Avraham Wein

The RIETS Hashkafah Series
Rabbi Daniel Z. Feldman, Series Editor

The Michael Scharf Publication Trust of Yeshiva University Press
Maggid Books

Mimini Mikhael
Essays on Yom Kippur and Teshuvah
First Edition, 2023

Maggid Books
An imprint of Koren Publishers Jerusalem Ltd.

POB 8531, New Milford, CT 06776-8531, USA
& POB 4044, Jerusalem 9104001, Israel
www.korenpub.com

The publication of this book was made possible
through the generous support of *The Jewish Book Trust.*

ISBN 978-1-59264-645-6, *hardcover*

A CIP catalogue record for this title is
available from the British Library

Printed and bound in the United States

עמודי תורה

הרב חיי בן ר׳ אברהם ז״ל

by his loving wife and family
Mrs. Ann Arbesfeld
Dr. Benjamin & Sara Arbesfeld & family
Mr. Eli & Michelle Salig & family
Dr. David Arbesfeld, Pnina Arbesfeld

In honor of our dear parents
Selma and Jacob Dyckman,
and Channa and Steve Wintner.

Ezra and Adena Dyckman

In honor of

הרב מיכאל רוזנצוייג שליט״א

by
The Berman Family, including the following talmidim:
Julius Berman
Zev Berman
Judy Berman
Elie Berman
Josh Berman
Daniel Berman
Shai Berman
Aryeh Berman

מחזקי תורה

לכבוד מורנו ורבנו הרב מיכאל רוזנצוייג שליט"א

We would like to express our heartfelt appreciation for your extraordinary commitment to teaching and spreading Torah for over three decades within our community. Your unwavering dedication to *talmud Torah* and your tireless efforts to impart your vast knowledge and wisdom to your students has had a profound and lasting impact on us, those privileged to have studied with you.

Your remarkable dedication to your students and your steadfast desire to raise their level of learning and *yiras shomayim* is truly inspiring. May we be blessed to continue learning together for many years.

With sincere gratitude and admiration,
the past and present attendees of the Queens Monday Night Shiur:

Dr. Benjy Arbesfeld
Simcha Axelrod
Zev S. Berman
Judy Hecht Berman
Rabbi Julius Berman
Baruch Dov Braun
Ari Clark
Ezra Dyckman
David Eis
Adam Flug
Michael Frank
Michael Gottesman
Dr. David Hurwitz
Jay Lisker
Dr. Zev Maybruch
Larry Rabinovich
Avi Rabinovich
Mayer Rydzinski
Akiva Sacknovitz
Eli Schick
Leon Well
Gerry Zahtz

Dedicated in honor of

מורנו ורבנו

הרב הגאון מיכאל רוזנצווייג שליט"א

whose guidance, encouragement, support, wisdom, and rigor have profoundly impacted the lives of thousands of students and their respective shuls, schools, communities, yeshivot, and batei midrash.

אשרינו שזכינו להתאבק בעפר רגליך ולשתות בצמא את דבריך.

By Rav Rosensweig's shiur assistants:

Rav Assaf Bednarsh
Rav Shalom Rosner
Rav Dr. Moti Novick
Rav Dr. Yosef Kalinsky
Rav Meir Welcher
Rav Avi Robinson
Rav Akiva Block
Rav Yehuda Chanales
Rav Dr. Yaakov Jaffe
Rav Daniel Rosenfeld
Elie Rosenberg
Rav Yehuda Turetsky
Rav Yoni Chambre
Rav Dr. Avi Block
Dr. Oren Wachstock
Rav Dr. Yosef Bronstein
Rav Willie Roth
Rav David Weiss
Rav Dr. Itamar Rosensweig
Rav Robbie Schrier
Rav Shua Katz
Rav Isaac Shulman
Rav Avraham Wein
Rav Avrumi Schonbrun
Rav Josh Kaufman
Rav Asher Finkelstein
Eitan Kaszovitz
Josh Appel

Dear Rabbi Rosensweig,

On behalf of the Fifth Avenue Synaoguge, we would like to congratulate you on the publication of this new *sefer, Mimini Mikhael.*

Thank you for your extraordinary dedication to teach a weekly Tuesday evening class at our synagogue for the past two-plus decades. Your brilliance and sterling character have left an indelible impression on all of us who have had the pleasure of learning with you.

We wish you continued success in all your future endeavors, and we look forward to learning from you at our synagogue for many years to come.

With gratitude and admiration,

Rabbi Sol Roth, Rabbi Emeritus
Cantor Joseph Malovany, Senior Cantor Emeritus
J. Ezra Merkin, Honorary President
Jacob D Gold, President
Larry Present, Trustee
Alan Harris, FAS Member
Joseph Guttman, FAS Member
Andrew Lowinger, FAS Member
Jacob Plitman, FAS Member
David Present, FAS Member
Henry Wollman, FAS Member

תומכי תורה

בהערכה *and in honor of*

Rabbi Michael Rosensweig

Terry and Gail Novetsky

With much gratitude and appreciation to

Rav Michael Rosensweig

For his many years of devotion in teaching Torah and its values – thirty-two years (and counting) for the Tuesday morning shiur.

Barbara and Simcha Hochman

Dear Rabbi Rosensweig,

Mazal tov on the publication of *Mimini Mikhael*!

Marilyn and I would like to thank you for always being there for our family yahrzeits.

You have given so graciously of your time to give *shiurim* at Congregation Rinat Yisrael, Teaneck, NJ, twice each year, as we marked our fathers' yahrzeits in the spring, and our mothers' yahrzeits in Elul.

We continue to benefit from your Torah through your two *talmidim*, Rabbi Schrier and Rabbi Strauchler, who are now rabbinic leaders at Congregation Bnai Yeshurun and Congregation Rinat Yisrael, respectively.

לעילוי נשמת

דוד אריה הכהן (י״א בניסן תשכ״ו)
ורחל בת הרב שלמה יקותיאל זלמן (כ״א באלול תשנ״ז)

לעילוי נשמת

יעקב שמואל בן משה דוד אריה (כ״ב באייר תש״ס)
ולאה בת משה (כ׳ באלול תשע״ב)

Wishing you continued success in your efforts to be *marbitz Torah*!

Dr. Joseph and Marilyn Solomon Bench

Dear Rabbi and Rebbetzin Rosensweig,

We are so proud to have learned from you in YU/Stern and beyond. We will forever cherish the time we have spent with you, and we are always yearning for more. Your tireless efforts on behalf of your students and the community at large are amazing and inspiring. We love you, and may Hashem give you the strength and wisdom to keep proliferating Torah through speaking and writing עד מאה ועשרים.

A Grateful Talmid

David and Talia Eis

*In loving memory of our grandparents,
whose dedication to a Torah life continues to inspire us.*

Joseph K. Miller
יוסף בן אהרן שמואל הי״ד

William T. and Edith Steinlauf
טרייטל זאב בן ברוך ז״ל ורכל בת ירמיהו ז״ל

Philip and Geraldine Eis
פנחס בן יעקב אשר ז״ל וגולדה בת ישראל דוד ז״ל

Rabbi Arnold B. Marans
הרב אברהם דב בן אהרן ז״ל

Li'iluy nishmas

Rabbi Dr. Jacob Reiner z"l,

who, along with his dear friend and colleague Rabbi Dr. Berel Rosensweig z"l, shaped countless lives in his role as both a rabbi and educator. We are so fortunate to have Rav Rosensweig as our Rebbe and to continue this bond through the generations.

Elisheva and Ariel Reiner

Daniel and Hindy Lifshitz
In memory of our grandparents

Moshe and Tzippora Lifshitz

Isaac and Bette Einhorn

Aaron Yitzchak and Sonia Bronstein

Yisrael Gershon and Perel Ruck

Dr. and Mrs. Gerald Zahtz
in memory of his mother

מאשה בת הרב אברהם שלמה ז״ל

Masha Zahtz Gellman z"l

נודבים

Sam and Yehudit Ash

Rabbi Dovid S. Asher, Keneseth Beth Israel – Richmond, VA

Henchy and Jerome Balsam

Shonnie and Yoni Chambre

Chaya and Daniel Fridman

Lynn and Aaron Kraft

Carol and Tuvia Lazar

Congregation Bnai Yeshurun:
Rabbi Elliot Schrier, Rabbi Ari Zahtz, and Rabbi Yosef Weinberger

Rav Aryeh Stechler and Heichal Hatorah

Aryeh and Shoshana Sova

Miriam and Adam Steiner

Nehama and Lawrence Teitelman

Rabbi Dovid Zirkind and Riverdale Jewish Center

Contents

YOM KIPPUR

Foreword

It is with tremendous joy that we present this exceptional volume by Rabbi Dr. Michael Rosensweig *shlit"a* on *teshuvah* and the period of the High Holy Days to our esteemed readers. Rabbi Rosensweig is renowned for his perspicacious insights and breathtaking analysis in all areas of Torah study. Multiple generations of students have merited to study at his feet, and his *shiur* at Yeshiva University/RIETS boasts an abundant and outstanding student base. This book captures his remarkable ability to engage, expound upon, and elucidate deep ideas in Jewish thought, Jewish law, and Talmudic exposition.

R. Joseph B. Soloveitchik *zt"l* would refer to the *teshuvah* process, which is a centerpiece of this volume, as a personality transformation (see Rambam, *Hilkhot Teshuvah* 2:4). I vividly remember the Rav likening the *teshuvah* experience to that of a boy who, against his father's instructions, throws a ball against a window of his house, causing the window to break, and then, after a period of estrangement, comes weeping to his father and declares, "I am not the same boy who broke the window! I am a different person now." Through a proper understanding and execution of *teshuvah,* we "grow up" over the course of a lifetime and continuously transform ourselves religiously, emotionally, and intellectually.

The Rambam (*Moreh Nevukhim* 3:17–18) discusses how the degree of an individual's Divine Providence is based on intellectual achievement; the higher one's intellectual plane, the closer his relationship with the Creator. Since the foundation of our ability to cleave to Hashem is the study and fulfillment of the words of the Torah (see *Hilkhot Teshuvah* 10:3–6), it seems appropriate to understand this statement of the Rambam in that context. Indeed, the Rambam (*Moreh Nevukhim*, ibid.) specifically relates intellectual perfection to one's level of piety. Through studying Torah on a high plane of intellectual sophistication, we strengthen our devotion and connection to the Almighty. This is the mandate articulated by our Sages: "*Tiheyu amelim ba-Torah*," toil mightily in understanding Torah (see, e.g., Rashi, *Vayikra* 26:3).

Rabbi Rosensweig is a paradigm of this ideal. Each of his ideas is meticulously developed through a careful analysis of source materials, comparisons with other texts, and multi-layered explanations rich in nuance, meaning, and purpose. As we seek to elevate ourselves through the *teshuvah* process, Rabbi Rosensweig enables us to access and develop our higher selves and move to a loftier plane of intellectual existence, suffused with the spiritual grandeur of the Torah and concomitantly a greater closeness to the Divine.

We are enormously indebted to Rabbi Rosensweig for writing this transformative treatise, and we look forward to many more of his contributions in the future. Our *yeshiva* and our community are truly enriched to have Rabbi Rosensweig in our midst to enlighten, elevate, and ennoble us in the service of Hashem.

We thank Rabbi Daniel Feldman for continuing his wonderful work as the Executive Editor of the RIETS Press, Avraham Wein for his superb editing in connection with this volume, and the RIETS leadership team of Rabbi Dr. Ari Berman, President of YU/RIETS, and Rabbi Menachem Penner, Dean of RIETS, for their dedication to the RIETS Press and to stellar Torah education for our community.

Yona Reiss
Director, RIETS Press

Editor's Preface

Every Sukkot, *mori ve-rabbi* Rav Rosensweig hosts a *simhat beit ha-sho'evah* in his family's *sukkah*. Each student shares a substantive *dvar Torah,* which R. Rosensweig subsequently comments on. One year, fittingly, I discussed the mitzvah of *kabbalat penei rabbo ba-regel* (the obligation to visit one's primary *rebbi* on the festivals). While some commentators understand the obligation as an opportunity to engage in Yom Tov-related Torah learning or a way to sanctify these holy days, Rambam adopts a different stance. Instead of including this *halakhah* in *Hilkhot Yom Tov,* he places it in *Hilkhot Talmud Torah* (5:7), in the section detailing the laws of honoring one's primary *rebbi.* Additionally, he links this mitzvah with the obligation of *amidah lifnei rabbo* (standing before one's *rebbi*). Clearly, Rambam views this mitzvah as an expression of one's more general obligation to honor his *rebbi.*

I noted in my *dvar Torah* that I remained puzzled by the underlying logic of Rambam's position. What is it about Yom Tov that prompts this specific expression of *kevod rabbo*? Rav Rosensweig answered that Yom Tov is a natural opportunity to express *kevod rabbo* because the *mo'adim* trigger a sense of nostalgia and appreciation for one's *rebbi.* It would thus be inconceivable and even inappropriate to fail to express *kavod* to someone who, through his teachings, enhanced one's entire experience of the *hag* to such a degree.

Rav Rosensweig shared that this obligation is a particularly special one for him, as he experienced this feeling each *hag* with his own *rebbi*, R. Joseph B. Soloveitchik. Although the Rav's *shiur* rarely deviated from discussing the *masekhet* being studied, prior to a *hag*, he delivered a *shiur* relating to the *hag*, and this, Rav Rosensweig remarked, continues to contribute immense meaning and perspective to the *hag* for him each year.

This explanation resonated deeply with me then and even more so now. My own Yom Tov experiences have been transformed by and are inextricably linked to the profound ideas Rav Rosensweig developed in his *shiurim* on the *mo'adim*, many of which appear in this book. My hope is that readers of this volume will enjoy a similar enrichment of their Yom Tov experiences.

I would like to make a few brief comments concerning Rav Rosensweig's methodology that may assist the reader in their journey through this *sefer*. The chapters of this volume clearly display many of the hallmark elements of the Brisker method of Talmudic study prominently found in the works of Rav Rosensweig's primary *rebbe'im* – R. Soloveitchik and especially R. Aharon Lichtenstein. These include a heavy focus on Rambam's positions, analysis of the underlying conceptual basis of the varying opinions on each topic, and precise conceptual classifications. Like R. Lichtenstein, Rav Rosensweig presents an extremely thorough treatment of each *sugya* and employs an extensive library of commentaries, especially *Rishonim*.

However, there are unique features of Rav Rosensweig's method of study that are worthy of mention. The following two are most salient. First, the reader will notice repeating key sources and themes throughout the chapters. While some of the repetition is undoubtedly an outgrowth of natural overlap between topics and the origin of these chapters as independent *shiurim*, this phenomenon primarily derives from and exemplifies a critical aspect of Rav Rosensweig's style of learning: identifying overarching themes and *hakirot* (conceptual distinctions) that interweave many individual topics into one larger *sugya*. This more sweeping focus of study, a meta-*sugya*, allows many standalone *sugyot* to coalesce under a broader topic because of their common network logic. This valuable next step in the development of the Brisker method of study is clearly demonstrated in this *sefer*.

Second, as previously mentioned, although Rav Rosensweig seeks to develop larger fundamental themes within these meta-topics, simultaneously the reader will notice an intense focus on seemingly minor details in these chapters. These two elements of his style not only do not contradict each other but also work in tandem. The narrow details help contribute to building the broader conceptual framework, but once the macroscopic themes have been developed, they allow for a deeper appreciation of the nuances and details of the minutiae within the related *halakhot*.

It has been a tremendous *zekhut* to work on this *sefer* and to be able to experience Rav Rosensweig's breadth of knowledge, depth of insight, and intellectual integrity so closely. In particular, I would like to thank my fellow *talmidim* who helped with various parts of bringing this *sefer* to print. Special recognition is warranted for two of Rav Rosensweig's outstanding *talmidim* who were particularly helpful during the writing and editing process: Rabbis Noach Goldstein and Yehoshua Katz.

May Hashem bless Rav Rosensweig and his wife with continued health and *nahat* from their children and grandchildren, *banim* who are his *talmidim* and *talmidim* who are like *banim*, and may the broader Torah community continue to benefit from his *harbatzat Torah* for many years to come.

Avraham Wein
Tevet 5783

Introduction

מימיני מיכאל: Essays on Yom Kippur and *Teshuvah*

"Mikra kodesh" – the most ubiquitous and consequential term employed in the Torah's depiction of the *mo'adim* (*Shemot* 12:16; *Vayikra* 23:1–44; *Bamidbar* 28:18, 25, 26, 29:1, 7, 12) – is somewhat obscure and perhaps even intentionally ambiguous, a testament to the multidimensional character of the *mo'adim*. It is unsurprising that the phrase stimulated vigorous exegesis, producing a wide range of different interpretations, each underscoring an important theme in festival commemoration.

While many commentators focus on the content and modes of observance on these special days – prayers, festive meals, formal attire, and the like[1] – Targum Onkelos and Targum Yonatan accentuate the very magnitude and character of these singular and sanctified days, rendering "*mikra kodesh*" as "מערע קדיש," a holy event. Ramban posits that the conception of "*mikra kodesh*" as a "*me'ora*" was inspired by the verse "*asher yikra etkhem be-aharit ha-yamim*" (*Bereishit* 49:1), which alludes to the pivotal, transformative experiences that will define the end of days.

1. See *Sifra* 12:4; *Sifrei, Pinehas* 147; Rashi, *Vayikra* 23:27; Rashi and Tosafot, *Shevuot* 13a, s.v. *lo kera'o*; Rashi, *Keritut* 7a, s.v. *mikra kodesh*; Ramban, *Vayikra* 23:2.

A "*me'ora*" is significantly more than an occurrence, anniversary, or even experience that affords opportunity to express thanks or to revisit the spiritual implications of past events. The term conveys a perspective that perceives singular spiritual experiences in our national history as transformative milestones, times invested with inherent sanctity (*kedushat ha-yom*), forces that shape our worldview and define and reinforce core halakhic principles and values. Indeed, the unique festival recitations in *tefillah* and *Birkat ha-Mazon* are referred to as "*mei-ein ha-me'ora*."

Elsewhere, Onkelos equates the verb form of *me'ora*, "דערעית," with "פגשתי," signaling a consequential encounter. This association further projects *mikra kodesh* as a memorable spiritual or divine encounter.[2] This supports the complementary theme, also developed and popularized by Rav Soloveitchik *zt"l*, that the festivals constitute an experience and manifestation of "*lifnei Hashem*" (*Vayikra* 23:28, 40; 16:30), being in the presence of God – a consequential halakhic category.

Further telling is Ramban's conclusion that the Targum's perspective on *mikra kodesh* entails the halakhic mandate emphasized by other commentators – that festival meals and attire must unequivocally attest to the sanctity of these milestones:

> ורבותינו אמרו ארעם במאכל ובמשתה ובכסות נקיה, כלומר שלא יהא חוקם אצלך כחוק שאר הימים. אבל תעשה להם מקרא של קודש לשנותם במאכל ובמלבוש מחול לקודש, וגם זה דעת אונקלוס.
>
> Our Sages taught: Distinguish them through food and drink and clean clothing – that is, that you should not treat them in the manner of ordinary days, but rather make them sacred events by transforming the profane into the sacred through food and dress. And this too is the view of Onkelos.

A final dimension of *mikra kodesh* as "*me'ora kadish*" is highlighted by Rashbam, who links the concept to the anticipation and prior affirmation of the *mo'ed*:

2. Onkelos, *Bereishit* 33:8. See also Onkelos, *Bereishit* 28:11, *Shemot* 4:27, 5:3, 20.

כל לשון קריאה שאצל מועדים לשון קביעת זמן הוא כמו קרא עלי מועד (איכה א:טו). וכן התרגום: מערע קדיש.

> The language of "*kri'ah*" in the context of the *mo'adim* refers to the establishment of a set time, as in the verse, "He has proclaimed a set time against me" (*Eikhah* 1:15). This is conveyed by the Targum: "*me'ora kadish.*"[3]

It is characteristic of the impact of these singular days, which define our aspirations and embody our destiny, that one cannot merely "happen" into them. Conscious and targeted preparation is a *sine qua non* for internalizing the seminal themes of *kedushat ha-yom* and for capitalizing on the spiritual opportunities afforded by festival observance. The requirement of previewing the halakhic details and concepts pertinent to each *mo'ed* facilitates a rigorous reflection on the special character and unique principles encapsulated in each unique festival.[4]

Although every *mo'ed* qualifies as "*mikra kodesh,*" Yom Kippur constitutes the quintessential or preeminent "*mikra kodesh.*" While the term is ordinarily employed in connection with the prohibition against the performance of "*melekhet avodah*" on each of the *mo'adim*, only on Yom Kippur is it applied to the more particular character of this most acute *kedushat ha-yom* and its singular imperative – "*ve-initem et nafshoteikhem* – you shall afflict your souls" (*Vayikra* 23:27; *Bamidbar* 29:7). It is surely no coincidence that the intrinsic sanctity of this day is also more pronounced. This is reflected in the definition of Yom Kippur as "*Shabbat Shabbaton*" (*Vayikra* 16:31, 23:32), as well as the fact that all elements of the day are presided over by the *Kohen Gadol*, who is permitted entrance into the otherwise impenetrable *Kodesh ha-Kodashim* (*Vayikra* 16:2). The explicit emphasis on "*lifnei Hashem*" (*Vayikra* 16:30, 23:28) as the telos of the day further reinforces the unparalleled acuity of "*mikra kodesh*" on this unique yet most consequential day of the calendar.

---

3. Rashbam, *Vayikra* 23:2. The *Zohar* and other sources (cited by *Ha-Ketav ve-Hakabbalah, Vayikra* 23:2) support this emphasis as well.
4. See *Megillah* 32a; *Pesahim* 6a.

The essays presented in this volume were initially formulated as *shiurim* presented in Yeshivat Rabbeinu Yitzchak Elchanan of Yeshiva University and in the broader community in advance of the *Yamim Nora'im,* in the spirit of *mikra'ei kodesh* in all its multiple dimensions. These *shiurim* were designed to highlight the inimitable *kedushat ha-yom* of Yom Kippur, to demonstrate how this heightened sanctity is concretized in specific norms and modes of observance, to underscore the pivotal institution of *teshuvah,* and to illuminate the opportunity afforded by Elul and the *Aseret Yemei Teshuvah* in cultivating a halakhically meaningful life inspired by the experience of "*lifnei Hashem.*" Preparing for the *Yamim Nora'im* through Torah study and halakhic analysis surely enhances the experience and maximizes the impact of this unique period, a significant facet of "*mikra kodesh*" itself.

Acknowledgments

I have merited to have exceptional *talmidim,* about whom I can honestly affirm: "*U-mitalmidai yoter mi-kulam.*" They are exemplary in their character and in their intense commitment to *talmud Torah* and to lives of Torah and *avodat Hashem.* A number of them, including sons and sons-in-law, contributed significantly to this project. I would like to thank R. David Mandelbaum, R. Yakir Forman, R. Isaac Shulman, R. Yaakov Schiff, R. Chanan Freilich, R. Robert Schrier, R. Elliot Schrier, R. Yonatan Mehlman, R. Asher Finkelstein, R. Ariel Rosensweig, R. Avigdor Rosensweig, R. Itamar Rosensweig, and R. Shlomo Friedman, each of whom generously invested significant time and effort in this project, particularly in the initial stages of converting the oral *shiurim* into written form. I am very appreciative of the additional efforts and editing of R. Yehoshua Katz and R. Noach Goldstein, which have greatly enhanced the final product.

R. Avraham Wein, a young *talmid hakham* and special *talmid,* spearheaded and orchestrated this project. He organized the cadre of talented and dedicated *talmidim* to transcribe and to render the audio recordings of each of the *shiurim* into text form, personally reviewed and often significantly reworked the material, and worked closely with me on the final drafts, which in some cases required extensive additional editing. His contribution was invaluable, and his dedication to the integrity of the material and to the realization of the goal was exceptional. He has shepherded this *sefer* through all its phases with great skill, extraordinary diligence, great personal devotion to the author, and admirable patience. It has been a true pleasure to work with Avraham and to experience his pervasive *menschlikhkeit*. I look forward to continuing this special collaboration, *le-hagdil Torah u-leha'adirah*.

I would like to acknowledge the generous support of R. Hyman Arbesfeld *z"l*, a true *tomekh Torah* and a wonderful family friend, and of R. Ezra Dyckman, a long-time cherished *talmid*, who facilitated formative work on this *sefer*. I also thank Yigal Segal of the Jewish Literacy Foundation for his assistance in this effort.

I am grateful for the participation of RIETS Press, and I thank R. Yona Reiss and R. Daniel Feldman for their assistance in facilitating this project. I appreciate R. Yaakov Werblowsky's close reading of the manuscript and his helpful comments and editing.

I am appreciative of the very professional and efficient efforts of Maggid Books in bringing this work to publication. I want to thank publisher Matthew Miller as well as Meira Mintz, Nechama Unterman, Ita Olesker, and R. David Silverstein for their meticulous editing of the manuscript, and Nachum Goldstein and Cobi Nadel for preparing the indexes. I am grateful to R. Reuven Ziegler, an early and much esteemed *talmid*, for his personal interest and for overseeing Maggid's involvement with this project.

This *sefer* is called מימיני מיכאל first and foremost to reflect my boundless gratitude for the *siyata di-shemaya* I have experienced in all dimensions of my life. The Targum and other commentators interpret the verse in *Tehillim* (80:18), "*Tehi yadekha al ish yeminekha* – May your hand be upon the man of Your right hand," as referring to one who is recipient of divine support and providence that enables a life of purpose characterized by the attainment of halakhic and spiritual growth.[5]

I have been privileged to be raised in a family devoted to *avodat Hashem* and *harbatzat ha-Torah*. I have been profoundly influenced by parents (R. Dr. Bernard and Rebbetzin Miriam Rosensweig *z"l*) and

5. See Radak and *Metzudat Tziyon* (in contrast to Rashi and Malbim), as well as the Targum: "על גבר דקיימת ליה ביד ימינך."

parents in-law (R. David and Prof. Yaffa Eliach *z"l*), who dedicated their careers and lives to *Klal Yisrael* and who contributed significantly to Jewish education and scholarship. I have been immeasurably blessed together with *ishti ke-gufi*, Professor Smadar Rosensweig, the full partner in all my endeavors, to raise a family of *banim u-venei banim osekim ba-Torah*. We are very proud of the achievements, admire the priorities, and cherish the special character of our children: R. Ariel and Jackie Rosensweig, R. David and Moriah Weiss, R. Dr. Itamar and Dr. Esty Rosensweig, R. Avigdor and Devorah Rosensweig, R. Chanan and Ayalah Freilich, Asher and Avigayil Finkelstein, and Etan and Elisheva Soclof. We treasure the growing bond with our wonderful grandchildren, Rena, Yonah, and Binyamin Rosensweig; Miri, Ashira, Shalva, and Azarya Weiss; Ayelet, Noam, and Adi Rosensweig; Nachshon Rosensweig; and Yaffa, Yitzchak, and Miri Freilich. We look forward with great anticipation to their continued growth as *benei* and *benot Torah*.

Beyond *hakarat ha-tov*, the title מימיני מיכאל also reflects the aspiration to merit a life defined by and immersed in rigorous *talmud Torah* and *avodat Hashem* that is an extension of and fiercely loyal to the principles and *mesorah* conveyed by my family and *rabbe'im*. The Talmud describes those who plumb the depth of halakhic knowledge as "מיימינין" who are worthy and "rightful" recipients of Torah wisdom.[6] Rashi clarifies that this entails rigor and purity of motive: "שמפשפשין טעמיהן בדקדוק ובודרין כימין המיומן למלאכה...אי נמי מיימינין בה עוסקים לשמה – For they search carefully for the explanations and examine as though with the right hand, which is adept at labor.... Alternatively, they toil in Torah study for its own sake."[7] In another passage, Rava declares that Torah knowledge is the elixir for spiritual health only for those who cultivate a מיימינין commitment: "למיימינין בה סמא דחיי, למשמאילים בה סמא דמותא – To those who are 'right-handed' in their approach to Torah, it is an elixir of life; to those

6. *Shabbat* 63a: "ת"ח המחדדין זל"ז בהלכה... זוכין לתורה שניתנה בימין שנאמר ותורך נר־ ראות ימינך...זוכין לדברים שנאמרו בימינה של תורה – Torah scholars who sharpen one another in matters of Halakhah...merit the Torah, which was given with the right hand, as the verse states, 'So that your right hand shall perform awesome things' (*Tehillim* 45:5)...and they merit the matters stated with regard to the right hand of the Torah."

7. Rashi, ad loc., s.v. *la-meyamnin*.

who are 'left-handed,' it is a drug of death."[8] Rashi again accentuates the intense effort to fathom and to internalize *devar Hashem*: "עסוקים בכל כחם וטרודים לדעת סודה כאדם המשתמש ביד ימינו שהיא עיקר – They are involved with all their might and engaged to know its secret, like a man who uses his right hand, the main one."[9] The term ימין is linguistically associated with affirmation (אמן), and commitment (as it is used in taking an oath), as well as with trustworthiness and loyalty (נאמן).[10]

I am immensely proud to be counted among the *talmidim* of *mori ve-rabbi* Ha-Rav Yosef Dov ha-Levi Soloveitchik *zt"l* and of *mori ve-rabbi* Ha-Rav Aharon Lichtenstein *zt"l,* towering *hakhmei mesorah,* giants of Torah knowledge and halakhic thought and paragons of *yirat Hashem* and personal integrity, whose transformative impact cannot be overstated. The worthy goal of striving to be one of the rigorous *meyamnin,* as well as a true *ne'eman,* a faithful trustee of a remarkable *mesorah,* is encapsulated by these inspiring role models.

I am also very grateful for my long and rich association with Yeshivat Rabbeinu Yitzchak Elchanan, my spiritual and intellectual home from a formative age and for many decades. The yeshiva has significantly facilitated my experience of "שבתי בבית ה׳ כל ימי חיי לחזות בנועם ה׳ ולבקר בהיכלו." In addition to being a conducive framework for personal growth, I have been afforded the singular opportunity to teach *havayot de-Abaye ve-Rava* and to explore the endlessly fascinating intricacies of *devar Hashem* with exceptionally diligent, idealistic, and receptive *talmidim.* It has been a privilege to witness their advancement in Torah and life and to forge the special bonds of "ושננתם לבניך - הרי אלו תלמידך – 'Teach them to your children' – this refers to your students."[11] I have personally experienced an added special dimension of this equation – the wonderful *zekhut* of having each of my sons and sons-in-law as *talmidim* as well. תהי ידך על איש ימינך, indeed!

Finally, I would like to dedicate this *sefer* of essays on the *Yamim Nora'im* in memory of my parents, R. Dr. Bernard Rosensweig, הרב דוב

8. *Shabbat* 88b.
9. Rashi, ad loc., s.v. *la-meyamnin.*
10. See also *Ha-Ketav ve-Hakabbalah, Shemot* 15:6.
11. *Sifrei* and Rashi, *Devarim* 6:7.

בער בן מאיר רוזנצווייג זצ״ל, and Rebbetzin Miriam Rosensweig, הרבנית מרים ברכה בת הרב מאיר יהושע ע״ה. Each of my parents was a singular personality with special qualities of mind and heart. Each was an indispensable and impactful force in my life and in the lives of each member of our family. The *demut deyuknam* (influential image) of my parents remains a very powerful presence for us all.

My father was a devoted *talmid* of Rav Soloveitchik *zt"l,* an influential national rabbinic leader, a dedicated communal *rav* for more than a half-century, and a beloved professor of Jewish History at Yeshiva University. He relished teaching Torah on various levels and lecturing on Jewish scholarship, but he particularly savored the challenge of preparing and presenting advanced Shabbat Shuvah and Shabbat ha-Gadol *derashot.* I recall vividly being profoundly inspired, even exhilarated, by my earliest exposure to the grandeur and depth of serious halakhic thought in these meticulously organized and formulated *shiurim.* My fascination and engagement with *Yamim Nora'im* themes are inextricably bound up with those formative experiences, but also merely exemplify my father's pivotal role in shaping my values, interests, and direction in life.

My mother, scion of a royal rabbinic family, a caring and involved rebbetzin, and an enthusiastic master teacher, was a rare combination of regal nobility and warmth, of *atzilut* and accessibility. Her sincerity, integrity, balance, *simhat ha-hayim,* and unbridled devotion to family are unforgettable and have struck deep roots in each of us. Her optimism, idealism, and understated deep faith particularly shone through on the *Yamim Nora'im.* My formative impressions of the ineffable atmosphere of transcendence on the *Yamim Nora'im* were imbibed from experiencing my mother's natural if unselfconscious posture during this inimitable period of the year.

My parents' legacy lives on in their considerable accomplishments and in their indelible imprint on the personalities of their children, grandchildren, and great-grandchildren, but also in the *mesorah* of principles, priorities, and values they imparted throughout their influential lives, both explicitly and subtly. May we continue to aspire to be מיימינין and נאמנים, consistent with and as a tribute to their memory. יהי זכרם ברוך.

Teshuvah

Chapter 1

Teshuvah and *Viduy*: The Ambitious Method of Coming Closer to Hashem

In describing the mitzvah of *teshuvah,* Rambam employs the term "*lifnei Hashem*" or "*lifnei ha-Kel*" ("before God") no fewer than three times (*Sefer ha-Mitzvot, aseh* 73; *koteret* to *Hilkhot Teshuvah; Hilkhot Teshuvah* 1:1). Given the phrase's rare usage and extraordinary implications, it is startling to see this phrase appear repeatedly in Rambam's characterization of *teshuvah.*[1] What is it about *teshuvah* that compels Rambam to remind us consistently that it must be done *lifnei Hashem*?

The answer to this question lies in a more complete understanding of *teshuvah* and its crucial role in the life of a committed *eved Hashem* (servant of God), as well as in understanding the interplay between *teshuvah* and *viduy* (confession).

1. The phrase *lifnei Hashem* is used in the Torah primarily in reference to the *mo'adim.* R. Soloveitchik emphasized the idea of *lifnei Hashem* as a signature theme of the *mo'adim* and as signifying and characterizing the experience of *simhat ha-regel* and *kedushat ha-zeman,* particularly in the *Mikdash.*

In his *koteret* (heading) to *Hilkhot Teshuvah,* Rambam summarizes the single mitzvah that he will discuss in this section:

> מצות עשה אחת, והוא שישוב החוטא מחטאו לפני ה׳ ויתודה.
>
> [This section includes] one positive commandment, which is that a sinner should return before Hashem from his sin and confess.

In this introduction, Rambam seems to indicate that the primary mitzvah discussed in this section is the mitzvah of *teshuvah,* with *viduy* constituting a component of that mitzvah. However, even a cursory glance in the body of *Hilkhot Teshuvah* and *Sefer ha-Mitzvot* indicates that this is not Rambam's view.

In *Hilkhot Teshuvah* 1:1, Rambam writes:

> כל מצות שבתורה בין עשה בין לא תעשה אם עבר אדם על אחת מהן בין בזדון בין בשגגה כשיעשה תשובה וישוב מחטאו חייב להתודות לפני הא-ל ברוך הוא.
>
> If one has violated any mitzvah in the Torah, whether a positive or negative commandment, whether done purposely or accidentally, *when he does* teshuvah *and returns from his sin,* he is obligated to confess before God, blessed be He.

In this context, Rambam seems to assume that it is axiomatic that *teshuvah* will occur; he subsequently codifies the obligation to say *viduy* in the context of the inevitable *teshuvah.* Similarly, in *Sefer ha-Mitzvot* (*aseh* 73), Rambam writes:

> היא שצונו להתודות על החטאים והעונות שחטאנו לפני הא-ל יתעלה ולאמר אותם עם התשובה.
>
> [The mitzvah is] that He commanded us to confess the sins and transgressions that we committed before God and to mention them together with doing *teshuvah.*

Here too, the primary mitzvah seems to be the *viduy*, while *teshuvah* is either assumed or considered to be an ancillary component of the *viduy*. How do we reconcile these two sources, which imply that the mitzvah is *viduy*, with the *koteret* to *Hilkhot Teshuvah*, which portrays *teshuvah* as the centerpiece of the mitzvah?

The Interplay between *Teshuvah* and *Viduy*: Three Approaches

In addressing this question, Mabit chooses to accentuate the *koteret* while deemphasizing the other two sources.[2] He asserts that Rambam did not intend to exclude the initiation of *teshuvah* as part of the mitzvah; rather, he simply wanted to emphasize that the mitzvah of *teshuvah* is incomplete until one does *viduy*. However, while this explanation is consistent with the language of Rambam in *Sefer ha-Mitzvot*, it is not as compatible with his formulation in *Hilkhot Teshuvah* 1:1.

Minhat Hinukh is so troubled by this enigma that he reaches the startling conclusion that there is no obligatory mitzvah of *teshuvah*. Rather, if one elects to do *teshuvah*, there is a mitzvah to express *viduy*. *Teshuvah*, according to this perspective, is perceived as a spiritual opportunity; however, one may choose to bypass *teshuvah* and remain in a state of *het* (sin).[3]

R. Soloveitchik strongly rejects this argument. On a textual level, he feels that *Minhat Hinukh*'s approach does not properly account for the *koteret*, which clearly conveys that there is a mitzvah to do *teshuvah*. More importantly, R. Soloveitchik believes *Minhat Hinukh*'s position to be philosophically and halakhically untenable. The Rav argues that it is inconceivable that *teshuvah* is merely discretionary. Just as the Torah condemns sin *a priori*,[4] it is equally repulsive, and hence inconceivable,

---

2. *Kiryat Sefer* 1:1.
3. *Minhat Hinukh*, mitzvah 364. *Minhat Hinukh* draws an analogy to the mitzvah of *gerushin* (among other *mitzvot*): One is not obligated to divorce his wife, but if one does divorce his wife, he fulfills a mitzvah if he does it in accordance with the laws of the Torah.
4. *Hazal* teach in numerous places (e.g. *Pesikta, Parashat Shelah*) that despite the Torah's phraseology in passages such as "*Im be-hukotai teilekhu* – If you follow My ordinances" (*Vayikra* 26:3), one should not mistakenly believe that the Torah is

to consider as halakhically legitimate the option of remaining in a state of sin.[5]

The Rav offers a different approach to solving this quandary in understanding Rambam.[6] We need not declare absolutely that Rambam thinks that either *teshuvah* or *viduy* is the mitzvah. Rather, Rambam is referring to two different motifs: the *ma'aseh* (action) of the mitzvah of *teshuvah* and the *kiyum* (inner fulfillment) of the mitzvah of *teshuvah*.[7] In certain cases, the method of performing a mitzvah is different from the effect that one creates through that performance. In fact, Rambam often emphasizes two different aspects in the *kotarot* and in the *halakhot* of *Mishneh Torah*, and our case is no exception. Thus, the *koteret*, which emphasizes *teshuvah*, refers to the *kiyum ha-mitzvah*, while in the *halakhah* and in *Sefer ha-Mitzvot*, Rambam is practical and writes that the method of doing *teshuvah*, the *ma'aseh ha-mitzvah*, is to say *viduy*.

This understanding of Rambam's opinion, although compelling, raises several issues. First, it is not clear that the dichotomy proposed by the Rav between *Sefer ha-Mitzvot* and the *koteret* is true in all cases. It

---

merely telling us the consequences of *aveirot* and that we may choose to do them if we so desire. Rather, the consequences delineated in these passages reflect the severity of the choices. There is an acceptable choice and an unacceptable choice.

5. A possible justification for *Minhat Hinukh*'s opinion is that he views *teshuvah* as an extraordinary opportunity that defies the causal relationship of *het*, and he therefore perceives it as a gift or option, as opposed to an obligation. If *teshuvah* is merely a way to expunge the effect of *het* and is not about enhancing the broader relationship with God, then each person may take the initiative to take advantage of it, but one is not required to do so.
6. *Al ha-Teshuvah*, 44–45.
7. The Rav presents numerous cases in which this dichotomy holds true. Two similar examples are the *mitzvot* of *tefillah* and *Keri'at Shema*. In both cases, the *ma'aseh ha-mitzvah* is strictly the verbalization of the words. However, in the case of *tefillah*, the *kiyum* is *avodah she-balev*, and in the case of *Keri'at Shema*, the *kiyum* is *kabbalat ol malkhut Shamayim*. Another example is the mitzvah of *aveilut*, where the *kiyum* is the *tza'ar* that one feels over the loss, while the *ma'aseh* consists of numerous actions or forms of conduct, both passive and active, that promote that end (*nihugei aveilut*). On this basis, the Rav explains that we mistakenly consider certain actions to be *issurei aveilut* (prohibited conduct) when they are in fact *kiyumei aveilut*, as abstaining from these actions engenders a certain effect that reinforces the sense of loss.

is not always the case that the *Sefer ha-Mitzvot* details only the *ma'aseh ha-mitzvah* to the exclusion of the *kiyum*. In *Sefer ha-Mitzvot,* Rambam succinctly captures the essence of a mitzvah, and he sometimes does delineate the *kiyum,* motifs, and themes of *mitzvot.*

In addition, in our case, Rambam also mentions *viduy* in the *koteret.* Why is *viduy* included in this framework if it defines only the *ma'aseh* and is disconnected from the *kiyum* of the mitzvah of *teshuvah*? Moreover, even were we to accept that *viduy* is the *ma'aseh ha-mitzvah* of *teshuvah,* it seems appropriate to ponder the purpose of this *ma'aseh.* What is it that *viduy* brings to the process that cannot be accomplished by *teshuvah* alone?

Further, I do not think that this approach does full justice to the formulation of Rambam in *Hilkhot Teshuvah* 1:1, where he writes that one is obligated to say *viduy, "ke-sheya'aseh teshuvah ve-yashuv mei-heto* – when he does *teshuvah* and returns from his sin." What is the purpose of this double formulation? It sounds as though there are two types or two levels of repentance that Rambam is trying to describe: doing *teshuvah* and returning from sin.

A problem of larger proportions emerges upon analyzing the broader evidence in Rambam's corpus. Although it is true that Rambam uses the term *hiyuv* in *Hilkhot Teshuvah* 1:1 only with respect to *viduy,* he does use the term with respect to *teshuvah* elsewhere in *Hilkhot Teshuvah.* In 2:7, in discussing the *teshuvah* on Yom Kippur, Rambam writes:

> יום הכפורים הוא זמן תשובה לכל ליחיד ולרבים והוא קץ מחילה וסליחה לישראל. לפיכך חייבים הכל לעשות תשובה ולהתודות ביום הכפורים.
>
> Yom ha-Kippurim is the time set aside for repentance for all, the individual as well as the many; for it is the apex of exoneration and pardon for Israel. Therefore, all are obligated to repent and confess on Yom ha-Kippurim.

Here, Rambam codifies an obligation to do *teshuvah* while simultaneously referring to *viduy.* If *teshuvah* is the *kiyum ba-lev* and Rambam in *Hilkhot Teshuvah* focuses exclusively on the method of achieving that, the *ma'aseh ha-mitzvah,* why does he emphasize *teshuvah* in this *halakhah*?

Moreover, since he employs the language of obligation with respect to *teshuvah* on Yom Kippur, why does Rambam not count two separate *mitzvot* of *teshuvah* in the *koteret* – one for *viduy* for the entire year and another for *teshuvah* on Yom Kippur? Finally, why does Rambam choose to discuss the obligation of *teshuvah* on Yom Kippur in *Hilkhot Teshuvah*, instead of in *Hilkhot Shevitat Asor*, where most of the *halakhot* of Yom Kippur are found? By choosing *Hilkhot Teshuvah* as the location to discuss this obligation, Rambam may be implying that the *teshuvah* of Yom Kippur relates more closely to *teshuvah* of the rest of the year than we might have thought.

In order to understand the relationship between *teshuvah* and *viduy*, we must first investigate various other challenging formulations in *Hilkhot Teshuvah*. By doing so, a pattern will emerge that will help us develop a solution to our questions.

The Singular Character of *Viduy*

The text of the *viduy*, as described by Rambam, is of vital importance in comprehending the nature of *viduy*. In the continuation of *Hilkhot Teshuvah* 1:1, Rambam writes:

> כיצד מתודין אומר אנא השם חטאתי עויתי פשעתי לפניך ועשיתי כך וכך והרי נחמתי ובושתי במעשי ולעולם איני חוזר לדבר זה. וזהו עיקרו של וידוי. וכל המרבה להתודות ומאריך בענין זה הרי זה משובח.
>
> How is the verbal confession made? The sinner says thus: "I beseech You, O Great Name! (*Anna Hashem*!) I have sinned (*hatati*); I have been obstinate (*aviti*); I have committed profanity against You (*pashati*), particularly in doing such and such. Now, behold! I regret and am ashamed of my actions; I will never relapse into this thing again." This is the elementary form of confession; whoever elaborates in confessing and extends this matter is praiseworthy.

We will begin with the first two words of Rambam's presentation of *viduy*: "*Anna Hashem*." These two words originate in the special *viduy* that the *Kohen Gadol* recited on Yom Kippur.[8] In contrast to Rambam, Rashi[9] and the *Sifra*[10] imply that these two words are unique to the *Kohen Gadol's viduy* on Yom Kippur. Additionally, in *Hilkhot Ma'aseh ha-Korbanot* (3:16), Rambam omits these two words when he codifies the text of the *viduy* that accompanies all other *korbanot* brought throughout the year. If these two words are indeed unique to the *viduy* of the *Kohen Gadol* on Yom Kippur, why does Rambam include them in the text of the *viduy* of *teshuvah* that we recite year round? This inclusion is neither obvious nor intuitive.

Another difficulty stems from Rambam's inclusion of three different words for sinning in the *viduy*: *hatati, aviti,* and *pashati. Minhat Hinukh* questions why all three of these words are necessary for a typical *viduy*. After all, these terms describe three entirely different types of sin that a person may commit. Would it not make more sense for a person's *viduy* to entail only the category of sin the person committed and for which they are doing *teshuvah*?[11]

The text of the *viduy* in *Hilkhot Teshuvah* 1:1 integrates several other components worth examining. Aside from the three categories of sin, the recitation of the *viduy* includes the concepts of *nehamah* (change of heart), *bushah* (shame), and *kabbalah al ha-atid* (resolution not to commit the same transgression in the future). This presentation differs from that of Rambam in *Hilkhot Teshuvah* 2:2, where he considers the definition of *teshuvah*:

8. *Yoma* 35b.

9. Rashi, *Yoma* 37a.

10. *Sifra, Parashat Aharei Mot, Parsheta* 3.

11. *Minhat Hinukh,* ibid. Due to this difficulty, *Minhat Hinukh* concludes that one would use all three of these verbs only if he had, in fact, committed and was doing *teshuvah* for all three types of sin. Otherwise, one should relate only the applicable type(s) of sin for his *teshuvah*. Accordingly, when Rambam lists all three categories in the text of his *viduy*, he is either referring to one who has committed all three categories or he is allowing the penitent to customize his *viduy* in accordance with the designations that are germane to his particular *teshuvah*. However, *Minhat Hinukh*'s suggestion does not appear to do justice to the words of Rambam.

ומה היא התשובה הוא שיעזוב החוטא חטאו ויסירו ממחשבתו ויגמור בלבו שלא יעשהו עוד שנאמר יעזוב רשע דרכו וגו׳. וכן יתנחם על שעבר שנאמר כי אחרי שובי נחמתי. ויעיד עליו יודע תעלומות שלא ישוב לזה החטא לעולם שנאמר ולא נאמר עוד אלהינו למעשה ידינו וגו׳. וצריך להתודות בשפתיו ולומר עניינות אלו שגמר בלבו.

What is repentance? The sinner shall cease sinning, remove sin from his thoughts, and wholeheartedly conclude not to return to it, as the verse states, "Let the wicked forsake his way" (*Yeshayahu* 55:7); so, too, shall he be remorseful on what was past, as the verse states, "Surely after I was turned, I repented" (*Yirmiyahu* 31:19). In addition, He who knows all secrets should testify about him that forever he will not turn to repeat that sin again, according to what it is said, "Say unto Him ... neither will we call any more the work of our hands our gods" (*Hoshe'a* 14:3–4). It is, moreover, essential that his confession shall be by spoken words of his lips, and all that which he concluded in his heart shall be formed in speech.

In this context, Rambam seems to define *nehamah* and *kabbalah al ha-atid* as distinct from the *viduy* that a person recites, and the concept of *bushah* is absent altogether from this formulation. It is essential to ascertain whether *Hilkhot Teshuvah* 1:1 and 2:2 are dealing with the same type of *teshuvah* and to investigate the differences if they are not, as the variation in formulation suggests.

A final question regarding *Hilkhot Teshuvah* 1:1 concerns the concluding phrase of the text quoted in the beginning of this section. Reminiscent of the obligation of *sippur yetzi'at Mitzrayim*, we are told that any additional effort in the daunting task of *viduy* ("*ve-kol ha-marbeh le-hitvadot*") is praiseworthy. What is it about the character of *viduy* that invites and invokes the use of such an obviously significant phrase?

Several broader questions about the concepts of *teshuvah* and *viduy* will enable us to ultimately paint a more comprehensive and satisfying picture of the interplay between the two concepts.

The *gemara* tells us that if a man marries a woman on condition that he is a *tzaddik*, the marriage takes effect even if this man is known to be a completely wicked person. How can this be? The *gemara* explains, "*shema hirher teshuvah be-da'ato* – perhaps he engaged in thoughts of *teshuvah*."[12] *Minhat Hinukh* asks that if, according to Rambam, it is only *viduy* and not *teshuvah* that constitutes the mitzvah, how can *hirhurei teshuvah,* mere thoughts of *teshuvah,* suffice to characterize a man as a *tzaddik* for the purposes of *kiddushin*? Should we not also require *viduy* in order for his *teshuvah* to have any halakhic efficacy?[13]

Finally, the very existence of the institution of *teshuvah* prompts Hida to question how a scenario can exist in which *beit din* may impose corporal punishment for transgression of a *mitzvat lo ta'aseh* (negative commandment). After all, since *teshuvah* is ostensibly a *mitzvat aseh* (positive commandment), shouldn't every single *lav* be considered *nitak la-aseh* (able to be rectified through a *mitzvat aseh*), in which case the *lav* does not incur *makkot*?[14] This *reductio ad absurdum* argument demonstrates the need for further careful thought about the core relationship between *teshuvah* and sin.

Two Levels of *Teshuvah*

A solution to the difficulties outlined above and the key to unlocking the proper perspective on *teshuvah* lies in the words of Ramban toward the end of his *Derashah le-Rosh ha-Shanah*. Ramban writes that when a person sins, his infraction transcends a single action and moment in time. As long as he does not redress his sin by means of *teshuvah,* he is *omed be-mirdo*; he persists in his active state of rebellion against Hashem. It is egregious to stand in the presence of the king while in a state of rebellion.

12. *Kiddushin* 49b.

13. *Minḥat Ḥinukh,* ibid. Mabit (*Kiryat Sefer, Hilkhot Teshuvah* 1:1) anticipated and preempted this question by explaining that while the mitzvah is *teshuvah, viduy* constitutes the *gemar ha-mitzvah* (completion of the mitzvah). In order for one to achieve the status of a *tzaddik, hirhurei teshuvah* can suffice. However, to complete the mitzvah and attain true and maximal *kapparah, viduy ba-feh* is absolutely necessary.

    The Rav, in one of his annual *teshuvah* lectures, answered *Minḥat Ḥinukh*'s question by explaining that the mitzvah of *teshuvah* and the status of being a *tzaddik* are two entirely different things. It is wholly possible to achieve the status of being a *tzaddik* (in this case, through *hirhurei teshuvah*) without having fulfilled the mitzvah of *teshuvah*. This idea will be explored further below.

14. *Ya'ir Ozen* 400:15:2.

We may infer from Ramban's words that the basic obligation of *teshuvah* does not stem from an independent mitzvah of *teshuvah* at all. Rather, sin itself obligates one to repent, lest he perpetuate a state of rebellion against Hashem. The impropriety, illegality, and rebellious implications of his original transgression necessitate that he rectify the situation and redeem his status as an *oved Hashem,* a religious persona.

Based on this analysis, we would reject the suggestion of *Minhat Hinukh* that it is acceptable for one to bypass the opportunity of *teshuvah* and remain in a state of *het.* Rambam certainly maintains that there is an obligation of *teshuvah.* However, he believes that the obligation of *teshuvah* stems from the sin itself, not from a separate mitzvah.[15]

Moreover, returning to Hida's question, it would be nonsensical to refer to a sin as a *lav ha-nitak la-aseh,* with the mitzvah of *teshuvah* as the subsequent *aseh.* This is because the *teshuvah* in which a person is *hayav* stems from the *lav* itself, not an ancillary *aseh.*

If this is the case, what is the purpose of the actual mitzvah of *teshuvah*? The mitzvah of *teshuvah* begins where *omed be-mirdo* ends. *Teshuvah* is the step beyond, the step that an aspirational *oved Hashem* takes once he has already neutralized his sin. This fits perfectly with the formulation of Rambam in *Hilkhot Teshuvah* 1:1, when he describes "*ke-sheya'aseh teshuvah ve-yashuv mei-heto* – when he does *teshuvah* and returns from his sin." This seemingly repetitive statement effectively describes two levels of *teshuvah*: simply neutralizing the sin that one has committed and then taking a much more ambitious step with regard to one's relationship with Hashem.

Mabit proposes that the source for Rambam's mitzvah of *viduy* comes from the verse "*Kehu imakhem devarim ve-shuvu el Hashem* – Take words with you and return to the Lord" (*Hoshe'a* 14:3).[16] If this is indeed Rambam's source, the context is particularly significant. The previous verse states, "*Shuva Yisrael ad Hashem Elokekha ki khashalta*

15. See the commentary of *Avodat ha-Melekh* (*Hilkhot Teshuvah* 1:1), who presents a similar approach.

16. Mabit, ibid. This contrasts with most other thinkers, who believe that the source for *viduy* is from the verse "*Ve-hitvadu et hatatam asher asu* – They shall confess the sins that they committed" (*Bamidbar* 5:7).

ba-avonekha – Return, Israel, to Hashem your God, because you have stumbled over your sins." The first *pasuk* speaks of returning "***ad** Hashem Elokekha*," referring to the initial step of *teshuvah*, the neutralization of sin and implied rebellion. This returns the transgressor to square one after a period of alienation due to sinfulness – "*ki khashalta ba-avonekha*." The next *pasuk* then aims higher, seeking to attain the spiritual ambition of "***el** Hashem*." This second level of *teshuvah* aspires to elevate one's status to the point at which one can boast of an intimate connection with Hashem. This level of *teshuvah* is accomplished via *viduy*, as Mabit points out.[17]

This second step of *teshuvah* is thus epitomized and encapsulated by the *viduy*. As noted above, Rambam's formulation of the text of the year-round *viduy* is identical with the *viduy* of the *Kohen Gadol* on Yom Kippur. Were the purpose of the *viduy* simply to neutralize one's sin and his status as *omed be-mirdo*, the formula of the *viduy* used when offering any other *korban* would suffice. It would not be necessary to include the three terms *hatati, aviti,* and *pashati* regardless of the sin; one could merely insert whichever terms are relevant to one's situation. However, if the mitzvah of *teshuvah* is intended to be transformative, to enable one to reach a higher status, it is compelling to argue that *viduy* must target beyond a specific sin. According to this view, the *viduy* is perceived as a vehicle for deep introspection, for critically examining how one could have become enmeshed in sin in the first place. *Viduy* affords the opportunity not merely to neutralize, but to capitalize on the *het*. The

---

17. It is fascinating that the *Sifra* (*Parashat Ha'azinu, piska* 306) interprets the "*devarim*" mentioned by Hoshe'a as referring to *talmud Torah*, connecting the verb "*kehu*" with other *pesukim* that either explicitly or obliquely refer to *talmud Torah*: "*Ki lekah tov natati lakhem, Torati al ta'azovu*" (*Mishlei* 4:2) and "*Ya'arof ka-matar lik'hi*" (*Devarim* 32:2). One may achieve the enviable status of "*ve-shuvu el Hashem*" specifically through the medium of *talmud Torah*. This is reminiscent of the opinion of R. Hayim Volozhiner (*Nefesh ha-Hayim* 4:31), who says that *teshuvah mei-ahavah* (whose lofty attributes are recounted in *Yoma* 86b) can be achieved only through *talmud Torah*. This idea is indicated by the juxtaposition of the phrases "*hashiveinu Avinu le-Toratekha*" and "*ve-hahazireinu bi-teshuvah sheleimah lefanekha*" in our daily *Shemoneh Esrei* prayers.

For a more extensive analysis of the relationship between *teshuvah, ahavat Hashem,* and *talmud Torah*, see the chapter "*Ahavat Hashem* and Talmud Torah: The Telos of *Teshuvah*."

sinner ensures that the *het*, while initially a step backward, will now be a catalyst toward a superior overall relationship with Hashem. The *viduy* of the *Kohen Gadol* on Yom Kippur is ideally suited to accomplish this goal, as are the three terms *hatati, aviti,* and *pashati,* which address the broader category of human missteps and are not restricted to the individual transgressions committed by the particular individual.

For this reason, Rambam emphasizes the praise due to one who puts extra effort into his *viduy*. The greater the quality and quantity of the *viduy,* the more it reflects the individual's keen self-appraisal and his deep understanding of the impetus of *teshuvah* in the first place. He is not simply attempting to restore his prior status. The transgressor realizes that *het* cannot be dismissed merely as a local misstep. He comes to realize that while sin causes a profound distancing from Hashem, aspirational *teshuvah* affords a tremendous opportunity to advance his spiritual persona, to come closer to Hashem than ever before.

This perspective also sheds light on the discrepancies between the presentation of *viduy* in the first and second chapters of *Hilkhot Teshuvah*. Chapter 1 deals with the aspirational second level of *teshuvah,* whereas chapter 2 deals with the basic phase of *teshuvah* that removes a person from the status of *omed be-mirdo*. Thus, the *viduy* in *Hilkhot Teshuvah* 1:1 includes the concept of *bushah,* even though it is not an integral component of basic *teshuvah,* as indicated by its omission from *Hilkhot Teshuvah* 2:1. In addition, the concepts of *kabbalah al ha-atid* and *nehamah* are integral to the *viduy* of the ambitious stage of *teshuvah* but are ancillary to the *viduy* of the elemental level of *teshuvah.*

While the *koteret* and *Sefer ha-Mitzvot* are ostensibly the venue for a succinct depiction or identification of the mitzvah, I believe that it can be consistently demonstrated that Rambam employs these frameworks to integrate details, including the method of performing the mitzvah, that he maintains specifically characterize Halakhah's perspective on a given theme.[18] Thus, it is fitting that Rambam mentions *viduy* in

18. This constitutes a general pattern in Rambam's formulations. For example, see the *koteret* to *Hilkhot Ishut,* where Rambam includes *ketubah* in the mitzvah of marriage, even though the institution of *ketubah* appears to be only *de-Rabbanan*. Rambam highlights *ketubah* in the *koteret* because the concept and theme of *ketubah* is what

both the *koteret* and *Sefer ha-Mitzvot,* because it is precisely the *viduy* that highlights and characterizes what is singular about this aspirational second level of *teshuvah.*

Viduy and Yom Kippur: Going Beyond Individual Sins

We were previously troubled by Rambam's decision to invoke the language of "obligation" with respect to *teshuvah* on Yom Kippur, even as he refrained from counting *teshuvah* on Yom Kippur as a separate mitzvah. Now that we have a clearer understanding of *viduy*'s special role, the solution to these difficulties quickly materializes. *Teshuvah* on Yom Kippur is not counted separately, because it and *viduy* throughout the year are two sides of the same coin. The purpose of *viduy* is not merely to neutralize any outstanding transgressions that one may have committed. Similarly, the goal of Yom Kippur is not simply to start with a clean slate, unsullied by the errors and missteps of the past year. Rather, the goal of both institutions is to elevate one's status as an *eved Hashem,* making the most of the opportunity to intensify one's relationship with Hashem.

Thus, it is no accident that Rambam utilizes the singular phrase "*lifnei Hashem/ha-Kel*" three times in reference to *viduy* and *teshuvah.* If there is any expression that perfectly encapsulates the character of Yom Kippur, it is "*lifnei Hashem.*" This phrase is used five times in the course of the Torah's discussion of Yom Kippur in *Parashat Aharei Mot*

---

separates and elevates the Jewish concept of marriage relative to the universal notion of marriage. Rambam's emphasis on the role of *kiddushin* in the context of *nissu'in* is also consistent with these themes.

Another example may be found in the *koteret* to *Hilkhot Gerushin,* where Rambam seemingly gratuitously incorporates the concept of *gerushin bi-khetav* (written divorce) in the *mitzva de-orayta* of *gerushin.* Again, this inclusion may reflect his view that the concept of *gerushin bi-khetav* highlights the unique character of *gerushin* as a whole. Rambam's inclusion of numerous *matirin,* such as *shehitah,* in the count of 613 *mitzvot,* a position that triggered much controversy and debate, may also be explained in this manner.

For more on these topics, see my "*Be-Inyan Shitat ha-Rambam be-Ketubah,*" *Beit Yitzhak* 26 (1994), 441; "*Be-Inyan Shitat ha-Rambam be-Mitzvat Kiddushin,*" *Hazon Nahum* (1998), 35; and "*Shitat ha-Rambam be-Inyan Ketav Yad be-Gittin, Kiddushin, u-Milveh,*" *Beit Yitzhak* 32 (2000), 63.

(Vayikra 16), culminating in the phrase, "*lifnei Hashem tit'haru* – you shall be purified in front of Hashem."[19] Yom Kippur's very essence is a day of being *lifnei Hashem*.

This characteristic of *lifnei Hashem* is manifest in myriad aspects of Yom Kippur. For example, part of the special *viduy* for Yom Kippur includes the *tefillah* of *Al Het*. The very first phrase of this lengthy confession is an acknowledgment and a plea for forgiveness for all the sins that we committed, whether willfully or by accident. The inclusion of *aveirot be-ones*, accidental sins, in our *viduy* is a curious one, as they do not appear to require *teshuvah* at all.[20] However, Yom Kippur is not merely a day on which one attempts to neutralize past sins. It is the time when one takes stock of his standing as an *eved Hashem*, attempting to repair the breach in the relationship between himself and his Creator while concurrently aspiring to elevate his status and upgrade his religiosity to achieve new heights. Thus, it is not surprising that we seek forgiveness and express regret and humiliation even for sins committed unwittingly or under duress.[21]

It is also not surprising that one could be obligated to do *teshuvah* even for sins for which he had previously atoned on prior Yom Kippurs.[22] The very association and identification with sin is anathema to the ambitious *oved Hashem*, even if there is no technical halakhic *ma'aseh aveirah* or legal culpability. The taint of transgression constitutes a certain

19. Rabbeinu Yonah (*Sha'arei Teshuvah* 2:14) suggests that this verse is the source for a separate mitzvah of *teshuvah* on Yom Kippur.

20. In *Hilkhot Teshuvah* 1:1, Rambam omits *aveirot be-ones* from his list of the sins for which a person must do *teshuvah*. Rambam's larger view is somewhat complex. See *Perush ha-Mishnayot, Yoma* 8:6.

21. In part, this depends on how we understand the concept of "*ones Rahmana patrei*." If this concept signifies not merely a *petur onesh* (exemption from punishment), but also that actions under duress do not legally constitute halakhic actions (*hafka'at ha-ma'aseh*), then it would appear completely unnecessary for one to seek forgiveness for sins committed through *ones*. However, one might still be mortified for being a vehicle for and tainted by sin, notwithstanding the absence of any legal culpability.

22. There is a dispute in the *beraita* in *Yoma* (86b) regarding whether such a requirement exists. Rambam (*Hilkhot Teshuvah* 2:8) rules in accordance with the opinion that one is obligated to do *teshuvah* in this scenario, but *Minhat Hinukh* (ibid.) is troubled by this conclusion.

pathology in its own right. It is still a "*mehitzah ha-mavdelet beino u-vein Kono*," an obstacle separating one from his Creator. One who values his relationship with Hashem will be impelled to mobilize all available resources to negate any vestigial barrier to facilitating the maximal bond with his Creator. That is the opportunity that *teshuvah* on Yom Kippur and *viduy* the entire year provides.

This approach may further explain the singular role of the *korban olah* (burnt-offering) in the Yom Kippur *viduy*. The *Al Het* list introduces *olah* violations before *hatat* (sin-offering) transgressions. This is perplexing, since the offering of *korban hatat* always precedes that of the *korban olah*.[23] However, it is the *olah* that uniquely captures the opportunity, ambition, and focus of Yom Kippur. Although the *hatat* focuses on neutralizing each individual sin, which is also a priority on Yom Kippur, it is the *olah* – which is totally consumed on the altar (*kalil la-Hashem*) – that conveys the total commitment of *kulo la-Hashem* (entirely for Hashem).[24]

Moreover, the *olah* addresses the totality of the religious personality and experience, as it is offered to compensate for the neglect of spiritual opportunity (*bitul mitzvot aseh*, failure to perform positive commandments) and for improper attitudes and intentions (*hirhurei aveirah*, thoughts of sin). It is therefore appropriate that the *korban* that most approximates and embodies the theme of Yom Kippur atones for these mistakes, even if they may not technically be triggered by a *ma'aseh aveirah*. It is natural that the *teshuvah* of Yom Kippur, which accentuates the *olah* theme, emphasizes the *korban olah* even as it includes the *korban hatat*.[25]

The *olah*'s priority over the *hatat* in the *viduy* may reflect an additional dimension as well. The *gemara* likens the *korban olah* to a *doron*, a gift to Hashem.[26] In general, the *korban hatat* precedes the *korban olah*,

---

23. *Zevahim* 7b; see parallel discussion in *Magen Avraham, Orah Hayim* 1:5.
24. See Ramban (*Vayikra* 1:4), who develops an approach to *korban olah* that is the basis for our approach. For a more extensive analysis of the *korban olah*, see my "*Be-Inyan Ritzuy Olah*," *Kol Tzvi* 13 (2011), 25.
25. For further development of this idea, see the chapter "The Unique *Teshuvah* of Yom Kippur," below.
26. *Zevahim* 7b.

because it is inappropriate and unacceptable to bring a gift to the king before one has first smoothed his relationship with the king, appropriately apologizing for past misdeeds. However, the very theme of Yom Kippur is the extraordinary opportunity to elevate one's spiritual profile by reorienting one's religious priorities and agenda – by giving God a gift, so to speak. The text of *Al Het* accentuates this emphasis and order by delineating *olah* violations before *hatat* transgressions.[27]

Teshuvah for Non-Jews

Several statements of *Hazal* indicate that *teshuvah* is limited to *Klal Yisrael.* Commenting on the verse "*Yisa Hashem panav eilekha* – May Hashem show favor to you" (*Devarim* 32:4), the *Midrash Tanhuma* states that while Hashem will show favoritism to those who engage in *teshuvah,* this preferential treatment applies only to Jews, not to gentiles. Similarly, *Sifri Zuta* says that *viduy* may be achieved only by Jews.[28]

---

27. This may also help us explain a curious *hava amina* in the *gemara* (*Zevahim* 6a). The *gemara* asks whether an animal that has been designated as a *korban olah* (*hafrashah*) may atone for the *ba'al ha-korban*'s neglect of a *mitzvat aseh* that took place before he actually offered the sacrifice (*hakravah*). A *korban hatat* would not atone in the analogous case, when a person committed a *hiyuv lav* after *hafrashah*. However, the *gemara* entertains the possibility that the *olah* would differ in this respect from the *hatat.* What evidence is there to signify such a discrepancy? The *gemara* suggests that just as a single *korban olah* may atone for several *hiyuvei aseh* (as opposed to a *korban hatat,* which can atone only for a single *het* at a time), it may similarly atone for the neglect of an additional *mitzvat aseh* after *hafrashah.*

   What is the connection between these two seemingly disparate points? I believe that the *gemara* is highlighting the core difference between *hatat* and *olah.* The *gemara* conveys that the purpose of the *hatat* is to negate the impact of a particular *ma'aseh aveirah,* in which case one would need a separate *korban hatat* for each additional *het,* and one would certainly not receive *kapparah* if he were to commit an additional *het* after *hafrashah.* However, a *korban olah* addresses the holistic religious personality and whether he is considered *ratzuy la-Hashem* (favorable before Hashem), as evidenced by its ability to cover the disregard of several *mitzvot aseh* at once (and, as we mentioned above, even *hirhurei aveirah*). The crux of the matter is about *who* he is, not *what* he has done. Therefore, the *gemara* briefly considers the possibility that the *olah* would even atone for one who had an additional episode of inattention toward a *mitzvat aseh* even after *hafrashah.*

28. *Sifri Zuta, Bamidbar* 4:4.

These two statements seem quite troubling and problematic, considering that one of the main storylines of the book of *Yonah* involves the capacity of a gentile nation to successfully do *teshuvah*. Moreover, the *mishnah* recounts how the city of Nineveh not only succeeded in its *teshuvah* quest, but also came to be regarded as a paradigm for honest and sincere *teshuvah* to which *Klal Yisrael* should aspire![29]

We may resolve this difficulty by invoking the previously described two levels of *teshuvah*. The basic notion of *teshuvah* is a universal concept. Any gentile who wishes to live a meaningful life must follow the seven Noahide commandments,[30] which themselves mandate the basic level of *teshuvah* when one inevitably errs. This is parallel to the *teshuvah* obligation when a Jew sins, an obligation that is generated by the *mitzvot* themselves. In the case of Nineveh, this *teshuvah* is symbolized by their leader's exhortation, "*Ve-yashuvu ish mi-darko ha-ra'ah u-min ha-hamas asher be-khapeihem* – Let each man return from his wicked ways and from the violence that is in their hands" (*Yonah* 3:8).[31] However, the additional and aspirational second level of *teshuvah*, one that can transform sins into heavenly favor because it upgrades the relationship with Hashem to previously unattained levels, is a *Klal Yisrael*-specific opportunity. *Teshuvah* certainly does not constitute an independent mitzvah for *Bnei Noah*. But according to the concept we have developed

29. *Ta'anit* 16a, codified in Rambam's *Hilkhot Ta'aniyot* 4:2.

30. These seven *mitzvot* may be more extensive and inclusive than they appear. *Sefer ha-Hinukh* (mitzvah 416) describes how the seven *mitzvot* are actually seven *categories* of *mitzvot* obligatory to gentiles. This perspective has its roots in the exchange between Abaye and Rava (*Sanhedrin* 74b) regarding the question of whether Noahides are obligated in martyrdom (*kiddush Hashem*).

31. If this is the case, it remains an open question why it was decided that we should read from this book on Yom Kippur. The simplest answer may be that while Yom Kippur's theme is the aspirational level of *teshuvah*, the foundational level is also of utmost importance, as we established earlier in our discussion of the *korbanot olah* and *hatat*. An alternative possibility is that it was chosen to teach us about Yonah's personal *teshuvah*. Finally, this story may also serve the purpose of teaching us about the scope and opportunity of *teshuvah*, as Hashem still wished for *teshuvah* even in a case in which it might ultimately cause harm to others or lead to a greater *hillul Hashem* in the future, as was the case with the people of Nineveh and their descendants.

that elemental *teshuvah* stems from the primal religious obligation itself, it applies to Noahides, as is attested to by the book of *Yonah*.

If this is the case, it is very appropriate that the *Sifri Zuta* specifically references *viduy* and its uniquely Jewish character. It highlights that the ambition inherent in *viduy* reflects the higher purpose and distinctive character of *Klal Yisrael*'s *teshuvah*.

Tzaddik Gamur vs. *Ba'al Teshuvah*

This idea may also illuminate the interesting interplay reflected in *Hazal*'s analysis of the relative statuses of the *ba'al teshuvah* (penitent) and the *tzaddik gamur* (completely righteous individual). The *gemara* informs us of the superiority of the *ba'al teshuvah* over the *tzaddik gamur*,[32] but it does not define and characterize the two terms, which leads to speculation about the differences between them. Further, it is certain that any *tzaddik* will occasionally stumble and fall prey to sin,[33] and the assumption is that he will subsequently engage in *teshuvah*. Thus, the very attempt to discern any significant difference between the *tzaddik gamur* and the *ba'al teshuvah* appears to be an exercise in futility, or at most a theoretical task.

I believe that the explanation is that the *ba'al teshuvah* is exactly what his moniker describes: He allows himself to be defined by his *teshuvah*. He is one who capitalizes on the opportunity provided by the circumstance of his alienation and *het* to resolve to never again allow himself to experience that situation.[34] He is therefore motivated to undergo a core reassessment and transformation to reconcile and strengthen his relationship with Hashem.

In response to *Minhat Hinukh*'s question about *hirhurei teshuvah*, it can now be suggested that just as *hirhurei teshuvah* may be enough to neutralize one's sin, *hirhurei teshuvah* may be sufficient to grant one the status of *tzaddik*. However, to become a true *ba'al teshuvah*, one is required to say *viduy* (which includes *nehamah*, *bushah*, and *kabbalah al*

32. *Berakhot* 34b; *Sanhedrin* 99a.
33. See *Kohelet* 7:20; *Mishlei* 24:16.
34. For further development of this theme, see the chapter "*Le-David* and *Teshuvah*: Achieving Clarity of Purpose."

ha-atid, along with the three levels of sin), given what it reflects about the scope and magnitude of the *teshuvah* process. This enables the *teshuvah* to define him going forward. The *viduy* of the *Kohen Gadol* on Yom Kippur is a *sine qua non* for achieving the aspiration of a *ba'al teshuvah.*

This heightened ambition of the *ba'al teshuvah* is reflected by a statement in the *gemara*[35] and codified by Rambam.[36] The *ba'al teshuvah* (or a "*ba'al teshuvah gemurah*" in Rambam) is defined as one who previously sinned, subsequently did *teshuvah,* and then had a second opportunity to engage in the same transgression (with circumstances similar to the first time) but nevertheless withstood the temptation. This concrete spiritual about-face, if it arises, may not be necessary to neutralize *het,* but it is necessary to attain the status of *ba'al teshuvah.*[37]

Rambam cites the *gemara* describing the superiority of the *ba'al teshuvah* over the *tzaddik gamur* in an interesting context. He introduces that *halakhah* by dismissing the notion that *teshuvah* applies exclusively to acts of sin. Instead, he contends that *teshuvah* extends even more significantly to values, inclinations, and emotions (such as anger, jealousy, or lust), dimensions that are indigenous to human personality. He emphasizes that one should not think that a *ba'al teshuvah* is inferior to the *tzaddik;* rather, "he is beloved and desired before Hashem, as if he never sinned at all." He then cites this *gemara* to reinforce his position that the stature of the *ba'al teshuvah* is far superior to that of the *tzaddik gamur.*[38] Now that we have demonstrated that *teshuvah*'s scope extends even to character traits and values, the hierarchy of *ba'al teshuvah* and *tzaddik gamur* is quite understandable.

There are several additional examples of *teshuvah*'s capacity to redefine the religious persona. The *gemara* states that in addition to the effectiveness of repentance, which enables the penitent's entry into the idyllic *Olam ha-Ba,* he also attains the elevated status of "*Rebbi.*"[39] This

35. *Yoma* 86b.
36. *Hilkhot Teshuvah* 2:1.
37. In that *halakhah,* Rambam has a clear hierarchy between a *ba'al teshuvah gemurah,* a *ba'al teshuvah,* and one who is merely "*nimhalin lo,*" forgiven. This again solidifies our theory of the several existing gradations of *teshuvah.*
38. *Hilkhot Teshuvah* 7:3.
39. *Avodah Zarah* 17a.

is not merely an honorific; the term "*Rebbi*" implies great stature in the world of Torah and Halakhah. Yet it is evidently an apt description of a *ba'al teshuvah*. In addition, the *gemara* says regarding *ba'alei teshuvah*, "Praiseworthy is our old age, which has atoned for our misspent youth."[40] Once again, these are indications of *teshuvah*'s far-reaching implications.[41]

Rambam refers to the possibility of transformative change through *teshuvah* numerous times throughout *Hilkhot Teshuvah*, especially in chapter 7. There, he poignantly expresses how a true *ba'al teshuvah* never puts the experience of *het* out of his mind, although one is forbidden to remind him of it.[42] The penitent, of his own initiative, must be omni-aware of his roots, previous challenges, and deficiencies. This is an interesting dialectic: One cannot remind him of his past misdeeds, but he naturally draws upon the fullness of his experience as a *ba'al teshuvah*.

Conclusion

We have seen that there is a tremendous gap between a *ba'al teshuvah* and one who merely does *teshuvah*, and even between a *ba'al teshuvah* and a *tzaddik gamur*. One's goal on Yom Kippur, as well as whenever engaging in *teshuvah* and *viduy* throughout the year,[43] should not be solely to become a *tzaddik*, but rather to achieve the pinnacle of becoming a *ba'al teshuvah*.

It is therefore quite fitting that in the crescendo of *Hilkhot Teshuvah* (chapter 10), Rambam defines and writes about the value of *avodah mei-ahavah* (service of Hashem motivated by love), as well as how one can achieve it. The role of *teshuvah* in achieving not only *avodah mi-yirah* (service motivated by fear) but *avodah mei-ahavah* is of utmost impor-

---

40. *Sukkah* 53a.

41. For another example highlighting Rambam's expansive perspective on *teshuvah*, see the chapter "*Mi-Darkhei ha-Teshuvah*: Authentic Repentance."

42. *Hilkhot Teshuvah* 7:8.

43. Yom Kippur is the single most unique day of the year, but it is also the most *relevant* day of the year. Maharsha (*Megillah* 32a) notes that Moshe Rabbeinu's enactment that one begin to review the *halakhot* of a particular festival in the preceding month was never articulated with respect to Rosh ha-Shanah and Yom Kippur. He explains that the theme of *teshuvah* that dominates this period belongs to the entire year, while Moshe's *takanah* applies only to themes that are unique to a particular festival.

tance. That is why it is a fitting conclusion to Rambam's *Sefer ha-Madda,* in which the essentials of *avodat Hashem* are discussed.[44] *Teshuvah* is the conclusion and culmination of what began with *Hilkhot Yesodei ha-Torah,* precisely because it has at the center of its ambition the potential transformation of even a *tzaddik gamur* into a *ba'al teshuvah gemurah.*

44. For a more extensive analysis of the placement of *Hilkhot Teshuvah* in *Sefer ha-Madda,* see the chapter "*Ahavat Hashem* and *Talmud Torah*: The Telos of *Teshuvah.*"

Chapter 2

An Alternative and Complementary Perspective on *Teshuvah*: Rabbeinu Yonah's *Sha'arei Teshuvah*

Introduction

As the first comprehensive compilation of laws of repentance, Rambam's *Hilkhot Teshuvah* was both novel and impactful. Due to its pioneering nature, all later works on *teshuvah* respond to, integrate, adapt, and sometimes diverge from Rambam's breakthrough work.[1] In this vein, Rabbeinu Yonah's *Sha'arei Teshuvah*, perhaps the second most prominent

1. These later works include Meiri's *Hibbur ha-Teshuvah*, Mabit's *Beit Elokim*, and Ran's *Derashot ha-Ran* (chapters 6, 9, and 10). Each of these is independently worthy of extensive treatment focused on the singular contributions of these seminal thinkers. Indeed, our discussion here is merely a cursory survey of the different emphases of Rambam and Rabbeinu Yonah; Rabbeinu Yonah's position is certainly deserving of more extensive analysis.

composition on *teshuvah,* confronts the challenge and opportunity of developing *hilkhot teshuvah* in a post-Rambam era.

Although Rambam's *Hilkhot Teshuvah* and Rabbeinu Yonah's *Sha'arei Teshuvah* share many common perspectives on *teshuvah* as a legal, conceptual, and experiential institution, these *ba'alei ha-mesorah* emphasize the character of *teshuvah* and its role in religious life in distinctive manners. Even a brief analysis of Rabbeinu Yonah's opening discussion in *Sha'arei Teshuvah* establishes a fundamentally different perspective on *teshuvah* than Rambam's view, especially in light of Rambam's striking editorial choices throughout the ten chapters of *Hilkhot Teshuvah.*

Rambam's Unique Perspective: *Teshuvah* as a Mode of *Avodat Hashem*

We might have anticipated that Rambam's *Hilkhot Teshuvah* would center on the specific details of how to react to sin and neutralize its deleterious effects. In truth, however, *Hilkhot Teshuvah* presents *teshuvah* as more than simply a strategy to address transgression.[2]

First of all, Rambam codifies *Hilkhot Teshuvah* as the conclusion of *Sefer ha-Madda,* the volume dedicated to the overlap of and interface between Halakhah and *hashkafah* (proper belief). Rambam conceivably could have integrated *Hilkhot Teshuvah* into a number of other contexts, such as *Hilkhot Shegagot, Hilkhot Avodat Yom ha-Kippurim,* or *Hilkhot Shevitat Asor*. Instead, Rambam insists that *Hilkhot Teshuvah* is an independent component and coda of *Sefer ha-Madda.*

Second, in *Hilkhot Teshuvah* itself, Rambam extensively discusses concepts we might have expected to be presented elsewhere. For example, chapter 5 of *Hilkhot Teshuvah* is allotted for Rambam's expansive comments on *behirah hofshit* (free will). Of course, free will is indispensable to the possibility and efficacy of *teshuvah;* it is a prerequisite for the obligation of *teshuvah* and its very existence. As such, Rambam's discussion of *behirah hofshit* in *Hilkhot Teshuvah* cannot be declared out of place. At the same time, however, we could have imagined the discussion of *behirah hofshit* in other contexts, including *Hilkhot Yesodei ha-Torah* or

2. For additional analysis, see the chapters "*Ahavat Hashem* and *Talmud Torah*: The Telos of *Teshuvah*" and "*Mi-Darkhei ha-Teshuvah*: Authentic Repentance."

Hilkhot De'ot. Why does Rambam devote an entire middle chapter, the apparent fulcrum of *Hilkhot Teshuvah,* to the notion of *behirah hofshit*?

Third, Rambam concludes *Hilkhot Teshuvah* on an intriguing note. Chapter 10, the final chapter, centers on the concepts of *ahavat Hashem* (love of God) and *avodat Hashem mei-ahavah* (serving God out of love) – to such an extent, in fact, that read independently, one might not recognize its context of *Hilkhot Teshuvah*! The climax of *Hilkhot Teshuvah* omits any mention of *teshuvah* itself and instead focuses on *ahavat Hashem* and its role in service of Hashem. The striking absence of the concept of *teshuvah mei-ahavah* (repentance out of love), which would have justified this placement as a substitution for the broader articulation of *ahavat Hashem,* reinforces this point.

Rambam's editorial choice is inherently perplexing, but it is even more intriguing when compounded by other evidence. Chapter 10 of *Hilkhot Teshuvah* is not Rambam's first mention of *ahavat Hashem*. Rambam begins his *Yad ha-Hazakah* with *Hilkhot Yesodei ha-Torah,* and after establishing the necessary existence and uniqueness of the *Ribbono Shel Olam* in chapter 1, Rambam elaborates immediately in chapter 2 on *ahavat Hashem* and *yirat Hashem*. Thus, not only does Rambam conclude *Hilkhot Teshuvah* by focusing entirely on *ahavat Hashem,* seemingly overlooking *teshuvah* itself, but he does so somewhat repetitively, having already discussed *ahavat Hashem* at the very beginning of *Sefer ha-Madda*! What compels Rambam to classify *avodah mei-ahavah* and *ahavat Hashem* as the pinnacle of *Hilkhot Teshuvah*?

Taken cumulatively, Rambam's decisions to include *Hilkhot Teshuvah* in *Sefer ha-Madda* and to integrate discussions of *behirah hofshit* and *avodah mei-ahavah* and *ahavat Hashem* into the fabric of *Hilkhot Teshuvah* suggest that Rambam perceives *teshuvah* not only as a narrow remedy to sin, but also as a broad form of religious observance that advances one's relationship with *Ha-Kadosh Barukh Hu*. Rambam's choice of placements impresses upon us his position that *teshuvah* constitutes a critical element of *avodat Hashem*. Genuine repentance targets and neutralizes sin and its implications, but thereby also catalyzes and facilitates man's opportunity to elevate his religious commitment, personality, and outlook.

Thus, *teshuvah* emerges as a central mode of *avodat Hashem*. As such, Rambam insists on discussing *teshuvah* as the culmination of *Sefer ha-Madda,* and he also expands *Hilkhot Teshuvah* to include topics whose relevance transcends *teshuvah.* The presentation in this context of *behirah hofshit,* which is indispensable to all facets of *avodat Hashem,* accentuates the role of *teshuvah* as a form of *avodat Hashem.* Most prominently, Rambam's choice to conclude *Hilkhot Teshuvah* with the concepts of *avodah mei-ahavah* and *ahavat Hashem* indicates that the ultimate purpose of *teshuvah* is not merely to expunge the effects of spiritually toxic *het,* but to promote a significantly more aspirational *ahavat Hashem.* In this respect, *teshuvah* also motivates and defines *avodat Hashem.*

Rambam's discussion of *ahavat Hashem* in the context of *Hilkhot Teshuvah* is not gratuitous; on the contrary, it recalibrates our understanding of *teshuvah* in its entirety. The final chapter of *Hilkhot Teshuvah* highlights the immense significance of *ahavat Hashem* and *avodat Hashem* as the telos of *teshuvah,* establishing the foundation to transition to Rambam's next *sefer, Sefer Ahavah,* which is introduced by the powerful expression of unambiguous and unconstrained *ahavah*: "*Mah ahavti Toratekha kol ha-yom hi sihati.*"

Zedonot Na'asot Lo Ki-Zekhuyot

Rambam's focus on *teshuvah* as a means of *avodat Hashem* is consistent with a conspicuous omission in *Hilkhot Teshuvah.* The *gemara* cites Reish Lakish's staggering contention that when one repents due to fear of Hashem, "*zedonot na'asot lo ki-shegagot*" – his intentional sins are rendered mistakes – but if one repents out of love of Hashem, "*zedonot na'asot lo ki-zekhuyot*" – his intentional sins are rendered merits.[3] This challenging statement, which is both intellectually puzzling and spiritually inspiring, would seem to be difficult to ignore by a codifier of the laws of *teshuvah.* Yet, Rambam omits any reference to it throughout his ten chapters of *Hilkhot Teshuvah*! Why does Rambam seemingly overlook the astounding potential to transform *zedonot* into *zekhuyot*?

Rambam eschewed the literal notion of "*zedonot na'asot lo ki-zekhuyot*" as an isolated, potentially misleading mystification of a crucial concept that might, ironically, also promote a narrow perspective on the scope and significance of *teshuvah.* He certainly perceived the

3. *Yoma* 86b.

significance of *teshuvah mei-ahavah* as the highest form of *teshuvah,* but precisely as a subset of the ideal *avodah mei-ahavah.* This inspired his dramatic decision to conclude all of *Hilkhot Teshuvah* and *Sefer ha-Madda* with the theme of *ahavat Hashem.* By broadening his presentation to include the ideal of serving Hashem out of love, Rambam further promoted the centrality of this theme. He thus accentuates that the spiritual alienation triggered by sin can engender a constructive appreciation of the existential need to repair and elevate one's bond with Hashem.

As a mode of *avodah mei-ahavah, teshuvah mei-ahavah* is the optimal way to serve *Ha-Kadosh Barukh Hu.* According to Rambam, "*na'asot lo ki-zekhuyot*" is the articulation of this very idea. *Teshuvah,* when executed consistently, broadly, and authentically, has the capacity to reinvigorate religious dedication. It impresses upon the transgressor the urgency of and an appreciation for the opportunity to stand "*lifnei Hashem*" (before God) and eliminate the obstruction that sin creates between man and his Creator. *Teshuvah* does not cause *zedonot* to turn into merits in a magical fashion. Rather, the net consequence of *teshuvah mei-ahavah* as a conscious process constructively enhances one's dedication and commitment to Torah life.

In truth, then, "*zedonot na'asot lo ki-zekhuyot*" is not absent from Rambam's *Hilkhot Teshuvah,* but rather implicitly central to his characterization of the telos of *teshuvah.*

Sha'arei Teshuvah: The *Hesed* of *Teshuvah*

Whereas Rambam's emphasis on *teshuvah* as a means of *avodat Hashem* portrays *teshuvah* as a natural dimension of religious observance, Rabbeinu Yonah paints *teshuvah* in a different light. This is evinced by his opening words in *Sha'arei Teshuvah*:

> מן הטובות אשר היטיב השם יתברך עם ברואיו, כי הכין להם הדרך לעלות מתוך פחת מעשיהם ולנוס מפח פשעיהם, לחשוך נפשם מני שחת ולהשיב מעליהם אפו, ולמדם והזהירם לשוב אליו כי יחטאו לו, לרוב טובו וישרו כי הוא ידע יצרם, שנאמר (תהלים כה:ח): "טוב וישר ה׳ על כן יורה חטאים בדרך", ואם הרבו לפשוע ולמרוד ובגד בוגדים בגדו, לא

סגר בעדם דלתי תשובה, שנאמר (ישעיה לא:ו): "שובו לאשר העמיקו סרה". ונאמר (ירמיה ג:כב): "שובו בנים שובבים ארפה משובותיכם".

Among Hashem's kindnesses to His creations is having prepared for them the way to rise from the pit of their deeds and to escape the trap of their offenses, to save themselves from destruction and to turn His wrath from them. In His great goodness and uprightness, He has taught and exhorted them to turn to Him upon having sinned against Him, for He knows the inclination of their hearts, as it is said, "Good and upright is Hashem; therefore, He instructs sinners in the way" (*Tehillim* 25:8). Even if they have offended and rebelled exceedingly and have been utterly faithless, He has not closed the doors of repentance to them, as it is said, "Turn unto Him against whom you have deeply rebelled" (*Yeshayahu* 31:6), and "Return, backsliding children; I will heal your backslidings" (*Yirmiyahu* 2:22).[4]

Rabbeinu Yonah's very first formulation, *"Min ha-tovot,"* stresses that *teshuvah* is unnatural and undeserved, a divine gift that can change one's trajectory in ways inconsistent with the natural fabric of life. Defining *teshuvah* as an act of divine beneficence, of *"rov tuvo,"* hearkens back to a comment of the Talmud Yerushalmi:

שאלו לחכמה חוטא מהו עונשו אמרו להם (משלי יג:כא) חטאים תרדף רעה. שאלו לנבואה חוטא מהו עונשו אמרה להן (יחזקאל יח:ד) הנפש החוטאת היא תמות. שאלו לקודשא בריך הוא: חוטא מהו עונשו אמר להן יעשו תשובה ויתכפר לו.

They asked Wisdom, "What is the punishment of a sinner?" It responded, "Evil will pursue sinners" (*Mishlei* 13:21). They asked Prophecy, "What is the punishment of a sinner?" It responded, "The sinful soul will perish" (*Yehezkel* 18:4). They asked the Holy

4. Translation adapted from the Feldheim edition of *Sha'arei Teshuvah*.

> One, blessed be He, "What is the punishment of a sinner?" He responded, "Let him repent and attain forgiveness."[5]

The Yerushalmi conveys the rule-breaking character of the concept of *teshuvah* and its apparent incompatibility with the principle of causality. According to the laws of cause and effect, repentance should be impossible. Thus, "*Hokhmah*" and "*Nevu'ah*" assume, quite sensibly, that sinners must suffer the consequences of their sins, since they cannot uproot the past. Hashem, however, establishes that *teshuvah* is possible, such that the existence of *teshuvah* reflects the goodness of God; it is "*min ha-tovot asher heitiv*."

To be sure, Rambam need not disagree with Rabbeinu Yonah's characterization of *teshuvah*, but the assessment of *teshuvah* as a *hesed* is not Rambam's focus.[6] Rambam does not emphasize the unnaturalness of *teshuvah*. Just as he refrains from citing explicitly the potential of "*na'asot lo zedonot ki-zekhuyot*," he does not highlight the Yerushalmi's presentation of *teshuvah* as inconsistent with the laws of nature. More central to Rambam is man's free choice and ability to change, the prerequisites that allow for the status of *teshuvah* as crucial to man's service of Hashem. While Rabbeinu Yonah's emphasis is on *teshuvah* as an extraordinary kindness that allows man to escape his tainted past, Rambam's emphasis is on *teshuvah* as a prospective means by which to further cement and uplift his *avodat Hashem* and achieve the peak of *avodah mei-ahavah*.

Other elements of Rabbeinu Yonah's initial formulation cohere as well with his perspective on *teshuvah* as *tovat Hashem*. Rabbeinu Yonah describes sin and its impact as that which traps and imprisons man, portending a bleak future, even ultimate destruction. Sin is spiritually toxic. It contaminates man's soul and places him in a spiritual swamp from

---

5. Yerushalmi *Makkot* 2:6.
6. Interestingly, even when Rambam eloquently marvels about the remarkable character of *teshuvah* (*Hilkhot Teshuvah* 7:7), he mostly focuses on the astonishing transformative impact or effect. Even in this context, he does not emphasize its miraculous, counter-causal nature, as formulated by the Yerushalmi, or its status as a divine gift, as recurrently articulated by Rabbeinu Yonah. I am not suggesting that Rambam disputes these motifs, but rather that his understanding of *teshuvah* as part of the fabric of *avodat Hashem* made it less urgent to project these emphases.

which he must extricate himself, his only lifeline the unearned opportunity to repent. Nonetheless, when man takes advantage of this divine *hesed,* he can be catapulted to spiritual levels he has yet to experience, in this respect parallel to Rambam's understanding of *na'asot lo ki-zekhuyot.*

Moreover, Rabbeinu Yonah accentuates the Torah's repeated warnings of the necessity of *teshuvah.* He recurrently emphasizes that *teshuvah* stems from Hashem's initiative, reinforcing his general approach that *teshuvah* is a gratuitous kindness:

> והוזהרנו על התשובה בכמה מקומות בתורה, והתבאר, כי התשובה מקובלת גם כי ישוב החוטא מרוב צרותיו, כל שכן אם ישוב מיראת השם ואהבתו, שנאמר (דברים ד, ל): "בצר לך ומצאוך כל הדברים האלה באחרית הימים ושבת עד ה׳ אלהיך ושמעת בקולו". והתבאר בתורה, כי יעזור ה׳ לשבים כאשר אין יד טבעם משגת ויחדש בקרבם רוח טהורה להשיג מעלת אהבתו, שנאמר (דברים ל, ב): "ושבת עד ה׳ אלהיך ושמעת בקולו ככל אשר אנכי מצוך היום אתה ובניך בכל לבבך ובכל נפשך".
>
> The Torah in many instances exhorts us in relation to repentance. It demonstrates that penance is accepted even when the sinner repents because of his many troubles, and all the more so when it proceeds from the fear and love of Hashem, as it is said, "In your distress, when all these things have come upon you, in the end of days, you will return to Hashem your God and hearken to His voice" (*Devarim* 4:30). And it is clear from the Torah that Hashem assists the penitent when he is limited by his nature and implants in him a spirit of purity, whereby he may attain the level of loving Him, as it is said, "And you shall return unto Hashem your God and hearken to His voice, according to all that I command you this day, you and your children, with all your heart and with all your soul" (ibid. 30:2).[7]

Rabbeinu Yonah underscores that *teshuvah* is often initiated by Hashem. The famous verse, "*Hashiveinu Hashem eilekha ve-nashuvah* – Hashem,

7. *Sha'arei Teshuvah* 1:1.

bring us back to You and we will return" (*Eikhah* 5:21), exemplifies this perspective. This divine initiative is a further expression of *teshuvah* as "*min ha-tovot.*" Although Rabbeinu Yonah, like Rambam, prioritizes *teshuvah mei-ahavah* over *teshuvah* prompted by suffering, he consistently conveys that the effectiveness of any and all *teshuvah* remains "*rov tovo.*"

The most striking difference between the respective orientations of Rambam and Rabbeinu Yonah pertains to viewing *teshuvah* either as a default natural component of religious life or as an extraordinary opportunity and independent obligation that requires warning and encouragement. Rabbeinu Yonah repeatedly asserts that Hashem instructs us about *teshuvah* and that the Torah ubiquitously warns and encourages us to capitalize on the opportunity for *teshuvah.* His concentration on *azharot ha-Torah* is unsurprising; it is consistent, after all, with his pervasive view that *teshuvah* is unnatural and counterintuitive, commanding man's attention by repeated emphasis. The Torah seeks to implant and entrench in man the recognition of the *hesed* of *teshuvah* and its profound potential.

Rambam, in keeping with his comprehensive stance that *teshuvah* is a natural and integral component of *avodat Hashem,* the coda of *Sefer ha-Madda,* presents a stark contrast. He conspicuously refrains from formulating the obligation of *teshuvah,* instead conveying the institution and its execution as a default given and shifting his focus to the mode of its methodology. In the first *halakhah* of *Hilkhot Teshuvah,* he writes:

> כל מצות שבתורה בין עשה בין לא תעשה אם עבר אדם על אחת מהן בין בזדון בין בשגגה כשיעשה תשובה וישוב מחטאו חייב להתודות לפני הא־ל ברוך הוא.
>
> If one has violated any mitzvah in the Torah, whether a positive or negative commandment, whether done purposely or accidentally, when he does *teshuvah* and returns from his sin, he is obligated to confess before God, blessed be He.[8]

8. *Hilkhot Teshuvah* 1:1.

Rambam presents the obligation associated with repentance as *viduy*, a celebrated position that demanded the attention of all Rambam commentators. Strikingly, the core imperative of repentance itself is merely assumed: "*ke-sheya'aseh teshuvah ve-yashuv mei-heto*." Consistent with this formulation, Rambam omits the obligation to repent in *Sefer ha-Mitzvot*, instead focusing on *viduy*.[9] These editorial choices reflect Rambam's perspective that *teshuvah* is simply a natural dimension of religious life, such that it needs no explicit commandment. The contrast to Rabbeinu Yonah, for whom *teshuvah* is an unnatural gift that cannot be taken for granted, could not be more stark. For Rabbeinu Yonah, the *azharot ha-Torah* that motivate man to engage in *teshuvah* are vital to his initiation and immersion into the repentance process.

The theme of *teshuvah* on Yom Kippur further reinforces this trend. In keeping with his tendency to formalize the obligatory aspect of *teshuvah*, Rabbeinu Yonah claims that there is a second, distinct commandment of *teshuvah* specifically on Yom Kippur:

> ומצות עשה מן התורה להעיר אדם את רוחו לחזור בתשובה ביום הכפורים שנאמר מכל חטאתיכם לפני ה׳ תטהרו. על כן הזהירנו הכתוב שנטהר לפני ה׳ בתשובתנו והוא יכפר עלינו ביום הזה לטהר אותנו.
>
> It is a positive commandment from the Torah for a man to arouse his spirit to repent on Yom Kippur, as it is stated, "From all your sins, you shall be pure before the Lord" (*Vayikra* 16:30). Therefore, the Torah warned us that we should purify ourselves before Hashem with our repentance, and He will atone for us on that day to purify us.[10]

9. *Sefer ha-Mitzvot, aseh* 73. Rambam's formulation in his *koteret* (heading) to *Hilkhot Teshuvah* is more complex: "מצות עשה אחת, והוא שישוב החוטא מחטאו לפני ה׳ ויתודה – There is one positive commandment, and it is for a sinner to repent from his sin before Hashem and confess." Here, it appears that the obligation includes two components: *teshuvah* and *viduy*. I discuss this topic at length in the first chapter, "*Teshuvah* and *Viduy*: The Ambitious Method of Coming Closer to Hashem."
10. *Sha'arei Teshuvah* 2:14; also see 4:17.

Rabbeinu Yonah's prooftext, "*lifnei Hashem tit'haru*," is noteworthy. The verse seems to promise purification as a result of Yom Kippur, not to legislate an imperative to purify oneself. Rabbeinu Yonah's innovative rendering reflects the extent to which he felt compelled to locate a source for this *teshuvah* obligation; since *teshuvah* is unnatural, all opportunities to capitalize on this gift must be made explicit.

In contrast, while Rambam does mention an obligation to do *teshuvah* on Yom Kippur – notably, the only time he formulates any type of *teshuvah* imperative – he is cursory and restrained:

> יום הכפורים הוא זמן תשובה לכל ליחיד ולרבים והוא קץ מחילה וסליחה לישראל לפיכך חייבים הכל לעשות תשובה ולהתודות ביום הכפורים.
>
> Yom ha-Kippurim is the time set aside for repentance for all, the individual as well as the many, for it is the apex of exoneration and pardon for Israel. Therefore, all are obligated to repent and confess on Yom ha-Kippurim.[11]

Rambam's formulation of "*lefikhakh*" is telling: The need to do *teshuvah* on Yom Kippur is simply an organic consequence of the time being opportune for achieving *selihah u-mehilah*. There is evidently no need to source this single example of a repentance imperative! Likewise, Rambam does not reference this obligation in the *koteret* (heading) to *Hilkhot Teshuvah*, and he certainly does not count it as an independent mitzvah in his *Sefer ha-Mitzvot*. This more subtle and limited presentation reflects Rambam's consistent perspective that *teshuvah* is a natural element of religious life. Yom Kippur – a singular expression, venue, and even pinnacle of *avodat Hashem* – naturally also incorporates a special expression of *teshuvah* as well.

Additionally, Rabbeinu Yonah's emphasis on the urgency and stakes of *teshuvah* and the danger of ignoring or bypassing the opportunity to repent is an important facet of his formulation – but not that of Rambam. Rabbeinu Yonah warns:

11. *Hilkhot Teshuvah* 2:7.

ודע, כי החוטא כאשר יתאחר לשוב מחטאתו יכבד עליו מאד ענשו בכל יום, כי הוא יודע כי יצא הקצף עליו ויש לו מנוס לנוס שמה, והמנוס הוא התשובה, והוא עומד במרדו והנו ברעתו, ובידו לצאת מתוך ההפכה, ולא יגור מפני האף והחמה, על כן רעתו רבה.

> The penalty of the sinner who defers repentance greatly intensifies itself each day, for he knows that anger has gone forth upon him and that there is a sanctuary to which he can flee, the sanctuary of repentance, and still he persists in his rebellion and continues in his evil. It is within his power to emerge from the turmoil, and still he does not fear the scorn and the wrath. His evil, therefore, is great.

Since *teshuvah* constitutes an act of divine generosity with incredible transformative capacity, one who rejects and squanders this opportunity to extricate from the tarnish of *het* descends into an even more precarious and problematic state.

Sha'arei Teshuvah, a work that exhorts man to take advantage of the *hesed* of *teshuvah,* thus emphasizes the peril of intransigently maintaining a state of rebellion. Although Rabbeinu Yonah's underscoring of the urgency to neutralize sin is not in opposition to Rambam's view of *teshuvah,* Rambam's *Hilkhot Teshuvah* does not reflect the same intense urgency to avoid spurning the divine kindness of *teshuvah,* focusing instead on the broader role and function of *teshuvah* as an organic part of one's *avodat Hashem.*[12]

12. Rambam and Rabbeinu Yonah also present distinctive views regarding the need to assess the classification and severity of a sin subject to *teshuvah.* Rambam (*Hilkhot Teshuvah* 1:1) ignores the requirement to grade the sin in question; *viduy* requires only that one identify a particular sin. In contrast, Rabbeinu Yonah (*Sha'arei Teshuvah* 3:1) repeatedly emphasizes how critical the evaluation of sin is to the *teshuvah* process. This different emphasis may derive from their respective conceptions of *teshuvah.* For Rambam, since the *teshuvah* process not only neutralizes individual transgressions but also reformulates one's relationship with Hashem, the stature of the individual sins that catalyze this process is less consequential. For Rabbeinu Yonah, in contrast, *teshuvah* is an opportunity to return from the depths of despair engendered by particular sins, and as such demands an awareness and reckoning with the specific nature of one's descent.

Taken in tandem, *Hilkhot Teshuvah* and *Sha'arei Teshuvah* provide mutually enhancing outlooks on the concepts and obligations of *teshuvah*. Notwithstanding their distinctive *teshuvah* orientations – and also due to them – the symbiotic contributions of Rambam and Rabbeinu Yonah guide our fulfillment and experience of *teshuvah*. They promote the singular experience of *teshuvah* – a divine gift that neutralizes past transgressions and at the same time charts a course to an enhanced spiritual relationship with Hashem, advancing us toward a future of *avodah mei-ahavah*.

Chapter 3
Mi-Darkhei ha-Teshuvah: Authentic Repentance

Of the many novel insights presented in Rambam's *Hilkhot Teshuvah,* Rambam's development of the "*darkhei ha-teshuvah,*" "the ways of repentance," is at the forefront. Rambam states:

> מדרכי התשובה להיות השב צועק תמיד לפני השם בבכי ובתחנונים ועושה צדקה כפי כחו ומתרחק הרבה מן הדבר שחטא בו ומשנה שמו כלומר אני אחר ואיני אותו האיש שעשה אותן המעשים ומשנה מעשיו כולן לטובה ולדרך ישרה וגולה ממקומו, שגלות מכפרת עון מפני שגורמת לו להכנע ולהיות עניו ושפל רוח.

> It is of the ways of *teshuvah* for the repentant to shout continuously before God with cries and supplications, for him to give charity according to his ability, for him to distance himself significantly from the matter with which he sinned, for him to change his name, as if to say, "I am a different person and not the person who committed those transgressions," for him to transform all of his ways into the good and straight, and for him to exile himself

from his place, for exile absolves sin, as it causes him to humble himself intensely.[1]

Rambam's formulation raises a variety of challenging questions.

First of all, what is the source for Rambam's description of "*darkhei ha-teshuvah*"? *Kesef Mishneh* assumes that Rambam's position is anchored in a comment of R. Yitzhak in *Rosh ha-Shanah*:

ואמר רבי יצחק: ארבעה דברים מקרעין גזר דינו של אדם, אלו הן: צדקה, צעקה, שינוי השם, ושינוי מעשה. צדקה - דכתיב (משלי י:ב) וצדקה תציל ממות, צעקה - דכתיב (תהלים קז:ו) ויצעקו אל ה׳ בצר להם וממצקותיהם יוציאם, שינוי השם - דכתיב (בראשית יז:טו) שרי אשתך לא תקרא את שמה שרי כי שרה שמה, וכתיב וברכתי אתה וגם נתתי ממנה לך בן, שינוי מעשה - דכתיב (יונה ג:י) וירא האלקים את מעשיהם, וכתיב וינחם האלקים על הרעה אשר דבר לעשות להם ולא עשה. ויש אומרים: אף שינוי מקום, דכתיב (בראשית יב:א) ויאמר ה׳ אל אברם לך לך מארצך, והדר ואעשך לגוי גדול.

And R. Yitzhak said: Four things uproot a man's fate, and these are the four: charity, screaming [in prayer], changing one's name, and changing one's deeds. Charity, as the verse states, "And charity will save from death" (*Mishlei* 10:2); screaming, as the verse states, "And they cried out to Hashem in distress, and He would deliver them from their distresses" (*Tehillim* 107:6); changing one's name, as the verse states, "As for Sarai your wife – do not call her name Sarai, for Sarah is her name," and it is written, "And I will bless her and also give you a son from her" (*Bereishit* 17:15); changing one's deeds, as the verse states, "And God saw their deeds," and it is written, "And God regretted the evil He said He would do to them and did not do it" (*Yonah* 3:10). And some say that even changing one's place uproots his fate, as the verse states, "And Hashem said to Avram, 'Go forth from your land,'"

1. Rambam, *Hilkhot Teshuvah* 2:4.

(*Bereishit* 12:1), and then He promised, "I will make you into a large nation" (ibid. 12:2).[2]

R. Yitzhak and the "*yesh omerim*" delineate all five of the various *darkhei ha-teshuvah* that Rambam records. Consequently, it is not surprising that *Kesef Mishneh* identifies R. Yitzhak's statement as Rambam's source. The context, however, is different in the two discussions. As Ritva notes, R. Yitzhak's "four things" are methods that can uproot one's fate. The act of changing one's name, in particular, divorces one from the astrological harm to which he is subject:

> **שינוי השם שמשנה שמו שאינו האיש בעל העבירות כדי שלא יזכירוהו לרעה, ובר מהכי דבטיל ונפיק מאצטגנינות דיליה כדרך שאמר באברהם (שבת קנו.).**
>
> The purpose of changing one's name is to declare that he is not the same person who committed sins in the past, and thereby prevent others from speaking negatively about him. And aside from this, another benefit of changing one's name is that his astrological fate is nullified and removed from him, as the *gemara* (*Shabbat* 156a) explains about Avraham.[3]

Yet, while R. Yitzhak's statement concerns the changing of one's *gezar din* (verdict), Rambam's statement concerns the acts of a repentant! The act of uprooting one's troubling destiny is certainly distinct in character from the act of repentance.

Kesef Mishneh himself accentuates Rambam's deviation from R. Yitzhak when he states:

> **ואל ה׳ דברים אלו רמז רבינו בדבריו אלה.**
>
> And our rabbi [Rambam] hints to these five things with these words.

2. *Rosh ha-Shanah* 16b.
3. Ritva, *Rosh ha-Shanah* 16b.

Clearly, *Kesef Mishneh* recognizes that Rambam does not quote R. Yitzhak's instruction, but rather only hints to it. Rambam reinvents the application of R. Yitzhak's words, and Rambam's comments therefore cannot be construed as a verbatim quotation. The source for Rambam is the *gemara* in *Rosh ha-Shanah*, but Rambam alters its meaning.

On what basis does Rambam diverge from the simple interpretation of R. Yitzhak's statement, broadening its scope to include not only *keri'at gezar din* but also *teshuvah*? What does Rambam's interpretation of the passage in *Rosh ha-Shanah* reflect about his understanding of the concept of *teshuvah*?

Lehem Mishneh notes another critical discrepancy between Rambam's comments and his apparent source:

> וכל החמשה הוזכרו בדברי רבינו...אף על פי דבגמרא אמרו דכל חד מנייהו סגי.
>
> And all five ways are mentioned in our rabbi's [Rambam's] words, even though the *gemara* states that one of the five is sufficient [to uproot one's fate].

If Rambam's source is the *gemara* in *Rosh ha-Shanah*, why does Rambam argue that all five of the behaviors detailed in the *gemara* are indispensable to the accomplishment of *darkhei ha-teshuvah*? After all, according to R. Yitzhak, only one of the five behaviors is necessary to uproot one's fate!

Perhaps a more basic question should be confronted as well. What is the meaning of Rambam's phrase, "*mi-darkhei ha-teshuvah*"? Rambam himself coins this terminology; it does not appear in the Mishnah or Gemara, and other *Rishonim* do not utilize it when discussing the same concept. Even Meiri, in *Hibbur ha-Teshuvah*, reformulates this idea. Lest we assume that Rambam's phraseology is merely coincidental, we must note that the phrase appears not only in *Hilkhot Teshuvah*, but also in *Hilkhot Ta'anit*:

> ודבר זה מדרכי התשובה הוא, שבזמן שתבוא צרה ויזעקו עליה ויריעו ידעו הכל שבגלל מעשיהם הרעים הורע להן ככתוב (ירמיהו ה:כה) עונותיכם הטו וגו׳, וזה הוא שיגרום להם להסיר הצרה מעליהם.

> And this is of the ways of *teshuvah*, that when suffering arises and they [*Klal Yisrael*] shout and blow trumpets, all will know that because of their bad deeds, they have been distressed, as the verse states, "Your sins have caused you to stray..." (*Yirmiyahu* 5:25), and this will cause them to remove the suffering from upon them.[4]

Rambam's usage of the same phrase in both *Hilkhot Teshuvah* and *Hilkhot Ta'anit* suggests that the phrase carries significant meaning; it is not simply a convenient way of describing the proper way to react to sin and a methodology for attaining forgiveness.[5] Rather, it is indicative of some broader concept and ideal. What are the full implications of *darkhei ha-teshuvah*?

To unpack the meaning of Rambam's *darkhei ha-teshuvah,* we begin by explaining Rambam's veering from the simple understanding of R. Yitzhak's comments. We can suggest two distinct, yet consistent, approaches.

First, in contradistinction to Ritva, Rambam may shy away from emphasizing astrological significance, especially in light of his broader rationalistic proclivities and specific rejection of this discipline. For Rambam, R. Yitzhak does focus on the uprooting of one's *gezar din,* but the method employed to uproot a *gezar din* demands the transformation of values, personality, and merit, rather than the alteration of one's astrological or mystical fate. It was natural for Rambam to apply R. Yitzhak's *keri'at gezar din* formula to a methodology of repentance, since repentance and *keri'at gezar din* share in common the need to transform one's personality and value system.[6]

4. *Hilkhot Ta'anit* 1:2.
5. See also *Hilkhot Teshuvah* 4:2, where Rambam again uses the term "*darkhei ha-teshuvah*" and mentions that which prevents one from accomplishing *darkhei ha-teshuvah.*
6. See *Shu"t ha-Rashba* 1:19. Rashba argues that exiling oneself from his locale, as R. Yitzhak advises, is beneficial not only for *shinuy mazal,* but also for attaining *kapparah* for one's sins. As we have suggested for Rambam, Rashba similarly does not limit the application of R. Yitzhak's advice to *shinuy mazal,* but rather includes attainment of *kapparah* as well.

Second, Rambam's application of R. Yitzhak's statement to *Hilkhot Teshuvah* reflects Rambam's tendency to broaden and expand throughout *Hilkhot Teshuvah.*[7] *Hilkhot Teshuvah,* the final section of *Sefer ha-Madda,* constitutes a climactic transition, bridging the ideas of *Sefer ha-Madda* with the ideas of *Sefer Ahavah. Hilkhot Teshuvah* emphasizes the ideal service of Hashem, a service motivated by *ahavah* and rooted in the proper legal philosophy of *Sefer ha-Madda.* For this reason, chapter 10 of *Hilkhot Teshuvah,* the section's final chapter, centers on the "*oved mei-ahavah,*"[8] the one who serves Hashem due to his love for Him. As evinced by Rambam's stance that the laws of *teshuvah* are the prerequisites for *avodah mei-ahavah,* Rambam defines and interprets the process of repentance in an all-encompassing fashion. *Teshuvah,* as the climax of *Sefer ha-Madda,* is not indispensable to man's life only because it facilitates his neutralizing of past sins; rather, *teshuvah,* at its finest, is an independently vital process, one that transforms a person into an *oved Hashem* and facilitates *avodah mei-ahavah.*[9]

Rambam's discussion of repentance for corrupt traits, values, and beliefs in the seventh chapter of *Hilkhot Teshuvah* further corroborates his broad understanding of repentance. Although Rambam records that true repentance includes the uprooting of certain emotions and traits, such as anger, hatred, and jealousy, this assertion is unsourced.[10] On what basis does Rambam justify his position? Additionally, we might question why Rambam waits until chapter 7 to discuss repentance focusing on character and personality; such discussion seems relevant to the core components of repentance, as outlined in chapters 1 and 2.

---

7. See the previous chapter, "An Alternative and Complementary Perspective on *Teshuvah*: Rabbeinu Yonah's *Sha'arei Teshuvah,*" which includes an analysis of the breadth and theme of Rambam's *Hilkhot Teshuvah.*
8. *Hilkhot Teshuvah* 10:2.
9. For a more extensive analysis of the tenth chapter of *Hilkhot Teshuvah,* see the chapter "*Ahavat Hashem* and *Talmud Torah*: The Telos of *Teshuvah.*"
10. *Hilkhot Teshuvah* 7:3. See *Migdal Oz,* ad loc., who suggests that Rambam's source is the concept of "*hirhurei aveirah kashu mei-aveirah*" (*Yoma* 29a). This suggestion, however, seems difficult, if not untenable; Rambam is explicit in his assertion that repentance must address not only thoughts of sin but also *middot ra'ot.*

Perhaps Rambam's understanding of *teshuvah,* as captured by his thesis of *darkhei ha-teshuvah,* explains these apparent anomalies. If *teshuvah* is necessary not only to counteract sin but also to propel man toward *avodah mei-ahavah,* then chapter 7 – which is dedicated to *ma'alat ha-teshuvah,* the greatness of repentance – is the most appropriate context in which to present repentance from traits. Rambam informs us that the greatness of repentance is precisely its transformative potential, but in order for *teshuvah* to achieve this ambition, it must be comprehensive; it must address both action and thought. Since *teshuvah,* in its most pristine form, is the laying of groundwork for service of Hashem *mei-ahavah,* no source is necessary to conclude that such *teshuvah* must encompass repentance that holistically addresses the entire personality.

Given Rambam's broad understanding of *teshuvah,* his reading of the passage in *Rosh ha-Shanah* emerges lucid and sensible. R. Yitzhak's statement advises one as to how to change his *gezar din*. Rambam intensifies and transforms R. Yitzhak's statement into "*darkhei ha-teshuvah,*" expanding its relevance beyond the uprooting of decrees and applying it to the institution of repentance as a whole. Rambam adds that as part of "*darkhei ha-teshuvah,*" one should not only shout, as R. Yitzhak advises for *keri'at gezar din,* but he should be "*tzo'ek tamid,*" shouting constantly. Moreover, he should not only yell, but he should yell "*bi-vkhi u-vetahanunim,*" with cries and pleas. One should not only give charity, as R. Yitzhak instructs, but he should do so "*ke-fi koho,*" according to his ability. He must not only distance himself from evil, but he must distance himself greatly – "*u-mitrahek harbeh.*" Finally, Rambam emphasizes that one must be "*meshaneh ma'asav kulan*"; he must change *all* of his ways.

Rambam's intensification of R. Yitzhak's instructions reflects Rambam's attitude toward them. For Rambam, they are part of *darkhei ha-teshuvah.* They are ways of motivating man toward and assisting him in self-evaluation and self-transformation. For *keri'at gezar din,* less intense shouting, charity, or changing of deeds may be sufficient, but for concrete repentance that leads to *avodah mei-ahavah,* intensification is necessary.

Furthermore, not only must these acts be strengthened qualitatively, but they must be bolstered quantitatively as well. Rambam, as *Lehem Mishneh* notes, requires all five actions as part of *darkhei ha-teshuvah*. For *keri'at gezar din*, one action may be sufficient, but for *teshuvah* that leads to *avodah mei-ahavah*, all five are necessary.

The motif of "*darkhei ha-teshuvah*" as a window into *teshuvah* dominates much of Rambam's *Hilkhot Teshuvah*. Interestingly, when Rambam articulates the well-known practice to increase giving of charity and multiply acts of kindness throughout the *Aseret Yemei Teshuvah*, the Ten Days of Repentance, he adds that the practice includes as well *"esek be-mitzvot*," involvement in *mitzvot*.[11] For Rambam, not only altruistic action should pervade the Ten Days; rather, the *ba'al teshuvah* must make extra effort to increase his punctiliousness regarding all commandments. Rambam's expansion of the scope of proper activity during the *Aseret Yemei Teshuvah* coheres precisely with his characterization of *"darkhei ha-teshuvah*." If *teshuvah* is not simply an accumulation of merits but also a process of personal transformation, one that directs and facilitates *avodah mei-ahavah*, then it must include intense involvement in all *mitzvot*.[12]

Thus, while they may seem innocuous on their surface, the "*darkhei ha-teshuvah*" are in fact the means, both quantitative and qualitative, that guide one on his path toward *avodah mei-ahavah*. This is not merely an itemized list of actions to take in order to achieve forgiveness. On the contrary, the phrase "*darkhei ha-teshuvah*," in its intensified form, signifies Rambam's all-encompassing understanding of *teshuvah*.[13]

---

11. *Hilkhot Teshuvah* 3:4.
12. See the chapter "Religious Stringency, Consistency, and the Implications of the *Aseret Yemei Teshuvah*."
13. See *Sefer Likkutim, Hilkhot Teshuvah* 3:3, who formulates the notion of repentance as "*takhlit bi-fnei atzmo*," a purpose in and of itself. Such a characterization highlights the approach to repentance not as solely a reaction to sin, but as a proactive effort to achieve *avodah mei-ahavah*.

Chapter 4

Teshuvah and Rebirth

S*hulhan Arukh* records the well-known practice to immerse in a *mikveh* prior to Yom Kippur:

> יכול לטבול וללקות מתי שירצה, רק שיהיה קודם הלילה; ואינו מברך על הטבילה.
>
> One may immerse and strike himself [as part of his fulfillment of *viduy*] whenever he desires, as long he does so prior to evening, and he should not recite a blessing on his immersion.[1]

Many have advanced suggestions as to the objective of the immersion prior to Yom Kippur.[2] Maharil offers a particularly striking explanation:

> טבילת ערב יום כפור אמר מהר"י סג"ל יש פוסקים לטבול אחר סעודת המפסקת בערב, כי עיקר הטבילה משום תשובה היא ויותר שיקרבנה

1. *Shulhan Arukh, Orah Hayim* 426:4.
2. See *Tur, Orah Hayim* 426, who quotes Rosh (*Yoma* 8:24) as entertaining the possibility that the practice is due to one's obligation to purify oneself prior to a holiday (*Rosh ha-Shanah* 16b). For extensive discussion of this practice, see the chapter "The Custom of Immersion and the Theme of Purification on Yom ha-Kippurim."

> לעצומו של יום יפה הדבר...וכן טבילת גר כשנתגייר טובלין אותו משום תשובה.
>
> Regarding immersion on the eve of Yom Kippur, Maharil states that according to some *Posekim*, one should immerse in the afternoon after the *se'udah ha-mafseket*, because the central purpose of his immersion is for the sake of repentance, and the closer his immersion is to the day [of Yom Kippur] itself, the better.... Similarly, when a convert immerses as part of his conversion, we immerse him for the sake of repentance.[3]

Maharil argues that one's immersion on the eve of Yom Kippur and a convert's immersion are both for the sake of *teshuvah*.

Darkhei Moshe refers to Maharil's view, but interprets it slightly differently:

> וכתב עוד מהרי"ל דאף על פי שטבל בערב ראש השנה ויודע שלא ראה קרי אפילו הכי יטבול בערב יום הכפורים משום תשובה כגר המתגייר.
>
> Maharil also wrote that although one immersed on *erev* Rosh ha-Shanah and knows that he did not experience a seminal emission afterward, nonetheless, he should immerse prior to Yom ha-Kippurim for the sake of repentance, like a convert at his conversion.[4]

According to *Darkhei Moshe*, the immersion of the eve of Yom Kippur and that of a convert not only share a common goal – repentance – but the immersion on *erev* Yom Kippur is actually intended to mimic the immersion of the convert. The *gemara* teaches that a convert experiences a type of rebirth at his conversion: "*Ger she-nitgayer ke-katan she-nolad damei* – A convert at his conversion is like a newborn child."[5] Similar to a convert, one who undergoes the process of repentance experiences a fundamental rebirth.

3. Maharil, *Hilkhot Erev Yom Kippur* 3.
4. *Darkhei Moshe, Orah Hayim* 606:3.
5. *Yevamot* 22a.

This understanding compels us to question the character of the rebirth of the repentant. What is the mechanism of such a rebirth, and what is its precise nature?

A response to these questions may be formulated by considering the uniqueness of *teshuvah*. The Yerushalmi states:

> שאלו לחכמה חוטא מהו עונשו אמרו להם (משלי יג:כא) חטאים תרדף רעה שאלו לנבואה חוטא מהו עונשו אמרה להן (יחזקאל יח:ד) הנפש החוטאת היא תמות שאלו לקודשא בריך הוא חוטא מהו עונשו אמר להן יעשו תשובה ויתכפר לו.
>
> They asked Wisdom, "What is the punishment of a sinner?" It responded, "Evil will pursue sinners" (*Mishlei* 13:21). They asked Prophecy, "What is the punishment of a sinner?" It responded, "The sinful soul will perish" (*Yehezkel* 18:4). They asked the Holy One, blessed be He, "What is the punishment of a sinner?" He responded, "Let him repent and attain forgiveness."[6]

The Yerushalmi expresses the innovative and rule-breaking character of the concept of *teshuvah*. According to laws of cause and effect, repentance should be impossible. Wisdom and Prophecy thus assume that sinners must suffer the consequences of their sins, as they cannot uproot the past. God, however, establishes *teshuvah* as a possibility. Repentance is based not on human logic, but on divine logic – perhaps divine generosity and compassion.

The uniqueness of *teshuvah* as described in the Yerushalmi presses us to formulate some understanding of its mechanism in human terms. Broadly speaking, we can suggest two approaches.

The first approach is that the efficacy of repentance is rooted in a distinctive view of time. Usually, the past is assumed to be inaccessible; the novel concept of *teshuvah* allows one to redeem or even rewrite one's past. *Teshuvah* proceeds on the assumption of access to the past.[7] This

6. Yerushalmi *Makkot* 2:6.
7. This is a prominent theme in R. Soloveitchik's *Al ha-Teshuvah* and relates to the Bergsonian theory of time. For a more extensive treatment of this topic, see the chapter

access, in turn, enables the neutralization, reconciliation, and even the revision of past transgressions. Repentance motivated by fear of God (*teshuvah mi-yirah*) or inspired by love of God (*teshuvah mei-ahavah*), each of which have the capacity to reframe previous misconduct,[8] exemplify this process.

The second understanding is that *teshuvah* is possible because *teshuvah* is transformational. This view is subtly articulated by Rambam. The penitent transforms himself to such an extent that he may declare, "*Eini oto ha-ish* – I am not that same person!"[9] If the penitent achieves this comprehensive transformation, he is no longer held accountable for sins of the past, the transgressions of his previous religious persona. It is this perspective that reflects the element of "rebirth" entailed in *teshuvah*. After the experience of *teshuvah,* one's past does not define or undermine one's present.

However, it is critical to emphasize that even as one undergoes a change of identity, Halakhah rejects the notion of a "born-again" Jew. No such concept exists in Judaism.[10] One's transformation through the process of *teshuvah* is limited and not absolute; one cannot fully divorce himself from his past. Rather, the authentic *ba'al teshuvah* is transformed

---

"*Ani le-Dodi ve-Dodi Li*: The Relationship Between Hashem and the Jewish People." It is worth noting that while the idea of this principle is particularly central and helpful in explaining several anomalies of *teshuvah,* it is a principle that is applicable to all elements of *kedushat ha-zeman,* and even to other categories of Halakhah. For example, the notions of *sippur* and *zekhirat yetzi'at Mitzrayim,* the reenactment of the *Aseret ha-Dibrot* on Shavu'ot, and the more general notion of *zakhor* that arises in various contexts are tied to this outlook on time. Moreover, this perspective on time also pertains to the notions of *zekhut avot* and the *brit* formulated in *Devarim* 29:14.

8. *Yoma* 86b.
9. *Hilkhot Teshuvah* 2:4. For an extensive treatment of this perspective, which Rambam characterizes as "*mi-darkhei ha-teshuvah,*" see the chapter "*Mi-Darkhei ha-Teshuvah*: Authentic Repentance." The themes developed in that chapter dovetail with the approach developed here.
10. See Maharal, *Netivot Olam, Netiv ha-Teshuvah* 8:1, who argues that heresy and *arayot* are sins that are so transformative that they are excluded from the process of *teshuvah* in the human world; repentance can be achieved only through death. Maharal's contention supports the notion that even the genuine *ba'al teshuvah* is still connected to his past; complete *teshuvah* from such defining sin would entail a total disconnection from the past, which is antithetical to authentic *teshuvah.*

while maintaining continuity with his past, both the constructive and the deplorable; his personal identity continues, but it is also transformed in the present.

It is significant that Rambam himself underscores this balance in ruling that on Yom Kippur, one should confess all of his sins, even transgressions from previous years. Sins from previous years are still a part of one's identity, even though they are no longer held against him.[11] Moreover, one cannot and does not elude or evade concrete punishment by means of *teshuvah*. *Teshuvah* is not a refuge from legal or moral responsibility, but rather a mechanism that actually assumes greater accountability, allowing for the reconciliation and sometimes even redemption of past infractions.[12]

This point marks the convergence of the two approaches we have delineated as conceptually underpinning the institution of *teshuvah*. Proportional, halakhically-mandated consequences contribute to and facilitate transformational *teshuvah* by integrating the problematic past with an unencumbered present and future.[13]

11. *Hilkhot Teshuvah* 2:8.
12. *Yoma* 86b, regarding "*avonot she-na'asot shegagot o zekhuyot.*"
13. The concept of *ger she-nitgayer ke-katan she-nolad damei*, although focused on a new legal status, similarly does not imply complete negation of the past. Conversion is not a pathway to avoid punishments for transgression of Noahide law, and notwithstanding the new identity of the *ger*, there are certain universalist *halakhot* (*onshin, peru u-revu*, and *yerushat bekhor*) that remain tied to his past (see *Yevamot* 22a, 48b, 62a; *Sanhedrin* 71b). It is worth noting that Maharil's formulation, in contrast to that of *Darkhei Moshe*, perceives *teshuvah* as the paradigm for transformation, underscoring the component of integration with the relevant parts of one's past. See also Ritva, *Ketubot* 3b.

Chapter 5

A Blueprint for *Teshuvah*

In *Parashat Nitzavim,* which is generally read just before Rosh ha-Shanah, the Torah records several crucial passages that depict the highs and lows of the national destiny of the Jewish People – the devastating impact of sin, exile, loss, and destruction (*Devarim* 29:19–27), as well as the equally impressive phenomenon of rebirth and return to prosperity and divine providence (ibid. 30:1–9). This broad description culminates with a direct reference to the *teshuvah* that will bring about this remarkable turn of events:

כי תשוב אל ה׳ אלוקיך בכל לבבך ובכל נפשך

> When you return to Hashem your God with all your heart and with all your soul. (Ibid. 30:10)

The Torah then dramatically introduces an ambiguous mitzvah:

> כי המצוה הזאת אשר אנכי מצוך היום לא נפלאת היא ממך ולא רחוקה היא. לא בשמים הוא לאמר מי יעלה לנו השמימה ויקחה לנו וישמענו אתה ונעשנה. ולא מעבר לים הוא לאמר מי יעבר לנו מעבר לים ויקחה לנו וישמענו אתה ונעשנה. כי קרוב אליך הדבר מאד בפיך ובלבבך לעשותו.

> For this mitzvah that I am commanding you today is not wondrous for you, nor is it distant. It is not in the heavens, such that you may say, "Who will ascend to the heavens and take it for us, and we will listen to it and do it!" And it is not across the sea, such that you may say, "Who will pass across the sea and take it for us, and we will listen to it and do it!" For this matter is very close to you; it is in your mouth and your heart, so that you can fulfill it. (Ibid. 30:11–14)

The unspecified imperative referred to here is clearly well within our grasp. But what mitzvah are the *pesukim* referring to?

In the continuation, the Torah presents the choice of life and good vs. death and evil (ibid. 30:15), conveying the urgency of the implementation of "*ha-mitzvah ha-zot*." Clearly, a major principle of Judaism is being projected here, but the identity of that principle is ambiguous.

The Talmud,[1] Rashi,[2] and Rambam[3] interpret this imperative as a reference to study of Torah. This opinion is readily understandable, as *talmud Torah* is deemed "*ke-neged kulam*," equivalent to all of the *mitzvot*.[4] Torah study is the source for Jewish education and values and is the most crucial institution that exists in Jewish life.

In contrast to this view, Ramban suggests that the "*mitzvah ha-zot*" is the obligation of *teshuvah*.[5] His reading is reinforced by an analysis of the context and language of the previous sections, which discusses the *teshuvah* of *Am Yisrael*. *Teshuvah* is the great principle that holds life and death in its hands; it is the mitzvah that is in our grasp and that every individual must strive to achieve.

Ramban's view is consistent with the prominence of *teshuvah* as a vehicle for personal, communal, and national transformation. *Hazal* considered the very existence and possibility of *teshuvah* as a gift, even a miracle. The ability to reinvent oneself by extricating oneself from past

1. *Eiruvin* 55a.
2. Rashi, *Devarim* 30:11.
3. *Hilkhot Talmud Torah* 3:8.
4. *Pe'ah* 1:1.
5. Ramban, *Devarim* 30:11.

behavioral patterns and by neutralizing sin and past inadequacy seems to be a philosophically problematic notion, as it denies moral and behavioral causality. This is particularly true of the more ambitious forms of *teshuvah mi-yirah* (repentance out of fear of Hashem) and *teshuvah mei-ahavah* (repentance out of love of Hashem), which have a remarkable transformative impact on the sin itself.[6] Yet, *teshuvah* is a centerpiece of the halakhic outlook; that man can and must mold his spiritual destiny is axiomatic. This is particularly urgent in the period beginning with Rosh ha-Shanah and concluding with Yom Kippur.[7]

An analysis of these *pesukim* according to Ramban's reading provides a blueprint for *teshuvah.* This passage contributes significantly to our understanding of the challenges and possibilities of *teshuvah,* and it illuminates the process and methodology of this crucial institution/ mitzvah.

Lo Rehokah Hi

One element of *teshuvah* emphasized in these *pesukim* is its accessibility. This point is conveyed repeatedly and emphatically in these verses: "It is not wondrous for you, nor is it distant.... For this matter is very close to you; it is in your mouth and your heart, so that you can fulfill it." Meiri begins his work on *teshuvah* (*Hibbur ha-Teshuvah*) by emphasizing the importance of not despairing in the quest for repentance. Being cognizant of our capacity to succeed not only dispels counterproductive frustration, but also reflects the nature of *teshuvah* and religious growth as meaningful challenges.

Furthermore, the Torah's intriguing formulations preclude and reject a decisive role for extraneous factors, while at the same time hinting at the obstacles that must and can be overcome. They underscore that misguided or overstated nostalgia and over-idealization of other eras or circumstances are generally counterproductive, unless they inspire and motivate, rather than frustrate by raising the bar to unattainable levels.

The concept of "*lo rehokah hi*" encourages man to reject the sense of frustration and hopelessness due to the apparently overwhelming

6. See *Yoma* 86a.
7. *Rosh ha-Shanah* 18a.

distance that separates between him and Hashem, particularly as a consequence of sin. This feeling can impede the effort toward *teshuvah.* The Torah perceives the formidability of the task as a catalyst for greater effort, as the experience of loss and distance underscores the negative effects of sin. Since man's purpose in the world is only to develop a relationship with Hashem, the sense of purposelessness and insignificance that results when one loses his spiritual bearings and anchor must trigger his motivation to return.

Lo Niflet Hi

The motif of "*lo niflet hi*" is equally important. In *Ish ha-Halakhah,* R. Soloveitchik's magnificent depiction of the uniqueness of halakhic Judaism, he contrasts what he calls standard Religious Man and Halakhic Man. He demonstrates that unlike other religions, Judaism first and foremost focuses on concrete this-worldly norms and the sanctification of the real world, not on mysticism and the flight to a more spiritual realm. The process of *teshuvah,* by extension, is neither mysterious nor mystical. It is rooted in the accessible exoteric categories of Halakhah. Man's ability to sanctify the mundane and the physical world that he inhabits is the basis for the laws of *berakhot* (blessings), *taharat ha-mishpahah* (family purity), and *Hoshen Mishpat,* the comprehensive code of civil law that governs every aspect of human interaction. Halakhah's vast scope contrasts with the laws of other religions, which focus almost exclusively on the more obvious "spiritual/ritual" sphere. The halakhic approach reflects not compromise of spirituality, but, to the contrary, a greater ambition.

In *teshuvah,* this consideration of "*lo niflet hi*" is particularly acute. Sin reflects man's failure to attain his lofty goal, having succumbed to the pressures or temptations of the concrete world. Yet, in the process of *teshuvah,* man is not called upon to reject the physical world, but rather to rededicate to the struggle and ambition to sanctify his existence and the world around him. *Teshuvah* is a rigorous, lengthy process, exoteric and human in every way.

Lo ba-Shamayim Hi

The concept of "*lo ba-shamayim*" further declares that Judaism, and by extension the process of *teshuvah,* does not demand an angelic or other-worldly posture, nor does it require perfection in either deed or commitment.

Importantly, this verse is invoked by *Hazal* in a celebrated passage establishing the principle of man's partnership with God in the development of the halakhic system.[8] The Talmud explains that precisely because of the perfection and self-sufficiency of the Torah given at Sinai, and due to its ambition for man's spiritual growth, there is no need for divine intervention in halakhic decision-making. The tools and methodology of interpretation and adjudication are all part of the Torah, and man is charged with implementing that system through its divinely ordained rules. The sincere halakhist who is properly trained in those rules and who is fully committed to Torah and *yirat Shamayim,* willing to surrender to its rule and sensibilities, becomes a significant partner in the endeavor of Torah, making divine intervention unnecessary: "*Lo ba-shamayim hi.*" The fact that the halakhist's sincere input is indispensable, even decisive, reflects Hashem's ambition for man, as well as the enormous responsibility that accompanies and is the basis for his prerogatives.

Man's significant, if subordinate, role in the world of Halakhah constitutes a leitmotif in the writings and thought of R. Soloveitchik. R. Soloveitchik contrasts Halakhic Man's creative contributions with the generally passive posture of the admired heroic figures of other religions. The Jewish view reflects man's inherent value and potential for spirituality and sanctity.

This remarkable perspective attesting to man's vast potential qualifies man *qua* man – not as an angel – as a candidate for the gift of *teshuvah.* Man need not relinquish his humanity in order to restore his relationship with Hashem. Instead, he needs to elevate and sanctify his physical and human dimension and channel it to Hashem's service. In Judaism, man is always superior to angels. Because of – not despite – his humanity, he is privileged to have and observe the Torah.

8. *Bava Metzia* 59a, regarding the "*tanur shel Ahnai.*"

Lo mei-Ever la-Yam Hi

At the same time, *teshuvah* is also not "*mei-ever la-yam*." One need not travel away from society in order to achieve it. Halakhah rejects a decisive normative role for the social-cultural environment in human behavior. This is most certainly not due to a denial of its profound impact. Indeed, the concept of "*shakhen ra*" (the influence of bad neighbors) and the admonition to avoid "*moshav leitzim*" (a clique of scoffers) are pervasive and powerful themes in *Hazal,* who were keenly sensitive to the power of environment and prevailing sensibilities and norms. Rather, it is a testament to the ability and obligation to overcome such negative influences; it attests to the dominant concept of personal responsibility, the foundation for all reward and punishment. Personal choice (*behirah hofshit*) stands at the center of *teshuvah*.[9] According to the halakhic view, man has the capacity, and therefore the obligation, to insulate himself from unacceptable attitudes and conduct. He must extricate himself from or overcome his environment when necessary by strengthening his inner world, which dictates his own responses, and when possible, he must help shape the world around him.[10] Yaakov Avinu indicated as much to his brother Esav when he declared that he was able to fulfill the six hundred thirteen commandments in Lavan's home.[11] He ultimately left that home when he felt Lavan's influence had become too intoxicating or confusing.

R. Soloveitchik often emphasized his belief that Judaism can thrive in any society given the proper *yirat Shamayim* and level of commitment.[12] This conviction is predicated on the theme that Torah and its values are capable of fortifying a person, providing a powerful foundation that enables man to meet his challenges.

9. Indeed, in Rambam's *Hilkhot Teshuvah,* the principle of *behirah hofshit* is discussed in the fifth and sixth of the ten chapters dedicated to *teshuvah.*
10. See Rambam, *Sefer ha-Mitzvot, aseh* 3.
11. See Rashi, *Bereishit* 32:5.
12. A strong example of this is the following comment: "Here God teaches a fundamental truth about Judaism. The wisdom and moral principles are recognizable and understandable in every location, in every country – even on the moon .... Judaism must also be taught outside Israel." See *Mesoras HaRav Chumash, Bereishit* 28:10.

Be-Fikha u-Vilevavkha

Finally, we turn from the challenge and misconceptions to the methodology. The words "*be-fikha u-vilevavkha la-asoto* – in your mouth and your heart, so that you can fulfill it," constitute a remarkable guarantee that notwithstanding all of the misconceptions, which are really reflections of enormous challenges, *teshuvah* is within man's grasp and can be attained with nothing more than the basic tools of his inner life.

The first of these tools is the power of prayer through articulation – "*be-fikha*." By virtue of a mechanism to reach Hashem and simultaneously achieve self-knowledge (as indicated by the word for prayer, the reflexive "*le-hitpallel*"), man is able to place his needs and relationship to his Creator in better perspective. According to Ramban, "*be-fikha*" also refers specifically to the *viduy*, the confession stage that is indispensable to *teshuvah*, as it formulates and concretizes man's failings, stripping away rationalization and denial and paving the way for honest introspection and ultimately for change.

The second component, "*bi-levavkha*," projects the emotional-intellectual resources of heart and mind that can reshape and regulate man's inner world and dictate his hierarchy of values and priorities. Finally, "*la-asoto*" establishes the role of actions that concretely implement the values of Torah through halakhic norms. The this-worldly nature of halakhic religious commitment alluded to above – which is not a concession to the physical world, but rather a reflection of higher spiritual ambition – demands that profound inner change be concretized into physical and measured actions that also impact upon others.

The promise of accessibility of *teshuvah* and the delineation of a well-defined program to achieve it does not dismiss or ignore the challenges and obstacles, as noted. Moreover, the *pesukim* indicate that success is contingent upon the intensity of one's commitment. As the *gemara* notes, one need not storm the heavens, simulate conditions of "*eiver la-yam*," or immerse oneself in esoteric study and mystical actions in order to attain the goal and gift of *teshuvah*. But one's devotion, dedication, and conviction to religious self-improvement must nevertheless match the intensity that would have been required had these radical, formidable standards been established as the *sine qua non* of *teshuvah*![13] The gift of accessibility and attainability should not be misconstrued or exploited as a license for a tepid or mediocre effort to achieve so crucial a goal.

At the culmination of the *teshuvah* period, on Yom Kippur, we withdraw temporarily from the physical world, imitating the angels on high by standing and declaring aloud, "*Barukh shem kevod malkhuto le-olam va-ed* – Blessed is the name of His glorious kingdom for all eternity." We do so precisely to project the intensity of our commitment, our willingness to go to any lengths if they are demanded, and to demonstrate that our more balanced spiritual program throughout the year springs from the same devotion that would have characterized a more ascetic and esoteric approach; it is just as passionate and tenacious.

In this sense, the simplicity of "*be-fikha u-vilevavkha la-asoto*" does not belie the absolute comprehensiveness and ambitiousness of the task. The willingness to scale the heavens in our efforts to refashion our relationship with Hashem, combined with the accessibility guaranteed by the Torah, challenge and inspire each of us to aspire to a complete *teshuvah*, as individuals and as a community, in the *Yamim Nora'im* period. The multidimensional program outlined in the Torah is the blueprint for personal and collective introspection and transformation.

13. *Eiruvin* 55a.

Teshuvah Sihot

Chapter 6
Le-David and *Teshuvah*: Achieving Clarity of Purpose

There is a custom to recite *Tehillim* 27, "*Le-David Hashem ori ve-yishi*," throughout the month of Elul. This practice is established by the *midrash*, which comments on the opening verse of the psalm:

> רבנין פתרי קרא בראש השנה וביום הכפורים. אורי בראש השנה, שהוא יום הדין, שנאמר והוציא כאור צדקך ומשפטך כצהרים. וישעי ביום הכפורים, שיושיענו וימחול לנו על כל עונותינו.

> The Sages interpreted this verse as referring to Rosh ha-Shanah and Yom Kippur. "*Ori* – my light" – on Rosh ha-Shanah, as it is the Day of Judgment, and another verse states, "He shall put forth your justice as the light, your judgment as the noonday" (*Tehillim* 37:6). "*Ve-yishi* – and my salvation" – on Yom Kippur, when He shall save us and forgive all our sins.[1]

1. *Midrash Tehillim* 27:4.

It seems, however, that what underlies the psalm's recitation during Elul runs deeper than its first few words. The psalm's central theme is highlighted in two crucial verses (27:3–4):

> אם תחנה עלי מחנה לא יירא לבי אם תקום עליו מלחמה בזאת אני בוטח. אחת שאלתי מאת ה׳ אותה אבקש שבתי בבית ה׳ כל ימי חיי לחזות בנעם ה׳ ולבקר בהיכלו.
>
> If a camp encamps against me, I shall not fear; if a war arises against me, in this I shall trust. One thing I have asked of God, it I shall request: to sit in the house of God all the days of my life, to gaze upon God's pleasure, and to visit His temple.

These verses seem disjointed. The first appears to relate to some promise from Hashem, the acknowledgment of which soothes the Jewish People and builds their confidence when they are distressed and besieged. But the second verse does not appear to describe any such panacea. Instead, it details a seemingly unrelated lofty ideal of frequenting Hashem's house.

Troubled by this juxtaposition, Rashi and Radak are motivated to find the antecedent of "*be-zot ani votei'ah* – in this I shall trust" in earlier verses. Ibn Ezra, however, cites a position that finds the reference of "*be-zot ani votei'ah*" in the request of the following verse. This approach, unlike that of Rashi and Radak, allows the verses to be read as one thought, with a colon between the verses: "In this I shall trust: [In that] one question I have asked of God…" What is the correlation between these two verses?

To understand how the request forms a basis for confidence and security, we must analyze the aspiration articulated in the verse – "*shivti be-veit Hashem* – to sit in the house of God."

Malbim focuses on the striking phrase "*otah avakeish* – it I shall request." A normal request, explains Malbim, consists of two separate components: the *bakashah* (request), which describes the goal of the petitioner, and the *she'eilah* (question), which details the strategy the petitioner hopes to adopt together with the other party. In this case, uniquely, the question functions as the request itself – "*ahat* ***sha'alti***…

otah ***avakeish.*** "To sit in the house of God all the days of my life" is simultaneously the method and objective.

The unity of *she'eilah* and *bakashah* expresses itself in a chronological sense as well. Malbim notes that the verse begins in the past tense – "I have asked" – but transitions to the future tense – "I will request." He explains that unlike situational requests, which are relevant only as long as a particular situation lasts, the request "to sit in the house of God" is timeless and ties together past and future.[2]

The timeless clarity of purpose afforded by the unity of *she'eilah* and *bakashah,* of means and ends, is precisely the oasis that provides confidence and security to the person in crisis. Tactics can, and often must, deliver reprieve in a particular situation. But a clear objective offers a broader sense of perspective; it brings long-term confidence and provides a greater sense of equanimity. One whose timeless goal is "*shivti be-veit Hashem,*" sitting in the house of God, understands the value and purpose in his life. Such a perspective allows him to weather any crisis.

This clarity of perspective is central to the concept of *teshuvah* and links this powerful psalm to the month of Elul. Indeed, this idea is expressed in one of the tenets of *teshuvah*:

> האומר אחטא ואשוב אחטא ואשוב אין מספיקין בידו לעשות תשובה.
>
> One who says, "I shall sin and then repent, I shall sin and then repent" is not provided the opportunity to do *teshuvah.*[3]

Meiri notes that this rule is counterintuitive in practice.[4] One whose sin is entirely rebellious, without any repentant intention, can later repent, but one whose failure is only temporary from the start is not afforded the opportunity to repent! To explain this phenomenon, Meiri focuses

2. Expressing a similar idea, Rashi (*Tehillim* 27:4) quotes one opinion that interprets the word "*u-levaker,*" to visit, as related to the word "*boker,*" morning. According to this interpretation, the speaker expresses a desire to visit God every morning and thus develop a persistent, long-term relationship.
3. *Yoma* 8:9.
4. *Hibbur ha-Teshuvah* , *Meishiv Nefesh* 1:3.

on cynicism and the built-in exploitation of *teshuvah* as the culprits that prevent its efficacy.

One who attempts to abuse *teshuvah* does not succeed in attaining it, because *teshuvah* is accomplished by gaining clarity of perspective, by unifying *she'eilah* and *bakashah*. If one instead intends to use *teshuvah* to overcome an imminent hurdle or to secure a positive divine verdict, but at the same time he wants to retain the right to lapse into sin, he has lost the unity of means and end. This betrayal of *teshuvah* turns it into a tactic instead of a perspective. "I shall sin and then repent" is inconsistent with the notion of *teshuvah* as a clear perspective, and its inefficacy is a result of that inconsistency, not merely a punishment for abusing the *teshuvah* process.

During the month of Elul, when we focus our thoughts toward *teshuvah*, we recite the psalm centered around the timeless, unambiguous ideal at the center of *teshuvah*: "To sit in the house of God." The clarity of purpose expressed by the unity of *she'eilah* and *bakashah* is the centerpiece of our Elul enterprise, the single factor "in which we shall trust."

Chapter 7

Ani le-Dodi ve-Dodi Li: The Relationship Between Hashem and the Jewish People

The *gemara* cites R. Elazar's comment that whenever a *zivug rishon* (first marriage) ends in divorce, the Temple altar sheds tears:

> אמר ר' אלעזר כל המגרש אשתו ראשונה אפילו מזבח מוריד עליו דמעות.
>
> R. Elazar says: Anyone who divorces his first wife, even the altar sheds tears over him.[1]

What is the connection between a first marriage and the altar that accounts for this emotional response?

Maharsha offers a very technical explanation:

1. *Gittin* 90b; *Sanhedrin* 22a.

> הוא משל כאלו המזבח בוכה עליו שהמגרש אשתו אשת נעורים ממעט אכילת זבחים דאשת הנעורים מצויה שמביאה קיני זיבה ולידה למזבח.
>
> It is as if the altar itself cries, because one who divorces the wife of his youth (*eshet ne'urim*) diminishes the amount of sacrificial offerings, as it is common for the wife of one's youth to bring childbirth and *zavah* offerings on the altar.[2]

A first marriage is more likely to produce children; a divorce thus likely reduces the quantity of childbirth and *zavah* offerings. In this respect, the altar is "upset," as its activity is diminished when a first marriage concludes in divorce.

While technically sound, this is obviously not a particularly inspirational interpretation. Elsewhere, Maharsha provides a more edifying explanation.[3] The *Nevi'im* and *Ketuvim* often invoke the relationship between a husband and wife as a metaphor for the relationship between Hashem and *Kenesset Yisrael*, the Jewish People. Maharsha explains that *zivug rishon* and *zivug sheni* (a second marriage) parallel the First and Second Temples. The degree of sanctity and quantity of sacrificial activity in the First Temple far surpassed that of the Second Temple. This decline, which is emblematic of the very quality of this lofty relationship, prompts the altar to "weep."

In parallel fashion, it can be suggested that the altar bemoans the tragedy of the *egel ha-zahav*, the golden calf, which marred the initial idealistic bond between the Jewish People and God. At Sinai, the Jewish People accepted the Torah, and the building of the *Mishkan* was intended to be the marital *huppah* and their shared dwelling place. In the midst of the wedding itself, the Jewish People sullied the fledgling relationship and desecrated that exclusive bond by constructing the golden calf.[4] In this metaphor, the distinction between *zivug rishon* and *zivug sheni* is a consequence of the sin of betrayal at the golden calf.

---

2. *Hiddushei Aggadot, Sanhedrin* 22a.
3. *Hiddushei Aggadot, Gittin* 90b.
4. For an exploration of the significance of the *het ha-egel*, see my "*Chet ha-Eigel*: A Catastrophic Theological and Ideological Lapse," available at torahweb.org.

The Broken Relationship

The idea that discord between a husband and wife is symbolic of a disconnect – even a rupture – in the relationship between Hashem and the Jewish People resonates throughout Jewish theology. The poignant metaphor of a wayward wife repentantly returning "*le-ishah ha-rishon*," to her first husband – symbolically casting *Klal Yisrael* as the wife who has betrayed Hashem, her faithful husband – is quite prominent throughout *Tanakh*.[5]

The marital bond paradigm of Hashem's relationship with the Jewish People is, of course, the dominant metaphor of *Shir ha-Shirim*.[6] It is therefore unsurprising that this *megillah* is also perceived as a source that calls for introspection and *teshuvah*, centering on the demands and opportunities of that relationship. In this context, we encounter a passionate declaration and articulation of devotion:

אני לדודי ודודי לי.

I am my beloved's and my beloved is mine. (*Shir ha-Shirim* 6:3)

Avudraham's insight, which was popularly cited by subsequent halakhic thinkers, is that the first letters of each word in this phrase form an acronym for אלול, the period that initiates intense reassessment of this special bond, thereby reinforcing this theme.[7]

Furthermore, the conceptual basis for the halakhic construct of *teshuvah mei-ahavah* (repentance motivated by love) is patterned after this seminal theme of *Shir ha-Shirim*.[8] Rambam explains that *ahavat Hashem*, love of God, is the highest level of religiosity that one can attain. This ideal is depicted dramatically as an all-encompassing, even (constructively) obsessive relationship between a husband and wife, whose mutual devotion is absolute. That intensely single-minded admiration,

5. See, for example, *Hoshe'a* 2:9: "*Eilkhah ve-ashuvah el ishi ha-rishon* – I will go and return to my first husband."
6. See Rambam, *Hilkhot Teshuvah* 10:3.
7. Avudraham, *Seder Tefillot Rosh ha-Shanah*, 260.
8. *Yoma* 86a.

devotion, and longing models how *Kenesset Yisrael* are to cultivate their feelings toward God.[9] Indeed, *Bah* cites the verse "*Ani le-dodi ve-dodi li*" as reflecting the *teshuvah mei-ahavah* performed during Elul.[10]

Thus, the casting of the relationship between *het* and *teshuvah*, sin and repentance, in terms of returning to one's first husband is a notion that deserves further attention and examination.

The Marital Relationship Between the Jewish People and Hashem

Let us begin by examining in greater depth the nature of this marital relationship. Following the pattern reflected by the numerous verses of *Tanakh*, metaphors describing this kind of marital relationship between the Jewish People and God abound in *Hazal*. *Hazal* understood the relationship between God and the Jewish People as a marriage in which the Torah serves as the marriage contract. Thus, for example, the *mishnah* explains that "*be-yom simhat libo* – the day of his heart's rejoicing" (*Shir ha-Shirim* 3:11) refers to the giving of the Torah,[11] and the *gemara* conflates the term "*morashah*" in the verse "*morashah kehillat Yaakov* – the heritage of the congregation of Yaakov" (*Devarim* 33:4) with the term "*me'orasah*," connoting betrothal.[12]

The verses in *Hoshe'a* 2:21–22 also relate to this theme:

> וארשתיך לי לעולם וארשתיך לי בצדק ובמשפט ובחסד וברחמים.
> וארשתיך לי לעולם וידעת את ה'.
>
> And I will betroth you forever; I will betroth you with righteousness and justice, and with goodness and mercy. And I will betroth you with faithfulness; then you shall know God.

These verses, recited daily in the final phase of donning *tefillin* and constituting the denouement of *Sefer Hoshe'a*, further confirm the betrothal

9. *Hilkhot Teshuvah* 10:2.
10. *Bah, Orah Hayim* 581:2.
11. *Ta'anit* 4:8.
12. *Pesahim* 49b; *Sanhedrin* 59a.

motif. This is the foundation for the Jewish People's commitment to the Torah; sin constitutes betrayal of this commitment. The altar itself shedding tears reflects the lost potential of the unrealized ideal, an ideal and a commitment characteristic of a fully realized marital relationship.

However, the metaphor of "*Eilkhah na el ishi ha-rishon* – I will return to my first husband" (*Hoshe'a* 2:9) demands closer scrutiny. While the marital paradigm is suggestive, its application here, when assessed by normative Halakhah, seems problematic. After all, betrayal of the marital bond, as in the instance of *sotah* (marital infidelity), precludes resumption of the marriage. Furthermore, there is an equally important and related distinction between the relationship of God and the Jewish People and even the most idyllic bond between a husband and wife: There is no capacity for *gerushin* (divorce) between *Klal Yisrael* and God, but notwithstanding the tears of the altar, divorce is at times a necessary option in the human domain.

R. Soloveitchik expounded on this important discrepancy and suggested two explanations.[13] First, although the partners in a human marriage aspire to become one entity (per *Bereishit* 2:24), the most personal dimensions of man's existential being cannot be fully shared with others.[14] The unbridgeable gap that remains provides the philosophical justification or basis for divorce. Even the most ideal marriage does not provide complete unity, and an imperfect union can therefore be dissolved. This restriction does not exist in man's relationship with God, as there is no distance between Creator and creation that cannot be spanned through service of God. Although philosophically the chasm

13. Joseph B. Soloveitchik, *Family Redeemed: Essays on Family Relationships* (NJ: Ktav Publishing House, 2000), 63.
14. In the history of creation, Havah was created from Adam (*Bereishit* 2:21). The *gemara* (*Ketubot* 8a) debates the details of this process, including whether man was created "*du partzufin*" or "*partzuf ehad*," with two faces or one. Ra'avad (introduction to *Ba'alei ha-Nefesh*) and Ramban (commentary on *Bereishit*) identify these factors as relevant to the respective capacities to facilitate an existential bond and forge a united identity with a spousal partner. This important conclusion is not incompatible with the Rav's insight that, in the final analysis, human beings cannot completely bridge this gap. Indeed, this manifestation of existential loneliness as part of the human condition is a prominent theme in the Rav's writings.

is greater and the gulf more unbridgeable, Torah study and observance are the divinely ordained guide and mechanism to bridge this gap.

We perceive the Torah as a divine gift "*le-zakkot et Yisrael* – to give merit to Israel."[15] Man's *devekut ba-Hashem* (cleaving to God) will by metaphysical and philosophical necessity always be circumscribed, but this gap is not a function of man's inability to share, but rather a fundamental theological reality of God's transcendence and infinitude. This is one distinction between human relationships and the relationship with God that precludes termination or divorce in the latter context.

The Rav advanced a second reason that the divine relationship is irrevocable. A meaningful physical human relationship is contingent upon sanctity, which is subject to desecration and destruction. For example, the Halakhah addresses the specific parameters of *ervat davar,* the grounds for divorce that constitute desecration in a framework of a marriage.[16] However, when it comes to God's relationship with the Jewish People, that bond is suffused with sanctity to such an extent that it withstands any abuse or challenge that taints or compromises it. This singular bond is hypersensitive to impropriety, dysfunction, and desecration, but simultaneously invulnerable to permanent breach or irrevocable disrepair. This relationship is more easily damaged and disappointed, but it can never be absolutely profaned or irrevocably tarnished.

Rashi explains this phenomenon in his commentary on *Shir ha-Shirim,* where he explains that the impression of darkness is sometimes only superficial. The sanctity that is the basis of the relationship between God and the Jewish People is permanent, and there therefore can be no *gerushin* between them.[17] This idea is expressed by *Yeshayahu* (50:1) when he remonstrates with the nation, reminding them that God

15. *Makkot* 3:16. Presumably, this merit transcends the means for reward and establishes the system of Halakhah as a Torah value system and as a methodology for bonding with God.
16. See *Gittin* 90a and *Family Redeemed,* 63–65, for the Rav's discussion of legitimate halakhic grounds for divorce. I hope to address elsewhere the relationship between the definition of *ervah* grounds for divorce and Halakhah's singular approach to the sanctity of marriage.
17. Rashi, *Shir ha-Shirim* 1:6, s.v. *she-shezafatni ha-shamesh.*

never divorced them; it was their improper behavior that alienated them from Him.

This relationship endures even in a time of destruction, when Jerusalem and *Klal Yisrael* are referred to figuratively as "*ke-almanah* – like a widow" (*Eikhah* 1:1), but never as a *gerushah*, a divorcee.[18] Furthermore, the Jewish People is only *compared* to a widow: "ke-*almanah*"; they are not really widowed. Rashi, quoting the interpretation of the *midrash* based on a careful reading of this verse, explains that it is possible for the Jewish People to return to God precisely because the nation's situation also differs from the actual *almanah* analogy.[19] In any case, irrespective of the transgression/desecration, there is certainly no equation to divorce. Indeed, even as the prophet Hoshe'a invokes the imagery of the marital paradigm of *erusin*, he declares unequivocally the divine promise that this particular betrothal is permanent: "*Ve-erastikh li le-olam* – And I shall betroth you to Me forever" (*Hoshe'a* 2:21).

In light of these explanations, the atypical elements and departures from classical marriage do not detract from the metaphor; they merely reflect an even more intense marital relationship. The discrepancies magnify further the characteristics associated with a marriage here.

Preserving the Relationship for the Long Term

There are consequences to the fact that the relationship between God and the Jewish People cannot be broken. On the one hand, the permanence of God's relationship with the Jewish People means that there is always the possibility of return; the door is always open. That is, of course, a very good thing. But this positive consideration also heightens the expectations and raises the stakes of this bond, magnifying even minor grievances within this treasured exclusive relationship. If two people share a lesser, casual relationship, neither will be particularly sensitive to a petty offense; damage to the relationship would require a more grave or acute transgression. Such relationships are typically conducive to a

18. Note also Rambam's view in *Hilkhot Beit ha-Behirah* 6:15–16 that the sanctity of the *Mikdash* and Yerushalayim always remains because it is the sanctity of the *Shekhinah*.
19. Rashi, *Eikhah* 1:1, s.v. *haitah ke-almanah*. For the original *midrash*, see *Midrash Eikhah* 1:1:3.

wider latitude of perceived insults that likely inflict less pain. In contrast, longer-term, higher-stakes relationships require far greater existential investment and effort. They demand a greater appreciation of context, and they necessitate some compromise or, at minimum, coping mechanisms to overcome or integrate differences. Absent the luxury to simply withdraw and abandon the relationship, a long-term perspective must be cultivated, especially since the capacity to inflict pain and exacerbate conflict is heightened.

This is one way to interpret the verse in *Amos* (3:2):

> רק אתכם יעדתי מכל משפחות האדמה על כן אפקד עליכם את כל עונותיכם.
>
> You alone have I singled out of all the families of the earth; that is why I will call you to account for all your iniquities.[20]

There are several levels of meaning to this *pasuk*. First, as *Hazal* frequently explain, the stakes are not as high for the other nations of the world as they are for the Jewish People, because God does not supervise or scrutinize the conduct of other nations as extensively.[21] As such, there is rarely an intermediate level of palliative or corrective punishment. Particularly egregious or degenerative transgressions typically engender severe punishment or even destruction, while relatively minor infractions are ignored or treated benignly. In sharp contrast, God scrutinizes *Klal Yisrael*'s conduct and holds them extensively accountable. *Hazal* perceive this as an extraordinary kindness reflecting the depth of the bond, even

20. The word "*yadati*" here has not only an intellectual connotation, but also an intimate connotation, consistent with its use throughout *Tanakh*. Interestingly, Rashi and *Metzudat David* interpret *yadati* as "*ahavti*," "I have loved."

21. This less ambitious spiritual expectation is, of course, also reflected in the differences between the seven-mitzvah and the six-hundred-thirteen-mitzvah system. It can be demonstrated that the discrepancy is qualitative and fundamental. Noahides are obligated to observe only a very basic and broad system of human religious values, while Halakhah is comprehensive and is intended to elevate all dimensions of Jewish life. Moreover, precisely when the two systems address the same broad obligation, the different spiritual orientations and agendas are acutely evident; for example, see *Sanhedrin* 56b. I hope to address this topic more extensively elsewhere.

as high expectations concomitantly may also imperil the relationship.[22] Indeed, the constant supervision constitutes a further kindness in that it enables the neutralization of lesser offenses before they cascade into unmanageable, unforgivable offenses. Ultimately, this approach secures the Jewish People's future by providing a defusing mechanism and a safety net to protect the precious relationship.

It is common wisdom that the key to a successful marriage is to stay on top of petty misunderstandings, differences, or offenses, preventing them from festering. If one tarries too long in addressing minor but vexing issues, divisions and distances eventually grow and become unbridgeable and irreparable. The verse in *Amos* accentuates our good fortune by telling us, "*Rak etkhem yadati mi-kol mishpehot ha-adamah.*" We alone, *Klal Yisrael*, have this special relationship with God. Therefore, "*efkod aleikhem et kol avonoteikhem*" – God is going to supervise us more closely.

An additional motif accentuated in this verse articulates the delicacy and high spiritual stakes of the relationship as a factor in dictating ubiquitous scrutiny. This scrutiny enables constructive accountability, which determines that even relatively peripheral violations of trust may constitute an act of *begidah* (betrayal).

The marital paradigm reflects this perspective acutely. This theme is conveyed by the Talmud's discussion of "*hikdihah tavshilo*" (she burned his food) and "*matza ishah na'ah heimenah*" (he found a more beautiful woman than her) as stimuli for divorce. The *zivug rishon* should be preserved at almost all costs. One method of accomplishing this is to make sure that small matters are neutralized and are not conflated with larger issues.[23] At the same time, apparently minor infractions, and even petty

22. See *Yevamot* 121b and *Bava Kama* 50a: "*Ha-Kadosh Barukh Hu medakdek im sevivav ke-hut ha-se'arah* – God is scrupulous with those around him even to the extent of a hairsbreadth." On the one hand, this reflects a higher expectation that triggers greater disappointment and disillusionment, but it also and especially reflects appreciation, generosity, and reward.

23. To be sure, a case could be made that if one has a closer relationship, one will be more forgiving with one's partner. Certainly this dialectic characterizes any intense, defining, authentic relationship. In one respect, greater flexibility is warranted, as one is loath to discard or abandon a precious and primary relationship that is rooted in

annoyances like *hikdihah tavshilo* or superficial distractions like *matza ishah na'ah heimenah,* may be valid grounds for divorce precisely because the standards defining this ideal relationship are lofty indeed. The fact that trivial factors and mercurial considerations sufficiently exacerbate what should be an existential, loyal, and substantive bond is inconsistent with these standards of sanctity. It reflects that the relationship is already deficient and has deteriorated.

Another implication of this verse from *Amos* is that strict halakhic accountability and the concrete threat of punishment for halakhic dereliction are actually advantageous for the Jewish People, as they encourage the critical process of *teshuvah* and repairing one's deeds. This is more important for the Jewish People's relationship with God than it is for the bond between God and the gentile nations. While repentance also applies to non-Jewish violations, its central role in Judaism defies comparison. *Teshuvah* for Jews is not merely the neutralization of outstanding sin; it is an indispensable process of *avodat Hashem* that entails broader introspection and enables a transgressor to redefine and elevate his relationship with God.[24]

This unique relationship between God and the Jewish People is further highlighted by Mabit's controversial assertion that notwithstanding the story of Yonah's mission to Nineveh, the obligation and parameters of *teshuvah* are unique to *Klal Yisrael.*[25] Mabit explains that Yonah

---

the past and inspired by a vision of a common future. However, this is also offset by greater expectations and the increased sting of perceived disloyalty and betrayal. A long-term relationship, and even more so a permanent bond, requires a strict code of conduct and core rules of engagement to safeguard and nurture the relationship for the long term. See Rashi, *Devarim* 29:12: "Because He has promised it unto you and has sworn unto your fathers not to exchange their descendants for another nation, for this reason He binds you by these oaths not to provoke Him to anger since He, on His part, cannot dissociate Himself from you." Rashi accentuates the need for meticulous boundaries to ensure the continuity and evolution of the bond. See also Radak, *Amos* 3:2, who emphasizes that the closer bond establishes that transgressions constitute a greater crime and that they engender greater pain given expectations and the emotional and historical investment that links the parties.

24. For a more extensive discussion of this topic, see the chapter "*Teshuvah* and *Viduy*: The Ambitious Method of Coming Closer to Hashem."

25. *Beit Elokim, Sha'ar ha-Teshuvah,* 13. While Mabit's approach is somewhat innovative,

does not actually call upon the people of Nineveh to repent; he simply informs them of the consequences of their transgressions. They take the initiative on their own to do *teshuvah* when they declare, "*Yashuvu ish mi-darko ha-ra'ah* – Let every man repent from his evil ways" (*Yonah* 3:8). Yonah hesitated to go to Nineveh because he thought *teshuvah* would be ineffective, since the comprehensive concept of *teshuvah* is restricted to *Klal Yisrael.* Of course, this assumption about the effectiveness of *teshuvah* for non-Jews was an error. Nevertheless, it is conceivable that the obligation to repent and the scope and centrality of *teshuvah* derives from the singular bond with the Jewish People. Certainly the category of *teshuvah mei-ahavah* – which has the capacity to transform willful transgressions into merits[26] – is a special prerogative for the Jewish People alone.[27]

The restriction of *teshuvah mei-ahavah* to the Jewish People stems from the dialectical nature of *teshuvah mei-ahavah.* The transformational power of *teshuvah mei-ahavah* appears to be a very surprising and even mystical idea. How could willful transgressions ever turn into merits? Upon further consideration, however, it reflects an intense and profound relationship that transcends particular moments and actions. The bond with the Jewish People spans thousands of years and includes inspiring highs, spiritual attainments, abysmal failures, and cataclysmic setbacks. It is marked by a history of disruption and reconnection, and it is, by definition, one that is irrevocable, no matter how intolerable present circumstances are.

---

the existence of qualitative differences and distinctions between Jewish and non-Jewish repentance is a more mainstream notion that is acutely reflected in the Midrash and other sources. See, for example, *Midrash Tanhuma, Devarim* 32:4. Mabit also presents the interesting suggestion that because of *Klal Yisrael*'s added obligation of 613 *mitzvot,* they need the obligation of *teshuvah,* as they are bound to sin. Mabit discusses other distinctions between the repentance of Jews and that of non-Jews as well (ibid. 14), noting that for Jews, *teshuvah* is effective both in this world and the next, whereas for the rest of the nations, it merely wards off punishment in this world. Mabit further argues that for the Jewish People, a mass *teshuvah* by the public (partially) atones even for individuals who do not participate in that *teshuvah,* whereas for other nations, *teshuvah* benefits only those who actually perform it.

26. *Yoma* 86b.

27. This is explicit in Mabit. See also the chapter "*Teshuvah* and *Viduy.*"

Again, the marital paradigm is instructive. An acute sense of alienation that stems from and accentuates distance and separation can also serve as a powerful catalyst for greater appreciation of one's absent partner, which can facilitate the urgency to strengthen the bond. The crisis of impending profound loss can turn willful transgressions into merits, particularly when there is a long and intense history that reinforces the absolute conviction of a future joint destiny. For this reason, a marital bond that is irrevocable, which survives even betrayal and precludes any kind of termination, certainly exemplifies this motif even more forcefully.

Understanding *Teshuvah*

The significance of the long-term underlying relationship also pertains to the components of *teshuvah*: *haratah* (regret), *bushah* (shame), and even *kabbalah al ha-atid* (commitment for the future). Although we become acquainted with these components of *teshuvah* at a formative age, reflecting upon them reveals that they are challenging to implement, contemplate, and even to comprehend.

True regret, for example, differs from a mere expression of "sorry." It requires profound, tortured regret and authentic humiliation, even mortification. The goal is not simply to assuage one's guilt and move forward, but to powerfully experience the magnitude of one's transgression, stimulating an existential crisis. The *teshuvah* process entails a core assessment of purpose and meaning that is completely incompatible with a superficial disavowal of transgressions that retains a trace of ambivalence regarding the sinful experience. Ideal *teshuvah* requires *haratah* – an unequivocal rejection of past experience as well as a clear future commitment. The sense of profound regret relates not only to one's self-perception, but also to one's image and reputation in the eyes of those who command one's love and respect, stimulating *bushah*. Even more so, the sinner can hardly tolerate the fact that there is no refuge from divine omniscience.

Authentic agonizing over the implications of an aberrant past, coming to grips with one's capacity for egregious conduct, constitutes not only a vehicle to neutralize past infractions, as repentance is typically understood, but also a transformative cathartic act of *avodat Hashem* that elevates the true penitent.

Kabbalah al ha-atid similarly goes beyond even a sincere resolution about the future. It requires that the penitent thoroughly reinvent his persona and reorder his values so that his present status will conform to his enlightened new reality and his commitment will preclude any predictable future lapse. One might question how *kabbalah al ha-atid* can be required for *teshuvah,* inasmuch as it entails a commitment absent knowledge of what tomorrow will bring and what influences will come to bear. Indeed, even if one can make a *kabbalah la-hoveh,* a commitment for the present, can one really sincerely undertake a *kabbalah al ha-atid*? While *kabbalah al ha-atid* can be understood narrowly as a sincere commitment for the future, it too can encompass much more.

The rigorous *teshuvah* program, comprised of these steps, is significantly facilitated by a national relationship with God that is very intense and complex, that is deeply rooted in the past and that will confidently stretch forever into the future. The Rav spoke extensively about Halakhah's dynamic view of time. Time in Halakhah is not static,[28] and the boundaries of the past and the future are rather blurry. Halakhic time consciousness defines how we relate to our national history as well as to pivotal halakhic institutions. This is true of the catastrophic events of destruction and mourning, and is equally applicable to the foundational experiences of Jewish life, such as the revelation at Sinai, which is referred to in the Torah in the present tense, and the exodus from Egypt, whose memory is ubiquitous.

This is further reflected in Moshe Rabbeinu's introduction of God to *Klal Yisrael* as the God who transcends time, as reflected in the Tetragrammaton (*Shemot* 6:6). For God, in a metaphysical sense, the past, present, and future converge; they are all one reality. His name connotes omnipresence in time – that He always was, is, and will be. The precise nuances of this concept are inherently beyond our cognitive grasp, but the Jewish People's relationship with God partakes of

28. See R. Soloveitchik's discussion of time consciousness and Henri Bergson's notion of time in his essay "Sacred and Profane," in *Shiurei ha-Rav,* ed. Joseph Epstein (New Jersey: Ktav, 1994), 14–25. Also see the many sources cited in Jeffrey Woolf, "Time Awareness as a Source of Spirituality in the Thought of Rabbi Joseph B. Soloveitchik," *Modern Judaism* 32:1 (February 2012), 54–75.

this permanence and timelessness.[29] For this reason, the institution of *teshuvah* can redeem the past and even elevate it. The very notion of *kabbalah al ha-atid* would be more tenuous if the bond between God and the Jewish People could be terminated. However, this relationship is governed by the promise of "*ve-erastikh li le-olam* – I will betroth you to Me forever." Because of the irrevocability of the relationship, which determines that at worst we will be *ke-almanah* and no more, because the relationship is enduring and timeless, it can withstand our limited knowledge and control of the future, enabling *kabbalah al ha-atid* to become a rigorous and integral part of *teshuvah*.

The Opportunity of Elul

The eternal nature of the relationship between God and the Jewish People has profound implications for the special *teshuvah* opportunity of the month of Elul. Avudraham's acronym explaining the name of the month has much more significance than is commonly thought; it reflects not only reciprocity, but also and especially the marital relationship described in *Shir ha-Shirim*. It thereby reflects the breadth and depth of *teshuvah* as a process of *avodat Hashem* that stems from that special relationship. *Bah*'s claim that *teshuvah mei-ahavah* is specifically connected to the *teshuvah* of Elul and precisely the theme of "*ani le-dodi ve-dodi li*" reinforces this motif.

This should motivate us to seize the opportunity of Elul. This period is dedicated not only to the narrow pursuit of merits that secure our physical survival, but is even more an opportunity to focus on this special bond that undergirds the purpose of existence and the concept of *teshuvah*.

29. For many, this concept is also the foundation for free choice, as it neutralizes the dilemma of divine foreknowledge. Free choice is the centerpiece of *teshuvah*, as reflected by Rambam's devotion of a chapter to it in the middle of *Hilkhot Teshuvah* (chapter 5). It should be noted that this is not Rambam's own solution to the quandary of divine foreknowledge.

Chapter 8
Ahavat Hashem and *Talmud Torah*: The Telos of *Teshuvah*

In the final chapter of *Hilkhot Teshuvah,* Rambam presents a variety of beautiful formulations regarding *ahavat Hashem*:

> העובד מאהבה עוסק בתורה ובמצות והולך בנתיבות החכמה...מפני שהוא אמת וסוף הטובה לבא בגללה. ומעלה זו היא מעלה גדולה מאד ואין כל חכם זוכה לה. והיא מעלת אברהם אבינו שקראו הקב"ה אוהבו לפי שלא עבד אלא מאהבה...וכיצד היא האהבה הראויה הוא שיאהב את ה' אהבה גדולה יתירה עזה מאוד עד שתהא נפשו קשורה באהבת ה' ונמצא שוגה בה תמיד כאלו חולה חולי האהבה... והוא ששלמה אמר דרך משל כי חולת אהבה אני. וכל שיר השירים משל הוא לענין זה.
>
> One who serves [God] out of love occupies himself in the Torah and the *mitzvot* and walks in the paths of wisdom ... because it is true, and ultimately, good will come because of it. This is a very high level, which is not merited by every wise man. It is the level

> of our Patriarch, Avraham, whom God described as "he who loved Me," for his service was only motivated by love...
>
> What is the proper [degree] of love? That a person should love Hashem with a very great and exceeding love until his soul is bound up in the love of Hashem. Thus, he will always be obsessed with this love as if he is lovesick.... This concept was implied by Shlomo when he stated, as a metaphor, "I am lovesick" (*Shir ha-Shirim* 2:5). [Indeed,] the totality of *Shir ha-Shirim* is a parable describing this [love].[1]

Rambam then addresses the progression from performing a mitzvah for ulterior motives to doing it for correct reasons. Rambam concludes *Hilkhot Teshuvah,* and by extension *Sefer ha-Madda,* with this concept.

Interestingly, Rambam then transitions into *Sefer Ahavah,* which he begins with the motto, *"Mah ahavti Toratekha kol ha-yom hi sihati* – How much do I love your Torah; it is [the subject of] my constant conversation" (*Tehillim* 119:97). Rambam thereby conjoins the first two books of the *Mishneh Torah* with the notion of *ahavat Hashem.* Why did Rambam conclude *Sefer ha-Madda,* and more importantly *Hilkhot Teshuvah,* with a chapter devoted to *ahavat Hashem*?

This is particularly noteworthy and surprising considering that Rambam devised and devoted an independent ten-chapter section to the laws of *teshuvah,* which are strewn throughout the Talmud without any cohesion, as the culmination of the first of the fourteen books of the *Yad ha-Hazakah,* his comprehensive and masterful halakhic magnum opus. Rambam expanded, reorganized, and invested pioneering effort in the formulation of these particular laws. Moreover, Rambam specifically elected to place *Hilkhot Teshuvah* in *Sefer ha-Madda,* forgoing the more obvious alternative of locating these laws in a narrower, if more obvious classification, such as *Hilkhot Shegagot, Avodat Yom ha-Kippurim,* or *Shevitat Asor* in *Sefer Zemanim.* The determination that *Hilkhot Teshuvah* is pivotal to *Sefer ha-Madda,* and even its appropriate coda, certainly requires clarification. It adds greater urgency to understanding

1. *Hilkhot Teshuvah* 10:2–3. For Rambam's full presentation of *ahavat Hashem,* see the entirety of *Hilkhot Teshuvah* 10:1–3.

this puzzling choice of dedicating the final chapter of *Hilkhot Teshuvah* and all of *Sefer ha-Madda* to the mitzvah of *ahavat Hashem*.

These questions are compounded by the fact that Rambam already codifies *ahavat Hashem* in *Hilkhot Yesodei ha-Torah* at the beginning of *Sefer ha-Madda,* together with the theological truths that a person is required to affirm to qualify as a believing Jew.[2] It is striking that despite having already addressed the concepts of *ahavah* and *yirah* at the very beginning of *Sefer ha-Madda,* he feels compelled to return to them at the culmination of *Sefer ha-Madda* in *Hilkhot Teshuvah.*[3]

Resolution of Rambam

A close examination of *Hilkhot Teshuvah* reveals Rambam's intentions. It is no coincidence that Rambam chose the culmination of *Hilkhot Teshuvah* to ruminate about *ahavat Hashem* and the motivation and ambition that both suffuse and engender it. By accentuating the importance of *ahavat Hashem,* by promoting it as an ideal, and by utilizing the metaphor of intense romantic love found in *Shir ha-Shirim,* Rambam effectively conveys that *ahavat Hashem* is of paramount importance to all elements of *avodat Hashem.* Simply put, Rambam's unusual presentation reflects his profound comprehension that *ahavat Hashem* is the ultimate telos of *teshuvah.* He thereby accentuates a perspective that undergirds his entire presentation and classification of *Hilkhot Teshuvah* and informs and reinforces his classificatory decision.

For Rambam, *teshuvah* is a necessary, natural component of *Sefer ha-Madda* and *Mishneh Torah* more broadly, as it is a mode of *avodat*

2. *Hilkhot Yesodei ha-Torah* 2:1–2. For Rambam, theological truths are essential because philosophical conformity is indispensable to halakhic observance. This is why he begins the entire *Mishneh Torah* with *Sefer ha-Madda* and its philosophical axioms. From the most elemental discussions of his foundational theology, Rambam transitions into *yirat Hashem* and *ahavat Hashem.*
3. Importantly, in *Hilkhot Yesodei ha-Torah,* Rambam does not treat each topic separately. In general, Rambam introduces a mitzvah, defines it, and then moves on to the next one. In this instance, however, he groups *ahavah* and *yirah* together and then explains both of them. Rambam's choice is predicated upon his stated view and belief that there is a seamless and continuous interaction between these two. *Yirah* leads to *ahavah* and *ahavah* leads to *yirah* in an ongoing cyclical process. Instead of being two opposite emotions, they are really two parts of one religious experience.

Hashem in and of itself. *Teshuvah* is not exclusively about neutralizing *het* (sin), but instead an act of *avodat Hashem* that leads to the highest level of religiosity.[4]

Furthermore, Rambam's decision to place *Hilkhot Teshuvah* in *Sefer ha-Madda* is even intuitive, because his goal is to integrate *teshuvah* with *avodat Hashem* throughout the year. *Teshuvah* is not simply a narrow response to sin; rather, it is itself a pinnacle of *avodat Hashem,* and therefore an obvious choice for the culmination of *Sefer ha-Madda.*

Rambam's choice to conjoin *Hilkhot Teshuvah* with *Sefer Ahavah* through the concept of *ahavat Hashem* flows consistently from this perspective. The transition to daily *mitzvot,* which are described in *Sefer Ahavah,* reinforces these themes and accentuates the broader relationship between man and Hashem that is also a key component of the process of *teshuvah. Hilkhot Teshuvah,* at the culmination of *Sefer ha-Madda,* is juxtaposed with *Hilkhot Keri'at Shema* at the beginning of *Sefer Ahavah.* The laws of *Keri'at Shema* encapsulate the comprehensiveness of *ahavat Hashem* – *"be-khol levavekha u-vekhol nafshekha u-vekhol me'odekha"* – and capture the mission of total religious and halakhic commitment, *kabbalat ol malkhut Shamayim.* This juxtaposition further broadens the motif of *teshuvah* and integrates it into the other primary institutions of *avodat Hashem.*[5]

4. Rambam was likely inspired by the *gemara* in *Yoma* (86b), which proclaims that *teshuvah mei-ahavah* transfigures an unintentional transgression into a *zekhut* (merit). Surprisingly, Rambam, who masterfully compiled and formulated *Hilkhot Teshuvah,* seemingly omits and ignores this remarkable assessment and idea that forcefully projects the ambitious capacity of *teshuvah,* a theme that he would seemingly enthusiastically embrace. It is striking that although Rambam quotes many of the *divrei aggadah* collected at the end of *Yoma,* he does not codify this particularly noteworthy idea. We can speculate that Rambam may have actually been providing an interpretation of this unusual *gemara* by placing *ahavat Hashem* as the final chapter of *Hilkhot Teshuvah,* thereby suggesting that *ahavat Hashem* should not be seen as primarily the methodology for *teshuvah,* but instead the ultimate goal. I have related to these themes in the chapter "*Ahavat Hashem* and *Talmud Torah*: The Telos of *Teshuvah*" and elsewhere (see https://www.torahweb.org/torah/2015/moadim/rros_elul.html).
5. Another example of Rambam broadening the motif of *teshuvah* is his treatment of *behirah hofshit,* a lynchpin concept in *avodat Hashem,* in the middle of *Hilkhot Teshuvah* (chapters 5–6).

Rambam's Consistency on *Ahavat Hashem*

Rambam's approach to *ahavat Hashem* is very consistent. In the passage from *Hilkhot Teshuvah* cited above, he refers to Avraham Avinu as the exemplar of *ahavat Hashem*, invoking the verse "Avraham, who loves Me" (*Yeshayahu* 41:8), the same verse he quotes in *Sefer ha-Mitzvot* when he discusses *ahavat Hashem*:

> והמצוה השלישית היא שצונו לאהבו יתעלה וזה שנתבונן ונשכיל מצותיו ופעולותיו עד שנשיגהו ונתענג בהשגתו תכלית התענוג וזאת היא האהבה המחוייבת... ולשון סיפרי (שם) ואהבת את ה׳ וכו׳ אהבהו על הבריות כאברהם אביך שנאמר ואת הנפש אשר עשו בחרן. ר"ל כמו שאברהם בעבור שהיה אוהב השם כמו שהעיד הכתוב (ישעי׳ מא) אברהם אוהבי שהיה גם כן לגודל השגתו דרש האנשים אל האמונה מחוזק אהבתו כן אתה אהוב אותו עד שתדרוש האנשים אליו:
>
> The third mitzvah is that we are commanded to love God, exalted be He – that is, to meditate upon and closely examine His commandments and His works in order to understand Him, and through this understanding to achieve a feeling of ecstasy. This is the kind of love that we are obligated to achieve.... [We see that this mitzvah includes spreading love for God to others from] the *Sifri*: "'You shall love Hashem' – make Him beloved among the creatures, as your father Avraham did, as it is written, 'The souls that he made in Haran' (*Bereishit* 12:5)." The meaning of this is that Avraham, as a result of his deep understanding of Hashem, acquired love for Hashem, as the verse testifies, "Avraham, who loved Me." This powerful love caused him to call out to all mankind to believe [in God]. So too, you shall love Him to the extent that you draw others to Him.[6]

Avraham Avinu is the model of *ahavat Hashem* for Rambam. In *Sefer ha-Mitzvot,* he describes a practically uncontrollable impulse, an overflowing sense of *ahavah,* which overtakes the person. Rambam depicts

6. *Sefer ha-Mitzvot, aseh* 3.

Avraham as the paradigm of an *ohev Hashem,* one whose infectious enthusiasm and exuberance to share Torah with others derived from an overflow of his own intoxication with the *Ribbono Shel Olam* and His Torah. The experience begins with a rational awareness, but it goes beyond that and becomes a religious experience. This is the foundation of Avraham's method and mission. Avraham's outreach activity was part and parcel of being "Avraham, who loves Me," reflecting an unrestrained and overflowing sense of purpose resulting from love of the Divine.

Talmud Torah and *Ahavat Hashem*

Rambam articulates unambiguously that the primary mechanism for achieving this state of *ahavat Hashem* is *talmud Torah* (Torah study). Exposure to the word of Hashem, both Torah and *mitzvot,* has a transcendent and transformative impact (if one does not resist it), which ultimately leads to *ahavah* and performance of *mitzvot lishmah,* for the sake of heaven.[7] Hence, Torah study and observance of *mitzvot* in their own right are the indispensable foundation for developing *ahavat Hashem* and fostering authentic *avodat Hashem* in the model of "*Avraham ohavi.*"

It is surely no coincidence that some commentators suggest that *teshuvah mi-ahavah* can be attained primarily through *talmud Torah.*[8] The connection that Rambam draws between *ahavat Hashem* and the study of Torah in *Sefer ha-Mitzvot,* as well as the way he describes the study of Torah in the tenth chapter of *Hilkhot Teshuvah,* is absolutely consistent with this idea, and indeed reinforces it.

Moreover, it is likely no coincidence that the verse Ramban identifies as the source for *teshuvah* is related to *talmud Torah* as well:

> כי המצוה הזאת אשר אנכי מצוך היום לא נפלאת הוא ממך ולא רחקה הוא.
>
> For this commandment that I command you this day, it is neither too hard for you nor far off. (*Devarim* 30:11)

7. *Hilkhot Teshuvah* 10:4–6.
8. See, in particular, the comments of R. Hayim of Volozhin, *Nefesh Ha-Hayim,* ch. 4, and Netziv, *Ha'amek Davar, Devarim* 4:2.

The *gemara* states explicitly that this verse refers to the mitzvah of *talmud Torah,*[9] and that is how Rambam codifies it as well.[10] Rambam was obviously keenly aware of these normative sources; by nevertheless identifying this verse as the source for *teshuvah,* he establishes that Torah study and *teshuvah* are two sides of the same coin. The intimate connection between *talmud Torah* and *teshuvah* supports the notion that *talmud Torah* is the basis for *teshuvah mei-ahavah.*

This perspective provides a framework for understanding why *talmud Torah* is so urgent and why it is so important that the undertaking of Torah study not be performed frivolously or even casually. While Torah study should engender joy, as "the precepts of Hashem are right, making the heart rejoice" (*Tehillim* 19:9),[11] Torah study should be pursued with reverence and seriousness. The perspective that *talmud Torah* is the means to connect with the Infinite as the most ambitious expression of *avodat Hashem* precludes a casual, careless, or trivial approach.[12]

Talmud Torah is both the foundation of the marital relationship between us and the *Ribbono Shel Olam* and the prime tool for building that relationship.[13] Thus, learning Torah is equal in importance to all the other *mitzvot.*[14] Moreover, the way one engages in it is critical as well; Torah study requires mind, heart, and soul, demanding the surrender and subordination of one's mindset and way of thinking to that of the Torah.

This highlights the importance of in-depth Torah study and analysis, which includes the attempt to uncover the subtleties within a topic and connections between topics. While it provides intellectual exhilaration, the excitement engendered by advanced *talmud Torah* is

9. *Eiruvin* 55a, also cited by Rashi, *Devarim,* ad loc.
10. *Hilkhot Talmud Torah* 3:8.
11. There are a number of strong formulations in the *Rishonim* and *Aharonim* that articulate this concept. For example, despite the general concept of "*mitzvot lav le-hanot nitnu*" (*mitzvot* were not given for physical benefit), R. Avraham min Ha-Har (*Nedarim* 48a) argues that this does not apply to *talmud Torah,* because joy is intrinsic to the experience. See also the introduction of *Avnei Nezer* to his *sefer Eglei Tal.*
12. See, for example, *Berakhot* 22a.
13. *Hazal* consistently parallel *kabbalat ha-Torah* to *erusin* and *nissu'in.* See, for example, *Vayikra Rabba, Aharei Mot* 20, and *Mekhilta de-Rabbi Yishmael, Parashat Yitro.*
14. *Pe'ah* 1:1.

secondary compared to the spiritual aspiration that accompanies it. At the end of the day, the enthusiasm that we exhibit, the attachment to the topic, the exploration of the options and the nuances, and the analysis of the expressions of the *Rishonim* and other texts are really about the enthusiastic relationship of *ahavat Hashem,* which not only impacts *teshuvah,* but is the basis for *avodat Hashem* and a broader Torah-infused perspective on life.

Those who share a bench in the *beit midrash,* study partners who learn together, form a bond based on transformative shared experiences. There can and should be abundant joy associated with the creative process, including initiative and personal contribution, but the ultimate goal is a transcendent one: fostering a community built on shared values and the belief in the importance of Torah study.

As we noted, Rambam concludes *Hilkhot Teshuvah* with *ahavat Hashem* and then transitions into *Sefer Ahavah.* Thus, *teshuvah* is not a concept restricted to Elul and the *Aseret Yemei Teshuvah* (the Ten Days of Repentance). Rather, it sets the tone for our relationship with Hashem throughout the entire year.[15]

---

15. When we understand *teshuvah* as a process that intensifies the relationship and provides the perspective that transcends sin, the otherwise mystifying and intriguing concept of "*na'asot ki-zekhuyot*" (sins become like merits) can be understood. The reality of sin can be a catalyst for a person to rectify his *avodat Hashem* and his relationship with Hashem more broadly, and that catalyst, in some sense, can become a "merit." See the chapter "An Alternative and Complementary Perspective on *Teshuvah*: Rabbeinu Yonah's *Sha'arei Teshuvah.*"

Chapter 9

Religious Stringency, Consistency, and the Implications of the *Aseret Yemei Teshuvah*

A Hypocritical Stringency?

Between Rosh ha-Shanah and Yom Kippur, there is a widespread practice to refrain from eating bread that was commercially baked by non-Jews, commonly referred to as *pat akum*. As opposed to food cooked by non-Jews (*bishul akum*), there is no explicit prohibition of commercial baked goods made by non-Jews throughout the year. Why do we limit ourselves to Jewish-made baked goods during this time period?

The Talmud Yerushalmi writes that a higher level of purity is required seven days out of the year, explaining that this demand is limited to only seven days because of the difficulty of remaining in this state for an entire year.[1] Ra'avyah cites a tradition regarding these seven days:

1. Yerushalmi *Shabbat* 1:3.

> גרסי' בירושלמי פרק קמא דשבת ר' חייא רבה מפקיד לרב אין אתה יכול מיכיל כל שתא בטהרה אכיל ואין לו תהא אכיל שבעה יומין בשבתא... וקבלתי שאלו שבעה ימים הם שבעה ימים שבין ראש השנה ליום הכיפורים.
>
> The Talmud Yerushalmi in the first chapter of *Masekhet Shabbat* states: "The Elder R. Hiya instructed Rav: If you are able to eat food in purity the entire year long, eat it. But if not, eat it in purity seven days during the year".... And I have received a tradition that these seven days refer to the seven days between Rosh ha-Shanah and Yom Kippur.[2]

Based on this, Rosh writes that the custom in Germany was to refrain from *pat akum* during the *Aseret Yemei Teshuvah,* even if one was generally lenient regarding this practice throughout the year.[3] This practice is likewise quoted by Rosh's son in the *Tur,* as well as by R. Yosef Karo in *Shulhan Arukh.*[4]

Although this provides a source for the practice, there is an inherent difficulty observed by R. Shmuel of Bamberg, quoted by R. Shimshon ben Tzadok in his *Tashbetz Katan.* It would be understandable to practice a heightened level of ritual purity during these days, since there is no general prohibition associated with eating while impure. But bread that is baked by non-Jews is potentially problematic throughout the year. Thus, refraining from consuming it for merely ten days a year may prove to be halakhically inconsistent. Accordingly, R. Shmuel argues that if one

2. Ra'avyah 2:529. There is nothing in the text of the Yerushalmi itself that indicates that it is referring to the *Aseret Yemei Teshuvah. Tur* (*Orah Hayim* 603:1) implicitly makes note of the irony that Rosh ha-Shanah is not included within the count of seven days. He argues that it would be superfluous to mandate being in a state of *taharah* on Rosh ha-Shanah, due to the general principle of "*hayav adam le-taher atzmo ba-regel*" (one is obligated to purify himself on the festivals) (*Rosh ha-Shanah* 16b). Regardless, the fact that this practice became so popular in Ashkenaz attests to and reflects either the credibility of the tradition or how embracing stringency as a theme of the *Aseret Yemei Teshuvah* resonated with these communities.
3. Rosh, *Rosh ha-Shanah* 4:14.
4. *Orah Hayim* 603:1.

observes this prohibition during the *Aseret Yemei Teshuvah,* he should be obligated to observe it throughout the year.[5]

R. Yosef Karo addresses this concern in his *Beit Yosef.*[6] He argues that *pat akum* cannot be considered a true prohibition, since it is not a blanket prohibition but is rather dependent on individual practice.[7] Therefore, when an individual opts to behave stringently and avoid *pat akum* during the *Aseret Yemei Teshuvah,* he obviously does not intend to accept the prohibition throughout the year.

This provides a technical solution to the halakhic problem of maintaining a stricter stance on *pat akum* during these ten days than the rest of the year. However, the fundamental difficulty with maintaining this inconsistent practice remains: Is it not insincere to maintain an enhanced level of observance during these days, when we face judgment for our sins? As an extreme example, if we were to observe halakhic law only during this time each year, our observance would obviously be hypocritical and meaningless. Why is the observance of *pat akum* during this period anything more than a disingenuous attempt to project good behavior when Hashem's scrutiny is more intense and the stakes for survival are more acute?

Moreover, if the purpose of observance during this time is to gain favor during the process of judgment, doesn't this stringency during *Aseret Yemei Teshuvah* risk highlighting our inadequate and lax behavior throughout the year? If we are able to achieve this more maximal level of observance, why do we not employ this more ideal standard all the time? By being particularly scrupulous during this time, we seem to underscore that our less impressive behavior during the year stems from complacency.

5. *Tashbetz Katan* 117.
6. *Beit Yosef, Orah Hayim* 603.
7. *Arukh ha-Shulhan* (603:2), in the spirit of *Beit Yosef*'s distinction (although he does not quote it), makes a parallel point that during the *Aseret Yemei Teshuvah,* one should not assume the practice of refraining from foods when there are *Posekim* who maintain that those foods are prohibited *min ha-din,* such as *hadash* or *basar be-lo sirkha,* because once one has refrained from eating such food, it is as if he has accepted the opinion of those who prohibit it. Hence, it would be halakhically inconsistent to eat it again after the *Aseret Yemei Teshuvah.*

The Nature of the *Aseret Yemei Teshuvah*

To answer these questions, we must better understand the nature of the *Aseret Yemei Teshuvah*.

In truth, the special status of these ten days stands on dubious ground. Unlike *Hol ha-Mo'ed*, or even the days between Pesah and Shavu'ot, there is no source in the Torah for the concept of a special status for these days. The *gemara*, however, quotes a verse in *Yeshayahu* (55:6) as a reference to the ten days between Rosh ha-Shanah and Yom Kippur: "*Dirshu Hashem be-himatz'o* – Seek out Hashem when He can be found."[8] In his codification of this *gemara*, Rambam explains that *teshuvah* and crying out are more effective during this time:

> אע"פ שהתשובה והצעקה יפה לעולם, בעשרה הימים שבין ראש השנה ויום הכפורים היא יפה ביותר ומתקבלת היא מיד שנאמר דרשו ה' בהמצאו.
>
> Even though repentance and crying out are always beneficial, during the ten days between Rosh ha-Shanah and Yom Kippur, they are particularly beneficial and immediately accepted, as the verse states, "Seek out Hashem when He can be found."[9]

This time period reflects the closeness of Hashem and the increased conduciveness of atonement. During these ten days, we are called upon to better ourselves and redefine our religious personas and spiritual goals through introspection and repentance.

This point is emphasized by Rambam in his codification of the laws of *teshuvah*. The *gemara* describes that a person should always view his meritorious deeds as equal with his transgressions; the performance of one more mitzvah or sin will determine his fate.[10] Although this *gemara* describes a general halakhic outlook of personal responsibility, Rambam associates it specifically with the days between Rosh ha-Shanah and Yom Kippur. Immediately after codifying this *gemara*, he describes how the *shofar* is meant to awaken us from our slumber and stir us to

---

8. *Rosh ha-Shanah* 18a; *Yevamot* 105a.
9. *Hilkhot Teshuvah* 2:6.
10. *Kiddushin* 40b.

reexamine our behavior, repent from our transgressions, and remember our Creator. Curiously, Rambam then concludes:

> ומפני ענין זה נהגו כל בית ישראל להרבות בצדקה ובמעשים טובים ולעסוק במצות מראש השנה ועד יום הכפורים יתר מכל השנה.
>
> Based on this, the Jewish People customarily increase their charity, good deeds, and involvement in *mitzvot* from Rosh ha-Shanah until Yom Kippur more than the rest of the year.[11]

Rambam viewed this *gemara,* which describes a generic attitude that a person should have toward every decision he makes, as a special dictum that applies to the *Aseret Yemei Teshuvah.* These ten days are not only a time of increased capacity for repentance and atonement, but a time when each decision we make is highlighted and scrutinized. If our decisions throughout the year can tilt the scales, then we have an even greater responsibility during the *Aseret Yemei Teshuvah* to act judiciously, because our actions are placed under the microscope and the effect of every decision becomes magnified.

Importantly, the *gemara* refers to ten days of *teshuvah*: "*Elu asarah yamim she-bein Rosh ha-Shanah ve-Yom ha-Kippurim* – These are the ten days between Rosh ha-Shanah and Yom Kippur."[12] This phrase includes the terminus days of Rosh ha-Shanah and Yom Kippur in the count. Thus, the days in between are not simply an accident of the calendar, intermediate days while we wait for the arrival of Yom Kippur. Rather, they are included in the unit of the "ten days between Rosh ha-Shanah and Yom Kippur." By including the boundary days, which are significant and independent holidays, the *gemara* indicates the cohesive and structured nature of this period. This unit of time forms a bridge that allows for a process of repentance and introspection that begins on Rosh

---

11. *Hilkhot Teshuvah* 3:4.
12. *Yevamot* 105a. The *gemara* uses the same phrase in *Berakhot* 12b when it explains the changes made to the *Shemoneh Esrei* during the *Aseret Yemei Teshuvah. Ein Ya'akov's* text of the *gemara* is "*she-miRosh ha-Shanah le-Yom ha-Kippurim.*" See also *Etz Yosef,* who perceives *Aseret Yemei Teshuvah* not merely as the time in between Rosh ha-Shanah and Yom Kippur, but as having intrinsic significance as a period of *teshuvah.*

ha-Shanah and terminates with Yom Kippur, a structure framed by the days of judgment and atonement.

Thus, it is not surprising that the Torah does not command the observance of ten days of *teshuvah*; there is no need for a formal commandment. A proper understanding of the *teshuvah* process, beginning with Rosh ha-Shanah and ending with Yom Kippur, dictates that there must be a cohesive unit of time that allows for the progression and development of our introspection and prayer between those two dates. Jumping from Rosh ha-Shanah to Yom Kippur without the intervening period that allows for this extended period of introspection and necessary religious advancement would preclude a meaningful experience of repentance.

Indeed, it is not surprising that some of the rules that govern Rosh ha-Shanah and Yom Kippur spill over into these ten days. Since the placement of these days between Rosh ha-Shanah and Yom Kippur integrates Rosh ha-Shanah and Yom Kippur into a unified process, the intervening days partially assume the character of Rosh ha-Shanah and Yom Kippur.

The Unique Character of *Shemoneh Esrei* During the *Aseret Yemei Teshuvah*

The "overflow" from Rosh ha-Shanah and Yom Kippur manifests in several halakhic contexts. First, we observe that the structure and content of *tefillah* is affected during the entire ten-day period. The *gemara* records an interesting debate regarding the *hatimah* (conclusion) of two *berakhot* of *Shemoneh Esrei* during this period:

> ואמר רבה בר חיננא סבא משמיה דרב: כל השנה כולה אדם מתפלל הא־ל הקדוש, מלך אוהב צדקה ומשפט, חוץ מעשרה ימים שבין ראש השנה ויום הכפורים שמתפלל המלך הקדוש והמלך המשפט. ורבי אלעזר אמר: אפילו אמר הא־ל הקדוש - יצא, שנאמר: ויגבה ה׳ צבאות במשפט והא־ל הקדוש נקדש בצדקה. אימתי ויגבה ה׳ צבאות במשפט - אלו עשרה ימים שמראש השנה ועד יום הכפורים, וקאמר הא־ל הקדוש. מאי הוה עלה? אמר רב יוסף: הא־ל הקדוש ומלך אוהב צדקה ומשפט; רבה אמר: המלך הקדוש והמלך המשפט. והלכתא כרבה.

> Rabbah bar Hinana Saba said in the name of Rav: Throughout the year, a person recites [in *Shemoneh Esrei*] the words "*ha-Kel ha-kadosh*" [at the end of the third *berakhah*] and "*Melekh ohev tzedakah u-mishpat*" [at the end of the tenth *berakhah*], except during the ten days between Rosh ha-Shanah and Yom Kippur, when one recites, "*ha-Melekh ha-kadosh*" and "*ha-Melekh ha-mishpat.*" R. Elazar stated: Even if one were to recite "*ha-Kel ha-kadosh*" [during these ten days], he would fulfill his obligation, as the verse states, "And the Lord of Hosts is exalted through justice, and the holy God (*ha-Kel ha-kadosh*) is sanctified through righteousness" (*Yeshayahu* 5:16). When is "the Lord of Hosts exalted through justice"? During the ten days between Rosh ha-Shanah and Yom Kippur. And yet the verse says, "*ha-Kel ha-kadosh.*" What is the conclusion? R. Yosef said: [One recites,] "*ha-Kel ha-kadosh*" and "*Melekh ohev tzedakah u-mishpat.*" Rabbah said: [One recites,] "*ha-Melekh ha-kadosh*" and "*ha-Melekh ha-mishpat.*" And the *halakhah* follows the opinion of Rabbah.[13]

Although the commentators debate whether R. Elazar maintains that it is sufficient or preferable to retain the text of "*ha-Kel ha-kadosh*" during this period, most explain that even he validates a *Shemoneh Esrei* that veers from the standard formulation during this period. In any event, the *gemara*'s conclusion is clear about this substitution in a very critical point in the *tefillah*, concluding that we rule in accordance with Rabbah. Rambam and others follow suit.[14]

The fact that the standard *hatimah* to the entire introductory section of *Shemoneh Esreh* is transformed during the *Aseret Yemei Teshuvah* is consistent with the view that this entire period has a certain status. This is particularly the case if the recitation of "*ha-Melekh ha-kadosh*" is

13. *Berakhot* 12b. It is noteworthy that there is a slight variation between the formulations used by Rabbah and R. Elazar when referring to the *Aseret Yemei Teshuvah* (*she-bein* vs. *she-miRosh*). This slight variation may indicate that their dispute is not necessarily tied exclusively to *hilkhot tefillah*, but is rather potentially about the extent to which this entire period constitutes a single unit.

14. *Hilkhot Tefillah* 2:18.

me'akev (obligatory) and retaining the regular text disqualifies the *Shemoneh Esrei*, as is the preponderant view among the *Rishonim*.[15]

This is particularly striking given that Halakhah does not generally permit any changes to the opening or concluding three *berakhot* of the *Amidah*. As the *gemara* states:

> לעולם אל ישאל אדם צרכיו לא בשלש ראשונות, ולא בשלש אחרונות, אלא באמצעיות.
>
> A person should never make personal requests in the first three *berakhot*, nor in the last three, but rather in the middle *berakhot*.[16]

In codifying this *gemara*, Rambam generalizes the rule to prohibit any changes to these three *berakhot*:

> שלש ראשונות ושלש אחרונות לעולם אין מוסיפין בהן ולא פוחתין מהן ואין משנין בהן דבר.
>
> One may never add to, remove from, or change in any way the first three and last three *berakhot*.[17]

In light of this ruling, it is surprising that we encounter numerous additions to the standard text of the opening and closing sections of *Shemoneh Esrei* during these ten days, beyond the *hatimah* of "*ha-Melekh ha-kadosh*,"

15. For example, see Tosafot, *Berakhot* 12b, and Rambam, *Hilkhot Tefillah* 10:13. Ba'al ha-Ma'or (*Berakhot* 6b in *dapei ha-Rif*) and the *Hakhmei Tzarfat* (cited in *Talmidei Rabbeinu Yonah, Berakhot* 6a–6b in *dapei ha-Rif*) argue that even according to Rabbah, the changes are only *le-khat'hilah* (ideally). Perhaps this opinion stems from a perspective that does not believe the *Aseret Yemei Teshuvah* to be particularly unique; hence, it is inconceivable that the standard applied year round would be invalid during this period. However, as noted, this contrasts with the view of the majority of the *Rishonim*, who insist upon this change during this period. Also see the discussion found in the commentary of *Talmidei Rabbeinu Yonah* (ibid.), who contend that the *nussah* of "*ha-Melekh ha-mishpat*" is not obligatory; only the word "*ha-Melekh*" is absolutely necessary.
16. *Berakhot* 33b.
17. *Hilkhot Tefillah* 1:9.

which is explicitly sanctioned in the Talmud. Rambam himself approvingly records the widespread practice of inserting the phrases of "*Zokhreinu*," "*Mi khamokha*," "*U-khetov*," and "*Be-sefer hayim*" in *Shemoneh Esrei* during the *Aseret Yemei Teshuvah*. He adds that there are even some who integrate the passage of "*U-vekhein tein pahdekha*" – a stirring composition reflecting the gravity of these days that is added to the third *berakhah* of the *Amidah* of Rosh ha-Shanah and Yom Kippur – into every *tefillah* throughout these ten days.[18]

Understandably, even the more common insertions met with considerable resistance. Behag argues that these additions constitute a violation of the principle that one should not ask for his needs during the three opening and three closing *berakhot* of *Shemoneh Esreh*.[19] Supporting his challenge, he cites the ruling in *Masekhet Soferim* that explicitly rejects the alteration of the first and last three *berakhot* on days other than Rosh ha-Shanah and Yom Kippur. Moreover, *Masekhet Soferim* registers significant ambivalence regarding tampering with the standard formula of these *berakhot*, begrudgingly noting that even Rosh ha-Shanah and Yom Kippur constitute an exception to this norm.[20] *Masekhet Soferim* unequivocally gives priority to the immutability and integrity of the opening and closing *berakhot*, even at the expense of the opportunity to further accentuate the singular character of the *Aseret Yemei Teshuvah* period.

Nonetheless, the custom recorded in *Mishneh Torah*, as well as by Tosafot and other halakhic authorities, does include additions and changes to the *Shemoneh Esrei* throughout the *Aseret Yemei Teshuvah*.[21] This is, in fact, the common practice throughout the Jewish world. Tosafot and other authorities even consider whether the omission of these insertions/revisions invalidates the *tefillah*, mandating a repetition

18. *Hilkhot Tefillah* 2:18–19.
19. Quoted in *Hagahot Maimoniyot*, *Hilkhot Tefillah* 2:19.
20. *Masekhet Soferim* 19:8. Interestingly, although the standard text of *Masekhet Soferim* states that we do not say "*Zikhronot*," Behag quotes *Masekhet Soferim* as stating that we do not say "*Zokhreinu*" during the first and last three *berakhot*. Gra's version of this text actually removes the term "*Zikhronot*" entirely.
21. Tosafot, *Berakhot* 12b, s.v. *le-hilkhata*.

of the *Shemoneh Esrei.*[22] If so, these revisions reflect not merely additions to the *Shemoneh Esrei,* like the passage of *Aneinu* on a fast day, but rather a restructuring of the entire *tefillah.* The *Shemoneh Esrei* that we recite during these ten days differs significantly from the *Shemoneh Esrei* recited throughout the year, and failure to accommodate the appropriate additions and changes is therefore just cause for invalidation. Just as one who omits a *berakhah* from his *tefillah* has undermined his fulfillment of the *Shemoneh Esrei* obligation, one who omits the special requests that characterize prayer during the *Aseret Yemei Teshuvah* does not fulfill his prayer obligation. Although the issue is vigorously debated even with respect to the non-Talmudic insertions, this perspective is generally accepted regarding the *halakhah* of "*ha-Melekh ha-kadosh.*"

The halakhic justification for disqualifying a *Shemoneh Esrei* absent the insertions for the *Aseret Yemei Teshuvah* lies in the nature of these ten days. Since the entire period is an integrated whole and the intervening days act as a bridge between Rosh ha-Shanah and Yom Kippur, they assume some facets of the terminus days. One may even argue that *Masekhet Soferim* is correct in principle that changes to the *Shemoneh Esrei* are justified only on Rosh ha-Shanah and Yom Kippur. However, with respect to the character of their *tefillot,* the intervening days are redefined by their contribution to and integration with Rosh ha-Shanah and Yom Kippur. Thus, although the ability to make these changes is justified by the special status of Rosh ha-Shanah and Yom Kippur, the *Aseret Yemei Teshuvah* are included in that exception, as they are substantively integrated into that motif.

A Singular Requirement for Individual Supplications

Indeed, much of the halakhic justification for the added insertions during the intervening days rests on the assumption that many of the Rosh ha-Shanah and Yom Kippur themes, and therefore the *halakhot* that embody them, apply throughout the entire period of *Aseret Yemei*

22. Tosafot (ibid.) argue that these changes are *le-ikuva* (obligatory); one must repeat *Shemoneh Esrei* if they are not inserted; see also *Hagahot Maimoniyot, Hilkhot Tefillah* 2:19. Rosh (*Berakhot* 1:16) argues that although these changes are *le-khat'hilah,* one need not repeat *Shemoneh Esrei* if they are omitted.

Teshuvah. By extension, we may validate other innovations to the standard *Shemoneh Esrei*.

Halakhic authorities were particularly troubled by the insertion of personal requests (*bakashot*) in the first and last sections of the *Shemoneh Esrei*, an apparent violation of the Talmudic dictum cited above. Some, such as Tosafot, neutralize this difficulty by noting the plural form of these requests ("*Zokhreinu*," etc.) and asserting a distinction between individual and collective/communal pleas.[23] Others, however, perceive the special allowance of personal supplication as consistent with the broader, singular nature of *tefillah* during this unique *teshuvah* period. For example, *Yad ha-Melekh* argues that personal requests are appropriate during this period, in which individual and collective pleas converge:

> אבל בעשרת ימי תשובה דאין חילוק בין יחיד לרבים וגם צרכי יחיד מתפללין בהם, על כן הוסיפו לתקן בשמונה עשרה תפלת זכרנו ובספר חיים, שהם תפלה בפני עצמה על בקשת חיים לבד.
>
> During the *Aseret Yemei Teshuvah*, when there is no difference between the individual and the collective and we pray for the needs of the individual, they instituted that we say the prayers of "*Zokhreinu*" and "*U-vesefer*," since they are independent prayers asking just for life.[24]

The blurring of the line between individual requests and communal needs is a principle that is ubiquitous in the *tefillot* of Rosh ha-Shanah and Yom Kippur – and, by extension, all the days in between.[25]

---

23. Tosafot, *Berakhot* 34a.
24. *Yad ha-Melekh, Hilkhot Tefillah* 2:18–19.
25. This is a convergence of the *gemarot* in *Rosh ha-Shanah* 18a, which equates the capacity of supplication and repentance of the individual during the *Aseret Yemei Teshuvah* to that of the community all year round (based on "*Dirshu Hashem be-himatz'o*"), and *Berakhot* 12b, which proclaims that the canons of *tefillah* are transformed during this period.

Fasting on Shabbat Shuvah

Perceiving these ten days as a singular unit, a bubble in time in which certain halakhic rules are refashioned and reimagined, can help explain an additional oddity of these ten days. At first glance, the Shabbat between Rosh ha-Shanah and Yom Kippur, Shabbat Shuvah, seems just like every other Shabbat of the year, but upon closer examination, two strange features emerge.

The first, cited by the *Tur*, is an astonishing practice in some Sephardic communities to recite *Selihot* on this Shabbat.[26] Generally, Halakhah forbids making requests on Shabbat.[27] How, then, do these communities justify the abundance of requests made during Shabbat *Selihot*? The *Tur* himself poses this difficulty and notes approvingly that Ashkenazic communities do not observe this practice. *Beit Yosef*, however, defends the Sephardic practice by invoking the *gemara*'s exception to the prohibition of making requests on Shabbat. The *gemara* permits supplications on Shabbat if the matter is urgent, such as when a city is under siege by an invading army or a community faces the threat of being inundated by an overflowing river. *Beit Yosef* argues that since prayer is readily accepted during the *Aseret Yemei Teshuvah* and the verdict of our judgment is issued on Yom Kippur, "*ein lekha davar nahutz yoteir mi-zeh* – there is no more pressing matter than this."[28] The emphasis on repentance and prayer during these days dictates the "crisis perspective" we should adopt, to the extent that we perceive our lives to be under a threat equivalent to (or perhaps even greater than) the danger of an invading army or flooding river![29]

A second apparent anomaly is a practice, advocated by R. Natronai Gaon and cited by Rosh, to fast on Shabbat Shuvah. He argues that

26. *Tur, Orah Hayim* 602.
27. See *Ta'anit* 19a.
28. *Beit Yosef, Orah Hayim* 602.
29. Once again, this reflects the convergence of the two motifs of *Aseret Yemei Teshuvah*. One is the capacity and necessity for successful supplication in a crisis environment ("*Dirshu Hashem be-himatz'o,*" per *Rosh ha-Shanah* 18a); the second is the sanctioned particularization of otherwise standard rules and texts of prayer during this opportune time (*Berakhot* 12b); see note 25 above.

other than the first day of Rosh ha-Shanah, on which there is a Biblical obligation to eat, one may fast every day of the *Aseret Yemei Teshuvah*:

> אמר מר רב נטרונאי גאון ביו"ט ראשון של ראש השנה אי אפשר לישב בו בתענית משום דמדאורייתא הוא. אבל ביו"ט שני ובשבת לית בהו קושיא משום דעשרה יומי אינון משונין מכל ימות השנה. לפיכך נוהגין רבותינו לישב בהן בתעניות בין בחול בין בשבת.
>
> R. Natronai Gaon writes that on the first day of Rosh ha-Shanah, it is impossible to fast, since it is a Torah-designated [festival, and it is therefore obligatory to eat]. But on the second day of Yom Tov and on Shabbat, there is no problem, since these ten days are different from the rest of the year. Therefore, our Rabbis are accustomed to fast during the week and on Shabbat.[30]

Rosh himself challenges this view:

> ודבריו תמוהין שאסר להתענות ביו"ט ראשון של ר"ה והתיר להתענות בשבת.
>
> His argument is very difficult to understand, as he prohibits fasting on the first day of Yom Tov but permits fasting on Shabbat.

Indeed, Rosh posits the opposite view: One should not fast on Shabbat, but one may be allowed to fast on Rosh ha-Shanah.

Rosh's position is supported by two considerations. First, one may challenge R. Natronai Gaon's lenient assumption about the prospect of fasting on Shabbat as compared to Yom Tov. *Sefer ha-Manhig* emphatically rejects this view of R. Natronai Gaon, since Shabbat also entails an obligation to eat, based on the verse, "*Ve-karata la-Shabbat oneg* – You shall call the Sabbath 'delight'" (*Yeshayahu* 58:13).[31] In fact, fasting on Shabbat is more problematic, since Shabbat's sanctity is more stringent

30. Rosh, *Rosh ha-Shanah* 4:14.
31. *Sefer ha-Manhig, Hilkhot Rosh ha-Shanah, siman* 1 (Mossad ha-Rav Kook ed., p. 303).

than that of Yom Tov, as evidenced by the absence of *heter okhel nefesh,* the license to engage in *melakhot* relating to food preparation.[32]

Rosh's argument is further fortified in light of the unique character of Rosh ha-Shanah as an atypical Yom Tov. Although there is an obligation to feast on Yom Tov in general, Rosh ha-Shanah's particular status as a day of "*yirah va-fahad,*" awe and fear,[33] may preclude, neutralize, or blunt this imperative.[34]

In light of Rosh's strong arguments, how does R. Natronai Gaon permit fasting on Shabbat? A careful look at R. Natronai Gaon's formulation reveals the answer:

> אבל ביו"ט שני ובשבת לית בהו קושיא משום דעשרה יומי אינון משונין מכל ימות השנה.
>
> However, on the second day of Yom Tov and Shabbat, there is no question [that fasting is permitted], because these ten days are different from the other days of the year.

The justification for fasting on Shabbat Shuvah is that the entire ten-day period is "different from the other days of the year."[35] The obligation to eat on a typical Shabbat is not a compelling paradigm for Shabbat Shuvah, because this particular Shabbat, like the entire *Aseret Yemei Teshuvah* period, is *sui generis.*

This perspective resolves both of Rosh's questions. We cannot dismiss R. Natronai's view due to the general prohibition of fasting of Shabbat and Yom Tov, because Shabbat Shuvah is an atypical Shabbat. Nor can we challenge R. Natronai's conclusion based on the unique

32. This reflects a perspective on *heter okhel nefesh* that links it to a more circumscribed concept of *issur melakhah,* rather than an allowance based on the urgency of *simhah* on Yom Tov.

33. Rambam, *Hilkhot Hanukah* 2:6.

34. For an extensive analysis of this topic, see the chapter in the second volume of this series, "The Halakhic Status of Rosh ha-Shanah as a Day of *Simhah.*"

35. It is noteworthy that R. Natronai echoes the formulation of "*meshuneh*" in *Masekhet Soferim* invoked to justify the phenomenon of deviating from the otherwise standardized *nussah ha-tefillah.*

nature of Rosh ha-Shanah, which may allow for fasting, since R. Natronai evidently perceives Shabbat Shuvah as an extension of Rosh ha-Shanah in this regard. In sum, Shabbat Shuvah assumes the character of the time period in which it is found.

Aseret Yemei Teshuvah: Defining the Rest of the Year

Let us take stock of our argument thus far. It is common practice in Jewish communities to observe certain stringencies during the *Aseret Yemei Teshuvah* between Rosh ha-Shanah and Yom Kippur. This poses two difficulties, one that is strictly halakhic and one that is more ideological and conceptual. First, the very behavior intended to reflect admirable zeal and intensified commitment to Torah observance may obligate future halakhic conduct. Moreover, as a short-term practice, it may be perceived as an empty or insincere gesture, even hypocritical or cynical.

We proceeded to note that the *Aseret Yemei Teshuvah* is not only a period that pragmatically motivates and inspires *teshuvah* in anticipation of a fateful judgment, but rather constitutes a unit in time that is both integrated with and a bridge between the respective *Yamim Nora'im*. These days are particularly conducive to and invested with an increased capacity for intensive introspection, the rigorous process of *teshuvah*, and the attainment of atonement. As such, the period between Rosh ha-Shanah and Yom Kippur is not merely an opportune time, but rather an inherent component of the *Yamim Nora'im* and their halakhic agenda. This perspective accounts for the rule-defying *halakhot* that govern the *tefillot* of the entire time period, as well as the unique character of Shabbat Shuvah, as highlighted by those authorities who permit or even demand fasting on this Shabbat.

This comprehensive view of the *Aseret Yemei Teshuvah* as an independent bubble in time, with its own accentuated themes and desired goals, can explain how the apparent insincerity and hypocrisy of increased stringency that is exclusive to this period is actually a constructive and sincere reflection of deep religious commitment and piety.

The halakhic view of *kedushat ha-zeman*, the sanctity of time and festivals, facilitates the ability to promote and accentuate various themes. These themes are certainly relevant to the entire year, but then they must be integrated with numerous other, and even competing, motifs.

For example, on Shavu'ot we emphasize the importance and centrality of Torah learning, on Sukkot we stress our reliance on Hashem, and on Pesah we highlight the active role of Divine Providence and the spiritual responsibility of freedom.[36] This concept is acutely at the core of Yom Kippur's role as "*ahat ba-shanah*" (unique in the year) in our religious existence. It is not inconsistent, cynical, or hypocritical to de-intensify or withdraw from a single-minded focus on these themes upon the holiday's end, returning to a broader and more balanced religious agenda. This transition merely constitutes the recognition that the reality of human nature and the extensive and ambitious demands of our broader religious existence do not allow for an exclusive sustained emphasis of particular motifs throughout the year. Other pressures and halakhic values compete for our attention and time. By singling out certain times of the year during which we focus exclusively and intensively on particular values, we demonstrate and more effectively promote their importance year round.

Similarly, during the *Aseret Yemei Teshuvah,* we emphasize our capacity to be fully engaged and intensively involved in *avodat Hashem*. Consequently, we embrace a stricter code of behavior that sincerely and accurately reflects our true spiritual personality and ambition. We certainly do not forsake these values upon the conclusion of the ten days; rather, we transition to a more comprehensive, but equally challenging, religious agenda. To try to live as a "Ten-Days Jew" throughout the year would force us to abandon or compromise other valuable and meaningful halakhic pursuits; it would actually detract from our ability and goal to live holistic and maximalist Jewish lives. Indeed, it would potentially undermine the broader telos of the *Aseret Yemei Teshuvah* itself, which is enhanced by its relevance throughout the year and as an indispensable component of the entire halakhic agenda.

Instead, the ten days between Rosh ha-Shanah and Yom Kippur demonstrate the capacity and commitment to unequivocal devotion to Hashem and halakhic life. Maintaining a stricter standard of ritual purity is an enthusiastic expression of excessive piety that is eminently

36. This is not intended to be an exhaustive list of the themes highlighted on different holidays or an attempt to identify the central themes of those holidays. It is merely a list of a few examples of themes emphasized at those periods in the calendar.

appropriate during this period of intense spiritual opportunity. This single-minded spiritual agenda establishes that our more balanced, nuanced behavior during the rest of the year is not a consequence of complacency, a lack of effort, or failure to engage passionately in *avodat Hashem*, but rather due to the fact that we also enthusiastically embrace the halakhic challenge of an ambitious balance, of a multi-faceted halakhic life.

The *Aseret Yemei Teshuvah* provide an opportunity, and thus a responsibility, to reveal and display our authentic spiritual identities and personas. Failure to capitalize on the opportunity of introspection, repentance, and performance of *mitzvot* afforded by this period significantly jeopardizes the legitimacy, and certainly the ideal, of our broader halakhic posture throughout the year. It casts doubt on whether the balance indeed stems from insufficient religious passion and commitment to halakhic life. During this time period, we have the opportunity to demonstrate that that balance actually constitutes a maximalist, if complex, halakhic lifestyle, one that is immeasurably enriched by the opportunity and phenomenon of the *Yamim Nora'im* and the *Aseret Yemei Teshuvah.*

Chapter 10

Moons, Marriages, and Court: Avoiding *Mitzvot* During the *Aseret Yemei Teshuvah*

The period of the *Aseret Yemei Teshuvah* is a time when maximal mitzvah performance is urgently encouraged.[1] Not only is it a particularly propitious period for *teshuvah,* but Rambam writes that each mitzvah has the potential to tip the scale for an individual – and even the entire world – toward *zekhut* (merit).[2] Notably, there is also a custom to take upon oneself more *humrot* (halakhic stringencies) during this time period.[3] Thus, it is rather astonishing that there are *minhagim* (customs) to refrain from performing certain *mitzvot* during this time period. What could possibly justify this phenomenon? Why would we

1. See Rambam, *Hilkhot Teshuvah* 2:6, who articulates this point.
2. *Hilkhot Teshuvah* 3:4.
3. For further discussion of the practice to adopt *humrot,* see the chapter "Religious Stringency, Consistency, and the Implications of the *Aseret Yemei Teshuvah.*"

be encouraged to temporarily abstain from these *mitzvot,* further sources of potential merit?

An analysis of these intriguing *minhagim* provides a window into the true character and purpose of the *Aseret Yemei Teshuvah.*

Kiddush Levanah

There is a debate among the authorities regarding the propriety of reciting *Kiddush Levanah* (the blessing upon seeing the new moon) prior to Yom Kippur. The common practice is to follow Rema's view to wait until *motza'ei* Yom Kippur.[4] *Levush* explains the basis for this custom:

> אין מקדשין הלבנה אלא עד אחר יום כיפור, מפני שאנו תלויין בדין וקדושה צריך להיות מתוך שמחת הלב, כן הוא המנהג.
>
> The custom is to wait to sanctify the new moon until after Yom Kippur, because we are suspended in judgment and sanctifying requires happiness. This is the common practice.[5]

Levush then approvingly quotes a sage who advances the compelling counter-argument that one should be particularly motivated to sanctify the moon during the *Aseret Yemei Teshuvah*:

> ואני שמעתי בשם גדול אחד שאדרבה טוב שיקדשו אותה בתוך עשרת ימי תשובה, כדי שתבא מצוה זו ותוסיף על זכיותינו הקודמות, ואולי תכריע היא את הכף לזכות ביום הדין, וסברא נכונה היא, כי זו היא משמחת הלבבות שתוסיף על זכיותינו ותכריעינו לזכות.
>
> I heard from one sage that on the contrary, it is preferable to sanctify the moon during this time, so as to add this mitzvah to our previous merits, and perhaps thereby tip the scales in favor of one's merits on the Day of Judgment. This is a correct suggestion, as adding to our merits and tipping the scales toward *zekhut* engenders a sense of happiness.

---

4. Rema, *Orah Hayim* 426:2, 602:1.
5. *Levush, Orah Hayim* 602. Rema (ibid.) also presents this reason.

Levush writes that it is actually more sensible to recite *Kiddush Levanah* during the *Aseret Yemei Teshuvah,* so as to increase our merits during this critical time.[6] *Eliyah Zuta* states the case even more strongly, contending that there is an additional factor that motivates reciting *Kiddush Levanah* prior to Yom Kippur:

> מעשה באחד שפגע בו עכו"ם בלילה ורצה עכו"ם להרגו, וביקש ממנו שיניחנו לעשות מצוה אחת קודם מותו ואח"כ יעשה אתו מה שלבו חפץ, והלבנה היתה בחידושה וקידשה בפניו בכוונה גדולה, ונעשה לו נס כשדלג וקפץ ג' פעמים כמנהג ונשאו הרוח וניצול ממנו. גם שמעתי ממנו שמי שיקדש הלבנה מיום שיקדש שוב לא ידאוג שימות באותו חודש מאותו יום ואילך ע"כ. הבאתי זה כאן ללמוד ממנה קצת ראיה ללבוש דיותר מסתברא לקדש קודם יו"כ, משום דנאמר כשם שלא ידאוג שימות באותו החודש כן לא יגזור עליו מיתה באותו חודש.
>
> There is a story of a person who encountered an idolater at night, and the idolater wished to kill him. The Jew requested from his captor that he be allowed to perform one mitzvah before his death, and afterward he could do as he wished. There was a new moon, and he proceeded to sanctify it before him. While jumping up and down three times, as is customary, a miracle occurred, and the wind picked him up and took him away to safety. I also heard that one who recites the sanctification of the moon is guaranteed to survive the month. I cite this to support *Levush*'s argument that it is better to sanctify the moon before Yom Kippur, for just as one need not worry that he will die that month [if he recites *Kiddush Levanah*], he need not be concerned that a decree of death will be issued against him in the coming month.[7]

---

6. *Levush* subsequently defends the common *minhag* and suggests that waiting to sanctify the moon until after Yom Kippur in order to recite it in a state of *simhah* itself may constitute a mitzvah. Thus, waiting accomplishes the same goal of accumulating *mitzvot* during the *Aseret Yemei Teshuvah.*
7. *Eliyah Zuta* 602:4.

Eliyah Zuta argues that there should specifically be an impetus to recite *Kiddush Levanah* during the *Aseret Yemei Teshuvah*, because this particular imperative is perceived by *Hazal* as promoting longevity. Rabbinic legends even project the miraculous impact of *Kiddush Levanah* in neutralizing danger and in securing life and well-being, such as guaranteed survival of the next month. Certainly such a mitzvah should constitute a high priority during the precarious period of the *Aseret Yemei Teshuvah*, when our lives hang in the balance!

The positions articulated by *Levush* and *Eliyah Zuta* appear very compelling, as it is intuitive that one should be intensely immersed in as many *mitzvot* as possible during the *Aseret Yemei Teshuvah*, especially those that facilitate and even guarantee ongoing survival. One can hardly conceive of a more ideal time for *Kiddush Levanah*! How, then, can we account for our custom to delay the performance of this consequential mitzvah during the *Aseret Yemei Teshuvah*? Why would one forgo this formidable and calming asset during this tense period? Does the impropriety of reciting *Kiddush Levanah* during a time of acute fear, uncertainty, and anxiety justify or even account for this curious abstention?

Court Cases

There is a similar debate regarding conducting court cases during the *Aseret Yemei Teshuvah*. *Levush* cites a surprising *minhag* to avoid trying court cases between disputants, proceeding to argue strongly against this custom:

> ויש נוהגין שלא לדון בין איש לחבירו בעשרת ימי תשובה, ונ״ל אדרבה יותר טוב הוא לדון ולפסוק הדין בין הבריות כדי שיהא השלום ביניהם ביום כיפור, ועוד הרי אמרו חז״ל (דב״ר ה, ד) במקום שיש דין אין דין ומקום שאין דין יש דין, ר״ל אם נעשה הדין למטה אין הדין למעלה, ואם אין נעשה למטה נעשה למעלה, וא״כ אם לא ידונו למטה הרי מדת הדין למעלה מתוחה עלינו ח״ו, על כן נ״ל שיותר טוב הוא לדון למטה ולהשקיט הדין שלמעלה.

> Some have the custom to not conduct court cases between man and his fellow during the *Aseret Yemei Teshuvah*. It seems to me

> that, on the contrary, it is better to judge and render decisions in human affairs [during this time], so that there may be peace among the parties on Yom Kippur. Moreover, our Sages have said (*Devarim Rabbah* 5:4): "Where there is justice, there is no judgment; and where there is no justice there is judgment." In other words, if we do justice on earth below, there is no judgment from above, but if there is no justice below, there is judgment above. This being the case, if we do not judge below, the attribute of divine justice will be directed toward us, God forbid! Therefore, it seems to me that it is better to judge below and silence the judgment above.[8]

Levush not only objects to the custom, but views it as counterintuitive. It is, in fact, particularly appropriate for court cases to be conducted during this time period, for two reasons. First of all, the resolution of disputes engenders peace within the community, a climate that is particularly conducive to the judgment of Yom Kippur. And second, there is a direct correlation between divine justice and the responsible, honest administration of halakhic courts. When halakhic courts judge efficiently and with integrity, God is inclined to favor our judgment as well.

Levush's argument is reasonable. Why should we miss the opportunity to capitalize on this supernatural phenomenon to burnish our credentials, to enhance our worthiness, and to silence harsh judgment before Yom Kippur?

Weddings

A third surprising custom is the discouragement of weddings during the *Aseret Yemei Teshuvah*. R. David Zvi Hoffman was asked whether it is permitted to get married during the *Aseret Yemei Teshuvah*.[9] He initiates his response by citing a *minhag* found in the *Sefer Mateh Efraim* and the *Kitzur Shulhan Arukh* that one should not get married during this time period. R. Hoffman then challenges the basis for this *minhag*, writing

8. *Levush, Orah Hayim* 603.
9. *Melamed le-Ho'il* 3:1. I thank my father, Rabbi Dr. Bernard Rosensweig *zt"l*, for introducing me to this source.

that he is unaware of any source supporting this practice. On the contrary, it is advisable to get married during this period, as fulfilling the mitzvah of *peru u-revu* may tip the scales in one's favor.[10]

Hokhmat Shlomo also makes reference to this *minhag*.[11] He evaluates the practice based on the principle that "when one gets married, all his sins are forgiven."[12] From this perspective, the *minhag* to specifically refrain from marriage during this crucial period, thereby squandering a significant advantage in one's campaign for *selihah* and *kapparah*, is astounding. Surely there could be no more opportune time than the *Aseret Yemei Teshuvah* for one to experience this type of spiritual rebirth! Why would we advocate against an act that engenders the forgiveness of sin?

The Character of the *Aseret Yemei Teshuvah*

Notwithstanding the merit of the arguments on both sides of these debates, the mere existence of these *minhagim* is intriguing and necessitates a closer examination of the themes and character of the *Aseret Yemei Teshuvah*.[13]

The period of the *Aseret Yemei Teshuvah*, rather than being perceived as simply a break between the two intense days of Rosh ha-Shanah and Yom Kippur, actually integrates with and forms a substantive unit of time with Rosh ha-Shanah and Yom Kippur. Importantly, the *gemara* describes these days as "*asarah yamim she-bein Rosh ha-Shanah ve-Yom ha-Kippurim* – the ten days between Rosh ha-Shanah and Yom Kippur."[14] In not referring to this period as seven days (the mathematically correct number), the *gemara* clearly seeks to integrate the terminus days of Rosh ha-Shanah and Yom Kippur into the rest of the *Aseret Yemei Teshuvah*, thereby indicating that they are meant to be considered as a unit. Further buttressing this perspective, there are various laws and *minhagim* that spill

---

10. Interestingly, in support of his position, R. Hoffman relates that he himself actually married during the *Aseret Yemei Teshuvah*. He notes that none of his teachers or friends objected!
11. *Hokhmat Shlomo* 602:1.
12. See *Yevamot* 63b; Yerushalmi *Bikkurim* 3:5.
13. I address the issues in this section extensively in the chapter "Religious Stringency, Consistency, and the Implications of the *Aseret Yemei Teshuvah*." As they are dealt with at length there, I have only briefly delineated them in this chapter.
14. *Rosh ha-Shanah* 18b; *Yevamot* 105a.

over from Rosh ha-Shanah and Yom Kippur into the rest of the *Aseret Yemei Teshuvah*, reflecting a substantive connection. Moreover, the *gemara* interprets the verse in *Yeshayahu* (55:6), "*Dirshu Hashem be-himatz'o* – Seek out Hashem when He is found," as a reference to the *Aseret Yemei Teshuvah*, reflecting that these days are ones when God is especially close, and they are singularly opportune for *teshuvah*.[15] Rambam elaborates that *teshuvah* and crying out are more appropriate and effective during this time:

> אע"פ שהתשובה והצעקה יפה לעולם, בעשרה הימים שבין ראש השנה ויום הכפורים היא יפה ביותר ומתקבלת היא מיד שנאמר דרשו ה' בהמצאו.
>
> Even though repentance and crying out are always beneficial, during the ten days between Rosh ha-Shanah and Yom Kippur they are particularly beneficial and immediately accepted, as the *pasuk* states, "Seek out Hashem when He can be found."[16]

Rambam explains that the *Aseret Yemei Teshuvah* are not simply an interruption between Rosh ha-Shanah and Yom Kippur, nor are they designed to function solely as days of preparation for Yom Kippur. Rather, they constitute a unique stretch of time designated for *teshuvah*.

The *Aseret Yemei Teshuvah* are clearly intended to function as a bridge between Rosh ha-Shanah and Yom Kippur dedicated to rigorous *teshuvah* through self-reflection, self-improvement, and religious transformation. Indeed, this theme is further reflected in the *pasuk* that *Hazal* cite as the source for the time period's power. "*Dirshu Hashem be-himatz'o kera'uhu bi-heyoto karov* – Seek out Hashem when He is found, call out to Him when he is near" is not focused on *selihah u-mehilah* (forgiveness) and one's future fate, but rather accentuates the opportunity and urgency of repairing one's general relationship with the *Ribbono Shel Olam*.

Understanding the *Minhagim*

With this understanding of the *Aseret Yemei Teshuvah*, the *minhagim* to avoid or delay certain *mitzvot* during this period emerge as entirely

15. *Rosh ha-Shanah* 18b.
16. *Hilkhot Teshuvah* 2:6.

comprehensible. It may be precisely due to their outsized and practical effectiveness in facilitating and even securing one's future fate that we are wary of these very *mitzvot*! Indeed, *Hokhmat Shlomo*, when addressing the prohibition to get married during the *Aseret Yemei Teshuvah*, explicitly articulates this perspective, albeit in a more limited fashion.[17] He asserts that the reason for abstaining from marriage during this period is precisely because marriage neutralizes one's past transgressions, eliminating some of the anxiety and uncertainty that serves as a constructive catalyst for deep introspection. He articulates a more pragmatic and narrower concern, arguing that pursuing *mitzvot* whose special merit apparently ensures one's future encroaches on the divine prerogative to render judgment during this period and borders on an act of insubordination – "*ke-merim yado ba-melekh.*" Abstaining from marriage during the *Aseret Yemei Teshuvah*, in contrast, promotes God's special judicial role and supports the focal point of "*itzumo shel Yom ha-Kippurim mekhaper* – the essence of the day of Yom Kippur itself atones."[18]

As noted, this perspective can be formulated more broadly. The *Posekim* were reticent about these particularly compelling *mitzvot* that trigger consequential reward not only to protect divine judicial prerogative, but especially to avoid subverting the very purpose of the *Aseret Yemei Teshuvah*. These *mitzvot*, unwittingly or subconsciously pursued for their reward, may temper the significance of Yom Kippur as a *yom selihah u-mehilah* by defusing the tension and diluting the charged environment that make the *Aseret Yemei Teshuvah* an ideal period of *heshbon ha-nefesh* (introspection). The *Aseret Yemei Teshuvah* – in the aftermath of the stirring, penetrating sound of the *shofar* – is both a time of crisis and of confidence, a necessary catalyst for spiritual reassessment and transformation that culminates on Yom Kippur, when individual and collective fates are sealed. The more intense immersion in *mitzvot* during this singular time is an expression of impassioned *avodat Hashem* and *ahavat Hashem*; as a method of further internalizing halakhic values that define one's spiritual personality, this is an indispensable dimension of *teshuvah*. The emphasis of certain *mitzvot* particularly associated with securing a

---

17. *Hokhmat Shlomo*, ibid.
18. See Rambam, *Hilkhot Teshuvah* 1:3.

good fate could possibly be misconstrued as an effort to bypass rigorous *heshbon ha-nefesh* and authentic core repentance in order to attain a verdict of *selihah u-mehilah* in a more circuitous and technical manner.

It may be noteworthy that *Hokhmat Shlomo* cites the *minhag* to delay *Kiddush Levanah* in conjunction with the *minhag* to refrain from marrying during this time. This may support our understanding that the two share a common theme: the discouragement of specific mitzvot that may prematurely defuse or mitigate the anxiety that one should constructively experience during the week between Rosh ha-Shanah and Yom Kippur, deflecting from the primary emphasis and goal of genuine change during this crucial period.[19]

---

19. In light of this analysis, we may speculate that the posture of reticence, in some cases even opposition, to two other prominent practices – *tashlikh* and *kapparot* – may stem from similar considerations. Attaining *kapparah* is always an urgent goal, but the discomfort with a *segulah-zekhuyot*-expedited route to neutralizing halakhic infractions that may distract from thorough introspection is an important counterweight. There is a subtle line distinguishing *tefillah* and acts that embody the negation of past misconduct, on the one hand, and other symbolic mechanisms that may neutralize the effects of transgression without addressing the core flaws that produced them, on the other. Indeed, many of the advocates of these customs emphasize that they constitute a form of *tefillah* or that they provoke *heshbon ha-nefesh* and precisely express and facilitate *teshuvah*.

The *minhag* of *tashlikh* is anchored in the verse in *Mikhah* (7:19) "*Ve-tashlikh bi-metzulot yam kol hatotam* – And you will cast all their sins into the depths of the sea." It first surfaces in the fifteenth-century works of Maharil and R. Yitzhak of Tarna, although an earlier hybrid of *kapparot* and *tashlikh* is already attributed to the *Ge'onim* and cited by Rashi (*Shabbat* 81b). Rema (*Orah Hayim* 583:2), *Levush,* and others endorsed and popularized this practice in their works. However, many Sephardic communities did not initially partake in *tashlikh* (until the seventeenth century, due to the effect of R. Hayim Vital's support), and the Vilna Gaon (*Ma'aseh Rav*, no. 202) is reported to have abstained from *tashlikh,* as did many of his followers. (*Arukh Ha-Shulhan*'s discouragement of *tashlikh* [*Orah Hayim* 583:4] is rooted in practical misgivings about the social interactions that occur during its performance, but it is likely that these would have been overridden or resolved had he found the practice compelling or otherwise unproblematic.)

It is noteworthy that *Levush* (*Orah Hayim* 596) and later authorities specifically underscored *tashlikh* as a *tefillah* and a stimulus of *hirhurei teshuvah.* They emphasized the link to the *akeidah,* invoking the *midrash* that Avraham carried Yitzhak through dangerously high waters in his eagerness to fulfill Hashem's charge and challenge. Fish entrapped and dependent on salvation came to be projected as an important

Rambam's Emphasis of Specific *Mitzvot*

Rambam's presentation of the core *mitzvot* to perform during the *Aseret Yemei Teshuvah* further bolsters our perspective. Rambam declares that in the aftermath of Rosh ha-Shanah, all of one's *zekhuyot* have already been calculated, leaving the fate of the "*beinoni*" for the coming year to be determined only by the effectiveness of his *teshuvah*.[20] However, in the very next *halakhah*, Rambam introduces the concept of blowing the *shofar* and writes that every individual must view himself and the entire world as if they are half-guilty and half-righteous, and the fate of the world is therefore dependent on his deeds. Rambam then continues:

> ומפני ענין זה, נהגו כל בית ישראל להרבות בצדקה ובמעשים טובים ולעסוק במצות מראש השנה ועד יוה"כ יתר מכל השנה.

---

metaphor for the indispensability of *teshuvah* during this period. Thus, many of the supporters of *tashlikh* implicitly distanced themselves from any impression that one could possibly bypass substantive *tefillah* and *teshuvah* in the effort to achieve the aspirational goals of the *Yamim Nora'im*.

The *minhag* of *kapparot* was particularly controversial. While many of the Ashkenazic authorities (Rosh, *Yoma* 8:23; Rema, *Orah Hayim* 605:1) embraced it, it elicited passionate opposition from some of the leading Sephardic scholars (Ramban, *Teshuvot ha-Rashba* 1:391, and others). In early printings of *Shulhan Arukh* (*Orah Hayim* 605), it was labeled a "*minhag shetut*" (foolish practice) in the chapter title! Although many of the objections involved specific halakhic concerns (*darkhei Emori, kodshim ba-hutz, safek neveilah*, etc.), it is highly conceivable that the very premise of the practice – that one can escape his fate by simple substitution, "*zeh halifati zeh temurati*" – was perceived as problematic and incompatible with promoting the urgency of rigorous *teshuvah*.

Again, it is significant that support for those who encouraged the *kapparot* practice includes references to the parallel perspective in *korbanot* (ironically exemplified by Ramban's celebrated comment on *Vayikra* 1:9) to preclude any misconception that the *minhag* is intended to bypass or shortcut the rigorous processes of *kapparah. Mori ve-rabbi* R. Aharon Lichtenstein *zt"l* notes that although there is some ambiguity regarding the perspective of the Brisker dynasty regarding *kapparot*, R. Soloveitchik and other members of his family were strongly against the custom and did not perform it. See *Mevakshei Panekha* (Tel Aviv, 2011), 245.

20. *Hilkhot Teshuvah* 3:3.

> Based on this, the Jewish People customarily increase their charity, good deeds, and involvement in *mitzvot* from Rosh ha-Shanah until Yom Kippur more than the rest of the year.[21]

Rambam's approving description of the practice of increasing performance of good deeds during the *Aseret Yemei Teshuvah* appears to contrast with his comments in the previous *halakhah*. First, he emphasizes the significance of *teshuvah* exclusively; in the next *halakhah*, he focuses instead on performing additional good deeds.

However, a closer analysis of Rambam's presentation demonstrates that his position remains coherent and consistent. Rambam's comments in the latter *halakhah* surely must be read in context of the former. The goal is the *teshuvah* initially described; the method for accomplishing *teshuvah* are detailed in the *halakhah* that follows. Furthermore, Rambam's portrayal of this practice includes an amplification of one's general "*esek be-mitzvot*" (involvement in *mitzvot*). If this practice were only for the sake of accumulating specific merits that tip the scales, the intensification of one's broader attitude toward *mitzvot* would be irrelevant. The requirement of "*esek be-mitzvot*" reflects a sincere aspiration for lasting attitudinal change. Finally, Rambam specifically references *mitzvot* that facilitate and expand sincere *teshuvah*, as reflected in the poignant declaration in the Rosh ha-Shanah and Yom Kippur prayer services: "*Teshuvah, tefillah*, and *tzedakah* remove the terrible decree."[22] Again, this reflects that *teshuvah* is the goal and the additional mitzvah performance subsequently advocated is a method for achieving that ambition. Thus, Rambam's recording of this practice further reinforces the perspective that the period of the *Aseret Yemei Teshuvah* is meant to be a time for lasting change that elevates one to the elite status of an *ohev Hashem*.[23]

---

21. Ibid. 3:4.
22. Notably, at the end of the very same *halakhah*, Rambam refers to an increase in prayer during this time as well. Again, this reflects the choice to prioritize specific *mitzvot* that are particularly apt for achieving proper *teshuvah*.
23. In other chapters in this volume, we discuss Rambam's important choice to place the laws of *ahavat Hashem* as the final chapter in *Hilkhot Teshuvah*. As I have argued there, this decision reflects Rambam's perspective that the pinnacle of *teshuvah* is reaching *ahavat Hashem*.

Yom Kippur

Chapter 11

Yom Kippur: The Quintessential Shabbat

In the list of festivals in *Parashat Emor,* the Torah refers to Yom Kippur as "*Shabbat Shabbaton* – the Sabbatical Sabbath" (*Vayikra* 23:32). The *gemara* views this phrase as the *azharah* (explicit prohibition) of eating on Yom Kippur:

> רב אחא בר יעקב אמר: יליף שבת שבתון משבת בראשית. מה להלן לא ענש אלא אם כן הזהיר, אף כאן לא ענש אלא אם כן הזהיר.
>
> R. Aha bar Yaakov said: One learns [about the nature of] *Shabbat Shabbaton* from the Shabbat of creation [i.e. the weekly Shabbat]. Just as the punishment [for violation] of the weekly Shabbat accompanies a prohibition, so too the punishment [for violation] of Yom Kippur accompanies a prohibition.[1]

Instead of treating "*Shabbat Shabbaton*" as a turn of phrase indicating the supreme holiness of Yom Kippur – the "Sabbath of all Sabbaths" – this

1. *Yoma* 81a.

passage assumes the expression indicates a substantive connection between Yom Kippur and Shabbat.

The *gemara* utilizes this connection to a surprising end, however. Of the two categories of prohibitions on Yom Kippur – *issur melakhah* (the prohibition of work) and *innuy* (affliction, i.e. the prohibition of eating, etc.) – only the former has any parallel on Shabbat, while the latter is entirely unique to Yom Kippur. We would thus have expected any substantive link to Shabbat to be limited to the *issur melakhah* component of Yom Kippur. Yet the *gemara* uses "*Shabbat Shabbaton*" as a source for the *azharah* related to the *innuy* component!

The Relationship between *Issur Melakhah* and *Innuy*

To understand this phenomenon, we must examine the Torah's presentation of Yom Kippur in *Parashat Emor*:

> וידבר ה׳ אל משה לאמר. אך בעשור לחדש השביעי הזה יום הכפרים הוא מקרא קדש יהיה לכם ועניתם את נפשותיכם והקרבתם אשה לה׳. וכל מלאכה לא תעשו בעצם היום הזה כי יום כפרים הוא לכפר עליכם לפני ה׳ אלקיכם. כי כל הנפש אשר לא תענה בעצם היום הזה ונכרתה מעמיה. וכל הנפש אשר תעשה כל מלאכה בעצם היום הזה והאבדתי את הנפש ההוא מקרב עמה. כל מלאכה לא תעשו חקת עולם לדרתיכם בכל משבתיכם. שבת שבתון הוא לכם ועניתם את נפשתיכם בתשעה לחדש בערב מערב עד ערב תשבתו שבתכם.
>
> Hashem spoke to Moshe, saying: However, the tenth day of this seventh month is Yom ha-Kippurim. It shall be a sacred occasion for you; you shall practice self-affliction, and you shall bring an offering by fire to Hashem. And you shall do no work throughout that day, for it is a Yom ha-Kippurim, on which expiation is made on your behalf before Hashem your God. Indeed, any person who is not afflicted throughout that day shall be cut off from his people. And whoever does any work throughout that day, I will cause that person to perish from among his people. Do no work whatsoever; it is a law for all time, throughout the ages in all your settlements. It shall be a *Shabbat Shabbaton* for you, and

> you shall practice self-affliction; on the ninth day of the month at evening, from evening to evening, you shall observe your Sabbath. (*Vayikra* 23:26–32)

The themes of *issur melakhah* and *innuy* feature prominently in these *pesukim*. Importantly, rather than treat them separately, the Torah oscillates between the two themes, as if to suggest they are interchangeable:

v.27 – *innuy*
v.28 – *issur melakhah*
v.29 – *innuy*
v.30 – *issur melakhah*
v.31 – *issur melakhah*
v.32 – *innuy*

Apparently, *issur melakhah* and *innuy* are not two separate components of Yom Kippur; they are two sides of the same coin. Thus, the *gemara* does not limit the implications of "*Shabbat Shabbaton*" to the *issur melakhah* component, for it is not truly a separate component. "*Shabbat Shabbaton*" applies to the entire *issur melakhah-innuy* complex.

Rambam evidently adopts this perspective as well. Rambam chose the title "*Hilkhot Shevitat Asor* – The Laws of the Cessation of the Tenth" for the section of *Mishneh Torah* dedicated to the laws of Yom Kippur.[2] The word "*shevitah*," cessation, connotes *issur melakhah*, yet the bulk of *Hilkhot Shevitat Asor* is dedicated to the laws of *innuy*. Moreover, Rambam uses the verb "*li-shbot*" to describe both refraining from *melakhah*[3] and refraining from food and drink.[4] In *Sefer ha-Mitzvot*, Rambam writes explicitly that "*Shabbat Shabbaton*" refers to *shevitah* of both types:

---

2. Rambam devotes two sections of *Mishneh Torah* to Yom Kippur. *Hilkhot Shevitat Asor* focuses on the *issur melakhah* and *innuy* prohibitions, whereas *Hilkhot Avodat Yom ha-Kippurim* details the *avodah* in the *Beit ha-Mikdash* on Yom Kippur. Yom Kippur also plays a role in *Hilkhot Teshuvah*, the only section in which Rambam mentions an obligation of *teshuvah* on Yom Kippur; see *Hilkhot Teshuvah* 2:7–8.
3. *Hilkhot Shevitat Asor* 1:1.
4. Ibid. 1:4.

> ושהשביתה מחויבת מאלו הפעולות כלם מאמרו בו (אמור כג) שבת שבתון הוא לכם ועניתם את נפשותיכם כאילו הוא יאמר שחובה בו השביתה המיוחדת במלאכות והמעשים והשביתה המיוחדת במזון הגוף וקיומו ולכן אמר שבת שבתון.
>
> Cessation (*shevitah*) of all these activities [the various types of *innuy*] is required from the verse "It is *Shabbat Shabbaton* for you, and you shall practice self-affliction." It is as if the verse states that the specific cessation of *melakhah* and activities, as well as the specific cessation of the body's food and nourishment, is a requirement of the day; therefore, the verse states, "*Shabbat Shabbaton*."[5]

This passage, in which Rambam mentions *issur melakhah* and *innuy* in one breath and interprets the phrase "*Shabbat Shabbaton*" as referring to both, clearly indicates that Rambam views the two aspects of the day as complementary components of the same concept.

Rambam continues to use "*li-shbot*" to describe the other forms of *innuy* on Yom Kippur:

> וכן למדנו מפי השמועה שאסור לרחוץ בו או לסוך או לנעול את הסנדל או לבעול, ומצוה לשבות מכל אלו כדרך ששובת מאכילה ושתייה שנאמר שבת שבתון שבת לענין אכילה ושבתון לענינים אלו.
>
> We also learn from the tradition that it is forbidden to bathe on the day, or to anoint oneself, or to wear shoes, or to have marital relations. It is a mitzvah to cease (*li-shbot*) all these activities, just as one ceases eating and drinking, as the *pasuk* states, "*Shabbat Shabbaton*": "*Shabbat*" regarding food and "*Shabbaton*" regarding these other matters.[6]

A variant text of the last line replaces "*akhilah*" with "*melakhah*":

> ...שנאמר שבת שבתון שבת לענין מלאכה ושבתון לענינים אלו.

5. *Sefer ha-Mitzvot, aseh* 164.
6. *Hilkhot Shevitat Asor* 1:5.

> ...as the *pasuk* states, "*Shabbat Shabbaton*": "*Shabbat*" regarding *melakhah* and "*Shabbaton*" regarding these other matters.

According to our text, Rambam repurposes the phrase "*Shabbat Shabbaton*," which he previously used in the context of *issur melakhah*, to refer to fasting and the other forms of *innuy*. The variant text is more remarkable; instead of connecting the other forms of *innuy* to fasting, Rambam connects them to *issur melakhah*. Regardless, both texts emphasize the interchangeability of *issur melakhah* and fasting as elements of one *halakhah*. As we noted, in *Sefer ha-Mitzvot*, Rambam explicitly remarks on the dual expression of "*Shabbat Shabbaton*" as referring to *issur melakhah* and *innuy*. We see here that this duality is apparent in the *Mishneh Torah* as well.

Yom Kippur as a Yom Tov

The pairing of the *issur melakhah* of Yom Kippur with *innuy* makes Yom Kippur unique among all the festivals described in *Parashat Emor* (*Vayikra* 23:4–44). The Torah's formulations in *Parashat Emor* suggest that this uniqueness is not incidental. There are two aspects to most festivals: the specific character of the *hag* (including *mitzvot* specific to the *hag*, such as eating *matzah* on Pesah) and the generic quality of "*mikra kodesh*." The *pesukim* in *Parashat Emor* suggest that Yom Kippur is unique in that it lacks the generic Yom Tov status.

Whenever the Torah uses the phrase "*mikra kodesh*" in describing each Yom Tov in *Parashat Emor*, it connects it to *issur melakhah*.[7] The *pesukim* describing Yom Kippur provide the only exception, as they relate the status of *mikra kodesh* specifically to *innuy*:

> אך בעשור לחדש השביעי הזה יום הכפרים הוא מקרא קדש יהיה לכם ועניתם את נפשותיכם...
>
> However, the tenth day of this seventh month is Yom ha-Kippurim. It shall be a sacred occasion for you; you shall practice self-denial... (*Vayikra* 23:27)[8]

7. This is true of the *pesukim* describing the festivals in *Parashat Pinehas* as well.
8. Once again, the *pesukim* in *Parashat Pinehas* are structured similarly.

Yom Kippur thus emerges as a different type of *mikra kodesh* than the other *mo'adim.*

In a similar vein, Ibn Ezra comments on the unusual usage of the negative qualifier "*akh,*" which begins the Torah's treatment of Yom Kippur:

> וטעם אך בעשור - בעבור שיום מקרא קדש יום שמחה.
>
> The reason for the phrase "*Akh be-asor* – But on the tenth" is that a day of "*mikra kodesh*" is [in every other context] a day of joy.[9]

According to Ibn Ezra, "*akh*" differentiates Yom Kippur from every other Yom Tov. Every Yom Tov is a day of joy; "*akh*" puts us on notice that the *mikra kodesh* of Yom Kippur is a *mikra kodesh* of *innuy,* as opposed to a *mikra kodesh* of festivity.

In divorcing the *issur melakhah* of Yom Kippur from "*mikra kodesh,*" the Torah attaches it to a different phrase:

> וכל מלאכה לא תעשו בעצם היום הזה כי יום כפרים הוא לכפר עליכם לפני ה׳ אלקיכם.
>
> You may do no work on that very day. For it is a Yom ha-Kippurim, in order to bring atonement for you before Hashem your God. (*Vayikra* 23:28)

Issur melakhah is part of the specific character of Yom Kippur, but neither the *mikra kodesh* aspect of Yom Kippur nor the *issur melakhah* is identical to its generic Yom Tov counterpart.

Rambam's treatment of Yom Kippur showcases particular sensitivity to these unique formulations in the *pesukim.* Unlike *Tur* and *Shulhan Arukh,* which integrate the laws of Yom Kippur with the laws of the other *mo'adim* (arranged chronologically),[10] Rambam's *Mishneh Torah* separates *Hilkhot Shevitat Asor,* the section dedicated to the laws

9. Ibn Ezra, *Vayikra* 23:27.

10. This arrangement matches the order in *Parashat Emor.*

of Yom Kippur, from *Hilkhot Shevitat Yom Tov,* the section dedicated to the laws of the other *mo'adim.* Moreover, Rambam clearly does not intend *Hilkhot Shevitat Asor* to be an appendix to *Hilkhot Yom Tov* explaining how Yom Kippur differs from a standard Yom Tov, as he places *Hilkhot Shevitat Asor* before *Hilkhot Yom Tov,* not after. Apparently, Rambam believes Yom Kippur does not belong in the category of Yom Tov.

Rambam adopts this perspective consistently. At the beginning of *Hilkhot Yom Tov,* Rambam lists the six Yom Tov days; he does not include Yom Kippur.[11] In *Mishneh Torah,* Rambam never intends the term "Yom Tov" to refer to Yom Kippur as well as the other *mo'adim.* Thus, whenever Rambam codifies a *halakhah* that applies to both Yom Tov and Yom Kippur, he specifies both.[12]

Yom Kippur's status as a Yom Tov has been discussed in a number of different contexts. For example, should one who must eat on Yom Kippur due to medical need recite *Ya'aleh ve-Yavo*? Following the opinion of Rosh, *Shulhan Arukh* rules that one should:

> חולה שאכל ביום הכיפורים ונתיישב דעתו בענין שיכול לברך צריך להזכיר של יום הכיפורים בברכת המזון שאומר יעלה ויבוא בבונה ירושלים.
>
> A sick person who ate on Yom Kippur and was able to recite *Birkat ha-Mazon* must mention Yom Kippur in *Birkat ha-Mazon* by saying *Ya'aleh ve-Yavo* in the *berakhah* of *Boneh Yerushalayim.*[13]

Magen Avraham demurs:

> ובש"ל כ' בשם הר"א כ"ץ כיון שהיום גרם לו איסור רק שפקוח נפש גורם לו היתר והוה לדידי' כחול אין בו לא קידוש ולא על הכוס ולא

11. *Hilkhot Yom Tov* 1:1. As we will discuss below, Rosh ha-Shanah has characteristics atypical of a *mo'ed;* in this respect, it is much like Yom Kippur. Nevertheless, Rambam does count Rosh ha-Shanah as a Yom Tov and includes it in the framework of *Hilkhot Yom Tov.*
12. For example, see *Hilkhot Shabbat* 29:23 (which we will quote below).
13. *Shulhan Arukh, Orah Hayim* 618:10.

> הזכרה בב"ה ואפי' רצה להזכיר אינו מזכיר דלא אשכחן הזכרה בב"ה אלא במקום שיש מצוה באכילתו עכ"ל, וכנ"ל.
>
> *Shibbolei ha-Leket* wrote in the name of R. A. Katz that because the day prohibits [food], and only the need to save his life permits it, it is for him like a weekday. It has no *Kiddush,* no need for a cup [of wine], and no mention in *Birkat ha-Mazon*. Even if he wishes to mention it, he may not, for we never allow special mention in *Birkat ha-Mazon* unless there is a mitzvah entailed in the eating. This opinion seems correct to me.[14]

Shulhan Arukh's ruling reflects the perspective that Yom Kippur, like every Yom Tov, is a day of two dimensions; it includes a generic Yom Tov dimension and a specific Yom Kippur dimension. When the two clash, the particular character of Yom Kippur dominates. Thus, although the Yom Tov dimension mandates a festive meal, the fast imposed by the Yom Kippur dimension prohibits it. But when the Yom Tov element is isolated from Yom Kippur – for example, when medical need removes the obligation to fast – it creates its own set of obligations, including the recitation of *Ya'aleh ve-Yavo*.

According to *Magen Avraham,* on the other hand, the generic Yom Tov character is completely absent on Yom Kippur. Without the fast, Yom Kippur remains "*ke-hol,*" like a weekday.

The same question animates several other debates, albeit more subtly. Thus, for example, the *gemara* questions whether Yom Kippur necessitates the recitation of the *berakhah* of *Sheheheyanu*.[15] Although the *gemara* concludes that it does, the reason remains ambiguous.

In discussing this issue, the Yerushalmi presents two opinions.[16] One maintains that *Sheheheyanu* on Yom Kippur is a function of the day's

14. *Magen Avraham,* ad loc.
15. *Eiruvin* 40b. Although the *gemara*'s question relates to both Rosh ha-Shanah and Yom Kippur, the conclusion regarding these two days may differ. Ra'avyah (*Hilkhot Eiruvin* 383; *Hilkhot Rosh ha-Shanah* 534) suggests that *Sheheheyanu* may be required on Rosh ha-Shanah but optional on Yom Kippur, whereas Rambam's formulation separates Yom Kippur, but not Rosh ha-Shanah, from the category of Yom Tov.
16. Yerushalmi *Pesahim* 10:5.

infrequency and not a function of any Yom Tov status. The other asserts that *Sheheheyanu* is a function of "*mikra kodesh*" and thus applies to any day designated as such, including Rosh ha-Shanah and Yom Kippur. In light of our analysis of the Torah's usage of "*mikra kodesh*" in the context of Yom Kippur, the latter opinion makes a significant claim that Yom Kippur shares the basic "*mikra kodesh*" status of every other Yom Tov.

Rabbeinu Yehonatan maintains that the requirement to recite *Sheheheyanu* is a function of *simhat Yom Tov*.[17] Rambam's formulation is more ambivalent:

כל לילי יום טוב ובליל יום הכפורים אומרים שהחיינו.

> On all Yom Tov evenings and on the evening of Yom Kippur, we recite *Sheheheyanu*.[18]

Rambam designates Yom Kippur outside of the category of "all Yom Tov evenings," consistent with his aforementioned position throughout *Mishneh Torah* not to refer to Yom Kippur as a Yom Tov.

There is an interesting practice, first recorded in the *siddur* of R. Amram Gaon, of fulfilling this obligation to recite *Sheheheyanu* on Yom Kippur specifically through the *sheli'ah tzibbur*'s recitation. The *Ge'onim*, *Rishonim*, and *Posekim* record divergent views regarding the desirability of fulfilling the requirement through individual recitation, suggesting various justifications for R. Amram Gaon's practice, which has mostly been accepted as the norm.[19] In addition to these various suggestions, the fact that there is complexity to the status of Yom Kippur as a *mo'ed*

17. Rabbeinu Yehonatan, *Eiruvin* 10b in *dapei ha-Rif*.
18. *Hilkhot Shabbat* 29:23.
19. See *Tur, Orah Hayim* 619, who argues that the reason the *sheli'ah tzibbur* recites the *berakhah* is in case there are individuals who have not yet recited *Sheheheyanu* themselves. (According to *Bah*, *Tur* is really explaining why the *berakhah* is recited before *Ma'ariv*, when everyone is present.) See also *Kol Bo* (68), who writes that it is actually preferable for individuals to recite the *berakhah* themselves, rather than relying on the *sheli'ah tzibbur*. *Beit Yosef*, however, notes that the practice in his time was not in accordance with the *Kol Bo*; *Magen Avraham* (619:3) writes similarly in the name of *Darkhei Moshe*. *Magen Avraham* cites *Shelah*, who refers to a precedent in the laws of *Havdalah*, when one individual makes a *berakhah* for everyone. *Mahatzit*

and to the role of *simhah* on this day may have contributed to the acceptance of integrating the requirement of *Sheheheyanu*.

Similar issues pervade the discussion of reciting *Hallel* on Yom Kippur. After establishing unique *korbanot, mo'ed* status, and *issur melakhah* as the criteria for *Hallel* recitation, the *gemara* inquires why we omit *Hallel* on Rosh ha-Shanah and Yom Kippur:

> ראש השנה ויום הכיפורים דאיקרו מועד ואיקדוש בעשיית מלאכה לימא! משום דר' אבהו, דאמר רבי אבהו, אמרו מלאכי השרת לפני הקב"ה: רבש"ע, מפני מה אין ישראל אומרים שירה לפניך בר"ה וביום הכפורים? אמר להן: אפשר, מלך יושב על כסא הדין וספרי חיים וספרי מתים פתוחין לפניו וישראל אומרים שירה לפני?
>
> [According to the previously established criteria, we should recite *Hallel*] on Rosh ha-Shanah and Yom Kippur, as they are called "*mo'ed*" and are sanctified by *issur melakhah*! [We omit *Hallel*] because of the statement of R. Avahu, as R. Avahu said: The ministering angels said before the Holy One, blessed be He, "Master of the World, why do *Bnei Yisrael* not say *Hallel* before You on Rosh ha-Shanah and Yom Kippur?" He responded, "Is it conceivable that the King sits on the throne of judgment and the books of life and death are open before Him, and *Bnei Yisrael* say *Hallel* before Me?!"[20]

In the initial stage, the *gemara* clearly assumes that Yom Kippur shares the status of every other Yom Tov regarding the recitation of *Hallel*. The question is if this assumption survives in the *gemara*'s answer. Perhaps Yom Kippur indeed has the status of Yom Tov, but the inappropriateness of *Hallel* recitation on the Day of Judgment overrides the requirement to recite *Hallel*. Alternatively, perhaps the fact that "the books of life

---

ha-Shekel notes that in that context, it is preferable for only one person to recite the *berakhah* due to the principle of "*be-rov am hadrat melekh*," and that may be relevant to the question of *Sheheheyanu* as well. See also *Eliyah Rabbah* on this topic.

20. *Arakhin* 10b.

and death are open" reflects that Yom Kippur does not have the status of Yom Tov at all.

Rambam assumes that the argument that "the books of life and death are open" is not a technicality, but rather refers to the very character of Rosh ha-Shanah and Yom Kippur:

> אבל ראש השנה ויום הכפורים אין בהן הלל לפי שהן ימי תשובה ויראה ופחד לא ימי שמחה יתירה.
>
> But on Rosh ha-Shanah and Yom Kippur, *Hallel* is omitted, because they are days of repentance, awe, and fear, not days of excessive joy.[21]

According to Rambam, we omit *Hallel* as a consequence of the nature of the day. The *simhah* component on these days is mitigated.

Although the *gemara*'s discussion treats Rosh ha-Shanah and Yom Kippur equally, the interpretation of the *gemara*'s conclusion may differ regarding the two days. Ran distinguishes between Rosh ha-Shanah and Yom Kippur regarding a question related to the *Hallel* issue:

> יש מן הגאונים ז"ל שכתבו דכיון שאין הלל בר"ה אם חל להיות בשבת אומרים בו צדקתך דכלל מסור בידם דכל יום שיש בו הלל אין אומרים בו צדקתך לפי שאומר אותו על צדוק הדין של משה וזה כיון שאין בו הלל שפיר דמי למימריה וגאונים אחרים חולקים ואומרים דר"ה נמי ר"ח הוא וכיון דבשאר ראשי חדשים לא אמרינן צדקתך אף בר"ה נמי לא אמרינן ליה וה"ר יהודה בר ברזילי אלברגילוני ז"ל כתב שאין אומרים צדקתך בראש השנה ויום הכפורים שחל להיות בשבת ולא אבינו מלכנו ומנהגנו עכשיו שלא לאמרו בראש השנה שחל להיות בשבת אבל אומר אותו ביום הכפורים שחל להיות בשבת ואפשר דטעמא משום דכיון דבר"ה איכא שמחה באכילה ושתיה כשאר ימים טובים לא אמרינן ביה צדקתך אבל ביוה"כ כיון שהוא יום ענוי אומרים אותו.

21. *Hilkhot Megillah Ve-Hanukah* 3:6.

> There are some *Ge'onim* who wrote that because there is no *Hallel* on Rosh ha-Shanah, if it falls on Shabbat, we recite *Tzidkatekha*. They believe in a general rule: On any day on which *Hallel* is recited, we do not recite *Tzidkatekha*, as it refers to the *tzidduk ha-din* of [the death of] Moshe [and is therefore inappropriate on a day of joy]. On this day [Rosh ha-Shanah], since there is no *Hallel*, it is perfectly appropriate to recite [*Tzidkatekha*]. Other *Ge'onim* disagree and claim that Rosh ha-Shanah is also Rosh Hodesh, and since we do not recite *Tzidkatekha* on any other Rosh Hodesh, we do not recite it on Rosh ha-Shanah either. R. Yehudah bar Barzilai al-Bargeloni wrote that we do not recite *Tzidkatekha* on Rosh ha-Shanah or Yom Kippur that falls on Shabbat, nor do we recite *Avinu Malkeinu*. Our custom now is not to recite it on Rosh ha-Shanah that falls on Shabbat, but we do recite it on Yom Kippur that falls on Shabbat. It is possible that the reasoning is that there is *simhah* on Rosh ha-Shanah in eating and drinking, like on every other Yom Tov, and we therefore do not recite *Tzidkatekha*, but on Yom Kippur, since it is a day of *innuy*, we recite it.[22]

According to Ran's conclusion, despite the lack of *Hallel*, Rosh ha-Shanah remains a day of *simhah*. The omission of *Hallel* is a mere technicality and does not indicate that we are allowed to recite the *Tzidkatekha Tzedek* prayer. The omission of *Hallel* on Yom Kippur, on the other hand, reflects that it is purely a day of awe and fear, not a Yom Tov, and the *Tzidkatekha Tzedek* prayer is thus appropriate.

Rabbeinu Yonah's opinion regarding the *erev* Yom Kippur meal provides the most striking expression of the Yom Tov aspect of Yom Kippur.[23] According to Rabbeinu Yonah, the *erev* Yom Kippur meal is in fact the Yom Tov meal for Yom Kippur.[24] This assertion seems to run counter to the view, hinted at in the *pesukim* and embraced by Rambam,

22. Ran, *Rosh ha-Shanah* 9a in *dapei ha-Rif*.

23. *Sha'arei Teshuvah* 4:9.

24. See also Ritva's formulation (*Rosh ha-Shanah* 9a) of Rabbeinu Yonah's opinion.

that Yom Kippur lacks any generic Yom Tov character. Nevertheless, even if we accept Rabbeinu Yonah's explanation of the *erev* Yom Kippur meal, we must still ask whether Yom Kippur itself retains any Yom Tov character. Is the meal pushed earlier merely because there is no way to express the Yom Tov aspect on Yom Kippur itself? Or does the meal's rescheduling reflect a separation of the Yom Tov aspect, which is now limited to *erev* Yom Kippur, from the day of Yom Kippur itself, which now lacks any Yom Tov character?[25]

Yom Kippur as a Shabbat

Not only does Rambam refrain from categorizing Yom Kippur as a Yom Tov, but he embraces the substantive connection between Yom Kippur and Shabbat we noted above. In Rambam's striking formulation:

הרי הוא כשבת לכל דבריו.

> [Yom Kippur] is like Shabbat in all matters.[26]

With regard to what matters is Yom Kippur like Shabbat, rather than Yom Tov?

Halakhah requires one to wear *kesut nekiyah* (clean clothing) on Yom Kippur, just as on Shabbat and Yom Tov. Rashi quotes *Sifra*, which derives the requirement from the words "*mikra kodesh*":

מקרא קדש - קדשהו בכסות נקיה ובתפלה, ובשאר ימים טובים במאכל ובמשתה ובכסות נקיה ובתפלה.

---

25. Thus, it remains unclear, for example, whether Rabbeinu Yonah would instruct one eating on Yom Kippur due to medical need to recite *Ya'aleh ve-Yavo*. If the meal is pushed earlier merely because the Yom Tov aspect is normally not expressed on Yom Kippur itself, this case provides an opportunity to express the Yom Tov aspect, and *Ya'aleh ve-Yavo* should be recited. If Yom Kippur retains no Yom Tov character, however, then when one eats, Yom Kippur itself is merely like a weekday, even though there was a *se'udat Yom Tov* on *erev* Yom Kippur.

26. *Hilkhot Shevitat Asor* 1:3.

> "*Mikra kodesh*" – Sanctify it [Yom Kippur] with clean clothing and with prayer, and on every other Yom Tov with food, drink, clean clothing, and prayer.[27]

The *gemara* provides a different source:

> אמר ליה ריש גלותא לרב המנונא: מאי דכתיב "ולקדוש ה' מכבד"? - אמר ליה: זה יום הכפורים, שאין בו לא אכילה ולא שתיה. אמרה תורה: כבדהו בכסות נקיה.
>
> The Exilarch asked R. Hamnuna: To what does the *pasuk* (*Yeshayahu* 58:13) "And [call] Hashem's holy day 'honored'" refer? He answered: This is Yom Kippur, which has neither eating nor drinking. Said the Torah: Honor it with clean clothing.[28]

The *pasuk* in *Yeshayahu* quoted by the *gemara* refers to Shabbat:

> אם תשיב משבת רגלך עשות חפצך ביום קדשי וקראת לשבת ענג ולקדוש ה' מכובד וכבדתו מעשות דרכיך ממצוא חפצך ודבר דבר.
>
> If you restrain your foot due to the Shabbat [and refrain from] pursuing your affairs on My holy day; if you call the Shabbat "delight" and Hashem's holy day "honored"; and if you honor it by not going your ways nor looking into your affairs or discussing the forbidden.

Remarkably, the *gemara* quotes a *pasuk* about Shabbat as the source of the *kesut nekiyah* requirement on Yom Kippur! Unlike *Sifra*'s source, which characterizes *kesut nekiyah* as a Yom Tov obligation applied to

---

27. Rashi, *Vayikra* 23:35. Although Rashi emphasizes the comparison to Yom Tov – *kesut nekiyah* and *tefillah* are the two expressions of *mikra kodesh* on Yom Tov that carry over to Yom Kippur – the passage in *Sifra* itself does not explicitly compare Yom Kippur and Yom Tov.
28. *Shabbat* 119a.

Yom Kippur, the *gemara*'s source identifies it as an extension of a Shabbat obligation.

The most obvious "Shabbat-like" *halakhah* on Yom Kippur is the all-encompassing *issur melakhah*; unlike on Yom Tov, there is no *heter okhel nefesh,* allowance to perform *melakhot* related to food preparation. This does not necessarily reflect a gap between Yom Kippur and Yom Tov, however. If we assume that the *heter okhel nefesh* is a result of the Yom Tov meal requirement, then on Yom Kippur, which lacks that requirement (due to the obligation of *innuy*), there is no reason for *heter okhel nefesh*. Indeed, Netziv presents this reason for Yom Kippur's lack of *heter okhel nefesh*:

> הוא טעם על איסור מלאכת אוכל נפש משום שאסור לאכול, מבואר הא אי היה מצוה לאכול ביוה"כ כמו בשאר מועדות, היו רשאין אע"ג שעונש מלאכה בכרת.
>
> This is the reason for the prohibition of *melakhah* related to food preparation – it is forbidden to eat. Thus, if it were a mitzvah to eat on Yom Kippur, as on other *mo'adim,* we would be permitted [to perform such *melakhah*], even though the prohibition of *melakhah* on Yom Kippur is [punishable by] *karet.*[29]

Sha'agat Aryeh similarly assumes that the mitzvah to eat on Yom Tov underlies the *heter okhel nefesh*. Based on this premise, he argues that one must eat, and therefore may not fast, on Rosh ha-Shanah, as the *heter okhel nefesh* applies on Rosh ha-Shanah.[30] Those who permit fasting on Rosh ha-Shanah, however, do not deny the *heter okhel nefesh* on that day; they must therefore maintain that the *heter okhel nefesh* and the mitzvah to eat on Yom Tov are unrelated.[31]

---

29. *Ha'amek Davar, Vayikra* 23:29.
30. *Sha'agat Aryeh* 102.
31. As an extreme example, *Sefer ha-Manhig* (*Hilkhot Rosh ha-Shanah* 1) quotes a source that postulates the opposite relationship to that claimed in *Sha'agat Aryeh*: *Heter okhel nefesh* is a reason to *allow* fasting, and fasting should thus be permitted on Rosh ha-Shanah but not on Shabbat.

Ramban explains that there are two sources for the *heter okhel nefesh*: the explicit allowance of *melekhet okhel nefesh* on Pesah (*Shemot* 12:16) and the designation "*melekhet avodah*" for that which is prohibited on Yom Tov.[32] In the discussions of the *mo'adim* in *Parashat Emor* and *Parashat Pinehas*, the term "*melekhet avodah*" appears in the context of every Yom Tov – but not Yom Kippur. According to Ramban, the Torah uses "*melekhet avodah*" when prohibiting *melakhot* excluding *melekhet okhel nefesh*, whereas the term "*kol melakhah*" is used to prohibit all *melakhot*.[33] It seems that Ramban believes an *issur melakhah* with *heter okhel nefesh* is an *issur melakhah* of a different nature than an *issur* "*kol melakhah*." Accordingly, it is noteworthy that the *issur melakhah* on Yom Kippur shares its nature with that of Shabbat, as opposed to that of Yom Tov.

This affinity of Yom Kippur to Shabbat carries over to other aspects of *issur melakhah* as well. The prohibition of carrying (*hotza'ah*) applies on Shabbat, but not Yom Tov. The *Amora'im* debate whether it applies on Yom Kippur,[34] and the overwhelming majority of *Rishonim* rule that it does.

Hiluk melakhot is another distinction between the *issur melakhah* of Shabbat and that of Yom Tov. According to the *mishnah*, under certain conditions, one who violates several *melakhot* on Shabbat brings a *korban hatat* for each *melakhah*.[35] This law of *hiluk melakhot* does not apply on Yom Tov.[36] Several *Aharonim* discuss whether Yom Kippur is like Shabbat or like Yom Tov in this regard.[37] This question partially depends on how natural the concept of *hiluk melakhot* is. *Minhat Hinukh* viewed *hiluk melakhot* as a *hiddush* unlikely to apply outside the context

32. Ramban, *Vayikra* 23:7.
33. The phrase "*kol melakhah*" appears in the context of Shabbat in both renditions of the Ten Commandments and in *Parashat Emor*; in the context of Yom Kippur, it appears in *Parashat Aharei Mot, Parashat Emor,* and *Parashat Pinehas*. The phrase also appears in *Parashat Bo* in the context of Pesah, but there it is explicitly qualified to exclude *melekhet okhel nefesh*.
34. *Keritot* 14a.
35. *Shabbat* 67b.
36. *Pesahim* 48a; *Makkot* 21b.
37. Including R. Akiva Eiger, *Sha'agat Aryeh, Minhat Hinukh, Beit ha-Levi, Pri Megadim,* and *Hatam Sofer*.

of Shabbat, where an explicit *gezeirat ha-katuv* mandates it.[38] Alternatively, *hiluk melakhot* may be a natural concept, and its inapplicability to Yom Tov may be the *hiddush*. A third approach would view *hiluk melakhot* as characteristic of the different natures of the *issurei melakhah* on Yom Tov and on Shabbat. As a function of "*mikra kodesh*" (as opposed to the specific motif of the *hag*), the *issur melakhah* on Yom Tov forms a single prohibition encompassing the various forms of *melakhah*, and a single *korban hatat* should therefore suffice for violation. In contrast, the *issur melakhah* on Shabbat is intrinsic to the day's theme (commemorating the culmination of creation), and each action defined as *melakhah* therefore has significance.[39] According to this last approach, the question of *hiluk melakhot* on Yom Kippur hinges on the nature of *issur melakhah* on Yom Kippur. If the *issur melakhah* of Yom Kippur truly mirrors that of Shabbat, *hiluk melakhot* should apply on Yom Kippur as well.

Another difference between Shabbat and Yom Tov arises from the ruling that "*mumar le-hallel et ha-Shabbat mumar le-khol ha-Torah kulah*" – one who rejects the sanctity of Shabbat and intentionally violates it is considered an apostate. This principle does not apply to Yom Tov. *Beit ha-Levi* questions whether it is the case that "*mumar le-hallel et Yom ha-Kippurim mumar le-khol ha-Torah kulah*." If this is the case, it reinforces the idea that "*Shabbat Shabbaton*" is more than simply a designation; it is a substantive placement of Yom Kippur into the category of Shabbat.[40]

The formulation of the *mishnah* suggests that Yom Kippur indeed belongs in such a category. When the *mishnah* seeks to differentiate Shabbat and Yom Tov, it states:

38. *Minhat Hinukh* 298:9.

39. This distinction may relate to the distinction of the *heter okhel nefesh* as well, if that reflects a difference in the natures of the *issurei melakhah* on Yom Tov and on Shabbat (as discussed above). On Yom Tov, *issur melakhah* and festive meals are both part of "*mikra kodesh*"; the *heter okhel nefesh* is a built-in exception to the *issur melakhah* as it emerges from the concept of *mikra kodesh*. On Shabbat, when *issur melakhah* is intrinsic, such an exception would be absurd.

40. This question also depends on the explanation of the severe status of the *mumar le-hallel et ha-Shabbat*; see below.

אין בין יום טוב לשבת אלא אוכל נפש בלבד.

> There is no difference between Yom Tov and Shabbat other than *okhel nefesh* alone.[41]

The *mishnah* could have focused on the different punishments for violating *issur melakhah* (death on Shabbat, lashes on Yom Tov), but instead it chose *heter okhel nefesh* as the defining distinction.[42] When it comes to differentiating between Shabbat and Yom Kippur, on the other hand, the *mishnah* focuses on the severity of the punishments:

אין בין שבת ליום הכיפורים אלא שזה זדונו בידי אדם וזה זדונו בכרת.

> There is no difference between Shabbat and Yom Kippur, except that the punishment for knowingly transgressing the former is meted out by man, while the punishment for knowingly transgressing the latter is *karet.*

By making this choice, the *mishnah* seems to be relaying that the gap between Shabbat and Yom Kippur is fundamentally smaller than the gap between Shabbat and Yom Tov.

Rambam was particularly impressed by these indications. As we noted above, organizationally, Rambam separates *Hilkhot Shevitat Asor* from *Hilkhot Yom Tov.* Instead, he places *Hilkhot Shevitat Asor* immediately after *Hilkhot Shabbat* and *Hilkhot Eiruvin* (an extension of *Hilkhot Shabbat*), thus linking Shabbat and Yom Kippur. More remarkably, Rambam articulates this link in a celebrated comment in *Hilkhot Eiruvin.*

On Shabbat and Yom Tov, the laws of *tehum* prohibit traveling beyond a certain radius of one's home. If one wishes to walk outside the allotted area, he may set up an *eiruv tehumin,* which in effect relocates his home and allows him to walk within a radius of the *eiruv*'s location.

---

41. *Megillah* 7b.
42. This choice supports the aforementioned position that the *heter okhel nefesh* is characteristic of a difference in the nature of the *issurei melakhah* on Shabbat and on Yom Tov and is not simply an outgrowth of the Yom Tov meal requirement.

If Shabbat and Yom Tov occur on consecutive days, there is a debate regarding whether they comprise "*shetei kedushot*," two holy periods, or "*kedushah ahat*," one holy period. In other words, can one set up two separate *eiruvin* in two separate locations, one to be effective for each "holy period," or is it the case that since there is no break between Shabbat and Yom Tov, the same *eiruv* must remain in effect for both days? Rambam (*Hilkhot Eiruvin* 8:5) rules that such a situation comprises "*shetei kedushot*," and one may therefore set up two separate *eiruvin*. But there is one exception:

> יום הכפורים שחל להיות ערב שבת או לאחר שבת בזמן שמקדשין על פי הראיה, יראה לי שהן כיום אחד וקדושה אחת הם.
>
> If Yom Kippur fell on the day before Shabbat or the day after Shabbat during the time period when the months were sanctified according to witnesses' testimony [and this arrangement was thus a calendrical possibility], it seems to me that they are like one day, and they comprise one holy period. (*Hilkhot Eiruvin* 8:10)

Rambam introduces this proclamation with the words "*yeira'eh li* – it seems to me," which indicate that he has no source for this ruling; it flows with absolute conviction from his total understanding of the concepts involved. Shabbat and Yom Kippur are conceptually inseparable. The *kedushah* of Shabbat and the *kedushah* of "*Shabbat Shabbaton*," when consecutive, must therefore combine to comprise a single extended holy period.

Accordingly, Rambam's proclamation that "Yom Kippur is like Shabbat in all matters" is not simply a factual statement. Rambam believes that the *kedushah* and *issur melakhah* of Yom Kippur share their natures with the *kedushah* and *issur melakhah* of Shabbat.

The Confluence of Yom Kippur and Shabbat

This relationship between Yom Kippur and Shabbat is particularly pronounced when the two coincide. The *gemara* records a debate regarding how many *korbenot hatat* one must bring if one performs *melakhah* on such a day. R. Yosse ha-Gelili requires two, one for violating Shabbat and one for violating Yom Kippur, whereas R. Akiva maintains that one suffices.[43] Ramban notes that R. Akiva elsewhere accepts the principle of "*issur hal al issur*," that one prohibition can set in on top of another prohibition. According to this principle, one who violates two convergent prohibitions is responsible for both. If so, one who simultaneously violates Shabbat and Yom Kippur should bring two *korbanot*! Why does R. Akiva require only one? Ramban's second answer highlights the uniqueness of the particular confluence of Shabbat and Yom Kippur:

> טעמיה דר' עקיבא הכא משום דשבת ויום הכפורים איסור אחד הוא ותרוייהו שבת מיקרו ושבתון כתיב בהו.
>
> R. Akiva's reason here is that Shabbat and Yom Kippur constitute a single prohibition. They are both called "*Shabbat*," and "*Shabbaton*" is written in the context of both.[44]

According to Ramban's exposition of R. Akiva's position, since Yom Kippur is "*Shabbat Shabbaton*," the *issur melakhah* of Shabbat and that of Yom Kippur are one and the same *issur*. Although Shabbat and Yom Kippur present two different ways to accomplish this *issur*, the confluence of Yom Kippur and Shabbat carries only this single *issur melakhah*, not two overlapping *issurim*.

The convergence of Shabbat and Yom Kippur also raises questions about the performance of the *avodah* in the *Beit ha-Mikdash*. On Yom Kippur, the *Kohen Gadol* must preside over the daily *korbenot tamid* as well as the special *korbanot* of Yom Kippur. Rambam avers that the same applies to the *korbanot* of Shabbat when Yom Kippur and Shabbat coincide:

> ואם היתה שבת אף מוסף שבת אין מקריב אותו אלא כהן גדול.

43. *Hullin* 101b.

44. *Hiddushei ha-Ramban, Hullin* 101b, s.v. *ve-Rabbi Yosse ha-Gelili.*

> If [Yom Kippur] was Shabbat, the *korban mussaf* of Shabbat also cannot be brought by anyone other than the *Kohen Gadol*.[45]

The commentators on Rambam note that this ruling does not appear anywhere in the Talmud Bavli or Talmud Yerushalmi. What, then, is Rambam's source?

Or Samei'ah points to a *gemara* that discusses the order in which various *korbanot* should be offered.[46] The *gemara* discusses a case of two *korbanot*, one more frequent (*tadir*) and the other holier (*mekudash*). Frequency and holiness should each, in principle, take precedence; which should come first if these two principles clash? In an attempt to prove that the frequent *korban* should come first, the *gemara* furnishes the example of Rosh Hodesh that coincides with Shabbat, on which the more frequent *korban mussaf* of Shabbat precedes the holier *korban mussaf* of Rosh Hodesh. But the *gemara* then rejects the premise that the *korban mussaf* of Rosh Hodesh is holier than the *korban mussaf* of Shabbat. If Rosh Hodesh can invest a certain level of *kedushah* in its own *korban*, it can invest the same level of *kedushah* in the *korban mussaf* of Shabbat brought on the same day.[47] This *gemara* teaches that two converging obligations sometimes integrate and thus mutually affect the other. The *korban mussaf* of Shabbat on Shabbat-Rosh Hodesh becomes a *korban* of Shabbat-Rosh Hodesh. Similarly, according to *Or Samei'ah*'s understanding of Rambam, the *korban mussaf* of Shabbat on Shabbat-Yom Kippur becomes a *korban* of Shabbat-Yom Kippur, and as such, only the *Kohen Gadol* can offer it.[48]

---

45. *Hilkhot Avodat Yom ha-Kippurim* 1:2.
46. *Zevahim* 91a.
47. The *gemara* makes similar comments about the *kedushah* of Shabbat affecting the *korban tamid* brought that day and the *kedushah* of Rosh ha-Shanah affecting the *korban mussaf* of Rosh Hodesh brought that day. It is interesting that the *gemara* felt the need to discuss all three cases separately. This highlights the differences between the cases. For example, every Shabbat has a *korban tamid*, but the fusion of Shabbat and Rosh Hodesh is a coincidence of the calendar. Nonetheless, the same integration of *kedushot* occurs.
48. *Or Samei'ah, Hilkhot Avodat Yom ha-Kippurim* 4:1. This integration of convergent days of *kedushah* applies to other areas of Halakhah as well. For example, according to one opinion in the *gemara* (*Beitzah* 17a), we should conclude the middle *bera-*

A second possibility is that Rambam's ruling stems from the unique status of the *avodah* of the *Kohen Gadol* on Yom Kippur. Perhaps it is not only the *korbanot* of Yom Kippur that require the *Kohen Gadol.* The Torah refers to Yom Kippur as "*ahat ba-shanah*," a singular day in the year (*Vayikra* 16:34) – a day that is critical for the entire year. The *Kohen Gadol,* the idealistic symbol of full dedication to the *Ribbono Shel Olam,* must be connected to the *avodah* in the *Mikdash* every day of the year.[49] On a regular day, we allow any *Kohen* to officiate, but only because we set the tone on the most critical day of the year and establish that the *korbanot* deserve the *Kohen Gadol*'s complete dedication to *Ha-Kadosh Barukh Hu.*[50] In order to set such a tone, the *Kohen Gadol* must preside over the totality of the *avodah* on Yom Kippur, including the *korbanot* offered for coincidental reasons, such as the *korban mussaf* of Shabbat.

A third option would see Rambam's ruling as stemming from the special connection between Shabbat and Yom Kippur and the way in which it expresses itself when the two days coincide. As we have already demonstrated through his organization of *Hilkhot Shevitat Asor* and his

khah of *Shemoneh Esrei* on Shabbat-Yom Tov with "*mekadesh Yisrael ve-haShabbat ve-haZemanim* – He who sanctifies Israel, and Shabbat, and the times," seemingly implying that *Bnei Yisrael* sanctify Shabbat as well as Yom Tov. Netziv (*Meromei Sadeh, Beitzah* 17a) cites the *gemara* in *Zevahim* 91a in explaining that we relate to the day as an integrated Shabbat-Yom Tov, whose occurrence requires *Bnei Yisrael*'s input. The same question of integrating *kedushot* animates other debates, such as whether one who omits *Ya'aleh ve-Yavo* on Shabbat-Rosh Hodesh must repeat *Birkat ha-Mazon*; the Rosh Hodesh component does not mandate repetition, but the integration with the Shabbat component may demand repetition even for omission of the Rosh Hodesh paragraph.

49. The *pasuk* "*min ha-Mikdash lo yeitzei*" (*Vayikra* 21:12) teaches that the *Kohen Gadol* does not leave the *Mikdash,* even if he is in a state of *aveilut.* The *Kohen Gadol* further connects himself to the daily *avodah* via his *korban minhat havitin,* of which he offers half at the beginning of the day of *avodah* and half at its conclusion, forming the bookends of the daily *avodah.*

50. The concept of "setting the tone" in *avodah* originates with the initiation of *korbanot* during the *milu'im* period, during which Moshe Rabbeinu officiated and then passed the baton to Aharon ha-Kohen, before a regular *Kohen* could perform *avodah.* Interestingly, the *gemara* in the beginning of *Yoma* presents several parallels and overlapping *halakhot* between Yom Kippur and the process of *milu'im,* suggesting that Yom Kippur serves as an annual re-initiation of the *avodah,* an appropriate time for highlighting the idealism of absolute dedication to the *Ribbono Shel Olam.*

novel ruling in *Hilkhot Eiruvin,* Rambam emphasizes and expands the link between Shabbat and *Shabbat Shabbaton.* Even if we do not accept *Or Samei'ah*'s contention that the general pattern of convergent *kedushot* suffices to require the *Kohen Gadol*'s involvement, perhaps the particular combination of Shabbat and *Shabbat Shabbaton* is conducive to integration.

This integration of Shabbat and Yom Kippur also affects the question of reciting *Kiddush* on Yom Kippur that falls on Shabbat. As we noted above, the *Posekim* debate whether one who eats out of medical necessity on Yom Kippur recites *Ya'aleh ve-Yavo.* There is a parallel debate regarding the recitation of *Kiddush* in such a situation. Interestingly, many *Posekim* who rule against reciting *Kiddush* on an ordinary Yom Kippur require *Kiddush* on Yom Kippur that falls on Shabbat. Even if the Yom Tov element of Yom Kippur is overridden or entirely lacking, and thus does not mandate *Kiddush,* the coincidental *Kiddush* obligation of Shabbat exists independently of Yom Kippur.[51]

This assertion is questionable, however, in light of Rambam's view of an integrated Shabbat-Yom Kippur. The Shabbat element of the day does not remain independent, and the integrated Shabbat-Yom Kippur may therefore not carry a *Kiddush* obligation.

Kenivat Yerek

The context of Rambam's formulation that "Yom Kippur is like Shabbat in all matters" is the *halakhah* of *kenivat yerek* (vegetable preparation):

> ומותר לקנב את הירק ביום הכפורים מן המנחה ולמעלה, ומהו הקינוב שיסיר את העלים המעופשות ויקצץ השאר ויתקן אותו לאכילה, וכן מפצעין באגוזין ומפרדין ברמונים מן המנחה ולמעלה מפני עגמת נפש, ויום הכפורים שחל להיות בשבת אסור בקניבת ירק ובפציעת אגוזים ובפרידת רמונים כל היום, וכבר נהגו העם בשנער ובמערב שלא יעשו אחד מכל אלו ביום הצום אלא הרי הוא כשבת לכל דבריו.

51. Alternatively, some *Posekim* explain that the Shabbat *Kiddush* obligation is *mi-deOrayta,* while the Yom Tov *Kiddush* obligation is *mi-deRabbanan.*

> It is permitted to do *kinuv* on [detached] vegetables on Yom ha-Kippurim from the afternoon and on. And what is *kinuv*? That he removes the rotten leaves and trims the rest and prepares the vegetable for eating. Similarly, it is permitted to crack open nuts and separate pomegranate seeds from the afternoon and on, because of the anguish of the soul [i.e. so that one will not have to do it after the fast, when he is very hungry]. When Yom Kippur falls on Shabbat, it is forbidden to trim a vegetable, crack nuts, or separate pomegranate seeds the whole day. But the people of Shin'ar [Babylonia] and the West [Eretz Yisrael] have already accepted not to do any of these activities on the day of the fast; rather it is like the Shabbat in all of its matters.[52]

Idiosyncratically, *kenivat yerek* is prohibited on Shabbat but permitted on Yom Kippur.[53] Thus, to understand the relationship between Shabbat and Yom Kippur, we must analyze this *halakhah*. Especially according to Rambam, who emphasizes the fundamental similarity of Yom Kippur and Shabbat, we must explain how and why *kenivat yerek* constitutes an exception.

Kenivat yerek is subject to a dispute in the *gemara*:

> אמר רבי זירא אמר רב הונא, ואמרי לה אמר רבי אבא אמר רב הונא: יום הכפורים שחל להיות בשבת - אסור בקניבת ירק. אמר רב מנא: תנא, מנין ליום הכפורים שחל להיות בשבת שאסור בקניבת ירק - תלמוד לומר שבתון - שבות. למאי? אילימא למלאכה - והכתיב לא תעשה כל מלאכה. אלא לאו - אקניבת ירק, שמע מינה. אמר רבי חייא בר אבא אמר רבי יוחנן: יום הכפורים שחל להיות בשבת - מותר בקניבת ירק. מיתיבי: מנין ליום הכפורים שחל להיות בשבת שאסור בקניבת ירק - תלמוד לומר שבתון - שבות למאי? אילימא למלאכה - והכתיב לא תעשה

52. *Hilkhot Shevitat Asor* 1:3.

53. "*Agmat nefesh*" is the *gemara*'s stated reason for allowing *kenivat yerek* on Yom Kippur. The *Rishonim* offer two opposite explanations of this phrase: that preparing vegetables makes it easier to fast because the meal is ready for immediately after Yom Kippur, and that preparing vegetables makes the fast more difficult and is an enhanced form of *innuy*.

כל מלאכה, אלא לאו בקניבת ירק! - לא, לעולם למלאכה, ולעבור עליה בעשה ולא תעשה.

R. Zeira said in the name of R. Huna, and some say R. Abba said in the name of R. Huna: On Yom Kippur that falls on Shabbat, *kenivat yerek* is prohibited. R. Mana quoted a *beraita*: What is the source that *kenivat yerek* is prohibited on Yom Kippur that falls on Shabbat? The *pasuk* states, "*Shabbaton*," which means "cease." To what does this refer? If it refers to *melakhah*, does not another *pasuk* already enjoin, "Do not do any *melakhah*"? Rather, it must refer to *kenivat yerek*. This is the proof [that *kenivat yerek* is prohibited]. R. Hiya bar Abba said in the name of R. Yohanan: On Yom Kippur that falls on Shabbat, *kenivat yerek* is permitted. But the following *beraita* challenges R. Yohanan's opinion: What is the source that *kenivat yerek* is prohibited on Yom Kippur that falls on Shabbat? The *pasuk* states, "*Shabbaton*," which means "cease." To what does this refer? If it refers to *melakhah*, does not another *pasuk* already enjoin, "Do not do any *melakhah*"? Rather, it must refer to *kenivat yerek*! No – [according to R. Yohanan,] truly the *pasuk* does refer to *melakhah*, [and the two *pesukim* both enjoin against *melakhah*] in order that the one who does *melakhah* violates both a positive and a negative commandment.[54]

Tosafot mitigate the chasm between Yom Kippur and Shabbat caused by *kenivat yerek*:

נראה לר"י דאסמכתא בעלמא הוא דאי מדאורייתא ביוה"כ נמי ליתסר.

Ri believed that ["*Shabbaton*," the source of the *kenivat yerek* prohibition,] is merely a hint [and is really only Rabbinically prohibited], for if [*kenivat yerek*] were Biblically [prohibited], it would be prohibited on Yom Kippur as well.[55]

54. *Shabbat* 114b.
55. Tosafot, ad loc.

If the word "*Shabbaton*" includes *kenivat yerek,* according to Tosafot, it should prohibit *kenivat yerek* on both Shabbat and Yom Kippur; after all, the word "*Shabbaton*" appears in the context of Yom Kippur as well. Whatever "*Shabbaton*" conveys on Shabbat, it conveys on Yom Kippur. Thus, *mi-deOrayta,* there is no reason to differentiate between Yom Kippur and Shabbat.

Sensitive to this difficulty, Rashi addresses the issue dramatically:

> ואף על גב דכתיב ביה נמי שבתון שבות - לאו ממלאכה הוא, אלא מכל דבר המעכב מלהתענות, מדסמכינן לועניתם, הכי דרשינן לה בפרק בתרא דיומא (עד:א) לרחיצה וסיכה ודומין להם.

> Even though "*Shabbaton*" also appears in [the context of Yom Kippur], it does not refer [in that context] to *melakhah,* but rather to those things that inhibit fasting, as the *pasuk* juxtaposes it to "*ve-initem* – you shall afflict." This is how the *pasuk* is interpreted in the last *perek* of *Yoma* – as [prohibiting] washing, anointing, and the like.[56]

Apparently, Rashi disputes Tosafot's conclusion that the derivation from "*Shabbaton*" is merely an *asmakhta.*[57] According to Rashi, although "*Shabbaton*" in the context of Shabbat refers to the *mitzvat aseh* of resting

---

56. Rashi, ad loc.

57. This dispute is part of a larger debate among the *Rishonim* about the nature of the category of *shevut,* of which *kenivat yerek* is seemingly an example. Any *shevut* prohibition is *mi-deRabbanan.* Ramban (*Vayikra* 23:24), however, writes that the *mitzvat aseh* of "*Shabbaton*" mandates keeping the spirit of the law of Shabbat in addition to the letter of the law. Thus, for example, if an individual keeps his business open on Shabbat without violating any *melakhot,* he would still violate the *mitzvat aseh* of "*Shabbaton.*" *Shevut* prohibitions, according to Ramban, uphold the spirit of Shabbat and are included in the *mitzvat aseh mi-deOrayta* of "*Shabbaton,*" even though the specific prohibitions are *mi-deRabbanan.* In relating to *kenivat yerek* as included *mi-deOrayta* in "*Shabbaton,*" Rashi seems to be taking a similar view. Rashi elsewhere (*Shemot* 12:16) seems to endorse such a perspective, as he quotes a *midrash* from the *Mekhilta* that interprets a *pasuk* as referring to *amira le-nokhri,* a *de-Rabbanan* prohibition. (Ironically, Ramban takes issue with Rashi's interpreting a *pasuk* as referring to a *de-Rabbanan* prohibition.)

from *melakhah* and prohibits extensions of *melakhah* (such as *kenivat yerek*), the same word in the context of Yom Kippur refers to ceasing and desisting from eating and prohibits extensions of *innuy*.[58] But how can the same word have different meanings in different contexts?

When we analyze Rambam's ruling about *kenivat yerek*, we find more puzzles. Rambam quotes a *minhag* to prohibit *kenivat yerek* on every Yom Kippur. This *minhag* has two possbile explanations: It may have grown out of concern that allowing *kenivat yerek* on a regular Yom Kippur would lead to violating the prohibition on Yom Kippur that falls on Shabbat, or it may be an attempt to match the *halakhot* of Yom Kippur and Shabbat; even if we have justification to permit *kenivat yerek* on Yom Kippur, the bigger picture views Yom Kippur as "*Shabbat Shabbaton*," with the same *halakhot* as Shabbat. Rambam in particular would find the latter explanation compelling, given that he is particularly sensitive to the substantive link between Yom Kippur and Shabbat, as we have demonstrated. The latter explanation also seems to be the intent of Rambam's striking formulation, "Yom Kippur is like Shabbat in all matters."

Yet the congruence of the *minhag* with Rambam's overall perspective on "*Shabbat Shabbaton*" makes it more difficult to understand the baseline *halakhah* that *kenivat yerek* is permitted on Yom Kippur but prohibited on Shabbat. Rambam cannot agree with Rashi's explanation, as he uses "*Shabbaton*" as the source for the *mitzvat aseh* of *issur melakhah* on Yom Kippur.[59] Nor is it likely he endorses Tosafot's solution that the *pasuk*'s prohibition of *kenivat yerek* is merely an *asmakhta*, as Rambam

58. *Hatam Sofer* argues that Rashi is asserting an even more radical idea. Since Rashi interprets "*Shabbaton*" in the context of Yom Kippur to refer to *innuy* and not *melakhah*, he must believe that there is no *mitzvat aseh* to desist from *melakhah* on Yom Kippur. (This position would stand in contrast to the standard position, expressed by Rambam in the beginning of *Hilkhot Shevitat Asor*, that both a *mitzvat aseh* and a *mitzvat lo ta'aseh* prohibit *melakhah* on Yom Kippur.) Such a ruling might be halakhically consequential. Usually, "*aseh doheh lo ta'aseh*," a *mitzvat aseh* overrides a *mitzvat lo ta'aseh*, but a *mitzvat aseh* does not override the *lo ta'aseh* of *melakhah* on Shabbat, because *melakhah* is both an *aseh* and a *lo ta'aseh*. If there is no *mitzvat aseh* on Yom Kippur, however, the standard rule of *aseh doheh lo ta'aseh* may apply, unless this is neutralized by the fact that Yom Kippur is a *lav she-yesh bo karet*, which is a matter of dispute among the *Rishonim*.

59. *Hilkhot Shevitat Asor* 1:1.

includes *shevut* prohibitions – a category that includes *kenivat yerek* – in the *mitzvat aseh* of refraining from *melakhah* on Shabbat.[60] How, then, can Rambam explain the *gemara*'s distinction between Shabbat and Yom Kippur?[61]

The Nature of *Issur Melakhah* on Yom Kippur

Before answering these questions about *kenivat yerek*, let us review what we have shown about Yom Kippur and its *issur melakhah*. We demonstrated the inseparability of the *issur melakhah* and *innuy* components of Yom Kippur, especially within Rambam's formulations, and we showed that this hybrid characterizes Yom Kippur as a unique type of *mikra kodesh*, lacking the generic *mikra kodesh* status of every Yom Tov. We then established, once again especially within Rambam's rulings, that the *issur melakhah* of Yom Kippur should be identified with the *issur melakhah* of Shabbat.

This identification requires explanation. We can challenge its sensibility from two different angles. First, the marriage of *issur melakhah* and *innuy* is completely absent on Shabbat. How can the hybridized *issur melakhah* of Yom Kippur compare to the pure *issur melakhah* of Shabbat? Second, the *issur melakhah* of Shabbat arises intrinsically, "*ki vo shavat mi-kol melakhto* – for on that day, [Hashem] rested from all His activity [of creation]" (*Bereishit* 2:3), whereas the *issur melakhah* of Yom Tov stems from the holiness of the day and the need to focus on spiritual matters.[62] Yom Kippur does not commemorate creation, so why

60. *Hilkhot Shabbat* 21:1. Some (but not all) of the commentators explain this comment of Rambam as aligning with Ramban's aforementioned position regarding the nature of *shevut*. Rambam's commentary in *Perush ha-Mishnayot* (*Beitzah* 5:2) also indicates that *shevut* prohibitions are under the rubric of the *mitzvat aseh*. Even though Rambam doesn't explicitly mention *kenivat yerek* in *Hilkhot Shabbat* 21:1, the most explicit *gemara* that includes a *shevut* prohibition in the *mitzvat aseh* is the *gemara* deriving the *kenivat yerek* prohibition from "*Shabbaton*," so it is unlikely that Rambam would treat *kenivat yerek* exceptionally as an *asmakhta* prohibition.

61. *Avnei Nezer* asks this question (in a slightly different way) in a responsum (*Hoshen Mishpat* 161) addressed to his father.

62. As noted above, the *pesukim* in *Parashat Emor* consistently connect the *issur melakhah* of Yom Tov to the phrase "*mikra kodesh*."

should its *issur melakhah* match the intrinsic *issur melakhah* of Shabbat instead of the extrinsic *issur melakhah* of Yom Tov?

Ibn Ezra sees the *issur melakhah* of Yom Kippur as uniquely related to the nature of that day:

> וטעם שלא יעשו מלאכה, שלא תהיינה הנפשות מתעסקות חוץ מבקשת כפור העונות.
>
> The reason they should not do *melakhah* is so that the souls are engrossed in nothing other than requesting atonement for their sins.[63]

According to Ibn Ezra, *melakhah* is inconsistent with what Yom Kippur is about. Ibn Ezra poses this in a functional manner, but by revisiting the connection between Shabbat and Yom Kippur, we can conceptualize the relevance of *issur melakhah* to Yom Kippur.

An interesting line in *Sifra* suggests that the link between Yom Kippur and Shabbat not only characterizes Yom Kippur, but redefines Shabbat as well:

> ומניין שיום הכיפורים אסור באכילה ובשתייה וברחיצה ובסיכה ובתשמיש המיטה ובנעילת הסנדל תלמוד לומר שבתון שבות, יכול תהא שבת בראשית אסורה בכולם תלמוד לומר שבתון הוא לכם ועיניתם, הוא אסור בכולן ואין שבת בראשית אסור בכולן.
>
> What is the source that eating, drinking, washing, anointing, having relations, and wearing shoes are prohibited on Yom Kippur? "*Shabbat Shabbaton*." Perhaps all these activities should also be prohibited on the Shabbat of creation [i.e. the weekly Shabbat]? To exclude this possibility, the verse says, "*It* is a *Shabbaton* for you, and you shall afflict." All these activities are prohibited on it, but not on the Shabbat of creation.[64]

---

63. Ibn Ezra, *Vayikra* 23:29.
64. *Sifra* 14.

Sifra entertains the seemingly peculiar possibility that since Yom Kippur is "*Shabbat Shabbaton,*" every Shabbat should obligate fasting and the other forms of *innuy*. This strongly accentuates the commonality between Shabbat and Yom Kippur, but in a way that requires explanation. Yom Kippur obligates *innuy* as part of the spirit of a day of awe; why should *innuy* apply to Shabbat as well?

This application of the link between Yom Kippur and Shabbat highlights an additional theme of Shabbat beyond the commemoration of creation. Shabbat plays such a central role in Halakhah that a *mumar le-hallel et ha-Shabbat* is a *mumar le-khol ha-Torah kulah*. Rashi's rationale for this principle is theological: The Shabbat violator implicitly denies creation.[65] Rambam, however, explains that Shabbat is "*ha-ot she-bein Ha-Kadosh Barukh Hu u-veineinu le-olam* – the eternal sign [of the covenant] between *Ha-Kadosh Barukh Hu* and us."[66] Shabbat is emblematic of the irrevocable marriage-like bond between Hashem and the Jewish People. Echoing this marriage, we enter Shabbat singing *Lekhah Dodi,* and many recite *Shir ha-Shirim* as well. Shabbat takes such an important place in Halakhah because Shabbat underscores our irrevocable bond with our Creator.

Shabbat Shabbaton expresses this theme even more strongly. On Yom Kippur, we reestablish an intimate relationship with *Ha-Kadosh Barukh Hu* through the opportunity to attain *mehilah* (atonement).[67]

---

65. Rashi, *Hullin* 5a.
66. *Hilkhot Shabbat* 30:15. As we noted above, *Beit ha-Levi* questions whether the rule of *mumar le-hallel et ha-Shabbat mumar le-khol ha-Torah kulah* applies to Yom Kippur as well. Rashi's theological concern of denying creation is absent on Yom Kippur, which does not commemorate creation, but Rambam's explanation may very well carry over to Yom Kippur. As we will explore, Yom Kippur is an indispensable day in establishing the stature of the relationship between Hashem and the Jewish People.
67. The period leading up to Yom Kippur – the month of Elul and the *Aseret Yemei Teshuvah* – comprises a unique opportunity to develop a relationship with the *Ribbono Shel Olam*. The acronym "*ani le-dodi ve-dodi li*" highlights the intimacy of this relationship in comparing it to that of husband and wife. Other *pesukim* that *Hazal* point to as relevant for this period, such as "*Dirshu Hashem be-himatz'o kera'uhu bi-heyoto karov,*" reflect the same idea. *Teshuvah,* a central theme on Yom Kippur, is made possible by this intimate relationship. According to Rambam (*Hilkhot Teshuvah,* ch. 10), the highest form of *teshuvah* – *teshuvah mei-ahavah* (*teshuvah* out

Bnei Yisrael received the second set of *luhot* on Yom Kippur, together with the ultimate *mehilah* of "*salahti ki-dvarekha,*" which reaffirmed their bond with Hashem even after the ultimate betrayal, the *egel ha-zahav* (golden calf).[68] As such, *Klal Yisrael* exhibits its total loyalty to the *Ribbono Shel Olam* annually on Yom Kippur. While the balance of *hetzyo la-Hashem ve-hetzyo lakhem* (half for you and half for Hashem) characterizes every Yom Tov,[69] the theme of Yom Kippur is *kulo la-Hashem,* total devotion to *Ha-Kadosh Barukh Hu.*

We exhibit *kulo la-Hashem* in multiple ways on Yom Kippur. The *Kohen Gadol,* who personifies complete dedication to *Ha-Kadosh Barukh Hu,* performs extensive *avodah* in the *Beit ha-Mikdash.* We focus our day on *tefillah.* We disengage from all normal human conduct, both the pleasures of food and drink and the activities of *melakhah.* It is in this sense that *innuy* and *issur melakhah* are two sides of the same coin, as we have demonstrated; they both contribute to the headiness of our single-minded focus on *kulo la-Hashem.*

We now understand why *Sifra* thought it possible that every Shabbat should obligate *innuy.* Every Shabbat, just like *Shabbat Shabbaton,* highlights our relationship with *Ha-Kadosh Barukh Hu.* Perhaps, then, the true method of *avodat Hashem* should be pure spirituality, total escape from the human element, including food and drink. *Sifra* concludes that such an approach is reserved for *Shabbat Shabbaton,*

---

of love) – is patterned after a marital relationship. The long-term, irrevocable bond makes it possible to redeem and redefine the past (cf. *Yoma* 86b) and thus secure the future.

68. The Torah recounts the building of the *Mishkan* twice, once before the *egel ha-zahav* story (in *Parashat Terumah* and *Parashat Tetzaveh*) and once after (in *Parashat Vayak'hel* and *Parashat Pekudei*). The *midrash* explains that the original account of the *Mishkan* represents an idyllic relationship between Hashem and the Jewish People, without any difficulties or betrayals. The repetition after the *egel ha-zahav* story expresses the ability of that bond to survive the betrayal of *egel ha-zahav.* Shabbat, another symbol of the same relationship, also appears both before and after the *egel ha-zahav* story.

69. See *Beitzah* 15b, where two *Tanna'im* debate the appropriate way to balance the spiritual and physical aspects of Yom Tov. R. Eliezer argues that a person should either sit and learn all day or eat and drink all day; R. Yehoshua advocates balancing the two, "*hetzyo la-Hashem ve-hetzyo lakhem.*"

which establishes the principle of *kulo la-Hashem* as our aspiration; the best methodology for achieving that goal on a weekly (and daily) basis is a *hetzyo la-Hashem ve-hetzyo lakhem*. On Yom Kippur, we prove that we are capable of outdoing the spirituality of the *malakhim*; we thus establish that our balance of spirituality and physicality the rest of the year is not based on compromise or mediocrity, but rather reflects a comprehensive worldview that recognizes conflicting ideal obligations.

A fascinating exchange in *Avnei Nezer* highlights this character of Yom Kippur.[70] If a person must eat meat on Shabbat for medical reasons, and no kosher meat is available, the *Rishonim* debate whether it is preferable for him to slaughter an animal, and thereby violate Shabbat, or eat *neveilah* meat. The Ra'avad argues that it is better to slaughter an animal. *Avnei Nezer*'s father reasons, however, that this preference applies only to Shabbat, but not to Yom Kippur. Shabbat is violated via an act of *hillul* of *kedushat Shabbat*, desecration of the sanctity of Shabbat, but this does not apply in a case of *piku'ah nefesh* (saving a life). The obligation of *innuy* on Yom Kippur, in contrast, has no relation to *kedushah*, and it is therefore preferable to violate the less severe prohibition of eating *neveilah*. *Avnei Nezer* disputes this distinction and argues that eating on Yom Kippur is a type of *hillul*, the equivalent of *melakhah* on Shabbat, as *kedushat Yom Kippur* demands separation from the material world. As such, both *innuy* and *issur melakhah* – which, as we have shown, are two expressions of the same requirement of spiritual focus – are intrinsic to *kedushat Yom Kippur*, just as *issur melakhah* is intrinsic to *kedushat Shabbat*.

This understanding of the link between Yom Kippur and Shabbat explains the similarities and differences in the *issurei melakhah*. *Issur melakhah* arises intrinsically on both Yom Kippur and Shabbat, which explains the *halakhot* of *hiluk melakhot* and the lack of the *heter okhel nefesh*. This is unlike on Yom Tov, when the *issur melakhah* arises extrinsically. On Shabbat, the prohibition of *melakhah* commemorates creation; on Yom Kippur, it arises as part of our single-minded spiritual focus on our relationship with Hashem. It thus attaches itself to *innuy*, another expression of *kulo la-Hashem*, on Yom Kippur but not on Shabbat.

70. *Avnei Nezer, Hoshen Mishpat* 161.

We can now return to the puzzles of *kenivat yerek*. According to Rashi, "*Shabbaton*" magnifies the quintessential character of the day. In the context of Shabbat, which commemorates creation, it refers to the *issur melakhah* on Shabbat; in the context of Yom Kippur, it refers to *innuy*. According to Rambam, "*Shabbaton*" on Yom Kippur refers to the hybrid of *innuy* and *issur melakhah*, and even as it refers to *melakhah*, it defies the application of the parallel "*Shabbaton*" of *melakhah* on Shabbat. Since the *issur melakhah* of Yom Kippur expresses the day's spiritual focus, and *kenivat yerek* either facilitates the ability to achieve spiritual focus or exacerbates the withdrawal from the physical, *kenivat yerek* enhances Yom Kippur and does not violate the spirit of its *issur melakhah*. On Shabbat, when each *melakhah* is objectively a defiance of the commemoration of creation, *kenivat yerek* flies in the face of the spirit of the day.

Symbolically, the *halakhah* of *ner she-shavat* highlights this distinction between the *shevitah* of Shabbat and the *shevitah* of Yom Kippur. After Yom Kippur, we use for *Havdalah* a flame that burned for the duration of Yom Kippur, whereas we light a new flame for *Havdalah* after Shabbat.[71] Lighting a new flame after Shabbat commemorates the creation of fire (which tradition tells us occurred on *motza'ei* Shabbat), and it therefore forms part of Shabbat's broader commemoration of creation. The *ner she-shavat* after Yom Kippur, on the other hand, highlights that lighting a fire is prohibited for the duration of Yom Kippur, as Yom Kippur lacks the *heter okhel nefesh*, unlike every other Yom Tov. If *heter okhel nefesh* stems merely from the requirement to eat on Yom Tov, there would seem to be no need to announce its absence on Yom Kippur through the *ner she-shavat*. But if the lack of *heter okhel nefesh* expresses the intrinsic nature of *issur melakhah* on Yom Kippur, the *ner she-shavat* highlights an important theme – the withdrawal from constructive *melakhah* and the purely spiritual focus of the day. The *ner she-shavat* thus captures the essence of Yom Kippur and calls attention to the difference between Yom Kippur and the creation-themed Shabbat.

---

71. There is a debate regarding whether *ner she-shavat* is required for *Havdalah* after Yom Kippur when it falls on Shabbat; see *Sha'ar ha-Tziyun* 624:9.

At the very beginning of our discussion, we analyzed the Torah's treatment of Yom Kippur in the section of *Parashat Emor* that details the *mo'adim*. Now that we have established the essential difference between Yom Kippur and the other festivals according to Rambam, we may ask a more basic question: If Yom Kippur lacks the status of Yom Tov, why do the *pesukim* list Yom Kippur among the *mo'adim*?

Perhaps in this respect, too, Yom Kippur is "*Shabbat Shabbaton*." The *mo'adim* list in *Parashat Emor* begins with Shabbat. The relevance of Shabbat to the list is an age-old question, which bothered *Hazal*, Rashi, Ramban, and many others. The *pesukim* seem to present Shabbat as "*tehilah le-mikra'ei kodesh*," the framework for the *mo'adim*. Shabbat is the indispensable paradigm of a *yom kodesh* (holy day). Thus, *issur melakhah* is exported (albeit with some adjustments) from Shabbat to Yom Tov; if Yom Tov is to be a "*mikra kodesh*," it must look like Shabbat. Even if Shabbat is an atypical *mo'ed* or not a *mo'ed* at all, Shabbat belongs in *Parashat Emor* because there could be no *mo'adim* were it not for Shabbat.

Yom Kippur, too, belongs on the list because there could be no *mo'adim* if not for Yom Kippur. If not for our demonstration of loyalty and capacity to outstrip the spirituality of the *malakhim*, the *mo'adim* could not have properly expressed the ideal balance of "*hetzyo la-Hashem ve-hetzyo lakhem*." Yom Kippur is indispensable for establishing the credentials of *Klal Yisrael*'s loyalty and developing a direct, intimate relationship between *Klal Yisrael* and the *Ribbono Shel Olam*. Just as Shabbat is the most critical day of the week, Yom Kippur is the most critical day of the *mo'adim* and the entire year.

Chapter 12
The Nature of *Innuy Nefesh* on Yom Kippur

Introduction

In the discussion of the festivals in *Parashat Emor,* the passage about Yom Kippur (*Vayikra* 23:28–32) is introduced with the word "*Akh* – However," immediately conveying that Yom Kippur is unique among the *mo'adim.* In the verses that follow, the description of Yom Kippur breaks from the mold of the other *mo'adim* in nearly every detail. Every aspect of the day is given a reason and a definition unique to Yom Kippur.

The passage about Rosh ha-Shanah exemplifies the standard presentation:

> וידבר ה׳ אל משה לאמר. דבר אל בני ישראל לאמר בחדש השביעי באחד לחדש יהיה לכם שבתון זכרון תרועה מקרא קדש. כל מלאכת עבדה לא תעשו והקרבתם אשה לה׳.
>
> And Hashem spoke to Moshe, saying: Speak to the children of Israel, saying: In the seventh month, in the first day of the month, shall be a day of rest, a remembrance with blasts of horns, a holy convocation (*mikra kodesh*). Do not do any work of labor

> (*melekhet avodah*), and bring an offering to Hashem. (*Vayikra* 23:23–25)

The pattern of identifying the holiday, followed by the status of *mikra kodesh*, a holy convocation, and finally the result of *issur melakhah*, proscription of work, holds true throughout this section.

Yom Kippur diverges sharply from this pattern, however:

> אך בעשור לחדש השביעי הזה יום הכפרים הוא מקרא קדש יהיה לכם ועניתם את נפשתיכם והקרבתם אשה לה׳: וכל מלאכה לא תעשו בעצם היום הזה כי יום כפרים הוא לכפר עליכם לפני ה׳ אלקיכם: כי כל הנפש אשר לא תענה בעצם היום הזה ונכרתה מעמיה: וכל הנפש אשר תעשה כל מלאכה בעצם היום הזה והאבדתי את הנפש ההוא מקרב עמה: כל מלאכה לא תעשו חקת עולם לדרתיכם בכל משבתיכם: שבת שבתון הוא לכם ועניתם את נפשתיכם בתשעה לחדש בערב מערב עד ערב תשבתו שבתכם:

> However, the tenth day of this seventh month is Yom ha-Kippurim. It shall be a sacred occasion for you; you shall practice self-denial, and you shall bring an offering by fire to Hashem. And you shall do no work throughout that day, for it is a Yom Kippurim, on which expiation is made on your behalf before Hashem your God. Indeed, any person who is not afflicted throughout that day shall be cut off from his people. And whoever does any work throughout that day, I will cause that person to perish from among his people. Do no work whatsoever; it is a law for all time, throughout the ages in all your settlements. It shall be a *Shabbat Shabbaton* for you, and you shall practice self-affliction; on the ninth day of the month at evening, from evening to evening, you shall observe your Sabbath. (Ibid. 26–32)

Regarding Yom Kippur, the declaration of status as "*mikra kodesh*" is followed not by "*kol melekhet avodah lo ta'asu* – you shall not do any work," but rather by "*ve-initem et nafshoteikhem* – you shall practice self-denial." Additionally, when the Torah prohibits *melakhah* on Yom Kippur, the reason given is directly linked to the nature of the day, "*ki Yom Kippurim hu* – for it is a Day of Atonement" (ibid. 23:28), and not because it is a "*mikra kodesh*." The Torah further connects the prohibition of *melakhah* with the obligation of *innuy* (affliction).[1]

The Torah repeats this three-part pattern whenever it discusses Yom Kippur. First, the Torah recurrently emphasizes the imperative of "*ve-initem et nafshoteikhem*" and refers to those who are in violation of their religious duty as "*kol nefesh asher lo te'uneh* – any soul that is not afflicted." Second, there is strikingly no explicit prohibition of "eating"; the formulation typically associated with all dietary infractions is completely omitted with respect to this very severe and pivotal transgression. Third, the Torah links *issur melakhah*, a generic manifestation in all other *mo'adim*, to the obligation of *innuy*.[2] We are thus informed that *innuy* and the specific nature of Yom Kippur pervade every aspect of the *hag*, leaving nothing defined by the generic or default *mo'ed* that is so impactful on other holidays.

The Positive Command of "*Ve-Initem et Nafshoteikhem*"

In addition to *innuy*'s role in defining and emphasizing Yom Kippur's singular character, there is another peculiar aspect to the Torah's use of *innuy*. The obligation to fast on Yom Kippur, as noted, is couched in positive terms, "*ve-initem et nafshoteikhem*," even though it would appear that the obligation is to *refrain* from eating and drinking. Would it not have been more accurate to describe *innuy nefesh* in negative terms, as a prohibition? Moreover, the Torah informs us explicitly that there is a punishment of *karet*, spiritual excision, for "*kol nefesh asher lo te'uneh*," and such a punishment should be a consequence of a *lo ta'aseh* (negative prohibition). Yet, the Torah speaks only of the positive command of *innuy*, and not of an *issur akhilah*, a prohibition to eat.

Reish Lakish is deeply bothered by this question and offers a very puzzling answer:

---

1. Throughout this passage, the Torah oscillates between these two themes, as if to suggest they are interchangeable. I address this topic more extensively in the chapter "Yom Kippur: The Quintessential Shabbat."
2. See *Vayikra* 16:29–31, 23:28–32; *Bamidbar* 29:7.

> אמר ריש לקיש: מפני מה לא נאמרה אזהרה בעינוי - משום דלא אפשר...
> מתקיף לה רב אשי: נכתוב: אל תסור מן העינוי! - קשיא.
>
> Reish Lakish said: Why does the Torah not formulate a negative precept regarding *innuy*? Because it is impossible to properly formulate in the negative.... R. Ashi asked: Why not write "do not refrain from *innuy*"? It is indeed a good question.[3]

Reish Lakish's answer is odd and reflects how glaring the Torah's choice of formulation is. The Torah is a divine work and certainly could have formulated *innuy* in the negative. As such, the *gemara* rejects Reish Lakish's opinion and offers several ways to formulate the requirement to fast on Yom Kippur as a *lo ta'aseh,* ultimately leaving unanswered the question of why the Torah wrote it as a positive commandment. Furthermore, the *gemara* concludes that there is an implicit *lo ta'aseh* based on the punishment of *karet,* but the Torah intentionally makes no explicit mention of it. Clearly, the Torah wants to unambiguously express the positive nature of the mitzvah of *innuy*.

In light of the positive nature of the command, the *gemara* requires a *derashah,* a Biblical derivation, to preclude an obligation to proactively physically afflict oneself:

> תנו רבנן: תענו את נפשתיכם, יכול ישב בחמה או בצנה כדי שיצטער, תלמוד לומר וכל מלאכה לא תעשו. מה מלאכה - שב ואל תעשה, אף ענוי נפש - שב ואל תעשה.
>
> Our Rabbis taught: [The Torah says] "Afflict your souls." One might have thought that he should sit in the sun or the cold in order to afflict himself; the Torah therefore writes [in the next phrase], "and you shall not do any *melakhah*." Just as one must be passive regarding *melakhah,* so too affliction of the spirit is accomplished in a passive manner.[4]

---

3. *Yoma* 81a.
4. *Yoma* 74b.

Thus, although *innuy* is physically passive, it is fundamentally a positive commandment. It is not merely that there is a prohibition to eat and drink on Yom Kippur; rather, one must accomplish and embrace the state of *innuy nefesh* on Yom Kippur.[5]

What is the nature of the obligation of *innuy*, and what does it tell us about the character of Yom Kippur, the day defined by "*ve-initem et nafshoteikhem*"?

Innuy Nefesh and Fasting

The primary component of the mitzvah of *innuy nefesh* obligates us to abstain from eating and drinking. How does it compare to other prohibitions of consumption?[6]

To answer this question, we must first address the nature of the fast of Yom Kippur and the locus of the mitzvah of *innuy*. One option would be to build on the model of most forbidden foods, where the object itself is prohibited. At the onset of Yom Kippur, all food becomes *ma'akhalot assurot* (forbidden food); the food itself is a *heftza shel issur*, an intrinsically prohibited object. Alternatively, the prohibition can be located not in the object, but on the person who does the eating, such that it is an *issur gavra*, a prohibition with respect to the individual.

The notion that *innuy* creates a universal *heftza shel issur* is logically difficult, and there is strong halakhic evidence against this view. The question of reciting *berakhot* on forbidden food exemplifies this. There

5. Rambam counts *innuy* twice in *Sefer ha-Mitzvot*, as both a positive and a negative commandment (*aseh* 164; *lo ta'aseh* 196). In *Mishneh Torah* (*Hilkhot Shevitat Asor* 1:4), he emphasizes the principle of "*ein oneshin ela im ken mazhirin*" to establish a virtual or implicit *lav*. In contrast, R. Sa'adiah Gaon counts only a positive imperative of "*ve-initem*" (*aseh* 55). This is consistent with his general methodology to count only a single mitzvah unless there are concrete halakhic differences distinguishing the *aseh* and *lav* iterations of a particular *halakhah*, as R. Yeruham Fishel Perlow expounds. While R. Perlow projects that R. Sa'adiah's default policy is to enumerate the *aseh*, he acknowledges and addresses numerous exceptions to this apparent rule. With respect to Yom Kippur, however, it is likely that R. Sa'adiah's decision is further impacted by the Torah's very unusual presentation. It is reasonable to speculate that this emphasis on the positive character of "*ve-initem*" was perceived as reflecting its fundamental character as well.
6. We use the word "consumption" in order to include *issurei hana'ah* in our study.

is a debate among the *Rishonim* if a person who ate *ma'akhalot assurot* should recite a *berakhah*. Rambam asserts that one does not make a *berakhah* on *ma'akhalot assurot*;[7] according to some authorities, this is true even when one is permitted to eat the food due to illness.[8] Ra'avad disputes this ruling, excluding only a *zimmun* for *ma'akhalot assurot* under all circumstances.[9] Ra'ah and Ritva enthusiastically embrace Rambam's stance and support it with evidence, logic, and conviction. Ra'ah writes:

> טעמא דמתני׳ בכל הני משום דבשום מאכל עבירה ליכא ברכה, ולא תימא דוקא זימון הוא דקאמר דהא קתני בהדיא בהדייהו והשמש שאכל פחות מכזית מי איכא למימר דזימון הוא דליכא אבל ברכה מברך בפחות מכזית אלא ודאי דאינו מברך כלל, דאם איתה בהני דלעיל דאכלי איסור דמברכי כלל פירושי הוה מפרשינן לה בגמרא, והדין נותן דאיך יברך אין זה מברך אלא מנאץ ואין זה אלא מזכיר עון, תדע לך הרי שהיה אוכל חזיר ונבלה יברך, ולא עוד [אלא] אפילו אוכל אותן בהיתר כגון חולה שיש בו סכנה וצריך להן אין לברך על אכילתו זאת, וכן כתב הרב ר׳ משה.
>
> The explanation for all the cases in the *mishnah* is that there is no *berakhah* said on any prohibited food. The *mishnah* is not merely listing the exclusions from *zimmun*, as evidenced by the listing of a servant who ate less than a volume of an olive, who is certainly not only excluded from *zimmun*, as he doesn't recite a *berakhah* [after eating] at all. If the cases of eating prohibited food [were different and] required a *berakhah*, the *gemara* would have clarified this. And it seems logical [that one does not make a *berakhah*], because this would be a curse rather than a blessing, as it references the sin that was committed. This is self-evident: Would anyone think to recite a *berakhah* upon eating pig or *neveilah* (a carcass)? Additionally, even if one were to be permitted to

7. *Hilkhot Berakhot* 1:19.
8. This seems to be the way that Ra'ah understands Rambam, it is possibly implied in *Teshuvot ha-Rashba* (1:794), and it is *Taz*'s conclusion (*Orah Hayim* 196:1). However, *Beit Yosef* (ibid. 196 and 204) maintains that Rambam would agree that when one is permitted to eat, he would make a *berakhah*. Rashbetz (*Berakhot* 45a) writes similarly.
9. It is unclear what Rambam or Ra'avad hold regarding making a *berakhah* when eating food on Yom Kippur.

> eat otherwise forbidden foods, such as when one is dangerously ill and needs to eat these items, he would still not make a *berakhah*. This is also the position of Rabbeinu Moshe [Rambam].[10]

Ra'ah and Ritva confidently extend this ruling to Rabbinic prohibitions, albeit with a qualification that illuminates their broader perspective on this topic and that provides us a window into our present discussion. Ra'ah states:

> וכן הדין בודאי באיסורין דרבנן באוכל אותן באיסור, אבל אוכל אותן בהיתר, כגון חולה שיש בו סכנה או מעשה שבת על ידי גוי בחולה שאין בו סכנה, נראה ודאי שמברך שכיון שהתירוהו והוא טעון ברכה מן התורה ודאי מברך, לפי [ש]היום מותר הוא לאכילה ומאכל זה מותר הוא אלא שנעשה בו מלאכת איסור.

> The *halakhah* is certainly the same regarding one who eats a Rabbinically prohibited food. However, if he has permission to eat it, such as if he is dangerously ill, or even if his illness is not life-threatening and he eats food prepared on Shabbat by a non-Jew, he would then make a *berakhah*, since on the level of the Torah's requirement, he must make a *berakhah* [in this case], as he is actually permitted to eat it in this case. [Regarding the case of food prepared on Shabbat,] food is permitted on Shabbat in general, and this foodstuff is inherently permitted, but would only be prohibited because of a prohibited act done to it.

Evidently, Biblical prohibitions inhere in the object itself, disqualifying a *berakhah* even when there is personal exemption due to preservation of life. However, Rabbinic infractions devolve only upon the *gavra*; a *berakhah* is therefore warranted whenever circumstances require or permit consumption.

In this light, we must assess Ra'ah's and Ritva's ruling regarding food consumed on Yom Kippur due to *piku'ah nefesh*, preservation of human life. Ritva writes:

10. Ra'ah, *Berakhot* 45a, s.v. *akhal tevel*.

> אבל מי שהוצרך לאכול ביום הכפורים מחמת חולי אעפ"י שמותר נראה ודאי דאין לו לברך כלל בין לפניו בין לאחריו דלאו הנאה הוא לו אלא צערא.
>
> However, it seems certain that one who must eat on Yom Kippur due to [life-endangering] illness, even though it is permissible to do so, he should not make a *berakhah* either before or after eating, because this is considered pain and not pleasure (*hana'ah*).[11]

Ra'ah and Ritva argue that technically food consumed on Yom Kippur due to *piku'ah nefesh* should mandate a *berakhah,* but nevertheless, no *berakhah* is forthcoming, because having to eat on Yom Kippur is spiritually painful; one derives no pleasure from it![12] The assertion that eating on Yom Kippur when halakhically necessary would in principle require a *berakhah* distinguishes the status of "*ve-initem*" from Biblical *ma'akhalot assurot,* equating it with Rabbinic *issurei gavra.* Furthermore, the astonishing insight that the command of "*ve-initem*" eliminates physical pleasure provides a critical perspective on the *kedushat ha-yom* of Yom Kippur.

There are two ways to view the *issur gavra* of eating on Yom Kippur. It is possible that the prohibition consists of the act of eating per se, a typical *issur ma'aseh akhilah.* However, the Torah's clear avoidance of framing the mitzvah in terms of eating, as well as the absence of an explicit negative commandment, suggest otherwise. In light of the positive nature of the mitzvah of *innuy,* it is compelling to conclude that consuming food on Yom Kippur contravenes its very *kedushat ha-yom.* The *issur* lies in failing to fulfill the defining *kiyum* of "*ve-initem*" precisely as the Torah depicts it: "*asher lo te'uneh.*"

---

11. Ritva, *Berakhot* 45a, s.v. *akhal tevel.*
12. In Ra'ah's commentary, he offers an alternative explanation, comparing all food on Yom Kippur to pig and *neveilah.* It is interesting to consider whether he means that everything falls into the category of *ma'akhalot assurot* and the prohibition pertains to the food itself and not the *gavra,* or if he intends that this distinction is immaterial to the question of the *berakhah* on Yom Kippur; it is still deemed *akhilat issur* even though it is technically *be-heter.*

The *gemara* in *Yoma* addresses the Torah's surprising omission of the term "*akhilah*," concluding that the Torah specifically did not use the term, because it sought to change the quantity of food one needs to eat in order to violate the prohibition:

> כל השיעורין כולן בכזית חוץ מטומאת אוכלין ששינה הכתוב במשמען ושינו חכמים בשיעורן וראיה לדבר יוה"כ מאי שינה הכתוב במשמעו (ויקרא כג, כט) מלא תעונה ומאי שינו חכמים בשיעוריה ככותבת.
>
> All *shiurim* (minimum measurements) [regarding food] are the size of an olive (*ke-zayit*), except for the size of food susceptible to *tumah*; since the Torah uses different wording in that context, the Rabbis determined that the *shiur* should be different. We find proof to this principle [that a variation in language implies a different *shiur*] in the context of Yom Kippur: The Torah uses different wording – "*lo te'uneh*" – and the Rabbis determined that the *shiur* is different – the size of a [thick] date (*kotevet*).[13]

Had the Torah prohibited "*akhilah*," consuming a *ke-zayit* would trigger the full violation, in conformity with the standard of other *ma'akhalot assurot*. Instead, the Torah speaks of "*innuy*," in order to establish a special threshold in this context. When it comes to Yom Kippur, it is forbidden to eat a quantity of a *kotevet ha-gasah*, a thick date, because that amount causes "*yetuvei da'atei*," settling of the mind (what would be referred to in Hebrew as "*yishuv ha-da'at*").

The *gemara*'s conclusion may imply two different approaches:

> The prohibition fundamentally conforms to *issur akhilah*, but it is quantitatively adjusted to a larger *shiur*.
>
> Alternatively, the Torah's distinctive usage rejects the paradigm of *ma'akhalot assurot* and even *issur akhilah* in favor of a more experiential focus, perhaps also more consistent with a *kiyum* than an *issur*. The obligation of *innuy nefesh*, a linchpin of the Yom

13. *Yoma* 80a–81a.

> Kippur experience, would be undermined by *miyatva da'atei*, and it therefore prompts an obligation to fast.

In order to sharpen our understanding of the obligation of *innuy*, we will analyze the rules prescribing *innuy* on Yom Kippur in light of the general laws governing eating in other halakhic frameworks.

Shiurim of Food on Yom Kippur

The *gemara* discusses the measurement one must consume in order to be liable for drinking on Yom Kippur:

> השותה מלא לוגמיו... מתקיף לה רבי זירא: מאי שנא אכילה - דכל חד וחד בככותבת, ומאי שנא שתיה דכל חד וחד בדידיה? אמר ליה אביי: קים להו לרבנן בככותבת דבהכי מיתבא דעתיה, בציר מהכי - לא מיתבא. בשתיה - בדידיה מיתבא דעתיה, בדחבריה לא מיתבא דעתיה.
>
> [The *shiur* for] one who drinks is a cheek full.... Rabbi Zeira asked: Why regarding eating is the *shiur* objectively set at the volume of a date, while for drinking the *shiur* is subjective? Abaye responded: The Rabbis ascertained that everyone's mind is [somewhat] settled by eating a date's-worth of food, but with respect to drinking, [the volume necessary to cause] *miyatva da'atei* is dependent on the drinker.[14]

Although *shiurim* in general are objective, Abaye stresses that the *shiurim* of Yom Kippur are fundamentally subjective. They are entirely determined by evaluating whether a particular individual would achieve the state of *miyatva da'atei*. This factor reinforces the impression that the mitzvah of "*innuy nefesh*" on Yom Kippur consists of an experiential dimension.

The *gemara* uses this principle to suggest a novel property of eating and drinking on Yom Kippur:

14. *Yoma* 80a–b.

ורבי יוחנן אמר אפילו תימא רבנן עד כאן לא קאמרי רבנן התם אלא לענין טומאה אבל הכא משום יתובי דעתיה הוא והאי לא קא מיתבא דעתיה.

> And R. Yohanan said: This *halakhah* [that eating and drinking do not combine to create a *shiur*] could even be true according to the Rabbis [who hold in another context that two items that independently have different *shiurim* can combine to form a single *shiur*], because we find that the Rabbis stated their position only regarding *tumah*, but here [when it comes to Yom Kippur], the *halakhah* depends on settling of the mind [*yetuvei da'atei*], and there is no settling of the mind in this case [of combining eating and drinking].[15]

In general, the *Rabbanan* maintain that the *shiurim* of food and drink can be combined to attain the minimum requisite amount. However, R. Yohanan suggests that despite this general approach, Yom Kippur might contravene this rule, since the prohibition revolves around the possibility of attenuating hunger and thirst, not around the formal violation of an objective act of eating. Since a combination of partial *shiurim* of food and drink would not effectively satiate, the normative rules of combining *shiurim* would be inadequate.[16]

The mode of *hana'ah* (physical pleasure) that violates *innuy* may also differ from that which triggers standard *issurei akhilah*. R. Yohanan and Reish Lakish argue as to whether *hana'at gerono*, enjoyment via the palate, or *hana'at mei'ayim*, pleasure by means of digestion, defines an *issur akhilah*.[17] *Minhat Hinukh* posits that the violation of *innuy* of Yom Kippur, which is measured by the standard of *miyatva da'atei*, should

15. *Yoma* 81a.
16. In a similar vein, immediately after the *gemara* explicitly dictates that sauce is considered to be part of food and combines to form a requisite *shiur* (*Yoma* 80b), Reish Lakish feels compelled to state that the same would be true even on Yom Kippur. The *gemara* explains that we might have thought that on Yom Kippur, this would be considered like combining food and drink; therefore, Reish Lakish relates that seasonings are part of the food and will contribute even to *miyatva da'atei*. This again reflects different requirements for halakhic consumption on Yom Kippur.
17. *Hullin* 103b.

depend on *hana'at mei'ayim* even according to R. Yohanan. He further speculates that *hana'at mei'ayim* even absent *hana'at gerono* may be culpable on Yom Kippur.[18] If *hana'at gerono* is generally a defining staple of *akhilah,* its insufficiency on Yom Kippur due to the principle of *yetuvei da'atei* betokens not only a quantitative technical adjustment, but an abandonment of the category of *akhilah* entirely. If it also engenders stringencies (*hana'at mei'ayim* instead of *hana'at gerono*), it certainly constitutes an important factor in the *kiyum* of "*ve-initem.*"

Minhat Hinukh queries why the *gemara* did not mention the necessary mode of *hana'at mei'ayim* alongside the *shiur* of *kotevet* as a *hiddush* derived from the Torah's use of "*ve-initem.*" He speculates that the *gemara* follows the rejected opinion of Reish Lakish, who always demands *hana'at mei'ayim.* However, a more fundamental solution presents itself based on our approach. The *gemara* is not narrowly identifying halakhic anomalies reflected by the Torah's singular formulation. The *shiur* of *yituvei da'atei* succinctly crystallizes that "*ve-initem*" constitutes a *kiyum,* a fulfillment of Yom Kippur's *kedushat ha-yom,* not an expansive yet conventional *issur akhilah.* It is therefore unsurprising that there are multiple manifestations of this broad, halakhically consequential perspective, including the type of *hana'ah* (*hana'at mei'ayim*) that is prohibited.

Even universal rules of *akhilah* evidently apply differently to *innuy nefesh.* The *gemara* in *Yoma* declares:

> אמר ריש לקיש האוכל אכילה גסה ביוה"כ פטור מ"ט (ויקרא כג:כט) אשר לא תעונה כתיב פרט למזיק.
>
> Reish Lakish said: One who eats an excessive meal on Yom Kippur is not liable. What is the reason? Because the verse states, "[He] who does not afflict himself," which excludes one is merely doing damage.[19]

18. *Minhat Hinukh* 313:2. A practical ramification of this analysis is the permissibility of artificial eating on Yom Kippur. See *Teshuvot Ahiezer* (3:61) for a discussion of this issue.

19. *Yoma* 80b.

A special *gezeirat ha-katuv* establishes that *akhilah gasah* – excessive consumption beyond the point of satiation – is exempt from punishment on Yom Kippur. But the *gemara* in *Yevamot* teaches that excessive eating never qualifies as halakhic consumption.[20] Why, then, is an independent source required to establish that Yom Kippur conforms to the standard rules of *akhilah*?

It is noteworthy that the *gemara* in *Yoma* invokes a parallel exemption with respect to *terumah*: "*Ki yokhal – perat le-mazik*." One who eats *terumah* in a damaging manner is not liable for eating *terumah*. *Gevurat Ari* questions why *terumah* is singled out from other *akhilah* prohibitions (*hametz, hadash, ma'aser sheni* outside the borders of Jerusalem) in this context, but he is curiously silent about the need for an independent source excluding Yom Kippur consumption. It is reasonable to conclude, especially in light of our analysis, that the criterion of *miyatva da'atei* that negates or disrupts *innuy nefesh* might not fully cohere with the requirements of *akhilah*.[21] It is therefore necessary to exclude excessive consumption from both *akhilah* and *yetuvei da'atei*. It is conceivable that even after the Talmud establishes a parallel exemption of *akhilah gasah* for *terumah* (and possibly, by proxy, *ma'akhalot assurot* generally) and Yom Kippur, the two applications still diverge.[22] This is subtly implied by Rashi's nuanced justification of the exemption on Yom Kippur:

---

20. *Yevamot* 40a.
21. The *sugya* in *Yevamot* 40a does not cohere with this perspective, as the *gemara* apparently equates the two categories by proving from the Yom Kippur exemption that *akhilah gasah* does not qualify as *akhilat korban*. At the same time, that text is consistent with the impulse in the *gemara* in *Yoma* to expand the exemption of *akhilah gasah* to encompass *terumah*, although the exclusive focus is Yom Kippur.
22. The precise definition and application of *akhilah gasah* is a matter of significant controversy. What standard of gratuitous, excessive, repugnant, or self-destructive consumption dictates this exemption? See, for example, Rashi and Tosafot Yeshanim, *Yoma* 80b; Tosafot and Tosafot Yeshanim, *Yevamot* 40a; as well as the commentaries ad loc. and in *Bava Kama* 110a, *Nazir* 23a, *Pesahim* 107b. Regarding Yom Kippur, see also the comments of *Beit Yosef* (612:6) and *Bah* (612:4). In light of our analysis, it is conceivable that we might apply different standards of *akhilah gasah* to different halakhic categories. Indeed, this approach might resolve some of the apparent discrepancies.

> פטור - דלא עבר על אשר לא תעונה שאף זה עינוי הוא שמזיק את עצמו.
>
> He is exempt – Since he has not violated, "[He] who does not afflict himself," because this is also affliction, as he is harming himself.[23]

Here, Rashi particularizes the Yom Kippur exemption by accentuating the fact that excessive consumption may actually constitute a *kiyum,* as it facilitates "*ve-initem.*" In his commentary on *Yoma,* Rashi projects a more moderate posture, emphasizing that "*lo te'uneh*" has been insufficiently disrupted by *akhilah gasah*:

> פרט למזיק - לזה שאינו מבטל ממנו שום עינוי על ידי אכילה זו אלא מזיק הוא את האוכלין ואת עצמו.
>
> Excluding a damager – [This refers] to this person, who does not detract from any affliction through this [excessive] eating; rather, he is damaging both the food and himself.[24]

In this context, even though Rashi introduces the consideration of "*hezek ha-okhel*" (damage to the food) that also may detract from qualifying as "*akhilah,*" he still emphasizes the factor of "*hezek ha-gavra*" (damage to the person) that specifically excludes it from being a contradiction of *innuy nefesh.* With respect to *terumah,* Rashi underscores only the desecration of *heftza shel terumah,* as the destructive personal effect is irrelevant to that halakhic category.[25]

The evidence suggests that Rambam, like Rashi, distinguishes between eating on Yom Kippur and *ma'akhalot assurot* regarding *akhilah gasah,* but Rambam provides different reasons for the exclusion of *akhilah gasah.* In *Hilkhot Terumah,* he posits that it is because the self-

---

23. *Yevamot* 40a, s.v. *patur* (first).
24. Rashi, *Yoma* 80b, s.v. *perat le-mazik.*
25. Rashi, ibid., s.v. *perat le-mazik* (second). At the same time, the focus on the *terumah* itself is a particularly acute factor in *Hilkhot Terumah,* as the halakhic evidence demonstrates that the significance of its *akhilah* is precisely as a *kiyum* in the *kedushat ha-heftza.*

inflicted damage changes the action into one of *nezek*, not *akhilah*.[26] In *Hilkhot Shevitat Asor*, however, he argues that *akhilah gasah* renders the excess food as inedible and therefore eliminates any status of "food" nourishment.[27] This discrepancy reinforces the conclusion that the standards of *yituvei da'atei* and "*asher lo te'uneh*" differ fundamentally from that of typical *issurei akhilah*.[28]

The Biblical prohibition against consuming a *hatzi shiur*, a partial measure, is *prima facie* equally applicable to *innuy nefesh* and *ma'akhalot assurot*, and possibly even other negative commandments.[29] Indeed, the primary discussion of *hatzi shiur* in the Talmud Bavli is found specifically in connection with violating Yom Kippur.[30] The violation of *innuy nefesh* is treated as part and parcel of the global prohibition of *hatzi shiur*. However, in light of our analysis of the nature of "*ve-initem*," it is

26. *Hilkhot Terumah* 10:8.

27. *Hilkhot Shevitat Asor* 2:7.

28. Rambam's stance on vinegar parallels his view on *akhilah gasah*. The *gemara* in *Yoma* (81b) rules that eating vinegar is not prohibited on Yom Kippur. However, the *gemara* in *Berakhot* (40b) dictates that vinegar requires a *berakhah* of *she-hakol*. The *Rishonim* contend with this apparent contradiction. Rosh (*Berakhot* 6:23) distinguishes between different types of vinegar, and Rabbeinu Yonah (*Berakhot* 40b, s.v. *al ha-hometz*) theorizes that a *berakhah rishonah* is required for any *hana'ah*, even one not considered *akhilah*, because of the principle of "*kol ha-neheneh min ha-olam ha-zeh be-lo berakhah ma'al*" (*Berakhot* 35a). See also my "*Be-Inyan Birkat she-Hakol*," *Yevul ha-Yovelot* (1986), 261–262. However, Rambam (*Hilkhot Berakhot* 8:8) requires a *berakhah* both before and after the consumption of vinegar, and he does not require that vinegar be mixed with water. Apparently, Rambam understood that the factor of *miyatva da'atei* raises the criterion of illegal consumption that disrupts "*ve-initem*" on Yom Kippur. This position is explicitly articulated by Meiri (*Berakhot* 36b), who, in distinguishing between Yom Kippur and *berakhot*, explains that violation of Yom Kippur requires "*akhilah she-meishiv et ha-nefesh*."

29. This discussion relates to a general debate regarding *hatzi shiur*. *Hakham Tzvi* (86) maintains that *hatzi shiur* applies exclusively to *ma'akhalot assurot* and not to other *issurim*. In contrast, Rashi (*Shabbat* 74a, s.v. *ve-khi*) argues that the prohibition of *hatzi shiur* applies in the context of *bishul* on Shabbat as well. *Mishneh le-Melekh* (*Hilkhot Shabbat* 18:1) argues that *hatzi shiur* applies to all thirty-nine *melakhot*; the *shiurim* that *Hazal* delineated are only relevant regarding bringing a *korban hatat*. See *Minhat Hinukh* 32:4, who discusses these positions at length.

30. *Yoma* 73b–74a.

logically compelling that the unique prohibition might deviate from the typical standard.

The Talmud anchors the violation of *hatzi shiur* in the consideration of *hazi le-itzterufei,* the fact that smaller quantities may combine to a requisite amount. There are generally two ways to understand the factor of *hazi le-itztarufei*:

a. As a Biblical *seyag,* a hedge against the real concern that one will complete the *shiur* and incur the full violation.[31]
b. As a way of establishing *hatzi shiur* itself as an innate *heftza shel issur* or as initiating the formal act of *akhilah,* albeit absent the quantity required for a full punishment. The fact that incremental, miniscule amounts accumulate and combine demonstrates that each discrete unit qualifies as a prohibited substance and possibly even as a consumption.[32]

If the underlying problem of *hatzi shiur* is its actual potential to combine to a complete *shiur,* then this principle applies equally to "*ve-initem*" on Yom Kippur as to other prohibitions. However, if *hazi le-itzterufei* is based on initiating the consumption of an *issur* or on the perspective that one is consuming a *heftza shel issur,* albeit in insufficient quantities

31. See Meiri, *Yoma* 73b, s.v. *hatzi shiur,* who writes:
שאף ר' יוחנן לא אמרה שהוא מן התורה אלא כיון דחזי לאיצטרופי והרי זה התחלת אכילת איסור אבל כשנשבע על חצי שיעור הרי הוא מגלה דעתו שאינו מכוין לצירוף.
See also his comments on *Shevu'ot* 21b, s.v. *mi she-amar*; 25a s.v. *mi-mah. Sha'agat Aryeh* (74) rejects any distinction between edible and inedible food with regard to *hatzi shiur,* based on the pragmatic understanding of *hazi le-itztarufei.* This view conforms with the other positions he articulates in *Gevurat Ari* (*Yoma* 73b, s.v. *Reish Lakish*; 74a, s.v. *hatzi shiur*) regarding the application of the principle "*ein issur hal al issur*" to *hatzi shiur* and the question of *hatzi shiur*'s applicability to *shiurim* that require simultaneity (as opposed to cumulative *shiurim*). Along these lines, numerous *Aharonim* debate the status of *hatzi shiur* in circumstances in which there is either insufficient time or available quantity to complete the requisite amount.
32. Rabbeinu Hananel presents a subtle but significant reformulation of the *gemara*'s explanation (*Yoma* 74a) of R. Yohanan's Biblical prohibition of *hatzi shiur,* rendering "כיון דחזי לאיצטרופי - איסורא קא אכיל" as "אכילה קרינא ביה," accentuating that even lesser quantities qualify as *akhilah.*

to be punished, then applying *hatzi shiur* to *innuy nefesh* may deviate from the halakhic default standard in either extreme. Since food is not intrinsically prohibited on Yom Kippur, but rather there is an obligation to embrace the *kiyum* of "*ve-initem et nafshoteikhem*," there is no *heftza shel issur* being consumed, and perhaps no objective *ma'aseh aveirah* either. According to this perspective, the *hatzi shiur* of Yom Kippur might be less problematic if the experience of *miyatva da'atei* that characterizes this prohibition specifically requires a full quantity. For the very reason that the *shiur* for "*ve-initem*" is unique (*kotevet ha-gasah*), the demand for a full measure may also be more rigorous.

Alternatively, perhaps any eating on Yom Kippur can be perceived as a serious, if incomplete, lapse in fulfilling the positive obligation to abstain from food as a mechanism to underscore exclusive spiritual focus. Even the consumption of just a *hatzi shiur* could represent a serious breach in our aspiration to achieve an ideal state of "*ve-initem et nafshoteikhem*" on this critical day.

The Yerushalmi states that Reish Lakish, who champions the opinion that *hatzi shiur* is merely a Rabbinical violation, agrees that in three cases, *hatzi shiur* is prohibited on a Biblical level:

a. with regard to *issurei hana'ah*, items from which it is forbidden to derive any pleasure;
b. when there is intent to complete a full *shiur*;
c. in the context of fulfilling "*ve-initem et nafshoteikhem*" on Yom Kippur.[33]

Although no *miyatva da'atei* has been achieved by eating a *hatzi shiur*, eating even a miniscule amount constitutes a failure to properly participate

33. Yerushalmi *Terumot* 6:1. *Sha'agat Aryeh* (*Gevurat Ari, Yoma* 73b, end of *s.v. ela*) notes that while the Talmud Yerushalmi's presentation is incompatible with that of the Talmud Bavli regarding Yom Kippur, as the very debate between Reish Lakish and R. Yohanan registers in the Bavli exclusively with regard to "*ve-initem*" on Yom Kippur, the Yerushalmi's distinction between *issur akhilah* and *issur hana'ah* may be normative. It is interesting that the third factor delineated by the Yerushalmi (intention to complete the *shiur*) echoes in the discussions of *Rishonim* and *Aharonim* regarding the character and scope of *hazi le-itztarufei*. See Meiri and *Gevurat Ari* cited above.

in the mitzvah of *innuy nefesh*. According to the Yerushalmi, *innuy nefesh* by definition requires not only technical compliance, but also uncompromising embrace of the ideal fulfillment of "*ve-initem.*"

The parallel but opposite perspective is identified by a doctrine of *Sefer ha-Hinukh,* who contends that it is permissible for one who is significantly ill but whose life is not imperiled to consume a *hatzi shiur* on Yom Kippur.[34] *Minhat Hinukh* notes that this view is apparently problematic, as *hatzi shiur* is a Biblical transgression, which is not typically violated due to standard illness.[35] Indeed, *Sefer ha-Hinukh* does not apply this leniency to other instances of *hatzi shiur*. However, since "*ve-initem*" and *miyatva da'atei* constitute a singularly spiritual approach to Yom Kippur's *kedushat ha-yom,* we can comprehend this innovative position. The *holeh*'s consumption in this case is rightly perceived as therapeutic, not as a casual attitude toward *innuy nefesh*. The fact that he refrains because of "*ve-initem*" from accumulating the full *shiur* actually reinforces his commitment to his embrace of the Yom Kippur ideal. Thus, it would be entirely permissible for him to eat for medicinal purposes, as long as he restricts his intake to avoid violating the *kiyum* of "*ve-initem*" on Yom Kippur by eating enough to reach the level of *miyatva da'atei.*[36] "*Ve-initem*" emerges as a mitzvah that fundamentally centers on the individual's experience of and perspective on Yom Kippur.[37]

---

34. *Sefer ha-Hinukh* 313.
35. *Minhat Hinukh* 313:8.
36. In *Sefer ha-Hinukh* (ibid.), there is another application of this principle that "*ve-initem*" diverges from the typical categories of *akhilah* regarding the *shiur tziruf* of *kedei akhilat peras*. Uniquely regarding Yom Kippur, *Sefer ha-Hinukh* presents *kedei akhilat peras* as a measure of time that distinguishes between two discrete consumptions, disrupting any additional combining of the requisite *shiur*. Typically, this period is perceived as defining an integrated single consumption. While the practical difference is often minute, the conceptual discrepancy between the two perspectives is significant. *Minhat Hinukh* (313:6) critiques this stance and is puzzled by its atypical nature. In light of *Sefer ha-Hinukh*'s view on the singular status of "*ve-initem*" regarding the allowance of *hatzi shiur* for a *holeh,* highlighting the distinctiveness of "*ve-initem*" relative to other *ma'akhalot assurot,* we can appreciate the consistency of *Sefer ha-Hinukh*'s approach.
37. We have demonstrated Yom Kippur's potential special status with respect to *hatzi shiur* – either *le-kula* or *le-humra* – by invoking evidence (Reish Lakish's view in Yerushalmi *Terumah, Sefer ha-Hinukh*'s stance on *holeh*) that is not halakhically

There is another major debate among the *Rishonim* regarding the halakhic status of unfit food, typically subject to a Rabbinical prohibition, on Yom Kippur. While Rambam records a prohibition, thereby equating the status of inedible food on Yom Kippur with other *ma'akhalot assurot*,[38] Ra'avyah permits it.[39] *Beit Yosef* speculates, without evidence,

normative. The issue of *hatzi shiur* on Yom Kippur remains, however, halakhically consequential, as the core perspectives on *hatzi shiur* – the pragmatic potential of *hazi le-itztarufei* or the intrinsic stature of *hatzi shiur* – are not mutually exclusive. It is conceivable that Yom Kippur's special status may dictate more expansive or restrictive parameters for applying *hatzi shiur* relative to other prohibitions. Based on our analysis, it is also conceivable that the higher threshold demands of Yom Kippur dictate that its *hatzi shiur* is exclusively pragmatic. This perspective conforms to *Sefer ha-Hinukh*'s orientation. At the same time, there is substantial basis to support the argument, also consistent with the Yerushalmi's understanding of Reish Lakish, that specifically the *hatzi shiur* of "*ve-initem*" transcends the Biblical *seyag* of *hazi le-itztarufei* and constitutes an intrinsic violation, although one that does not trigger punishment. Either of these conclusions would justify significant normative divergence from *hatzi shiur* of other *issurim*.

Moreover, there is an additional debate about the nature of the prohibition of *hatzi shiur* that may particularly resonate with respect to Yom Kippur. While some *Rishonim* perceive *hatzi shiur* as an extension of the particular *issur* in question, others argue that this violation is a generic one; all *hatzi shiur* violations constitute a single transgression, divorced from the particular context. (See the two views in Ramban's *Torat ha-Adam, Sha'ar ha-Meihush, Inyan ha-Sakanah* 4, and *Hiddushei ha-Ramban, Yoma* 82a, with respect to the question of whether "*ma'akhilin oto ha-kal ha-kal*" applies to *hatzi shiur*.) R. Soloveitchik reported that his father, R. Moshe Soloveitchik, speculated regarding whether one who ate less than a *shiur* on Yom Kippur could still receive an *aliyah*, for although he has violated the generic prohibition of *hatzi shiur*, he did not impinge on the particular *kiyum of* "*ve-initem*." This conclusion is based on the premise that *hatzi shiur* does not constitute a violation of a specific infraction and that eating on Yom Kippur is a typical manifestation of the *issur hatzi shiur*. In light of our analysis, however, we may speculate whether "*ve-initem*," relative to other *issurim*, is likely to be a more generic or specific *issur*. The issue of "*ha-kal ha-kal*" and other practical differences would also hinge on this question.

A striking expression of the principle that an insufficient quantity undermines the specific identity can be found in the doctrine of R. Yonah (*Berakhot* 38b) that in the absence of a sufficient quantity, all foods mandate a *birkat she-hakol*. See my "*Be-Inyan Birkat she-Hakol*," *Yevul ha-Yovelot*, 252–256.

38. *Hilkhot Shevitat Asor* 2:5.

39. Ra'avyah, no. 861. Our assumption here is that Ra'avyah's allowance is limited to Yom Kippur. See Ra'avyah, no. 456, regarding the factors of "*she-lo kederekh akhilah*"

that Ra'avyah could only have permitted the consumption of quality-compromised food (*akhilah she-einah re'uyah*) that was also lacking the requisite *kotevet* quantity.[40] *Bah* emphatically rejects this justification, despite expressing his bewilderment that Yom Kippur consumption could possibly diverge so significantly from classical *issurei akhilah*.[41] It is reasonable to conclude that Ra'avyah embraced the notion that the difference in quantity – *ke-zayit* vs. *kotevet* – highlights a very different orientation for the *kiyum* of "*ve-initem*," as we have developed. In his view, this difference impacts the quality of *akhilat Yom ha-Kippurim* as well.[42]

Bah's analysis and novel conclusion, despite limiting the scope of Ra'avyah's allowance, actually reinforces this approach. He posits, based purely on conviction, that Ra'avyah would never have allowed *akhilah she-einah re'uyah* designed to mitigate the effects of the fast itself to neutralize "*ve-initem*" ("*le-vatel ra'av ve-tzama*"). Only if there is some other legitimate need or benefit does this allowance prevail, and then even only in small quantities (though above the *shiur*). The very notion that motivation influences the permissibility of consumption on Yom Kippur and that quantity (beyond the *shiur*) is a factor, independent of

---

and "*she-lo ke-derekh hana'ah*," which may imply a more universal position. *Sha'agat Aryeh* (74) links Ra'avyah's views on unfit food (*she-eino ra'uy*) and *she-lo ke-derekh*, though he himself distinguishes between them. Later, *Sha'agat Aryeh* (end of 75) identifies a potential discrepancy regarding the *Tur*'s view on unfit food on Yom Kippur versus other prohibited consumptions.

40. *Beit Yosef* 612:6.

41. *Bah* 612:6. He does posit that Ra'avyah's exemption neutralizes the problem of swallowing saliva on Yom Kippur. Other *Posekim* legitimize this action by distinguishing between *beli'ah* (swallowing) and *akhilah*.

42. See also *Arukh ha-Shulhan*'s comment (612:6) that even those who generally rule that *reiha milta* (aromas from food have significance) would abstain from applying this principle to "*ve-initem*" on Yom Kippur. He argues that relative to *ma'akhalot assurot*, violation of "*ve-initem*" requires a more concrete physical experience. He states:

ביום הכפורים לא נאסרה אלא דבר שהגוף נהנה...לאפוקי שארי איסורים שאין להנשמה ליהנות מן האיסור. לכך בהם הריח אסור אם ריחא מילתא הוא.

This formulation is particularly interesting given that the Torah emphasizes *innuy nefesh*, "affliction of the *soul*." It is also possible that *reiha milta* requires that the *heftza shel okhel* be intrinsically forbidden, a factor absent in "*ve-initem*."

the objective standards of consumption, reaffirms the conclusion that "*ve-initem*" is a *kiyum*, a way of relating to the demands of Yom Kippur.[43]

While *Sha'agat Aryeh* unequivocally rejects Ra'avyah's lenient position on the consumption of unfit food on Yom Kippur, even in the context of illness, he advances a novel stringent ruling that may parallel Ra'avyah's thinking, proscribing even unconventional ingestion of food ("*she-lo ke-derekh akhilah ve-hana'ah*") on Yom Kippur.[44] His conclusion derives from the Torah's avoidance of the term "*akhilah*" in the Yom Kippur context. Although the Talmud enumerates only *kila'ei ha-kerem* and *basar be-halav* as exceptions to the requirement of conventional ingestion for liability, *Sha'agat Aryeh* concludes that unconventional ingestion is forbidden on Yom Kippur as well.[45] Evidently, *Sha'agat Aryeh* intuited

---

43. Alternatively, one could speculate that *Bah*'s explanation is anchored in the notion of *ahsheveih* (conferring upon an object an elevated status through thought or action). However, the question of motivation should be immaterial to application of that principle. *Bah*'s perspective on the Ra'avyah is anchored in the position of Rabbeinu Yeruham (*Helekha-Adam* 7:2, cited also by *Bah* 612:6), which he prominently quotes at the end of this section. R. Yeruham rules that several of the allowances on Yom Kippur are limited to a minimal (yet above the *shiur*) quantity of consumption. *Bah* extrapolated from R. Yeruham's language that increased quantity could even generate a Biblical violation of "*ve-innitem*":

> ותימה למה יתחייב בהרבה כיון שאינן ראויין לאכילה ואנן אכילה בעינן וליכא...ואפשר דטעמא דאוכלין שאינן ראויין לאכילה דפטור הוא מפני שאינו נהנה מהם ולא תעונה כתיב פרט למזיק וזה כיון שאכל הרבה ושבר רעבונו וריוה צמאו הרי נהנה מהם ואכילה ושתייה ראויה לו קרינן ביה...דבדידיה תלי מילתא אי מותיב דעתיה בהכי אם לאו.

The question and response precisely capture the issue we have been contending with – the relationship between Yom Kippur and other prohibited *akhilot*. It is significant that *Bah* invokes the exemption of *akhilah gasah*, a leniency, in order to underscore the singular stringency of Yom Kippur with respect to the impact of increased quantity. Moreover, in his conclusion, he fully integrates his previous analysis of Ra'avyah by positing that R. Yeruham's increased quantity is synonymous with his own notion of the motivation to relieve the "*ve-initem*" experience. *Bah*'s comments are consistent with his aforementioned novel view.

Beit Yosef notes that R. Yeruham's position stems from the discussion of *hometz* (*Yoma* 81b), and he is troubled that Rambam (*Hilkhot Shevitat Asor* 2:5, 6) omits that *gemara*. Either way, it is likely that the idea of increased quantities (beyond the *shiur*) is a factor only in those specific cases, notwithstanding R. Yeruham's significant expansion.

44. *Sha'agat Aryeh* 74–76; *Gevurat Ari, Yoma* 80b, *milu'im*, s.v. *nikhtov*.

45. *Pesahim* 24b.

that the Torah's singular formulations of "*ve-initem*" and "*lo te'uneh*" not merely convey the higher quantitative requirement of *kotevet* vs. *ke-zayit*, but revise the very character of the *issur* of eating on Yom Kippur.[46]

Conclusion

We have seen that Yom Kippur is singled out in the Torah's presentation of the *mo'adim*; it is defined not as a *mikra kodesh*, but as a day of *innuy nefesh*. Our analysis of "*ve-initem*" has further demonstrated that this is a fundamentally positive mitzvah, a spiritual opportunity that is entirely distinct from other prohibitions of eating. Instead of prohibiting eating or requiring physical suffering, the mitzvah demands that we immerse ourselves in a state of *innuy nefesh*. Physicality must be studiously avoided in all of its forms, and *yetuvei da'atei*, which would destroy this mental state of "*ve-initem et nafshoteikhem*," must be avoided.

What state of being are we pursuing on Yom Kippur?

She'iltot argues that Yom Kippur cancels *aveilut* because it is a day of joy.[47] Similarly, Rabbeinu Yehonatan posits that Yom Kippur necessitates a *birkat ha-zeman*, an expression of joy.[48] Clearly, suffering is not the theme of Yom Kippur. Nor can *innuy nefesh* be primarily about prohibiting eating or afflicting oneself as a method of self-flagellation. Quite the opposite, the dissonance of eating on Yom Kippur is so painful that Ra'ah and Ritva rule that no *birkat ha-nehenin* can be recited on food eaten on Yom Kippur even in a state of permissibility, because no *hana'ah* has occurred!

---

46. *Sha'agat Aryeh* further argues that this conclusion establishes the "*ve-initem*" infraction as an *issur mosif* (not merely *issur kolel*) vis-à-vis the transgression of *neveilah*, etc. His discussion of *Yoma* 81a, where the Talmud speculates why the Torah avoided the *akhilah* usage regarding Yom Kippur, is reminiscent of *Minhat Hinukh*'s examination of *hana'at gerono* and *hana'at mei'ayim*. It is also particularly noteworthy, in light of our previous assessment of *akhilah gasah* on Yom Kippur, that *Sha'agat Aryeh* specifically contrasts the stringency of *she-lo ke-derekh* with the leniency of *akhilah gasah*. It is interesting that the Talmud (*Yoma* 81a), seemingly gratuitously, integrates the status of *akhilah gasah* and *she-lo ke-derekh* in the consumption of *terumah*.
47. *She'iltot, she'ilta* 15.
48. Rabbeinu Yonatan, *Eiruvin* 10b in the *dapei ha-Rif*, s.v. *ekra*.

In order to embrace the spiritual opportunity of Yom Kippur, we must extricate ourselves from physicality.[49] This is beautifully captured by Ritva, who writes:

> אלא שגזירת הכתוב הוא לפרוש בו ביום מתאוות גופניות שנהיה כמלאכים.
>
> Rather, it is a Biblical decree to refrain on that day [Yom Kippur] from physical desires, so that we will be like angels.[50]

As demonstrated, the *halakhot* of *innuy nefesh* define eating and food on Yom Kippur by their interference with one's immersion in spirituality. The absolute spiritual focus demanded by the mitzvah of "*ve-initem*" is the essence of Yom Kippur.

Indeed, the very *kedushat ha-yom* and full *issur melakhah* of Yom Kippur (which includes *melekhet okhel nefesh*[51]) are generated by the spiritual aspiration of the day represented by the *kiyum* of *innuy nefesh*. Rambam consistently formulates an intricate link between *innuy nefesh* and *issur melakhah* by associating the obligations and integrating the two distinct *mitzvot* into one rubric, depicting each as a *shevitah* imperative:

> מצות עשה לשבת ממלאכה בעשור לחדש השביעי שנאמר (ויקרא כג:לב) "שבת שבתון הוא לכם"...מצות עשה אחרת יש ביום הכפורים והיא לשבת בו מאכילה ושתיה שנאמר (ויקרא טז:כט) "תענו את נפשתיכם".
>
> There is a positive commandment to rest from labor on the tenth of the seventh month [Tishrei], as the verse states, "It shall be a Sabbath of rest for you"... Another positive command concerning Yom Kippur requires us to rest from eating or drinking on that day, as it is written: "You shall afflict yourselves" (*Vayikra* 16:29).[52]

49. See *Sefer ha-Hinukh* 313. Although he also speaks specifically of the effect of excess physicality on atonement, he primarily focuses on the broader theme of spiritual focus as an indispensable way of capitalizing on the opportunity of Yom Kippur.

50. Ritva, *Rosh ha-Shanah* 9a.

51. See the chapter "Yom Kippur: The Quintessential Shabbat."

52. *Hilkhot Shevitat Asor* 1:1, 4. See also *Hilkhot Shevitat Asor* 1:6, where Rambam also invokes the term "*shevut*" and seemingly gratuitously links *issur melakhah*

In this respect, Rambam precisely mirrors the emphasis of the Torah's presentation of these two obligations.

Yom Kippur is a day when we refrain, desist, and even disengage from all physicality, including creative *melakhah* and even the elemental and essential physical sustenance of eating and drinking, as well as adopt additional *innuyim* to embrace the special potential of the day.

Yom Kippur is the day of a stark choice between the *se'ir ha-na'aseh bi-fnim* and the *se'ir ha-mishtalei'ah,* between the goat dedicated to God and the one sent over a cliff – the day on which we demonstrate our absolute devotion to Hashem. On Yom Kippur, we have a once-a-year opportunity to establish that we are capable of devoting ourselves *kulo la-Hashem* on a level superior to that of the angels. *Innuy* is the mitzvah to completely immerse ourselves in the day's spirituality and to dedicate ourselves entirely to serving Hashem.

There is an unfortunate popular misconception that Yom Kippur is a punishment, a dreaded day that focuses on self-abnegation. This superficial and skewed perspective is unconducive to seizing the rare spiritual opportunity of this singular, remarkable day.[53] Observing

---

and *innuy nefesh.* He finds it necessary in his code to preclude the misconception that "*ve-initem*" would extend only to the daytime of Yom Kippur by invoking the parallel *issur melakhah* on Shabbat: "כשם ששבות מלאכה בו בין ביום ובין בלילה, כך שבות לענוי בין ביום בין בלילה." He then introduces the institution of *tosefet kedushah* specifically with respect to *innuy nefesh.* There is a debate between *Maggid Mishneh, Lehem Mishneh,* and other commentators regarding whether *tosefet kedushah* also extends to *issur melakhah* or is confined to the mitzvah of "*ve-initem.*" The view that conflates *issur melakhah* and "*ve-initem*" on this matter further reinforces the link between these two *shevitot.* If Rambam intended to confine *tosefet* to "*ve-initem,*" it is still striking that this singular manifestation of "*ve-initem*" follows an introduction that accentuates the link between the *shevitot.*

See also *Hilkhot Shevitat Asor* 1:5 according to the old-printed and Yemenite manuscripts (as opposed to the Frankel edition), according to which Rambam may have linked the *innuyim* and *issur melakhah.* See also the intriguing debate between Rashi (*Shabbat* 114b, s.v. *assur*) and Tosafot (ibid. s.v. *ela*) regarding the relationship between the *shevitot* of *melakhah/innuy nefesh* on Yom Kippur and that of Shabbat.

53. This perspective is often associated with and fueled by sources that view *innuy* as afflicting oneself as a type of punishment in order to serve as a *kapparah, viduy,* or even *korban.* In the view of some *mefarshim,* "*ve-initem*" is intended to be a direct contrast to the *simhah* and *oneg* of ordinary *yamim tovim.* See the comments of

Yom Kippur is an opportunity that we cherish and treasure. It is a day to anticipate, not dread and bemoan.[54]

R. Soloveitchik once approvingly quoted a comment by the Kotzker Rebbe that captures this positive view of Yom Kippur: "Tishah be-Av is such a bitter day, how is it possible to eat? Yom Kippur is such a wonderful day, why would one need to eat?"[55] It is no coincidence that "*ve-initem et nafshoteikhem*" in its positive form – which represents the headiness, inspiration, and spiritual heights of Yom Kippur – is at the core of the Torah's presentation of this wonderful day.[56]

Rashbam, Sforno, and R. Hirsch, *Vayikra* 23:27; and Ibn Ezra, *Vayikra* 16:29. Another striking formulation can be found in *Tefillah Zakah,* composed by *Hayei Adam,* which states: "May the fast be regarded as if we had offered our body upon the altar" (see Orthodox Union Yom Kippur *Mahzor,* p. 54). However, I believe that this association is a misreading of these sources. They are not meant to be taken as encouraging dreading Yom Kippur because of the fast, but rather as perspectives on how to understand the purpose of the fast. Furthermore, those sources are not mutually exclusive of our perspective that *innuy* is really a *kiyum* in Yom Kippur and contributes to the ambitious character of the day. To the extent that *innuy* is not about self-abnegation but rather a downgrading of physicality, many of these themes are consistent with our perspective.

54. Rabbeinu Yonah (*Sha'arei Teshuvah* 4:8) implicitly presents this perspective in his discussion of the pre-Yom Kippur *se'udah*:

    אמרו רבותינו זכרונם לברכה כל הקובע סעודה בערב יוה"כ כאלו נצטוה להתענות תשיעי ועשירי והתענה בהם. כי הראה שמחתו בהגיע זמן כפרתו.

55. Boston Lecture, September 9, 1971. See the commentary adapted from R. Soloveitchik's teachings in the Orthodox Union's Yom Kippur *Mahzor,* 55. In *Darosh Darash Yosef* (Urim, 2011), 472, R. Avishai David quotes a similar formulation from R. Soloveitchik: "The Rav answered that Tishah be-Av is too bitter for sleep and Yom Kippur is too sweet for sleep."
56. The concept of *tosefet Yom ha-Kippurim* also reflects these themes. See the chapter "*Tosefet Yom Kippur*: The Lasting Impact of a Singular Day."

Chapter 13
Tosefet Yom Kippur: The Lasting Impact of a Singular Day

YOM KIPPUR AS A YOM TOV

Introduction

Each of the *mo'adim* has a dual character. On the one hand, each is a unique expression of its own theme (e.g. Pesah as *Hag ha-Matzot*). On the other hand, each *mo'ed* also fits into the generic, broader category of Yom Tov. In the Torah, this generic Yom Tov aspect is signified by the phrase "*mikra kodesh* – a holy convocation," followed by its consequence: "*Kol melekhet avodah lo ta'asu* – You shall not do any work" (*Vayikra* 23:24–25, 23:35). This is the case for every single one of the *mo'adim* with one prominent exception: Yom Kippur. Regarding Yom Kippur, the Torah consistently links "*mikra kodesh*" to a theme specific to Yom Kippur: "*Ve-initem et nafshoteikhem* – You shall afflict your souls" (ibid. 23:27).[1] Furthermore, when the Torah does mention the prohibition

1. See also *Bamidbar* 29:7.

of *melakhah* on Yom Kippur, it links it to the specific nature of the day: "*Ki Yom Kippurim hu* – For it is a Day of Atonement" (ibid. 23:28–32). Moreover, the Torah describes Yom Kippur as a day that is by definition unique, "*ahat ba-shanah* – singular in the year" (*Vayikra* 16:34).[2]

In light of the Torah's repeated emphasis of Yom Kippur's uniqueness, we must ask whether the day of Yom Kippur also encompasses a dimension of generic Yom Tov: Is it completely *sui generis*, or does it share some elements of classic Yom Tov as well?

One of the classic features of Yom Tov is a requirement to feast. Thus, one possible expression of a generic Yom Tov element in Yom Kippur could be evidence of tension between the general obligation to eat on a Yom Tov and the prohibition to eat on Yom Kippur. In rare circumstances, there could even be potential to actualize an underlying obligation to eat.

Indeed, the *Rishonim* debate whether or not a *holeh mesukan* – a person who must eat for medical reasons on Yom Kippur – is obligated in the standard trappings of a Yom Tov meal, such as *Kiddush, lehem mishneh*, and the recitation of *Ya'aleh ve-Yavo* in *Birkat ha-Mazon.*[3]

The Rambam does not address this issue. However, I believe that in light of Rambam's staunch advocacy for the uniqueness of Yom Kippur, he would rule out the possibility of reciting *Kiddush* or *Ya'aleh ve-Yavo*. The more one subscribes to the idea that Yom Kippur is truly singular, the more unlikely the prospect that Yom Kippur has an undercurrent of standard Yom Tov.

In *Mishneh Torah*, Rambam classifies Yom Kippur with its own section, after *Hilkhot Shabbat* (and *Eiruvin*), which is only afterward followed by *Hilkhot Yom Tov*. Additionally, Rambam begins *Hilkhot Yom Tov* by enumerating all of the *mo'adim* that he considers "Yom Tov," and he notably omits Yom Kippur:

2. See also *Shemot* 30:10. See the chapter "The Relationship between Yom Kippur and the Rest of the Year."
3. Rosh (cited in *Tur, Orah Hayim* 618) and *Hagahot Maimoniyot* (*Hilkhot Berakhot* 2:5) state that one must recite *Ya'aleh ve-Yavo* in this case, while Rashba (*Shu"t ha-Rashba* 1:794), *Shibbolei ha-Leket* (312), and others argue that one should not. See also *Beit Yosef, Orah Hayim* 618:10, *Shulhan Arukh* 618:10, and the commentaries there for a discussion of the various elements that would or would not apply.

> ששת ימים האלו...שהן ראשון ושביעי של פסח וראשון ושמיני של חג הסוכות וביום חג השבועות ובאחד לחדש השביעי הן הנקראין ימים טובים...
>
> These six days...namely the first and seventh days of Pesah, the first and eighth day of Sukkot, Shavu'ot, and Rosh ha-Shanah, are called "*Yamim Tovim*."[4]

Since Rambam clearly isolates Yom Kippur from the other *Yamim Tovim*, it follows that even those compelled to eat on Yom Kippur would abstain from the typical accouterments of a Yom Tov meal.

Erev Yom Kippur

One may further evaluate Yom Kippur's relationship to general Yom Tov by examining the special requirements of *erev* Yom Kippur. The *gemara* states:

> "ועניתם את נפשותיכם בתשעה," וכי בתשעה מתענין? והלא בעשירי מתענין! אלא לומר לך: כל האוכל ושותה בתשיעי - מעלה עליו הכתוב כאלו התענה תשיעי ועשירי.
>
> "And you shall afflict your souls on the ninth" (*Vayikra* 23:43) – Do we fast on the ninth? We fast on the tenth! It is [phrased this way] to teach that anyone who eats and drinks on the ninth is considered as if he fasted on both the ninth and tenth.[5]

There are several approaches to explain the phenomenon of an obligatory festive meal prior to Yom Kippur. Many *Rishonim* propose a pragmatic explanation: Preparatory eating facilitates the capacity to fast.[6] Thus, the pre-Yom Kippur feast constitutes an investment in the subsequent obligation of "*ve-initem et nafshoteikhem*," afflicting oneself.[7]

4. *Hilkhot Yom Tov* 1:1.
5. *Yoma* 81b.
6. See Ritva, *Rosh ha-Shanah* 9a, s.v. *ke-ilu hitaneh*; Rashi, *Yoma* 81b.
7. This view underscores the prominence of "*ve-initem*," as it is rare for the Torah to

However, Rabbeinu Yonah posits that the *erev* Yom Kippur meal represents an independent demand. It is actually the *se'udat Yom Tov* of Yom Kippur that was necessarily relocated in advance of the *kedushat ha-yom* only because of its absolute incompatibility with the fast that dominates and defines the day.[8] While not as acute as demanding *Kiddush* on Yom Kippur for a *holeh mesukan,* Rabbeinu Yonah's view conveys the propriety of a theoretical *se'udat Yom Kippur.*

In sharp contrast, Rambam omits any mention of the *erev* Yom Kippur *se'udah* in *Hilkhot Shevitat Asor*. Instead, he codifies this meal in *Hilkhot Nedarim,*[9] a clear indication that he views the meal as extraneous, or at least peripheral, to the Yom Kippur experience.

Tosefet Yom Tov

Tosefet Yom ha-Kippurim, a temporal expansion of the laws of sanctity on Yom Kippur, may further test the possible Yom Tov motif of Yom Kippur. Examining this principle also provides an illuminating window into the possible convergence of diverse *kedushot* (sanctities). Moreover, the

---

formalize the preparation for a mitzvah. Moreover, the formulation that declares that the feast is tantamount to extending the fast into a two-day event is particularly striking and significant, highlighting just how urgent and indispensable "*ve-initem*" is to *itzumo shel yom,* establishing the paramount goal of Yom Kippur. The extra investment and effort to secure proper compliance is evidently also a *kiyum* in *kulo la-Hashem,* the *leitmotif* of "*ve-initem.*" See the chapter "The Nature of *Innuy Nefesh* on Yom Kippur."

8. See *Sha'arei Teshuvah* 4:9. Ritva (ibid.) cites Rabbeinu Yonah, but formulates his position differently. There, he compares the *erev* Yom Kippur meal to that of Rosh ha-Shanah, which is interesting in light of the ambivalence of *simhah* on Rosh ha-Shanah. See the chapter in the next volume of this series regarding the halakhic status of Rosh ha-Shanah as a day of *simhah*. Furthermore, Rabbeinu Yonah does not actually contend that *se'udat erev Yom Kippur* is a relocated *se'udah* (similar to a *se'udah* on Rosh ha-Shanah or Yom Tov), but instead emphasizes that Yom Kippur is a day of sanctity and *simhah* deserving of a *se'udah*.

   The formulation that the feast and fast constitute an integrated *kiyum* of "*ve-initem*" ("*ke'ilu mitaneh teshi'i ve-asiri*") requires further clarification, given that the feast is Yom Tov-centered. Perhaps the fact that "*ve-initem*" allows for the Yom Tov motif, despite displacing it in practice, accentuates both the prominence and status of the fast, as well its positive, inspirational character.

9. See *Hilkhot Nedarim* 3:9.

concept of *tosefet Yom ha-Kippurim,* in addition to clarifying the Yom Tov dimension of Yom Kippur, may highlight a core theme of Yom Kippur that uniquely differentiates it from Shabbat and the other *Yamim Tovim.*

We will first address the implications for the Yom Tov component of Yom Kippur.

If Yom Kippur entails a Yom Tov aspect that is suppressed by the more dominant particular demands of Yom Kippur, why is it not possible to selectively isolate the generic Yom Tov dimension from the more specific Yom Kippur theme of "*ve-innitem*" – which precludes *Kiddush* and *se'udah,* for example – and to implement them during the period of *tosefet Yom ha-Kippurim*?[10] A derivative of this creative suggestion (in the case of Shabbat-Yom Kippur) was addressed by the *Rishonim* and elaborated upon by R. Yosef Engel.[11] This proposal is anchored in several challengeable premises, and the failure of any one of these premises would preclude its acceptance.

The idea begins with the assumption that a singular Yom Kippur includes a generic Yom Tov component, an issue that we have already demonstrated is fiercely debated by the *Rishonim* and *Posekim.* Moreover, it projects that this generic *mo'ed* motif is distinct from, and therefore theoretically separable from, the primary Yom Kippur manifestations of the day. This is not necessarily true; although the day's practical

10. On the surface, it seems that the Talmud itself addresses and resolves this question. In the context of examining the requirement of *birkat ha-zeman* (*Sheheheyanu*) on Yom Kippur, the *gemara* (*Eiruvin* 40b) explicitly excludes the possibility that one could articulate *birkat ha-zeman* in conjunction with drinking wine, by virtue of the fact that "כיון דאמר זמן...ואסר ליה." Once one has recited the *berakhah,* thereby sanctifying the day, the *tosefet kedushah* already triggers the full complement of "*ve-initem*" restrictions of Yom Kippur, precluding any kind of drink. However, it should be noted that the Talmud is not discussing the potential of separating the diverse generic Yom Tov and Yom Kippur requirements, but is focusing on *Kiddush* of Yom Kippur, which specifically addresses the singular sanctity of Yom Kippur itself. This leaves open the question of the separation of two distinct *kedushot* or mitzvot. R. Yosef Engel (*Eiruvin* ad loc.) understood that Roke'ah (214) invokes this *gemara* to prove that the convergence of Yom Kippur and Shabbat cannot be separated by *tosefet Shabbat. Tanya Rabbati* (78) also excludes the splitting of *tosefet Shabbat* from *tosefet Yom Kippur,* although on more technical grounds.
11. See *Gilyonei ha-Shas, Yoma* 81b, *Eiruvin* 40b.

expressions are mostly suppressed or eclipsed by the more dominant demands of "*ve-initem*" and the theme of *kulo la-Hashem*, it is entirely conceivable that the Yom Tov dimension is holistically integrated into the very fabric of Yom Kippur. The undercurrent of *simhat ha-mo'ed* or *kedushat ha-mo'ed* may in fact be an indispensable linchpin for Yom Kippur's special *kiyumim* and *kedushah*. The fact that their classic manifestations are overridden on Yom Kippur may further constitute a vital aspect and acute expression of Yom Kippur's unique character, *kedushah*, and *itzumo shel yom*.[12]

In addition, the suggestion that one might accomplish or fulfill the classic Yom Tov requirements of Yom Kippur, unfettered by the counter-pressure of *innuy nefesh*, by initially employing *tosefet Yom Kippur* selectively to allow expression of the Yom Tov obligations posits that *tosefet kedushah* is not a holistic, integrated temporal extension, but rather a category that can be flexibly and discretely applied.

This proposition demands a brief analysis of the broader scope and character of *tosefet Yom Tov*.[13] Most authorities agree that *tosefet Yom Tov/Shabbat* does not fully revise time by altering the calendar date (vis-à-vis issues distinct from initiating the sanctified period in question) or advancing the onset of nighttime.[14] However, there is significant debate regarding whether it merely advances halakhic obligations and imposes

12. One might speculate that the singular *kedushat ha-yom* of "*itzumo shel yom shemekhaper*," which underpins the day and the concept of time on Yom Kippur, itself is manifest by defying the canons of time, bursting out of the confines of a twenty-four-hour day.

13. This is an extensive topic that demands more comprehensive treatment, but for our present purposes, it is sufficient to highlight and survey several of the issues.

14. Thus, one cannot recite *Keri'at Shema* yet, despite having accepted the *kedushah* of the next day. However, one can recite *Ma'ariv* of the festival or Shabbat, since it is linked to the *kedushat ha-yom*. This point is underscored by Maharshal in his responsa (13, 68), in which he explores the scope of *tosefet Shabbat* with regard to *sefirat ha-omer* and Shemini Atzeret. We will examine his view below. It is noteworthy that *Taz* (*Orah Hayim* 668:1) concedes this conclusion, but dismisses its relevance to their debate. See also *Berakhot* 27a–b regarding advancing *Ma'ariv* of Shabbat and *motza'ei* Shabbat, as well as *Kiddush* and *Havdalah*. As the *Aharonim* note, the applications to *motza'ei* Shabbat suggest that the advanced recitations are unrelated to a true shift in halakhic time, since Shabbat cannot be constricted. (See, however,

prohibitions or actually initiates the *mo'ed* period and constitutes sanctified time that fully integrates with the authentic onset of the *yom kodesh*. If we view *tosefet kedushah* as the halakhic advancement of sanctified time, that precludes a piecemeal application to individual applications or *mitzvot* that derive from the same *kedushat ha-zeman*.

We may further speculate as to whether two coinciding or converging *kedushot ha-yom* may be separated with respect to *tosefet kedushah*. In addition to the question of the interrelation of the two *kedushot* (how coincidental, mutually dependent, or enhancing they are), the possibility of separating *kedushot* would depend on the extent to which the halakhic calendar day has been initiated. If we are ushering in a new halakhic day, it would be inconsistent to do so only selectively.

On the other hand, the view that *tosefet Yom Tov* focuses on advancing obligations and prohibitions but does not purport to advance the clock or the calendar may justify applying a more specific and discrete *tosefet kedushah*. This might allow discriminating even among *mitzvot* and prohibitions engendered by a single *kedushat ha-yom* (as some *Aharonim* speculate), and it certainly lends credence to the idea of separating independent, albeit converging, *kedushot ha-yom*.[15]

Shevut Yaakov, Orah Hayim 8, and the critique of *Gilyonei ha-Shas, Berakhot* 27a.) Nevertheless, this does not preclude the prominent normative position that *tosefet Shabbat* or *Yom Tov* is an authentic temporal expansion.

The inability to advance *mitzvot* that are contingent upon "nighttime" may also dictate that the mitzvah of eating *matzah*, and possibly other expressions related to *sippur yetzi'at Mitzrayim*, cannot be accomplished before dark. See Tosafot, *Pesahim* 99b, s.v. *mi-sheteheshakh*, and Rosh, *Berakhot* 4:6. Some commentators perceive this issue in the Haggadah's exclusion of "*yakhol mi-be'od yom*."

As for the relationship between the periods of *tosefet kedushah* and *bein ha-shemashot*, see *Teshuvot Hakham Tzvi*, no. 11, and the rejoinder of *Gilyonei ha-Shas, Berakhot* 27a.

15. There is perhaps still room to distinguish coincidental (Shabbat-Yom Kippur) and definitional (Yom Tov-Yom Kippur) convergences. Moreover, *kedushat Shabbat* is also not intrinsically linked to the change in calendar date.

The status of Tishah be-Av is intriguing. See *Pesahim* 54a–b, where the Talmud weighs the day's relationship with Yom Kippur, and regarding which the authorities debate if there is a full prohibition already at *bein ha-shemashot* and even a concept of *tosefet* derived from Yom Kippur, notwithstanding the absence of *kedushat ha-yom*.

Netziv was asked (*Meishiv Davar* 2:73) if *tosefet Yom Tov* qualifies as Yom Tov with

Some of these issues are encapsulated in a wide-ranging, impassioned debate between *Taz* and Maharshal, although they are already implicit in earlier discussions of *tosefet kedushah* and are explored further in subsequent investigations of this theme.

Maharshal asserts that one should not apply *tosefet Yom Tov* to Shemini Atzeret, as doing so would trigger a halakhic paradox: One would have to make a blessing of "*leishev ba-sukkah*" on Shemini Atzeret, since it is still technically Sukkot![16] While Maharshal does not propose a selective application of *kedushat ha-zeman* that distinguishes different manifestations that typically stem from a single *kedushat ha-yom*, he does assume that the *kedushat ha-yom* of two different days and festivals (Sukkot and Shemini Atzeret) can theoretically coexist, although this paradox may prove halakhically intolerable. The anticipation and early initiation of *tosefet kedushah* apparently cannot banish the previous *kedushat ha-yom* or its halakhic expressions. Thus, Maharshal certainly does not perceive *tosefet kedushah* as altering the calendar even vis-à-vis *kedushat ha-yom*, certainly not at the expense of a prevailing *kedushah* identity.

One might distinguish between this singular confluence of Shemini Atzeret and Sukkot and ushering in a *tosefet* that operates in the absence of a competing *kedushah*. However, Maharshal's presentation militates against this distinction. The fact that Maharshal's view of *tosefet kedushah* does not focus on the full early onset of the next day does not necessarily dictate that *tosefet* is limited to the implementation of *mitzvot* and the imposition of *issurim*, and is therefore possibly conducive to a discrete application of *tosefet kedushah*. However, by precluding the

---

respect to *aveilut* – if being informed of a loss during that time frame postpones or enables the subsequent onset of full calendrical Yom Tov to negate the *shivah*. He notes that according to Rambam, *tosefet Yom Tov* is apparently restricted to Yom Kippur alone. Primarily, however, he weighs whether *tosefet* applies selectively – if it applies only to abstaining from *melakhah* or if it extends also to *simhat Yom Tov*, the determining factor for *aveilut*. Although Netziv ignores it, Tosafot (*Ketubot* 47a, s.v. *di-massar*) registers two views on the status of *simhat Yom Tov* during the *tosefet* period. The issue involves getting married during *tosefet Yom Tov*, given the consideration of "*ein me'arvin simhah be-simhah*."

16. *Maharshal*, responsa 68.

more holistic notion of *tosefet Yom Tov,* Maharshal's position opens the door to such an approach.

In contrast to *Maharshal, Taz* argues that *tosefet* triggers the next calendar day of *kedushah,* prematurely terminating the Sukkot holiday.[17] It is unlikely that *Taz,* who advocates for a *tosefet Yom Tov* that revises the calendar even at the expense of the prevailing *kedushat ha-yom,* would countenance any selective employment of *tosefet Yom Tov.*

R. Yosef Engel, addressing the possibility of a selective *tosefet kedushah,* invokes the confluence of Shabbat and Yom Kippur to demonstrate the need for a comprehensive, consistent, and integrated *tosefet kedushah.*[18] He argues that the fact that we do not counsel the prior initiation of Shabbat in order to fulfill *oneg Shabbat* in advance of the onset of Yom Kippur and the "*ve-initem*" requirement is incompatible with a more artificial and discrete posture regarding *tosefet kedushah.* Certainly, he would have even more vehemently objected to the proposition that one could possibly divide Yom Kippur's own generic Yom Tov component from its primary particularistic theme.

With respect to the coincidence of Yom Kippur and Shabbat, it is noteworthy that R. Yosef Engel assumes that discrete *kedushot* retain their independent character even when they converge with one another. Thus, the *kedushat ha-yom* of Shabbat triggers its typical demand of *oneg Shabbat,* albeit one that cannot be realized in practice, even when it coincides with Yom Kippur. R. Engel does not consider the possibility that a confluence of different *kedushot* generates a revised, integrated, and enhanced status that transcends the sum of its parts.

This may be true generally; it also may be contingent upon the particular *kedushot* that intersect and therefore interact. This phenomenon is exemplified by some discussions regarding the proper formula to convey, and possibly identify, the convergence of Shabbat-Yom Tov.[19] In the *nussah ha-tefillah* on Shabbat, we typically conclude the middle

17. *Taz, Orah Hayim* 668:1. As noted previously, *Taz* adds that this only changes the calendar day; the status of day and night remains unaffected, and therefore one must still repeat *Keri'at Shema* during the nighttime.

18. *Gilyonei ha-Shas, Yoma* 81a.

19. For another example of integrated *kedushot,* see the chapter in the next volume of this series discussing Rosh ha-Shanah's special relationship with Rosh Hodesh.

berakhah with "*mekadesh ha-Shabbat* – He who sanctifies Shabbat." On Yom Tov, we employ the phrase "*mekadesh Yisrael ve-hazemanim* – He who sanctifies Israel and the times." The Talmud explains that the distinctive *hatimot* (conclusions) reflect two different emphases and orientations of the respective *yemei kedushah*. Whereas *kedushat ha-Shabbat* has been fixed from the onset of creation ("*kavi'a ve-kayma mi-sheshet yemei bereishit*"), *Klal Yisrael* plays a vital role in sanctifying Yom Tov, by means of *kiddush ha-hodesh*. Given this premise, the *gemara* explores the appropriate terminology when Shabbat and Yom Tov coincide:

> תני תנא קמיה דרבינא: מקדש ישראל והשבת והזמנים. אמר ליה: אטו שבת ישראל מקדשי ליה? והא שבת מקדשא וקיימא! אלא אימא: מקדש השבת ישראל והזמנים.
>
> A teacher of *beraitot* taught before Ravina: [When Shabbat and Yom Tov coincide, we conclude the *berakhah* with] "*mekadesh Yisrael ve-haShabbat ve-hazemanim* – He who sanctifies Israel, and Shabbat, and the times." [Ravina] responded to him: Does Israel sanctify Shabbat? The *kedushah* of Shabbat is automatic! [It is therefore incorrect to mention Israel before Shabbat in the *berakhah*'s conclusion.] Rather, formulate it as: "*mekadesh ha-Shabbat Yisrael ve-hazemanim* – He who sanctifies Shabbat, Israel, and the times."[20]

Ravina's argument is so compelling that most commentators dismiss the original suggestion as simply an error. However, Netziv ascribes significance to the tentative perspective:

> קשה לי להאי תנא דלית ליה סברא דשבת מקדשא וקיימא, א"כ נימא בכל שבת מקדש ישראל והשבת, ומאי איריא דוקא בשבת שחל ביו"ט. ונראה עפ"י הא דאי' בזבחים דף צ"א א' דקדושת מועד מהני גם על שבת, ועיין שם ברש"י ז"ל בד"ה מוספי כו'. אם כן מבואר דמיתוסף מקדושת יום טוב על קדושת השבת, ומשו"ה ס"ל דשייך לברך מקדש

20. *Beitzah* 17a.

ישראל והשבת והזמנים [מצד ההוספה], משא"כ בכל שבתות. ואנן לא קיי"ל הכי, אלא שאין לברך על הוספה זו, רק על עיקר קדושת השבת:

I find this difficult, as according to the *beraita*'s view that does not apply the logic that *kedushat Shabbat* is automatic, we should recite "*mekadesh Yisrael ve-haShabbat* – He who sanctifies Israel and Shabbat," on every Shabbat. Why specifically when Shabbat and Yom Tov coincide [do we include "Israel" in the *berakhah*]? It seems that (as we see in the *gemara* in *Zevahim* 91a and Rashi ad loc.), the *kedushah* of Yom Tov impacts Shabbat as well. Thus, some of *kedushat Yom Tov* is integrated into *kedushat Shabbat*, and it consequently is appropriate to recite "*mekadesh Yisrael ve-haShabbat ve-hazemanim* – He who sanctifies Israel, and Shabbat, and the times" (due to this addition), while this is not the case on every other Shabbat. This is not our practice; rather we do not make a *berakhah* on the addition, but only on the main *kedushat Shabbat*.[21]

Netziv supports this principle of spiritual convergence by citing the *gemara* in *Zevahim*, which discusses the changed status of *korbanot* when special days converge. This buttresses his contention that when two days of *kedushah* coincide, they also somewhat integrate.[22] We do not relate to the convergence of Shabbat and Yom Tov as a calendrical coincidence; rather, we ascribe to it a status of an integrated Shabbat-Yom Tov, with each aspect impacting the other. Since the input of *Klal Yisrael* (through *kiddush ha-hodesh*) is a precondition for Shabbat-Yom

21. *Meromei Sadeh, Beitzah* 17a.

22. The *gemara* (*Zevahim* 91a) declares that the ubiquitous daily *korban tamid* assumes the elevated sanctified status equal to that of a Shabbat *korban mussaf* by virtue of the fact that it is offered on Shabbat: "אטו שבת למוספין אהני לתמידין לא אהני." The same principle redefines the stature of other convergent *korbanot* – the *mussaf* of Rosh Hodesh and Shabbat, as well as the *mussaf* of Rosh Hodesh and Rosh ha-Shanah. Netziv's specific insight would be better demonstrated by a confluence of Shabbat and *mo'ed*. It is noteworthy that he does emphasize the convergence of Shabbat and *mo'ed*, technically absent in the *gemara*, by subtly invoking Rashi's emphasis that *mussaf Rosh Hodesh* is officially defined as a *mo'ed korban*.

Tov to occur, it is valid to posit that it would be appropriate to recite "*mekadesh Yisrael ve-haShabbat ve-hazemanim.*" Although our normative practice rejects this specific conclusion, Netziv emphasizes that we still embrace the principle that the sanctities of Shabbat and Yom Tov are mutually enhancing. This remains a cogent concept despite the fact that the *hatimat ha-berakhah* of this joint convergent *kedushah* emphasizes the absolute stability and divine anchor of Shabbat.[23]

In the same vein, Shabbat and Yom Kippur may coalesce into a convergent *kedushat ha-yom,* thereby rendering it impossible to split the *tosefet kedushah* of *kedushat Shabbat* and *kedushat Yom Kippur.*[24]

---

23. The concept of the convergence of *kedushat ha-zeman* is further supported by the *gemara* (*Eiruvin* 38a; *Beitzah* 4a), which records a debate about the status of consecutive days of *kedushah* – Shabbat followed by Yom Tov or vice versa (*kedushah ahat* or *shetei kedushot*). The notion that contiguity or an extended, uninterrupted period of *kedushah* per se is halakhically consequential and integrative with respect to *nolad* ("*beitzah she-noldah ba-zeh assurah ba-zeh*"), *eiruvei tehumin,* and other issues presupposes a broader principle of *kedushah ahat.* This *kedushah* is likely even more intensely manifest when the respective *kedushot* actually coincide. See Rashi, Responsa 103:2, who upholds this ruling. Although the preponderant Rabbinic consensus rules against the view of *kedushah ahat,* it remains plausible that this principle prevails when the *kedushot* are simultaneous rather than consecutive.

24. Another context that exemplifies this phenomenon is the confluence of Rosh Hodesh and Shabbat. As one is not obligated to eat a meal with bread on Rosh Hodesh, one who omits *Ya'aleh ve-Yavo* need not repeat *Birkat ha-Mazon* (*Berakhot* 49a). On Shabbat or Yom Tov, however, the obligatory meal dictates that one must repeat *Birkat ha-Mazon* if he omitted *Retzeh* or *Ya'aleh ve-Yavo*. What if one forgets *Ya'aleh ve-Yavo* (but not *Retzeh*) on Shabbat-Rosh Hodesh? According to most *Posekim,* the absence of the Rosh Hodesh addition does not mandate a repetition of *Birkat ha-Mazon.* According to some *Rishonim* (cited by Meiri, *Berakhot* 49b), however, one should repeat *Birkat ha-Mazon* in this scenario. One possible explanation revolves around the principle adduced from *Zevahim* 91a. If the convergence of Shabbat and Rosh Hodesh is not a calendrical coincidence, but rather an opportunity to integrate the themes of Shabbat and Rosh Hodesh into more than the sum of its parts, the Shabbat meal, which necessitates the bread, assumes the status of a Shabbat-Rosh Hodesh repast. *Ya'aleh ve-Yavo* defines this obligatory festive meal almost as much as *Retzeh* does, notwithstanding the fact that it is the Shabbat motif that elevates the standards.

    There are numerous halakhic issues brought about by the confluence of Shabbat and Rosh Hodesh. As mentioned in our previous discussion of *Zevahim* 91a, Rosh Hodesh-Shabbat is one of the explicit applications of the convergence principle. The

Shabbat Shabbaton: The Special Bond Between Yom Kippur and Shabbat

Indeed, the fact that the Torah designates Yom Kippur as "*Shabbat Shabbaton*" (*Vayikra* 23:32) increases the prospect that these two overlapping *kedushot* may be particularly amenable to blend together in a halakhically consequential way that is mutually transformative, further precluding any discrete application of *tosefet kedushah*. We will briefly sample some of the numerous links between Yom Kippur and Shabbat to further substantiate the idea that their respective *kedushot* are particularly conducive, and even compatible, to spiritual convergence.

The special bond between Yom Kippur and Shabbat is ubiquitous.[25] Like Shabbat, Yom Kippur is the only *mo'ed* that has the full complement of *issur melakhah*; there is no exclusion of *melekhet okhel nefesh*. While some attribute the absence of the *heter okhel nefesh* on Yom Kippur to the practical implications of "*ve-initem et nafshoteikhem*,"[26] others perceive that the expansive *issur melakhah* stems from Yom Kippur's *kedushat ha-yom* and its character as *Shabbat Shabbaton*.[27] In any case, the affinity between Shabbat and Yom Kippur regarding the very issue that the *mishnah* identifies as the distinguishing factor between Shabbat and Yom Tov – "*Ein bein Yom Tov le-Shabbat ela okhel nefesh*

---

fact that this convergence draws upon two sources of temporal sanctity – Shabbat, *tehilah le-mikra'ei kodesh*," and Rosh Hodesh, "*asher tikre'u otam be-mo'adam*" – has numerous halakhic expressions and implications, which I hope to address elsewhere.

25. This issue is explored at length in the chapter "Yom Kippur: The Quintessential Shabbat." Additional parallel questions include whether it is necessary to use a *ner she-shavat* on *motza'ei* Shabbat-Yom Kippur and the status of *hadlakat neirot* for Shabbat-Yom Kippur. There are a variety of views regarding these practices, some of which are particular to the character and requirements of the specific application, but some of which also reflect the broader convergence theme.
26. See *Sha'agat Aryeh* 102, who bases the permissibility of *melekhet okhel nefesh* on the mitzvah of *simhat Yom Tov*. See also Netziv, *Ha'amek Davar*, *Vayikra* 23:27.
27. See Ramban, *Vayikra* 23:7, and *Sefer ha-Manhig* (*Hilkhot Rosh ha-Shanah* 1). This perspective is likely informed by Yom Kippur's special status of *Shabbat Shabbaton* and the conceptual implications of the mitzvah of "*ve-initem*," as we have developed in the chapter "The Nature of *Innuy Nefesh* on Yom Kippur."

bilvad"[28] – is likely a defining factor in both *kedushat Yom ha-Kippurim* and *kedushat Shabbat.*[29]

It is noteworthy that the *mishnah* asserts that the only distinction between the two epic manifestations of *kedushat ha-yom, kedushat Shabbat* and *kedushat Yom ha-Kippurim,* is the severity of the penalty for violation (*sekilah* vs. *karet*).[30] Moreover, like Shabbat, and in sharp contrast to the other festivals, abstaining from *melakhah* constitutes an inherent facet of Yom Kippur's sanctified status. As noted above, the Torah connects the prohibition of *melakhah* on Yom Kippur to the core identity of the day and to its other primary motif, "*ve-initem,*" in contrast to the other *mo'adim,* where it stems from the generic status of *mikra kodesh.* The Talmud cites the view of R. Akiva that even though the Halakhah generally adopts the principle of "*ein issur hal al issur*" (one prohibition does not apply on top of an earlier prohibition), this principle does not apply when Yom Kippur coincides with Shabbat.[31] Thus, one who accidentally violated a *melakhah* on Shabbat-Yom Kippur brings two separate *korbanot hatat.* Ramban suggests the following explanation:

> טעמיה דר' עקיבא הכא משום דשבת ויום הכפורים איסור אחד הוא ותרוייהו שבת מיקרו ושבתון כתיב בהו.
>
> R. Akiva's reasoning here is that Shabbat and Yom Kippur are one prohibition; they are both called "Shabbat" and are depicted as "*Shabbaton.*" [Hence, one violation does not preclude the other.][32]

Similarly, Rambam rules that while typically consecutive days of distinct *kedushot ha-zeman* are treated as "*shetei kedushot,*" as independent rather than as integrated *kedushot,* this is not true regarding Shabbat and Yom

28. *Megillah* 7b.
29. The apparently outsized importance of *ner she-shavat,* which underscores the prohibition of even *melekhet okhel nefesh* of Yom Kippur in the context of the termination of its *kedushat ha-yom* (*Havdalah*), accentuates this point.
30. *Megillah* 7b.
31. *Hullin* 101b.
32. *Hiddushei ha-Ramban, Hullin* 101b, s.v. *ve-Rabbi Yosse ha-Gelili.*

Kippur, which establish a single consecutive period of sanctity, at least with respect to *eiruvei tehumin*:

> יום הכפורים שחל להיות ערב שבת או לאחר שבת בזמן שמקדשין על פי הראיה יראה לי שהן כיום אחד וקדושה אחת הם.
>
> If Yom Kippur fell on the day before Shabbat or the day after Shabbat during the time period when the months were sanctified according to witnesses' testimony [and this arrangement was thus a calendrical possibility], it seems to me that they are like one day, and they comprise one holy period.[33]

Rambam's insertion of the phrase "*yeira'eh li* – it appears to me" is noteworthy, as it reflects his acknowledgment that his conclusion is unsourced. It derives from his broader halakhic conviction based upon his comprehensive understanding of the character of *kedushat Shabbat, kedushat Yom ha-Kippurim,* and their interaction. This analysis further affirms Rambam's editorial/organizational decision to classify *Hilkhot Shevitat Asor* immediately following *Hilkhot Shabbat* and *Eiruvin,* prior to and separate from *Hilkhot Yom Tov*. His omission of Yom ha-Kippurim from the list of *Yamim Tovim* is consistent with this posture.[34]

Furthermore, Rambam rules that on Shabbat-Yom Kippur, the *Kohen Gadol* is personally obligated to preside over the *mussaf* of Shabbat along with all the *korbanot* of Yom Kippur.[35] Here too, Rambam's conclusion appears unsourced, informed perhaps by his already established conviction that when the two days coincide, Shabbat fully integrates with Yom Kippur. Thus, the Shabbat *korbanot* become integrated as Yom Kippur sacrifices, all of which require the exclusive ministration of the *Kohen Gadol.*[36]

33. *Hilkhot Eiruvin* 8:10.
34. *Hilkhot Yom Tov* 1:2.
35. *Avodat Yom ha-Kippurim* 1:2.
36. Based on Rambam, *Or Samei'ah* (*Hilkhot Avodat Yom ha-Kippurim* 4:1) rules that a *holeh mesukan* who must eat on Shabbat-Yom Kippur would still not recite the *Kiddush* of Shabbat. He concludes that all overlapping *kedushot* enhance one another and integrate, invoking the previously noted *gemara* in *Zevahim* 91a without qualify-

In any case, the fact that *kedushat Yom Kippur* is particularly proximate to *kedushat Shabbat* further disputes the notion that one might selectively apply *tosefet kedushah* only to *kedushat Shabbat* when it coincides with Yom Kippur, even if such selectivity were possible from the general perspective of *tosefet kedushah.*

The proposition discussed by R. Yaakov Engel and others to employ *tosefet Yom ha-Kippurim* in order to achieve coinciding Shabbat or generic Yom Tov *se'udot* or in order to accomplish other *kiyumim* thus emerges as untenable on multiple grounds.

TOSEFET YOM KIPPUR

Tosefet Yom Kippur vs. *Tosefet Shabbat* and *Yom Tov*

We began our analysis by focusing on the distinctive *kedushat ha-yom* of Yom Kippur, which distinguishes it from all the other *mo'adim*. We introduced the principle of *tosefet kedushah* as part of our exploration of the scope of Yom Kippur's uniqueness, endeavoring to discern whether Yom Kippur includes a generic Yom Tov component at all, whether it can be isolated from the primary identity of *itzumo shel yom/"ve-innitem,"* and how the conjunction of Shabbat and Yom Kippur reflects these core questions. We will now turn our attention to the source and scope of *tosefet kedushah* to determine whether the singular *kedushat ha-yom* of Yom Kippur is expressed in this application as well.

In our previous discussion, we assumed that the institution and character of *tosefet kedushah* is itself generic and equally applicable to all types of *kedushat ha-yom*. However, perhaps *tosefet Yom Kippur* is unique, a manifestation of the singular *kedushat ha-yom* of Yom Kippur itself.

---

ing the interrelationship of different *kedushot ha-yom*. However, it is possible that Rambam's innovative ruling reflects the specifically unique relationship between Shabbat and Yom Kippur.

There are two other possible explanations of Rambam's innovative conclusion relating to the role of the *Kohen Gadol* on Yom Kippur and the interrelationship between *temidim* and *mussafim* on Shabbat. These are addressed in the chapter "Yom Kippur: The Day of the *Kohen Gadol*."

The *gemara* in *Yoma* provides the source for the concept of *tosefet kedushah*:

> ועניתם את נפשתיכם בתשעה לחדש, יכול יתחיל ויתענה בתשעה - תלמוד לומר בערב. אי בערב - יכול משתחשך - תלמוד לומר בתשעה. הא כיצד? מתחיל ומתענה מבעוד יום. מכאן שמוסיפין מחול על הקודש. ואין לי אלא בכניסתו, ביציאתו מנין? תלמוד לומר מערב עד ערב. ואין לי אלא יום הכפורים, שבתות מניין?...ימים טובים מנין?...כל מקום שנאמר שבות - מוסיפין מחול על הקודש.
>
> "And you shall afflict your spirit on the ninth of the month" (*Vayikra* 23:32) – This might imply that one must fast on the ninth; the Torah therefore adds, "at night." You might then have thought only after nightfall [the tenth]; the Torah therefore states, "on the ninth." How can this be? One must begin the fast while it is still day. From here we learn that we add from the mundane onto the holy [day]. So far, we only know [that this must be done] at its inception; from where do we know at its conclusion? The Torah therefore states, "from evening until evening." Heretofore, we know [that this is so] only regarding Yom Kippur; how do we know Shabbat...how do we know Yom Tov?... In every context in which the Torah refers to "rest," we add from the mundane to the holy.[37]

It is striking that *tosefet kedushah* is explicitly derived and specifically applied only with respect to Yom Kippur. Only then, *qua* the generic concept of *shevut,* is it extended to encompass *tosefet Shabbat* and *tosefet Yom Tov* as well.

Rambam further accentuates the special link to Yom Kippur, as he astoundingly records *tosefet kedushah* exclusively in connection with Yom Kippur. In fact, he explicates *tosefet kedushah* only with regard to the *innuyim* of Yom Kippur:

37. *Yoma* 81b.

כשם ששבות מלאכה בו בין ביום בין בלילה כך שבות לעינוי בין ביום בין בלילה, וצריך להוסיף מחול על הקדש בכניסתו וביציאתו שנאמר ועניתם את נפשותיכם בתשעה לחדש בערב, כלומר התחיל לצום ולהתענות מערב תשעה הסמוך לעשירי, וכן ביציאה שוהה בעינויו מעט מלילי אחד עשר סמוך לעשירי שנאמר מערב עד ערב תשבתו שבתכם.

> Just as one is required to rest from *melakhah* [on Yom Kippur] both during the day and night, so too, "resting" regarding affliction applies both during the day and night. Additionally, one must add from the mundane to the sacred both at the onset and conclusion [of Yom Kippur], as the *pasuk* states, "And you shall afflict your souls on the ninth of the month in the evening" – meaning: Begin to fast and afflict yourself from the evening of the night close to the onset of the tenth. Similarly, at the conclusion [of Yom Kippur], one must continue the affliction slightly into the eleventh close to the tenth, as the *pasuk* states, "From evening to evening you shall rest."[38]

The commentators on *Mishneh Torah* struggle to explain how Rambam's striking omissions cohere with the *sugya* in *Yoma,* which seems to ultimately extend *tosefet* to include *melekhet Yom ha-Kippurim,* as well as *kedushat Shabbat* and *Yom Tov.*[39] They debate if Rambam actually excludes *tosefet* either from *melekhet Yom ha-Kippurim* or *kedushat Shabbat* and *Yom Tov,* or if he simply emphasizes the more classic and acute instantiation of this institution. Regardless of how the problem is resolved, it seems certain that Rambam's controversial view, or at least his emphasis, derives from his broader understanding of the unique nature of Yom Kippur, as previously developed. Indeed, even according to the consensus halakhic position that applies *tosefet kedushah* to Shabbat and Yom Tov as well, it remains noteworthy that the explicit and core source for all *tosefet kedushah* is Yom Kippur.

38. *Hilkhot Shevitat Asor* 1:6.
39. See, for example, the commentary of *Maggid Mishneh,* ad loc.

Importantly, the *gemara* in *Beitzah* assumes as self-evident that women are obligated in *tosefet Yom Kippur*.[40] *Pri Megadim* contends that the Yom Kippur obligation, which also extends to women, by definition entails *tosefet* as well.[41] Implicitly, *Pri Megadim* is arguing that *tosefet innuy* is a fundamental and inseparable part of Yom Kippur.[42] However, *Pri Megadim* does not justify or even explicate this underlying assumption. Why is *tosefet* such an integral part of Yom Kippur?

"*Ve-Initem et Nafshoteikhem*"

The answer lies in the Torah's formulation of the mitzvah of "*ve-initem et nafshoteikhem* – and you shall afflict your souls."[43] The *gemara* is troubled by the Torah's positive formulation of the obligation to fast on Yom Kippur.[44] Since the mitzvah of "*ve-initem*" constitutes a severe prohibition that dictates abstaining from eating and drinking,[45] shouldn't the Torah have described *innuy nefesh* in negative terms?[46] The *gemara* ultimately leaves the question unanswered. Moreover, given the positive nature of the command, the *gemara* even requires a *derashah* to preclude an obligation to physically afflict oneself.[47] Thus, although "*ve-initem*" is halakhically applied in a manner that is physically passive, it is fundamentally a positive commandment. It is not merely that there is a prohibition to

40. *Beitzah* 30a.
41. *Pri Megadim, Mishbetzot Zahav, Orah Hayim* 608:1.
42. Additionally, *Pri Megadim* notes (*Eshel Avraham, Orah Hayim* 608, s.v. *tosefet*) that even if we apply *tosefet kedushah* to both *innuy* and *melakhah,* the additional *issur melakhah* would only attain the status of "*issura be-alma min ha-Torah,*" while *innuy* would be a genuine "*issur aseh meforash.*" This again reflects the significance *Pri Megadim* attributes to *tosefet Yom Kippur* as an expression particularly of "*ve-initem et nafshoteikhem.*"

    It is interesting to compare this question to the controversial issue of women's obligation in the feast of *erev* Yom Kippur. Is *tosefet Yom ha-Kippurim* more integrative and more of a core expression, technically or conceptually, of "*ve-initem*"?
43. For an extensive analysis of this mitzvah, see the chapter "The Nature of *Innuy Nefesh* on Yom Kippur."
44. *Yoma* 81a.
45. See the *gemara*, ibid., and *Hilkhot Shevitat Asor* 1:1–2.
46. The *gemara* further notes that the positive formulation is particularly unusual given the punishment of *karet* entailed.
47. *Yoma* 74b.

eat and drink on Yom Kippur; rather, Yom Kippur is a time when we embrace spirituality and immerse ourselves in a challenge of "*ve-initem et nafshoteikhem*." It is a day on which we imitate the angels and partake in the inspirational paradigm and experience of *kulo la-Hashem*. Abstinence from physicality is an important facet of creating that environment.

We can now appreciate the core contribution of *tosefet kedushah* specifically on Yom Kippur, and especially as applied to the theme of *tosefet* to "*ve-initem*" according to Rambam's view. By initiating the fast early and extending it after nightfall on *motza'ei* Yom Kippur, *tosefet Yom ha-Kippurim* transforms passive abstinence into an action and *kiyum* of "*ve-initem et nafshoteikhem*." Furthermore, the expansion and early initiation triggered by *tosefet Yom ha-Kippurim* underscores that we do not perceive Yom Kippur as oppressive, albeit necessary, but rather view it as an extraordinary spiritual opportunity to be enthusiastically anticipated and embraced.

These themes may be further emphasized by the *erev* Yom Kippur feast discussed above. The pre-fast feast and the fast-expansion are superficially antithetical phenomena. Upon reflection, however, they also significantly overlap and even emerge as parallel institutions in many respects. We invest in the facilitation of the fast, and we inject motifs and a spirit of Yom Tov, including joy and confidence, alongside "*ve-initem et nafshoteikhem*." And we further create a sharp and abrupt transition from obligatory feast to early fast, which gives concrete definition to an otherwise amorphous passive process of abstention from physicality. Thus, the pre-Yom Kippur feast provides an effective framework for *tosefet innuy* and the *kiyum* of "*ve-initem et nafshoteikhem*."

Yom Kippur and the Rest of the Year

Additionally, *tosefet Yom Kippur* reflects the idea that we must prepare for Yom Kippur and that Yom Kippur's impact must extend throughout the rest of the year.[48] Yom Kippur is a day of contrasts and elemental stark choices that establish our authentic spiritual credentials and our

48. On other *mo'adim*, there is an obligation of *linah*, to remain in Yerushalayim the night after the conclusion of the festival. However (according to Rambam), only Yom Kippur has full-fledged *tosefet*, through which Yom Kippur itself continues.

core identity as beings created *be-tzelem Elokim*. Yom Kippur presents us with mutually exclusive paradigms and options, forcing us to choose between the goat offered inside the Holy of Holies and the goat banished to *Azazel*. On Yom Kippur, we are provided with the opportunity to demonstrate our absolute devotion and loyalty to Hashem. Through the vehicles of *innuy, tefillah,* and *teshuvah,* we are inspired to cultivate the persona and atmosphere of *kulo la-Hashem* on a level that is superior to that of the angels.

Tosefet kedushah, the literal expansion of Yom Kippur into a pre- and post-Yom Kippur reality, is the ultimate symbol of this crucial dialectic.[49] The *Aseret Yemei Teshuvah* are a buildup to Yom Kippur; immediately after Yom Kippur, we initiate the construction of the *sukkah* as a manifestation of the concrete and tangible impact of Yom Kippur on the rest of the year. Yom Kippur impacts upon the other *mo'adim* as well. Precisely because it reflects our capacity for and celebration of the ideal *kulo la-Hashem,* it also validates the balance and the nuance of the other *mo'adim*. The *kulo la-Hashem* of Yom Kippur reflects that the "*hetzyo la-Hashem ve-hetzyo lakhem*" of the other *mo'adim* and the rest of the year is a legitimate and principled position, rather than a tepid compromise. *Tosefet Yom ha-Kippurim* is so integral to Yom Kippur, as *Pri Megadim* argued, precisely because the extension of Yom Kippur into the rest of the year accurately encapsulates Yom Kippur's very character and telos.[50]

---

49. Yom Kippur does not entail the usual requirement of teaching its *halakhot* thirty days in advance. Maharsha (*Hiddushei Aggadot, Megillah* 32a) explains that we do so only on days that stand apart from the rest of the year. Since Rosh ha-Shanah and Yom Kippur embody themes of the whole year, they do not need to be reintroduced.
50. *Tosefet Yom ha-Kippurim* also emphasizes the important role of Judaism's perception of time in *teshuvah*. As I have explored at length in the chapter "*Ani le-Dodi ve-Dodi Li*: The Relationship Between Hashem and the Jewish People," Judaism has a unique notion of time and believes in the merging of past, present, and future. This notion serves as the foundation and justification for *teshuvah,* which is predicated on the seemingly impossible effort to rewrite history. Therefore, it is quite fitting that Yom Kippur entails a *tosefet,* a piece of both the past and the future, and integrates it into the *kedushat ha-yom*. For a discussion of this point, see R. Joseph B. Soloveitchik, *Out of the Whirlwind* (New Jersey: Ktav, 2003), 17.

Chapter 14

The Relationship Between Yom Kippur and the Rest of the Year

Although the Torah repeatedly describes Yom Kippur as "*ahat ba-shanah*," unique in the year, and hence the most unusual day of the year (*Shemot* 30:10; *Vayikra* 16:34), some of the unusual phenomena of Yom Kippur strikingly find expression throughout the year. An analysis of this phenomenon demonstrates that it is precisely the relevance of these phenomena to the rest of the year that is responsible for their more intense manifestation on Yom Kippur. A number of examples illustrate this point.

The *Kohen Gadol*'s Obligation to Marry Only One Woman

The *gemara* in *Yoma* states that the *Kohen Gadol* must be married exclusively to one woman, rather than multiple wives. This *halakhah* is stated only with regard to Yom Kippur.[1] The implication of the *gemara* is that theoretically, the *Kohen Gadol* could marry additional women during the

1. *Yoma* 13a.

rest of the year, as long as he divorced them before Yom Kippur. However, in *Hilkhot Issurei Bi'ah*, Rambam rules that this *halakhah* applies throughout the year:

> מצות עשה על כהן גדול שישא נערה בתולה, ומשתבגור תאסר עליו שנאמר והוא אשה בבתוליה יקח, אשה לא קטנה, בבתוליה ולא בוגרת, הא כיצד יצאת מכלל קטנות ולכלל בגרות לא באה זו נערה, ואינו נושא שתי נשים לעולם כאחת שנאמר אשה אחת ולא שתים.
>
> It is a positive mitzvah for a *Kohen Gadol* to marry a virgin maiden (*na'arah*), and when she matures, she becomes prohibited to him, as the *pasuk* states, "And he shall take a virgin woman" (*Vayikra* 21:13). "Woman" excludes a child [and] "virgin" excludes a woman who has matured. What is implied? That she left childhood and has not yet achieved maturity, which refers to a *na'arah*. And he may not be married to two women simultaneously, as the *pasuk* states, "a woman," which implies one and not two.[2]

Ra'avad attacks Rambam's ruling and questions its source. He notes that the Talmud's only source for this *halakhah* is the verse commanding the *Kohen Gadol* to atone for himself and his "house" on Yom Kippur (*Vayikra* 16:6), which the Talmud explains refers to his wife – in the singular. How, then, does Rambam expand the application of this marital limitation, applying it to the whole year?

Furthermore, *Minhat Hinukh* points out that it is striking that Rambam omits this disqualification of more than a single wife specifically in the context of the Yom Kippur *avodah*.[3] In other words, Rambam not only extends this *halakhah* year round, but also neglects the origins of this requirement in the Yom Kippur *avodah*! This striking omission in *Hilkhot Avodat Yom ha-Kippurim* led *Minhat Hinukh* to further accuse Rambam of ignoring this requirement.

---

2. *Hilkhot Issurei Bi'ah* 17:13.
3. *Minhat Hinukh* 185:7. Rambam does reference the need for a *Kohen Gadol* to be married in *Hilkhot Avodat Yom ha-Kippurim* 1:2, but not the prohibition of having more than one wife.

In *Hilkhot Klei ha-Mikdash,* Rambam does in fact codify that the *Kohen Gadol* may not perform the Yom Kippur *avodah* if he is married to multiple women,[4] somewhat mitigating *Minhat Hinukh*'s severe critique. At the same time, the fact that Rambam extended this Yom Kippur requirement to a more general application in that he downplayed its connection to Yom Kippur by strategically excluding it from *Hilkhot Avodat Yom ha-Kippurim* – thus triggering *Minhat Hinukh*'s misconception of his actual view – requires clarification.

Another difficulty in Rambam's stance on multiple wives for the *Kohen Gadol* is worth noting and might further illuminate his view and suggest an approach regarding his perspective. Rambam maintains that in order to generally disqualify a *Kohen* from the Temple service, prohibited unions (i.e. to a divorcee) require *kiddushin* and consummation of the union (*kiddesh u-va'al*).[5] However, it appears that the *Kohen Gadol* is not allowed to marry more than one wife even if there is no consummation of the union. Moreover, Rambam does not suggest that the violation of this multiple-wife infraction disqualifies the *Kohen Gadol* in the year-round *avodah.*

R. Soloveitchik proposed a beautiful explanation for these anomalies.[6] Rambam's opinion in *Hilkhot Issurei Bi'ah* that the *Kohen Gadol* must be married to only one woman year round is not disconnected from the requirement on Yom Kippur. Rather, it bespeaks a more intense, intricate, and ambitious understanding of the relationship between Yom Kippur and the rest of the year. Rambam posits that for the entire year, a *Kohen Gadol* must be in a state in which he is qualified to enter the *Kodesh ha-Kodashim* (Holy of Holies) and perform the Yom Kippur *avodah.* His status all year is defined by his special opportunity on Yom Kippur.[7]

---

4. *Hilkhot Klei ha-Mikdash* 5:10.
5. *Hilkhot Issurei Bi'ah* 17:2.
6. See *Shiurei Ha-Grid, Avodat Yom ha-Kippurim,* 32–33.
7. An understanding of the *Kohen Gadol*'s broader role and limited responsibilities during the year may further substantiate the Rav's suggestion. In general, the special status of the *Kohen Gadol* in the *avodah* is reflected in only two primary laws. The first is the daily responsibility of the *Kohen Gadol* to bring a *minhat havitin;* the second is the almost exclusive role he plays in *avodat Yom ha-Kippurim.* Although there are other laws pertaining to the *Kohen Gadol* in the *avodah,* such as being

Rambam's deeply held conviction about the nature of the *Kohen Gadol* and his special affinity to *avodat Yom ha-Kippurim* renders superfluous the need for a source for the *halakhah* in *Hilkhot Issurei Bi'ah*. Moreover, this explains why even mere *ishut,* absent *kiddesh u-va'al,* constitutes a violation. This is not a disqualification related to prohibited marriage, like the general prohibitions against marrying a widow or divorcee. Rather, it is a specific *halakhah* related to the Yom Kippur *avodah* that is extended all year round due to the status and qualification of the *Kohen Gadol,* and as such is sufficiently determined by the status of *nissu'in*.

The Rav's suggestion can be taken one step further, albeit in an opposite direction.[8] As noted, Rambam does, in fact, unequivocally explicate the *Kohen Gadol*'s *avodat Yom ha-Kippurim* disqualification due to multiple wives, neutralizing *Minhat Hinukh*'s primary objection, but it is surely consequential that he bypassed the anticipated natural venue and chose to state that *halakhah* in the broader *Hilkhot Klei ha-Mikdash*. I suggest that although this *halakhah* is connected to and even stems from Yom Kippur, Rambam's point is that there is a dual connection between *kol ha-shanah* and Yom Kippur: If this *halakhah* did not apply at least as an ideal year round (mandating its inclusion in *Hilkhot Issurei Bi'ah*), it would not have had the increased capacity to invalidate the *avodah* on Yom Kippur. While the uniqueness of Yom Kippur intensifies

---

makriv onen (*Horayot* 3:5) and *notel be-rosh* (*Yoma* 1:2), those are prerogatives, not obligations. Other laws that apply to the *Kohen Gadol* (not being *metamei le-metim,* his death as *motzei* from *galut,* his added limitations in terms of marriage, living in Yerushalayim, and being around the *Mikdash*) do not relate to his presence in the *avodah.* Furthermore, on the *tzibbur* level, his exclusive obligation is presiding over the *avodat Yom ha-Kippurim.* In light of the limited year-round responsibilities of the *Kohen Gadol,* R. Soloveitchik's suggestion that the *Kohen Gadol* is perpetually defined by his Yom Kippur service is much more compelling. In line with my suggestion below, perhaps we can argue that just as Yom Kippur cannot exist in a vacuum and must be connected to the rest of the year, the *Kohen Gadol* is required to bring the daily offering of the *minhat havitin* so that his presence is not isolated to the day of Yom Kippur.

8. While our suggestion sufficiently explains and enhances our understanding of the aforementioned issues in Rambam, the two explanations are not mutually exclusive and in fact complement each other.

and impacts the halakhic categories of *kol ha-shanah,* spiritual consistency demands that these halakhic ideals must also be *rooted* in these year-round categories. Rambam codifies the particular ramifications of this law for Yom Kippur in *Hilkhot Klei ha-Mikdash,* in the general context of the requirements for the *Beit ha-Mikdash,* to teach that the *ahat ba-shanah* is on a continuum with *kol ha-shanah,* even as it constitutes its intensification. This law not only requires the *Kohen Gadol* to maintain a year-round state of preparedness for *ahat ba-shanah,* as the Rav noted, but also dictates that the *ahat ba-shanah* is continuous with and an intensification of *kol ha-shanah.*

Application to *Viduy*

This approach may also explain some anomalies of *viduy* (confession) of Yom Kippur. The role of *viduy* on Yom Kippur is subject to much discussion, and there are discrepancies in Rambam's presentation of *viduy* in the *teshuvah* process of Yom Kippur, relative to the general year-long requirement and character of this pivotal component of *teshuvah.*

Rambam describes a concise Yom Kippur *viduy* in *Hilkhot Teshuvah*:

> הוידוי שנהגו בו כל ישראל 'אבל אנחנו חטאנו (כולנו)' והוא עיקר הוידוי.
>
> The *viduy* that all of the Jewish People are accustomed to [say], "But we have sinned," is the main part of *viduy.*[9]

However, earlier in *Hilkhot Teshuvah,* addressing classical *viduy* in the *teshuvah* process, Rambam describes a very expansive *viduy* that requires a detailed enumeration of one's sins:

> כיצד מתודין? אומר, 'אנא השם חטאתי עויתי פשעתי לפניך ועשיתי כך וכך והרי נחמתי ובושתי במעשי ולעולם איני חוזר לדבר זה', וזהו עיקרו של וידוי.

9. *Hilkhot Teshuvah* 2:8.

> How does one confess? He states, "I implore You, God; I sinned, I transgressed, I committed iniquity before You by doing such-and-such. Behold, I regret and am embarrassed about my deeds, and I promise never to repeat this act again." These are the essential elements of *viduy*.[10]

Moreover, when Rambam introduces the Yom Kippur *viduy* of "But we have sinned," it is in the context of asserting that even though *teshuvah* applies year round, there is a special obligation to initiate *teshuvah* on Yom Kippur. Indeed, he argues that the fact that Yom Kippur is an auspicious time for *teshuvah,* both for individuals and all of Israel, triggers an imperative to do *teshuvah* on Yom Kippur:

> יום הכיפורים הוא זמן תשובה לכל ליחיד ולרבים והוא קץ מחילה וסליחה לישראל. לפיכך חייבים הכל לעשות תשובה ולהתודות ביום הכפורים.
>
> Yom ha-Kippurim is the time set aside for repentance for all, the individual as well as the many, for it is the apex of exoneration and pardon for Israel. Therefore, all are obligated to repent and confess on the Day of Atonement.[11]

Yet, the very next *halakhah* establishes "We have sinned" as a sufficient, if minimalist, Yom Kippur *viduy*. Why does the special urgency, opportunity, and status of *teshuvah* on Yom Kippur specifically mandate a less robust role for *viduy*?

Moreover, the *halakhah* clearly projects two manifestations and models of *viduy,* in general as well as on Yom Kippur. There is the *viduy* of *teshuvah,* whose central role Rambam emphasizes in the introduction to *Hilkhot Teshuvah,* the beginning of the first chapter of *Hilkhot Teshuvah,* and in *Sefer ha-Mitzvot*.[12] There is also a separate institution of *viduy* that accompanies *avodat ha-korbanot* and that is particularly meaningful as part of the sequence of *avodat Yom ha-Kippurim*. In the

10. Ibid. 1:1.
11. Ibid. 2:7.
12. *Sefer ha-Mitzvot, aseh* 75.

introduction to *Hilkhot Avodat Yom ha-Kippurim*, Rambam speaks about executing the elaborate *avodah* according to a precise order,[13] and he then proceeds to mention *viduy*:

> הלכות עבודת יום הכפורים. מצות עשה אחת, והיא שיעשה מעשה יום הכפורים כולו על הסדר כמו שכתוב בפרשת אחרי מות, הקרבנות, והוידויין, ושילוח השעיר, ושאר העבודות.
>
> These are the laws of the *avodah* of Yom Kippur. They include one positive mitzvah – to do the entire service of Yom Kippur in order, as it is written in *Parashat Aharei Mot*, including the sacrifices, the confessions, the sending of the goat, and the remainder of the service.

Evidently, the *Kohen Gadol*'s *viduy* on Yom Kippur is part of the *seder ha-yom*, the order of the day.

Indeed, in the context of the *gemara*'s discussion of the indispensable components of the *avodah*,[14] Rashi and Rambam include the *viduyim*. *Sefer Yerei'im* specifically mentions that the contemporary *viduy* recited on Yom Kippur is patterned after the *viduy* of the *Kohen Gadol* on Yom Kippur, which is a requirement of the *avodah*, disconnected from *teshuvah*.[15] According to Rebbi, even though both Yom Kippur and the *se'ir ha-mishtalei'ah* atone for sins even in the absence of *teshuvah*, there is still a requirement of *viduy*.[16] As such, it seems that *viduy* is both part of the *seder avodat Yom ha-Kippurim* and part of the process of *teshuvah*.

However, these are not two completely separate categories. There is a particularly significant link between the Yom Kippur *avodah* and the year-round *teshuvah*. Indeed, Rambam's central projection of the idea of *viduy* as the basis for *teshuvah* throughout the year actually appears to be based on the *viduy* of the *Kohen Gadol* on Yom Kippur.[17] It is not

13. See the chapter "Yom Kippur: The Day of the *Kohen Gadol*" for further exposition.
14. *Yoma* 60.
15. *Sefer Yerei'im* 263.
16. *Shevu'ot* 13a.
17. See the chapter "Teshuvah and Viduy: The Ambitious Method of Coming Closer to Hashem.

the *viduy* recited over other sacrifices,[18] but rather the *Kohen Gadol's* Yom Kippur *viduy* – "Please, Hashem, I have sinned before You" – that forms the basis for the *viduy* in *Hilkhot Teshuvah.*

On the one hand, Rambam views *viduy* and *teshuvah* on Yom Kippur as distinct. Only on Yom Kippur does he record a positive obligation to repent, and only regarding *teshuvah* on Yom Kippur does he articulate such a minimalist formulation of *viduy.*[19] At the same time, it is extremely consequential that the *viduy* that is unique to the *Kohen Gadol's avodat Yom ha-Kippurim* is the foundation for *teshuvah* of *kol ha-shanah.*

The totality of Rambam's presentation indicates that there is a special and prominent requirement for the *Kohen Gadol* to say *viduy* in the framework of the *avodah* on Yom Kippur and that this *viduy* is the inspiration for *teshuvah* throughout the year, yet *viduy's* role in the *teshuvah* process of Yom Kippur is de-emphasized. How can all three concepts be true?

Other considerations aside, once again, we can detect the pattern of *ahat ba-shanah* interacting with *kol ha-shanah.* Invoking the status and stature of the role of the *Kohen Gadol* in the *avodah* of Yom Kippur is a source of inspiration and spiritual ambition that defines *teshuvah* all year round. At the same time, the fact that Yom Kippur generates an *independent* obligation to initiate *teshuvah,* reflecting its singular status, eliminates and renders superfluous the need for an extensive *viduy.* To really appreciate the uniqueness of Yom Kippur and its impact, one must appreciate that it is designed and intended to have a transformative impact on the rest of the year, while also understanding that Yom Kippur's singular agenda and manifestations could not exist or be spiritually influential in a vacuum. Yom Kippur necessarily connects and interacts with halakhic values and motifs that are indispensable all year round.

---

18. *Hilkhot Ma'aseh ha-Korbanot* 3:15.

19. Also see the discussion of *Avodat ha-Melekh,* who argues with *Lehem Mishneh's* (2:8) technical resolution of Rambam's opinion. While some interpret this as a succinct reference to the full *viduy,* a more compelling reading is that Rambam is projecting a reduced *viduy* requirement.

"I Will Sin and Yom Kippur Will Atone"

The *mishnah* states:

> אחטא ואשוב, אחטא ואשוב, אין מספיקין בידו לעשות תשובה. אחטא ויום הכפורים מכפר, אין יום הכפורים מכפר.
>
> One who says, "I will sin, and then repent; I will sin [again], and then repent," will not receive an opportunity to repent. [For one who says,] "I will sin, and Yom Kippur will atone," Yom Kippur will not atone.[20]

Two principles are expressed in this *mishnah,* but notwithstanding their similarity, there is an important difference between them.

The first ruling declares that one who plans future transgressions assuming subsequent repentance is denied the opportunity to pursue a successful or effective repentance. This assertion is eminently reasonable, as repentance is a process and state of mind that demands a high level of sincerity, which is certainly incompatible with the sensibility of "*eheta ve-ashuv.*" Moreover, *teshuvah* is a singular divine gift that allows one to reorient his persona and begin anew. The particularly egregious and even grotesque posture of "*eheta ve-ashuv*" exploits and thereby forfeits this manifestation of divine mercy by transforming *teshuvah* into a catalyst for sin.

The second assertion proclaims that Yom Kippur's special capacity of atonement, which may (according to some authorities) exist even absent *teshuvah,* is not unqualified. A policy that cynically integrates the advantageous prospect of the singular atonement that derives from *itzumo shel yom* into one's schedule of halakhic infractions invalidates that atonement (*eino mekhaper*); it is not merely rendered unconducive (*ein maspikin be-yado*).

The subtle distinction between the respective exploitations of *teshuvah* and of Yom Kippur atonement is intriguing and somewhat unanticipated, given the different dynamics represented by each. We could readily predict the vulnerability of *teshuvah* to exploitation or

20. *Yoma* 8:9.

manipulation, but it is surprising that the *kapparah* of Yom Kippur, which may take effect even absent *teshuvah*, could be withheld.

It is noteworthy that, notwithstanding his celebrated hypersensitivity to nuances in the formulations of Rabbinic law, Rambam equates the two statements, extending the consequence of the future futility of *teshuvah* to an abusive posture on the atonement opportunity and capacity of Yom Kippur as well:

> עשרים וארבעה דברים מעכבין את התשובה. ארבעה מהן עוון גדול; והעושה אחד מארבעתן - אין הקדוש ברוך הוא מספיק בידו לעשות תשובה, לפי גודל חטאו...והאומר אחטא ואשוב; ובכלל זה האומר אחטא, ויום הכיפורים מכפר.
>
> Twenty-four different transgressions withhold the acceptance of repentance. Four of these are of great iniquity, and whoever commits one of them, the Holy One, blessed is He, provides no means for him to repent, due to the enormity of his sin.... One who says, "I will sin and then repent"; included in this category is one who says, "I will sin and Yom Kippur will atone [for me]."[21]

The complex relationship between Yom Kippur and the rest of the year that we have explored may account for Rambam's implicit conviction that these two phenomena are necessarily parallel and linked. As noted, it is particularly Rambam's view that the ideal of Yom Kippur and the core standard of *avodat Hashem* that prevails year round are always interrelated.

One who anticipates future transgressions predicated on the neutralizing capacity of accessible repentance transforms this divine gift from an antidote into a cause of sin, negating the very essence of that prized opportunity. By the same token, Rambam's view of Yom Kippur as a day and a process that, even if technically lacking the requirement of *teshuvah*, is an indispensable vehicle of personal transformation that parallels *teshuvah* equally precludes the very capacity of accessing

---

21. *Hilkhot Teshuvah* 4:1.

teshuvah itself. In any case, his view on this matter reflects and reinforces the dialectic of *ahat ba-shanah.*

At the same time, our analysis may also justify the subtle differences in the *mishnah*'s formulation that distinguish normative *teshuvah* from the atonement of Yom Kippur. The anticipation of a return to sin undermines the sincerity and quality of the process of *teshuvah,* rendering it ineffectual. Consequently, the opportunity of a future neutralizing *teshuvah* is appropriately withheld. However, one who relies on a future Yom Kippur to neutralize his planned year-round transgressions reveals an ideology that is completely antithetical to the principles that underpin Yom Kippur and its *itzumo shel yom.* By divorcing Yom Kippur's capacity for atonement from daily conduct, one displays not only ignorance, but a fundamental rejection of Yom Kippur's dialectical reflection of *ahat ba-shanah.* For such an individual, the atonement power of *itzumo shel yom* becomes utterly invalidated.

The theme of *ahat ba-shanah,* embodying the uniqueness of the day as a vehicle to encourage and reinforce high halakhic aspirations that constitute a lofty spiritual lifestyle, requires a commitment to uphold and upgrade Torah standards *kol ha-shanah,* the entire year. Only one who is completely insensitive to the authentic meaning and opportunity of Yom ha-Kippurim could possibly articulate the ideology of "I will sin and Yom Kippur will atone," a statement whose absurdity we can firmly comprehend.

Chapter 15

Yom Kippur: The Day of the *Kohen Gadol*

The *Kohen Gadol*'s Yom Kippur Service

The idea that the *Kohen Gadol* is the pivotal figure of the Yom Kippur service manifests itself in numerous ways. Most prominently, the verses in the beginning of *Parashat Aharei Mot* that describe the service repeatedly emphasize the role of Aharon, the paradigmatic *Kohen Gadol*. Furthermore, the *Kohen Gadol* wears unique garments for the special services of the day inside the *Kodesh ha-Kodashim* (Holy of Holies). All year round, he wears four garments of gold in addition to his four white linen garments, but the Torah instructs that when he enters the *Kodesh ha-Kodashim* on Yom Kippur, he must wear an all-linen uniform that more closely resembles the uniform of a regular *Kohen* (*Vayikra* 16:5). Indeed, the *halakhah* asserts that these garments may never be worn again after the *Kohen Gadol* completes the service, further highlighting his singular status on Yom Kippur.[1]

Most importantly, the *Kohen Gadol* presides over the services of the day. Of course, only the *Kohen Gadol* is allowed entry into the inner recesses of the Holy of Holies, with the incense and the blood of the

1. See *Yoma* 12b.

sacrifices sprinkled there (namely, that of his own bull and the people's sin-offering). However, most *Rishonim* rule that the *Kohen Gadol* also must perform *all* of the services of the day,[2] including the *tamid* and *mussaf* offerings, the burning of the daily incense, and the lighting of the *menorah*.[3]

However, there is a fascinating tension in these laws. On the one hand, the *Kohen Gadol*'s unique Yom Kippur vestments and his responsibility for the entire service in the *Beit ha-Mikdash* highlight the unique role he plays on this day. Ironically, however, they simultaneously seem to dilute the gap between the *Kohen Gadol* and the other *Kohanim*, as well as the gap between the exclusive service for Yom Kippur and the other, generic offerings brought on that day. Why is it that the special linen vestments worn by the *Kohen Gadol* on Yom Kippur, ostensibly intended to accentuate his unique standing, make him look more like an ordinary *Kohen Hedyot* than at any other time of the year?

The *Kohen Gadol*'s role in the *avodat ha-yom* is even more puzzling. This is especially pronounced according to the formulation of Rambam at the beginning of *Hilkhot Avodat Yom ha-Kippurim*:

> ביום הצום מקריבין תמיד בשחר ותמיד בין הערבים כסדר כל יום ויום, ומקריבין מוסף היום פר ואיל ושבעה כבשים כולן עולות, ושעיר חטאת נעשה בחוץ והוא נאכל לערב. ועוד מקריבין יתר על מוסף זה, פר בן בקר לחטאת והוא נשרף, ואיל לעולה, ושניהם משל כהן גדול, ואיל הבא משל צבור האמור בפרשת אחרי מות, והוא האיל האמור בחומש הפקודים בכלל המוסף, והוא הנקרא איל העם, ועוד מביאין משל צבור שני שעירי עזים, אחד קרב חטאת והוא נשרף, והשני שעיר המשתלח.

2. Rambam, *Hilkhot Avodat Yom ha-Kippurim* 1:2. See also *Ba'al ha-Ma'or* and *Milhamot Hashem, Yoma* 1a in the *dapei ha-Rif*, and Ritva, *Yoma* 12b, s.v. *ki ata Rav Dimi*.
3. The theme of the central role of the *Kohen Gadol* on Yom Kippur has echoes beyond the service in the *Mikdash*. Reflecting the connection between the world of *korbanot* and the world of *tefillah*, the *Kohen Gadol*'s importance on Yom Kippur is expressed in the Yom Kippur *tefillah*. One example is the custom recorded by Rema (*Orah Hayim* 581:1) to require the *sheli'ah tzibbur* during the High Holy Days period to be married, since the *Kohen Gadol* must be married. For another interesting example, see *Arukh ha-Shulhan, Orah Hayim* 581:5.

> נמצאו כל הבהמות הקרבים ביום זה חמש עשרה: שני תמידין, ופר, ושני אילים ושבעה כבשים כולם עולות, ושני שעירים חטאת אחד נעשה בחוץ ונאכל לערב והשני נעשה בפנים ונשרף, ופר כהן גדול לחטאת והוא נשרף.
>
> On the day of the fast, they offer the morning *tamid* and afternoon *tamid*, as is the schedule of every single day, and for the day's *mussaf* offering, they bring a bull, a ram, and seven sheep as burnt-offerings, and a goat for a sin-offering that is brought outside [the Sanctuary], and it is eaten in the evening. In addition to this *mussaf*, they bring a bull as a sin-offering that is entirely burnt and a ram as an burnt-offering, both of which are supplied by the *Kohen Gadol*, and a ram supplied by the public, as is recorded in *Parashat Aharei Mot*; this is the same ram that is mentioned in the book of *Bamidbar* included in the *mussaf* offering, and it is called "the people's ram." The public also supplies two goats; one is offered as a sin-offering and is burnt, and the other is the goat that is sent away. Thus, we find that there are fifteen animals offered in total on this day: two *temidim*, a bull, two rams, and seven sheep – these are all burnt-offerings – two goats as sin-offerings – one offered outside the sanctuary and eaten in the evening and the second offered inside the Sanctuary and burnt – and the *Kohen Gadol*'s bull as a sin-offering, which is burnt.[4]

Any literary critic will emphasize the importance of immediately commanding the audience's interest. Thus, we would expect Rambam, the masterful formulator, to begin *Hilkhot Avodat Yom ha-Kippurim* by drawing attention to the unique aspects of the Yom Kippur service – entering the *Kodesh ha-Kodashim*, sprinkling the blood on the *kapporet*, etc. Remarkably, however, Rambam instead seems to go out of his way to emphasize the generic aspects of the *avodat Yom ha-Kippurim*.

He begins by using the general term "*Be-yom ha-tzom* – On the day of the fast," instead of "*Be-Yom ha-Kippurim*."[5] This surprising pattern of understated exposition continues, as following the introduction, the

---

4. *Avodat Yom ha-Kippurim* 1:1.
5. The phrase also appears in *Hilkhot Klei ha-Mikdash* 5:10, 8:5.

first sacrifice mentioned is not one of the unique offerings brought inside the *Kodesh ha-Kodashim*, but rather the *korban tamid*! Moreover, Rambam seemingly superfluously adds that the *tamid* is brought the same way it is brought every other day of the year. He proceeds to write that the Yom Kippur service includes a *mussaf* offering, again like every other festival. Finally, Rambam adds that "in addition to this *mussaf*," a number of other sacrifices are offered. Those other sacrifices are the unique Yom Kippur offerings, the crux of the day's entire service – yet he presents them almost as an afterthought! Rambam concludes the first *halakhah* by summarizing that the total sum of animals sacrificed on Yom Kippur is fifteen – an unnecessary and self-evident computation – and he then repeats the entire list, which seems completely gratuitous.

This motif continues in the second *halakhah*:

> עבודת כל חמש עשרה בהמות אלו הקריבין ביום זה אינה אלא בכהן גדול בלבד, אחד כהן המשוח בשמן המשחה או המרובה בבגדים. ואם היתה שבת אף מוסף שבת אין מקריב אותו אלא כהן גדול, וכן שאר העבודות של יום זה כגון הקטרת הקטורת של כל יום והטבת הנרות הכל עשוי בכהן גדול נשוי שנאמר וכפר בעדו ובעד ביתו ביתו זו אשתו.
>
> The service for all of these fifteen animals brought on this day is performed exclusively by the *Kohen Gadol*. It does not matter if he was consecrated by the anointing oil or by wearing the larger number of garments. If it was Shabbat, even the Shabbat-*mussaf* may only be offered by the *Kohen Gadol*. Likewise, all of the other services of this day, such as burning the daily incense and trimming the lamps, are performed by a married *Kohen Gadol*, as the verse states, "He shall atone for himself and for his house" (*Vayikra* 16:6) – "his house" is his wife.

Rambam groups the fifteen offerings together, writing that they all must be offered by the *Kohen Gadol*, without any differentiation. Next, he rules that the *Kohen Gadol* must also be the one to offer the *mussaf* for Shabbat when it coincides with Yom Kippur. This innovative ruling is quietly insinuated squarely in the middle of the *halakhah*, as if it were completely obvious. In fact, there is no explicit source for this conclusion. Indeed, one could logically distinguish between the *tamid* offerings, which are offered on every single Yom Kippur and thus could be understood as an essential part of the day's service, and the *mussaf* of Shabbat, which certainly seems extrinsic to it.[6]

Yom Kippur and the Rest of the Year

The idea that seems to drive Rambam's codification is the relationship between Yom Kippur and the rest of the year. On the one hand, Yom Kippur is an absolutely unique day in the calendar, as the Torah highlights by describing it as "*ahat ba-shanah*" (*Shemot* 30:10; *Vayikra* 16:34).[7] It is a day of complete religious intensity, of entering *lifnai ve-lifnim* to the *Kodesh ha-Kodashim*, of fasting and of *kulo la-Hashem*. At the same time, however, it is imperative that Yom Kippur not stand completely independent from the rest of the year.

---

6. *Or Samei'ah, Avodat Yom ha-Kippurim* 4:1, makes the fascinating suggestion that Rambam's ruling is based on *Zevahim* 90b–91a, which discusses which of two offerings should take precedence: the one brought more frequently or the one with more sanctity. The *gemara* attempts to prove that higher frequency outweighs higher sanctity, since the morning *tamid* is brought on Shabbat before the *mussaf*, even though the *mussaf* carries additional sanctity as part of the Shabbat service relative to the daily *tamid* offering. However, the *gemara* rejects this proof, because in truth, the Shabbat *tamid* also acquires the sanctity of Shabbat. Thus, argues *Or Samei'ah*, it emerges that all of the sacrifices brought on a festival are integrated, even those that are not brought specifically because of the festival. Likewise, when Shabbat coincides with Yom Kippur, the Shabbat *mussaf* is integrated with the other Yom Kippur sacrifices, and it therefore must be offered by the *Kohen Gadol*.

   However, this comparison is debatable. Although the *tamid* is not offered because of Shabbat, it is brought on every single Shabbat. Thus, it is reasonable that the Shabbat *tamid* is defined as part of the Shabbat service. In contrast, the confluence of Yom Kippur and the Shabbat *mussaf* is merely a calendrical coincidence, such that Rambam's claim that the Shabbat *mussaf* is integrated into the Yom Kippur service and thus requires the *Kohen Gadol* remains unproven. (*Or Samei'ah* has an alternative solution for Rambam that is immune to this argument.)

   Alternatively, we might argue that Shabbat and Yom Kippur, which the Torah calls "*Shabbat Shabbaton*" (*Vayikra* 23:32), may be particularly eligible for integration due to their shared themes. See the chapter "Yom Kippur: The Quintessential Shabbat."
7. It is quite telling that "*ahat ba-shanah*" is the concluding phrase in the *parashah* of *avodat Yom ha-Kippurim*.

One way that this duality is expressed is through the relationship of the various components of the Yom Kippur service. The core of the service is the part unique to Yom Kippur that is performed inside the *Kodesh ha-Kodashim*. However, Rambam begins *Hilkhot Avodat Yom ha-Kippurim* by emphasizing that *all* of the various services of the day are integrated. Everything falls under the rubric of "*avodat Yom ha-Kippurim*" – both the unique aspects of the service and its more generic components – because the entire goal of Yom Kippur is to connect the day's unique spiritual ambition to that of the rest of the year.

Therefore, Rambam goes out of his way to accentuate the status of the *tamid* and *mussaf* offerings as part of the Yom Kippur service, almost seeming to downgrade its central, unique sacrifices. Likewise, by repeating and tallying all of the various animals offered in a single sequence, Rambam highlights their integration.

Rambam stresses the balance between exclusivity and integration in a second critical component of Yom Kippur as well: the role of the *Kohen Gadol*. Yom Kippur is the day of the *Kohen Gadol*. Indeed, this is likely the reason that Rambam rules that the *Kohen Gadol* must even offer the Shabbat *mussaf* when Yom Kippur falls on Shabbat. Yom Kippur demands that the *Kohen Gadol*, who embodies singular qualities, exclusively preside over all facets of this day, even extending beyond the "Yom Kippur service" as narrowly construed.

The *Kohen Gadol*'s comprehensive role in the Yom Kippur service appears to render the rest of *Klal Yisrael* as mere spectators, watching passively and from a distance as the *Kohen Gadol* achieves atonement on their behalf. It is to preclude this misconception that Rambam begins the laws of the Yom Kippur service in the *Beit ha-Mikdash* by referring to Yom Kippur as "*yom ha-tzom*." By highlighting that Yom Kippur is a fast that devolves upon each and every Jew, the laws of which Rambam already codified in *Hilkhot Shevitat Asor* in *Sefer Zemanim*, Rambam accentuates the holistic dimension of this day, emphasizing that those *halakhot* are inextricably linked to *Hilkhot Avodat Yom ha-Kippurim*. As exotic and inaccessible as the Yom Kippur service may seem, as much as it seems that the people passively receive vicarious atonement through the activities of the *Kohen Gadol*, it is particularly critical to remember that this is still "*be-yom ha-tzom.*" The fasting and *teshuvah* of every Jew is a critical component for the day's atonement.

The singular status of the *Kohen Gadol* on Yom Kippur reinforces this duality. Even as he clearly has a uniquely hegemonic role on Yom Kippur, some of the seemingly ironic laws we have seen express a certain accessibility to the routine *avodah* of the rest of the year, as well as a measure of affinity to his fellow *Kohanim*. He wears a singular wardrobe for this *avodah,* but at the same time it is comprised of the white linen that all *Kohanim* wear during the year. Likewise, his duties during the day are not limited to sacrificing the unique Yom Kippur offerings, but extend to the generic, year-round offerings as well.

The Role of the *Kohen Gadol*

To be sure, even as the requirement for the *Kohen Gadol* to perform the generic aspects of the Yom Kippur service bridges that day to the rest of the year, it reinforces even more that it is specifically the *Kohen Gadol* who presides over everything. This singular reality requires explanation. At the same time, the other *Kohanim* and the rest of *Klal Yisrael* do not have an active part to play in the Yom Kippur service. Are they simply detached observers, or do they have a greater role?

The general role of the *Kohen Gadol* is one that embodies the theme of Yom Kippur: "*kulo la-Hashem.*" There are a number of laws that distinguish the *Kohen Gadol* and highlight the intensity of his devotion and dedication to God.

In some respects, the *Kohen Gadol* must surrender his personal life for the sake of the *tzibbur* and the *Ribbono Shel Olam*. His personal and professional lives are inextricably linked. This is most notably captured by a verse in *Parashat Emor*:

> ומן המקדש לא יצא ולא יחלל את מקדש אלקיו כי שמן משחת אלקיו עליו אני ה׳.
>
> He shall not leave the sanctuary, and he shall not profane the sanctuary of his God, for the distinction of his God's anointing oil is upon him; I am Hashem. (*Vayikra* 21:12)

All other *Kohanim* may not serve in the *Mikdash* when one of their close relatives passes away, when they have the status of *onen*, and any sacrifices they offer during that time are disqualified.[8] In contrast, the *Kohen Gadol* continues to officiate even as an *onen*. Even the most intense moments of personal loss do not excuse him from his post: "He shall not leave the sanctuary."

Another area that highlights the *Kohen Gadol*'s unceasingly active status relates to the *sha'atnez* (mixture of wool and linen) in the *bigdei kehunah*. The *avnet* (belt), one of the four standard *bigdei kehunah* worn by every *Kohen*, contained *sha'atnez*.[9] Obviously, the *Kohanim* may wear the *avnet* while they are serving in the *Beit ha-Mikdash*, but Rambam and Ra'avad seem to disagree regarding whether they may do so when they are not on active duty.[10] Rambam rules that a *Kohen Hedyot* may only wear the *bigdei kehunah* while actually serving in the *Mikdash*, because that fulfills a *mitzvat aseh*; if he wears them at any other time, he is liable for lashes. Ra'avad, however, allows a *Kohen Hedyot* to wear the *bigdei kehunah* any time that he is in the *Mikdash*. One thing that seems clear, although not explicit, is that Rambam distinguishes between a *Kohen Hedyot* and the *Kohen Gadol*: the latter may wear the *bigdei kehunah* even though he is not actively serving.[11] Why should there be this difference?

One idea advanced by *Beit ha-Levi* and developed by Rav Soloveitchik is that for the *Kohen Gadol*, the wearing of the *bigdei kehunah* itself is an act of service.[12] The garments are not mere accoutrements or mechanisms for the service; wearing them is itself an *avodah*.[13] However, Radvaz offers another explanation, which in truth may serve as the foundation for *Beit ha-Levi*'s idea. He suggests that the constant allowance for the *Kohen Gadol* to wear *bigdei kehunah* stems from the verse "*u-min ha-Mikdash lo yetzei*." The *Kohen Gadol*, certainly when in the *Mikdash*, is always ready for service; he is permanently on call. His entire essence

8. See the *mishnah*, *Zevahim* 15b, and the ensuing Talmudic discussion on 16a.
9. See *Yoma* 12b; *Hilkhot Klei ha-Mikdash* 8:1.
10. *Hilkhot Klei ha-Mikdash* 8:12; *Hilkhot Kilayim* 10:32.
11. See Radvaz and *Kesef Mishneh*, *Hilkhot Kilayim* 10:32.
12. *Beit ha-Levi* 1:3:2; *Shiurei ha-Grid: Kuntres Avodat Yom ha-Kippurim*, 22–24.
13. This idea must be reconciled with the rule that "*bi-zeman she-bigdeihem aleihem, kehunatam aleihem; ein bigdeihem aleihem, ein kehunatam aleihem*" (*Zevahim* 17b).

is one of "*min ha-Mikdash lo yetzei.*" Therefore, there is simply no such thing as a time that he is not engaged in service. Consequently, there is no time that he may not wear the *bigdei kehunah*.

Rambam has another ruling that highlights this idea. The *Kohen Gadol* brings a daily meal-offering called the *minhat havitin*, which consists of a dozen loaves. In a controversial opinion, Rambam asserts that he brings half of each loaf in the morning and the other half in the afternoon.[14] Thus, in a sense, he spends the entire day engaged with the service of the *minhat havitin*. The idea is that even if the *Kohen Gadol* is not actually physically active the entire day, he is always, symbolically, in the midst of *avodah*.[15]

If that is the case, it is easy to appreciate why the *Kohen Gadol* is the symbol of Yom Kippur. While in general we rule that the festivals are celebrated in a balanced manner – *hetzyo la-Hashem ve-hetzyo lakhem*, half for God and half for man[16] – Yom Kippur is the day of the year that accentuates the idea of *kulo la-Hashem*. At least one day a year must be dedicated to establishing our *kulo la-Hashem* credentials. Against the background of that core commitment, the equilibrium and synthesis of *hetzyo la-Hashem ve-hetzyo lakhem* is an ideal expression of halakhic maximalism, a testament to the scope and impact of *avodat Hashem*, not a concession or compromise to man's spiritual inadequacy. Thus, the singular day of Yom Kippur is the linchpin for halakhic commitment at all times.

The perfect person to symbolize this dedication is the *Kohen Gadol*. After all, the essence of his persona as *Kohen Gadol* conveys the notion of *kulo la-Hashem*. The *Kohen Gadol* does not actually work

14. *Hilkhot Ma'aseh ha-Korbanot* 13:4; see Ra'avad, ad loc.
15. For an expanded discussion of this topic, see my article "*Shitat ha-Rambam be-Inyan Minhat Havitin*," *Kol Tzvi* 9, 14–23. This is acutely demonstrated by Rambam's codification of the *halakhot* of *minhat havitin* in *Hilkhot Temidin u-Mussafin* 13:4. It is also reinforced by his view that the apportionment between the daily and afternoon halves need not be precise. Ra'avad is puzzled, even dismayed, by the very notion that a *korban* mandate can be satisfied by approximation. This position, however, is consistent with and further confirms the conclusion that for Rambam, the *minhat havitin* constitutes an extended single *avodah*, whose segments combines for the full *shiur*.
16. *Beitzah* 15b.

actively all the time during the year, but he nevertheless stands for the ethos of *min ha-Mikdash lo yetzei*. It is surely consequential that the *Kohen Gadol*'s obligations, aside from the aforementioned daily *minhat havitin*, are focused almost exclusively on Yom Kippur.

Yom Kippur is the day of the *Kohen Gadol* in two interconnected ways: It is a day that defines his purpose and role,[17] but equally, the day demands and is itself contingent upon his leadership and persona. Yom Kippur and all that it accomplishes is inconceivable absent the *Kohen Gadol*, the symbol of total dedication to the *Ribbono Shel Olam*.

The *Kohen Gadol* and the People

In *Hilkhot Klei ha-Mikdash*, Rambam rules that the *Kohen Gadol* must be appointed by the *Sanhedrin ha-Gadol* (Great Sanhedrin) of seventy-one judges.[18] However, it is puzzling that this ruling appears only in *Hilkhot Klei ha-Mikdash*. The Rambam enumerates the various activities that require the Great Sanhedrin in *Hilkhot Sanhedrin*, such as judging a false prophet or appointing a king, but there he ignores the appointment of the *Kohen Gadol*.[19] *Lehem Mishneh* questions why Rambam does not include appointing the *Kohen Gadol* in that list, but he does not resolve the matter.

R. Yitzhak Zev Soloveitchik writes that the Sanhedrin's role in appointing a king differs fundamentally from its role in appointing a *Kohen Gadol*.[20] He notes that unlike the king, there is no source in the Talmud for the requirement of the Sanhedrin to appoint a *Kohen Gadol*; the *Tosefta* simply presents it as an accepted fact. Furthermore, the appointment of a king requires the dual participation of the Sanhedrin and of a prophet, while the *Kohen Gadol* is appointed by the Sanhedrin alone.[21]

---

17. See the chapter "The Relationship between Yom Kippur and the Rest of the Year" for further explication of this idea.
18. *Hilkhot Klei ha-Mikdash* 4:15.
19. *Hilkhot Sanhedrin* 5:1.
20. *Hiddushei Maran Riz ha-Levi, Sanhedrin* 5:1.
21. See *Sifrei, Devarim* 157:15; Rambam, *Hilkhot Melakhim* 1:3; Radvaz, ad loc. The distinction between *Kohen Gadol* and *melekh* is even more basic: There is no verse parallel to "*som tasim alekha melekh*" (*Devarim* 17:15), the imperative of anointing a

The Gri"z explains that appointing a king and appointing a *Kohen Gadol* fall under two distinct roles that the Sanhedrin plays. Appointing a king requires judicial approval. The judiciary must endorse the political appointment of the king, as it falls under the category of "*kol ha-davar ha-gadol yavi'u eilekha* – all grave matters they shall bring before you" (*Shemot* 18:22). Weighty matters for *Klal Yisrael* require the Rabbinic Supreme Court, and choosing a king qualifies as such, mandating the involvement of the Sanhedrin. However when it comes to the *Kohen Gadol*'s appointment, there is nothing juridical about the role of the Sanhedrin. In truth, it is the nation's prerogative to select a *Kohen Gadol*. The Sanhedrin here operates exclusively in a second capacity: as the representative body for all of *Klal Yisrael*. Whenever a decision or action by the entire nation is required, the Sanhedrin frequently serves as their representatives to execute that

---

king, regarding the appointment of the *Kohen Gadol*. Indeed, there is no comparable mitzvah in the scheme of Rambam, *Sefer ha-Hinukh*, *Smag*, etc. In fact, Rambam's presentation (*Hilkhot Klei ha-Mikdash* 4:12) assumes the institution and details the installation methodology without explicating the charge to undertake this process. Moreover, it is noteworthy that Rambam integrates his treatment of the *Kohen Gadol* within his prior broader discussion of the distinctive classes, beginning with the *Levi'im* (ch. 3), extending to regular *Kohanim* (ch. 4), and then finally examining the *Kohen Gadol* at the apex of this hierarchy (ch. 5). Unlike the king, who inherently stands apart, the *Kohen Gadol*, though qualitatively distinct in status and function, is depicted as "*ha-gadol mei-ehav*"; his status issues from his hierarchical role vis-à-vis his brethren and the rest of *shevet Levi*.

It is conceivable that the *Kohen Gadol*'s pervasive status on Yom Kippur, which also entails specific representation and expiation of the whole population of the *Kohanim* on his "personal" *par*, may account for these discrepancies. As noted, the *Kohen Gadol* not only dominates this day, but is appointed in this measure precisely for this purpose. His appointment, as well as the character of his relationships with the other *Kohanim*, *shevet Levi*, and *Klal Yisrael*, are intertwined with the *kedushat ha-yom* of Yom Kippur, in sharp contrast to the *melekh*. Hence, there may be no need for an independent source or obligation to appoint a *Kohen Gadol*, as his primary role is subsumed under the rubric of the Yom Kippur obligations.

The enduring status of a replacement *Kohen Gadol* on Yom Kippur, although attributed as an application of "*ma'alin be-kodesh ve-ein moridin*," as well as the special appointment protocol on Yom Kippur itself, further underscore this connection. See *Hilkhot Avodat Yom ha-Kippurim* 5:13 and my "*Be-Inyan Yom ha-Kippurim ke-Yomo Shel ha-Kohen ha-Gadol: Petihah le-Masekhet Yoma*," *Kol Tzvi* 18 (2017), 24–49.

action.[22] They are the Electoral College, as it were, selecting a *Kohen Gadol* as the representatives of the people, rather than as an independent body.

It is fascinating that the office of the *Kohen Gadol*, which seems designed as a practically unattainable ideal for the general public and apparently focuses on the most esoteric dimensions of Jewish law, is actually anything but. The people appoint the *Kohen Gadol.*[23] In some religious cultures, the independent high priest assumes an exclusive role, while the common man remains a passive bystander who attains vicarious spiritual benefit. In contrast, *Kehunah Gedolah* and its message of total devotion to the *Ribbono Shel Olam* are closely linked to the entirety of *Klal Yisrael* through the appointment process.

Thus, when the *Kohen Gadol* not only presides over but actually performs the entire Yom Kippur service, he does not operate independently from the rest of the *tzibbur*. The people observing him are not detached bystanders; they are part of the process.[24]

Serving in the Place of Aharon

This can be taken one step further. Until now we have discussed the dominant role of the *Kohen Gadol* in the Yom Kippur service. However, is the focus truly on the *Kohen Gadol*? In the verses in *Parashat Aharei Mot*, the repeated emphasis is specifically on Aharon ha-Kohen:

---

22. For an elaboration of this concept and other examples, see the Rav's article, "*Kevi'at ha-Mo'adim al pi ha-Re'iyah ve-al pi ha-Heshbon*," *Kovetz Hiddushei Torah*, 47–65 (esp. 51–52); *Iggerot Ha-Grid*, 79–90. See also Rav Hirsch's commentary to *Devarim* 16:18, s.v. *titen lekha*, and *Ha'amek Davar*, ad loc. Also see my "*Be-Inyan Semikhah u-Semikhat Zekeinim*," *Beit Yitzhak* 21 (1989), 91–101.
23. *Or ha-Hayim* (*Vayikra* 21:1) notes that several laws specific to *Kohanim* are surprisingly also directed to *Klal Yisrael*. This may reflect the deep connection between *Bnei Yisrael* and the realm of *kehunah*, and particularly with the *Kohen Gadol*.
24. This provides a different perspective on the status of *hishtakhava'ah* (communal prostration) and the presence of the nation in the *azarah* on Yom Kippur, as well as other manifestations of the anticipation and responsive posture of *Klal Yisrael*. See *Yoma* 55b; Rambam, *Hilkhot Avodat Yom ha-Kippurim* 2:7.

וידבר ה׳ אל משה אחרי מות שני בני אהרן בקרבתם לפני ה׳ וימתו. ויאמר ה׳ אל משה דבר אל אהרן אחיך ואל יבא בכל עת אל הקדש מבית לפרכת אל פני הכפרת אשר על הארן ולא ימות כי בענן אראה על הכפרת. בזאת יבא אהרן אל הקדש בפר בן בקר לחטאת ואיל לעלה.

> Hashem spoke to Moshe after the death of Aharon's two sons, when they approached before Hashem and died. Hashem said to Moshe: Tell your brother Aharon that he may not come at all times into the Sanctuary within the curtain, in front of the cover that is upon the ark, and he will not die; for I appear in the cloud over the cover. With this shall Aharon come into the Sanctuary: with a bull of the herd for a sin-offering and a ram for a burnt-offering. (*Vayikra* 16:1–3)

This can partially be attributed to the historical dimension of these *pesukim,* as the rigorous protocol that enables entry into the *Kodesh ha-Kodashim* constitutes a corrective for the tragic misconduct of Aharon's sons. However, as the passage continues to elaborate the Yom Kippur service, the repeated emphasis of Aharon ha-Kohen becomes even more striking, as it appears progressively more gratuitous. While the intricate *avodat Yom ha-Kippurim* service is being formulated for all generations, the Torah only refers more generically to the *Kohen Gadol* at the very conclusion of its presentation:

וכפר הכהן אשר ימשח אתו ואשר ימלא את ידו לכהן תחת אביו ולבש את בגדי הבד בגדי הקדש

> And the *Kohen* who is anointed and who is given the authority to serve in place of his father shall bring atonement, and he shall wear the linen clothes, the holy clothes. (*Vayikra* 16:22)

Even then, the Torah accentuates the function as a stand-in for his predecessor, Aharon ha-Kohen.

The Rav notes that the hymn "*Atah Konantah,*" the *nussah Sefard* narration of the Yom Kippur service that is the centerpiece of *tefillat Mussaf,* speaks of the *Kohen Gadol* as Aharon's stand-in:

תחת אהרן מגזעו יעמד לשרת לפניך ביום הסליחה.

> In the place of Aharon, one from his stock shall stand to serve before You on the day of forgiveness.

The Rav posits that this phrase, in conjunction with the Torah's aforementioned singular presentation, articulates this notion as a distinct halakhic concept: The role of the *Kohen Gadol* on Yom Kippur stems not merely from his status as *Kohen Gadol,* but by virtue of the fact that he assumes the mantle of Aharon ha-Kohen.[25]

The Rav explains that this perspective may clarify Ra'avad's thinking in his debate with Rambam about the procedure of appointing the *Kohen Gadol.* A *Kohen* can be elevated to the high priesthood either by being anointed with the *shemen ha-mishhah* that was designated by Moshe or by wearing the *Kohen Gadol*'s special garments. Rambam writes that the *Kohen* must be anointed with the oil or wear the garments every day for seven days, but if he served as *Kohen Gadol* before the seventh day, his service is not disqualified, since he truly achieved this status the first time he began this process. Ra'avad notes that Rambam clearly implies that ideally, the *Kohen Gadol* is supposed to abstain from service during the entire seven-day initiation period, but Ra'avad argues that there is no logical or textual basis for such a claim. Ra'avad himself rules that the new *Kohen Gadol* can generally serve from the first day of his consecration; the evidence for an ideal seven-day waiting period is restricted to his special performance of the Yom Kippur service.[26]

The argument is intriguing. However, both positions need to confront the same dilemma: If the *Kohen Gadol* receives his status from the first moment of his consecration, what do the next seven days add, such that according to Ra'avad he is now ideally credentialed to perform the Yom Kippur service and according to Rambam he can now serve in general as a *Kohen Gadol*? The difficulty is more challenging for Ra'avad's view, as the *Kohen Gadol*'s unconstrained license already prevails.

---

25. See *Shiurei ha-Grid,* 8–15.

26. *Hilkhot Klei ha-Mikdash* 4:13.

The Rav contends that the added dimension is the status of serving in the place of Aharon. According to Ra'avad, the requirement for this status is closely connected to the ability to perform the Yom Kippur service. Normally, the initial exposure to the *shemen ha-mishhah* or to the *Kohen Gadol*'s unique vestments creates the status of *Kohen Gadol*. However, serving on Yom Kippur requires more than the mere status of *Kohen Gadol*; he must substitute for the persona of Aharon as well. Since Aharon himself was consecrated over a full seven-day period,[27] the descendant who aims to assume his position must do so as well.

An alternative explanation of Ra'avad's position would reinforce the previous conclusion that *avodat Yom ha-Kippurim* is the central *raison d'etre* of the *Kohen Gadol*, even the source of his stature and status. Hence, the more ideal seven-day protocol is mandated specifically for this *avodah*. It is conceivable that even according to Rambam, the ideal seven-day period is connected with *avodat Yom ha-Kippurim*. Perhaps it is Rambam's view, given the centrality of *avodat Yom ha-Kippurim* to the institution of the *Kohen Gadol*, that qualification for that *avodah* ideally dictates the process of *minuy Kohen Gadol* all year round.[28]

The idea of the paradigmatic role of Aharon ha-Kohen is significantly amplified by the Midrash, and even more by the Gra. The passage in *Parashat Aharei Mot* never explicitly states that Aharon may enter the *Kodesh ha-Kodashim* only on Yom Kippur; it states only that he may enter exclusively when he performs the service described. Commenting on the verse "With this shall Aharon come into the Sanctuary" (*Vayikra* 16:3), Rashi writes that both conditions are actually necessary, and the Ramban adopts the same view. However, a fascinating *midrash* teaches that Moshe was informed of Aharon's expanded license to enter the *Kodesh ha-Kodashim* at will, provided that he adhered to the proper protocols:

> אמר הקדוש ברוך הוא למשה לא כשם שאתה סבור, לא עת לשעה ולא עת ליום ולא עת לשנה ולא עת לי"ב שנה ולא עת לשבעים שנה ולא עת לעולם אלא בכל שעה שהוא רוצה ליכנס יכנס רק שיכנס בסדר הזה.

27. See *Vayikra* 8:33.
28. See my "*Be-Inyan Yom ha-Kippurim ke-Yomo Shel ha-Kohen ha-Gadol*" and the discussion of R. Hayim Soloveitchik's opinion there.

> Hashem said to Moshe: It is not as you think. This [the proper way to enter the *Kodesh ha-Kodashim*] is not one time per hour, or one time per day, or one time per year, or one time per twelve years, or one time per seventy years, or one time for all eternity. Rather, at any time that he wants to enter, he may enter, but he must do so with this procedure.[29]

The simple reading of the *midrash* is that this expanded license applies exclusively to Aharon ha-Kohen, and this is how the Gra understood it.[30] Aharon can frequent the *Kodesh ha-Kodashim* at will, as long as he follows the protocols enumerated in the *parashah*; every other *Kohen Gadol* can enter only on Yom Kippur. The Gra notes that this is, in fact, the straightforward interpretation of the verses. The entire passage, which refers repeatedly to Aharon, does not refer to Yom Kippur. Only at the conclusion of the *parashah,* when the Torah finally identifies the institution of the *Kehunah Gedolah,* does the Torah explicitly mention Yom Kippur.

The *midrash* does not explain why this dichotomy should exist, but given our previous analysis, we may suggest that it is due to Aharon's status as the paradigmatic *Kohen Gadol.* Subsequent *Kohanim Gedolim* may enter the *Kodesh ha-Kodashim* with the status of the substitute of Aharon, but they may do so only on Yom Kippur. Alternatively, there may be two different mechanisms that enable piercing the privacy of the most intimate chambers of the *Mikdash* – one connected to the persona and prerogatives of Aharon and the other sanctioned by the character and urgency of *avodat Yom ha-Kippurim* and *kedushat ha-yom.*

The Gra quotes this *midrash* to explain two puzzles in the *parashah.* First, all the *mussaf* offerings for Yom Kippur appear exclusively in *Parashat Pinehas* (*Bamidbar* 29:7), except for the ram brought by the public, which is also referenced in *Parashat Aharei Mot* (*Vayikra* 16:5).[31]

---

29. *Vayikra Rabbah* 21:7.
30. *Kol Eliyahu,* no. 83. See also the conclusion to *Hilkhot Aveilut Matzeivat Moshe,* printed at the end of *Hokhmat Adam.* This contrasts with the view of *Meshekh Hokhmah,* who perceives this license as a function of that generation, as opposed to the persona of Aharon ha-Kohen.
31. See *Yoma* 72b.

Why does that offering alone appear here? Second, according to the Oral Law, the sequence of the *pesukim* does not perfectly adhere to the actual sequence of events on Yom Kippur. The *gemara* states that the entire Yom Kippur service is written sequentially except for one verse, *Vayikra* 16:23, in which Aharon returns one final time to the *Kodesh ha-Kodashim*. According to the Oral Law, this was done at a later phase of the *avodah* than actually appears in the Torah. The net result is that the *Kohen Gadol* would undergo five ritual immersions and ten sanctifications of his hands and feet, instead of the three and six that appear in the text of the Written Law.[32] This constitutes a very strange phenomenon. Why would the Torah intentionally misrepresent the process by ignoring the precise order? Indeed, both the Talmud and Rambam discuss the "*seder avodat Yom ha-Kippurim*," the precise order of the Yom Kippur service. The emphasis on *seder*, rigorous structure and order, appears incompatible with an imprecise presentation in the Written Law.

The Gra explains that there are two different services under discussion – the standard *Kohen Gadol*'s Yom Kippur service and Aharon's personal service whenever he wished to enter the *Kodesh ha-Kodashim*. Although the people's ram is part of the Yom Kippur *mussaf*, it appears in *Parashat Aharei Mot* as well because that ram is also a precondition for Aharon's personal entry. The ram thus has two functions: It is part of the Yom Kippur *mussaf*, and it is also a service component required for accessing the inner recesses of the Sanctuary. If Aharon were to enter the *Kodesh ha-Kodashim* on a day other than Yom Kippur, there would be no *mussaf* sacrifices, but he would still need to offer the ram to sanction his entry. Likewise, Aharon's entry required only three immersions and six sanctifications; the tradition demanding five and ten applies only to the Yom Kippur service.

Aharon ha-Kohen: The Paradigmatic Figure of Yom Kippur

We have demonstrated that there are two forms of the Yom Kippur service – the permanent one for all generations to perform only on Yom Kippur and the special one available to Aharon alone. But we are left

32. *Yoma* 32a, cited by Rashi, *Vayikra* 16:23.

with one pressing question. Why would the Torah specifically focus in the *Torah she-Bikhtav* on Aharon's exceptional service, rather than the typical *avodat Yom ha-Kippurim* that would be performed yearly throughout the rest of history as the centerpiece of the most consequential day of the calendar?

The solution to this puzzle reinforces the idea we have developed: The *Kohen Gadol* on Yom Kippur is tasked with assuming Aharon's function and persona. Aharon is the true paradigm, both for *kenisah lifnai ve-lifnim* , accessing the innermost precincts of *kedushat ha-makom,* as well as for executing the *seder ha-avodah,* which, in conjunction with *itzumo shel yom,* remarkably produces national atonement on Yom Kippur. Every subsequent *Kohen Gadol* may aspire to these transcendent attainments only by invoking the precedent and channeling the singular spiritual persona of Aharon ha-Kohen. The Torah conveys Aharon's prominence in these processes by deliberately and repeatedly personalizing his role and by obliquely hinting, by means of the textual subtly of a three-*tevilah avodah,* that he alone enjoyed the prerogative of unrestricted, year-round access to the *Kodesh ha-Kodashim.* This emphasis, in turn, further and more precisely illuminates the normative role of the *Kohen Gadol* every Yom Kippur, inspired by the model of Aharon ha-Kohen.

Aharon's preeminence in the *avodah* provokes an equally intriguing question: Why wasn't Moshe Rabbeinu chosen to execute this most sensitive task and to embody this sacred and pivotal vehicle of national expiation? The ubiquitous theme of *kulo la-Hashem* on Yom Kippur intensifies our query. Moshe Rabbeinu, more than any other figure, exemplifies the ethos of *kulo la-Hashem.* He was the greatest of all prophets, the recipient of the *luhot* and the Written Torah, the Torah scholar of the greatest magnitude, repository of the oral tradition, and first in the chain of the *mesorah,* and he likely could enter the *Kodesh ha-Kodashim* without restrictions.[33] Moreover, temperamentally, his tenacious, unbending "*yikov ha-din et ha-har*" posture credentialed him as an implacable, uncompromising idealist,[34] particularly suited to this motif of *kulo la-Hashem.* This principled approach was acutely

33. See *Yalkut Shimoni* 571:9; *Kli Yakar, Vayikra* 16:1–2.

34. See *Sanhedrin* 6b.

demonstrated through his political and spiritual leadership. Furthermore, Yom Kippur historically is the date when Hashem forgave *Klal Yisrael* for the sin of the golden calf – a crucial atonement that was achieved through the intercession of none other than Moshe Rabbeinu! Why, then, is Aharon ha-Kohen, and not Moshe Rabbeinu, the model personality for Yom Kippur?

Here, too, the solution is anchored in a perspective previously developed. Yom Kippur is not a day of passive spectating or vicarious atonement. Moshe's inimitable persona and his unattainable religious stature are precisely what disqualify him from being the pivotal figure of Yom Kippur.[35] If Moshe Rabbeinu were to be the paradigmatic Yom Kippur personality, the rest of *Klal Yisrael* necessarily would merely be watching from a distance. Notwithstanding its high aspirations, Yom Kippur is by definition an accessible halakhic institution. Indeed, this most singular and consequential day of the year is also its most relevant, as it establishes the potential to harness human spirituality in a way that surpasses even celestial devotion. Thus, it is necessary for the ideal *Kohen Gadol* – whose role is so deeply intertwined with the day of Yom Kippur – to couple his *kulo la-Hashem* devotion with an intimate link to the broader nation.[36]

In this regard, there could be no more exemplary figure than Aharon ha-Kohen. Aharon was seamlessly able to integrate being *kulo la-Hashem* with immense identification with and closeness to the people. Aharon's life poignantly demonstrated his capability of absolute commitment to Hashem. When called upon even in tragic moments, Aharon could suppress the most basic human instincts. "*Va-yidom Aharon* – Aharon was silent" (*Vayikra* 10:3) after the devastating loss of his

---

35. This was the basis for Aharon's and Miriam's initial rebuke of Moshe (*Bamidbar* 12:1–2), as they believed he had surrendered too much of his humanity. See Rashi, ad loc., and *Sifrei, Bamidbar* 99.

36. It can be argued that the reason Moshe was tasked with being the initial *Kohen Gadol* during the period of the *milu'im* was in order to cement its primary *kulo la-Shem* character. It was subsequently preferable for Aharon to assume the permanent position. This may resolve Radvaz's objection to Ra'avad's view in *Hilkhot Klei ha-Mikdash* (4:13) where he assumes that Moshe's service was due to Aharon's lack of availability. However, in fact, Moshe's initiating role may have been determinative.

children, and notably, it was specifically "after the death of Aharon's two sons" that he received the command, "With this shall Aharon enter the Sanctuary" (ibid. 16:1, 3).

Yet, there is no ambiguity that Aharon's defining characteristic and legacy was his accessibility, connection to, and empathy for the people. Aharon earned the epithet of "*ohev shalom ve-rodef shalom, ohev et ha-beriyot u-mekarvan la-Torah* – a lover of peace and a pursuer of peace, one who would love people and bring them closer to Torah" for his legendary devotion to *Klal Yisrael.*[37] Even his greatest misstep in navigating the episode of the golden calf likely stemmed from and attested to his profound attachment to the people.[38] The Talmud further highlights Aharon's unique interpersonal devotion, as he projected peaceful *pesharah* (legal compromise) as an ideal.[39] As Rashi notes, who else but Aharon ha-Kohen could have triggered the moving organic communal reaction of "*va-yivku et Aharon sheloshim yom kol Beit Yisrael* – and the entire House of Israel wept for Aharon for thirty days" (*Bamidbar* 20:29)?[40] Perhaps it is initially counterintuitive that the *Kohen Gadol*, whose primary focus is *Mikdash*-related matters such as *korbanot* (sacrifices) and *taharot* (purity), is the leader closer to the people, but understood within the perspective developed regarding Yom Kippur, it emerges as entirely sensible.[41]

Moreover, the *Kohen Gadol* – "*ha-kohen ha-gadol mei-ehav*" (*Vayikra* 21:10) – emerged from and was designed to be the head of the house of *Kehunah*. It is significant that his personal *par* and *viduy* on Yom Kippur encompasses and also atones for his extended *Kohanim* family.[42] These

---

37. *Avot* 1:12.
38. See Rashi, *Shemot* 32:5, and *Pirkei de-Rabbi Eliezer* 45.
39. *Sanhedrin* 6b. There is evidence that the *pesharah* model is a more flexible expression of justice, rather than an abdication of it. See also *Yad Ramah* and other *Rishonim* (ad loc.) on the relationship between *pesharah* and *betzi'ah*.
40. Rashi, *Bamidbar* 20:29, citing the *midrash*.
41. For a broader discussion of why Moshe was not permanently assigned the position of *Kohen Gadol* and was instead destined for political leadership, see my articles "Moshe Rabbeinu's Legacy of Leadership" and "The Leadership Partnership of Moshe and Aharon," available at torahweb.org.
42. *Hazal* (*Yoma* 44a) interpret the *pasuk* "*ve-khiper ba'ado u-ve'ad beito*" (*Vayikra* 16:17), as referring to the *Kohen Gadol*'s household and his priestly brethren.

relationships attest to and ensure his empathy for the fate of others.[43] In contrast, Moshe Rabbeinu's completely singular status in prophecy, leadership, and personal stature – "*Lo ken avdi Moshe*" (*Bamidbar* 12:7; *Devarim* 34:10) – preclude this role.

The institution of the *Kohen Gadol,* as someone appointed by and for *Klal Yisrael,* attaches the nation to the ideal of *kulo la-Hashem* all year round, and particularly on Yom Kippur. Thus, the *Kohen Gadol* must be able to straddle both worlds, connecting to the people while simultaneously occupying a higher spiritual existence as a figure of emulation. That combination, inspiringly embodied by Aharon, is what the *Kohen Gadol* strives for as he presides over the Yom Kippur service "in the place of Aharon."

43. See note 16 where I discuss this issue as well. The fact that the *Kohen Gadol,* particularly on Yom Kippur, must be married further reinforces both the theme of his humanity as well as his empathy for others. Nothing captures these themes more acutely than the spousal bond. The contrast with other religions, in which celibacy is a *sine qua non* for spiritual leadership, is striking. The importance of the *Kohen Gadol*'s marital status is emphasized in Rambam's matter-of-fact presentation and in his novel perspective of the *Kohen Gadol*'s marital obligation year round (*Hilkhot Avodat Yom ha-Kippurim* 1:2; see also *Hilkhot Klei ha-Mikdash* 5:10 and *Hilkhot Issurei Bi'ah* 17:13). See also the chapter "The Relationship Between Yom Kippur and the Rest of the Year."

    In this respect as well, Moshe, who distanced himself from his marriage, differs from the paradigm of the classic *Kohen Gadol.* It is further intriguing to note the prominent view in *Hazal* (e.g. *Vayikra Rabbah* 20:9) that identifies the rejection of marriage due to its incompatibility with spirituality as the central flaw that doomed the entry of Nadav and Avihu into the *Kodesh ha-Kodoshim.* For exploration of this mistake, see the commentaries of *Hatam Sofer* and *Ktav Sofer* on that passage.

Chapter 16

The Unique *Teshuvah* of Yom Kippur

Rambam writes in *Hilkhot Teshuvah* that because Yom Kippur provides a unique opportunity for *teshuvah*, it also precipitates a demand for *teshuvah*:

> יום הכפורים הוא זמן תשובה לכל ליחיד ולרבים והוא קץ מחילה וסליחה לישראל, לפיכך חייבים הכל לעשות תשובה ולהתודות ביום הכפורים.
>
> Yom ha-Kippurim is the time set aside for repentance for all, the individual as well as the many; for it is the apex of exoneration and pardon for Israel. Therefore, all are obligated to repent and confess on Yom ha-Kippurim.[1]

Rambam's formulation presents a surprising and complex relationship between the *teshuvah* of Yom Kippur and the *teshuvah* of the rest of the year. Several points highlight this:

1. *Hilkhot Teshuvah* 2:7.

1. This is the only time in *Hilkhot Teshuvah* (and in the entire *Yad ha-Hazakah,* for that matter) that Rambam records an actual obligation to do *teshuvah.* When Rambam presents the standard mitzvah of *teshuvah* (*Sefer ha-Mitzvot, aseh* 73; *Hilkhot Teshuvah* 1:1), he specifically formulates an obligation to perform *viduy* (confession) when doing *teshuvah,* but never an imperative of *teshuvah* itself.[2]
2. Given Rambam's special demand for *teshuvah* on Yom Kippur, we would expect a reference to it in his codification of the laws of Yom Kippur (either *Hilkhot Shevitat Asor* or *Hilkhot Avodat Yom ha-Kippurim*). However, he curiously mentions it only in *Hilkhot Teshuvah.*
3. Rambam writes in the *koteret* (preamble) that *Hilkhot Teshuvah* contains only one of the six hundred and thirteen *mitzvot*: the mitzvah of *viduy* in the context of *teshuvah* year round. Evidently, the unique obligation of *teshuvah* on Yom Kippur is somehow subsumed under the larger mitzvah, even though – as demonstrated – it features a different, more expansive imperative that contrasts to the daily norm of *viduy.*

Rambam was not alone in conceptualizing a complex relationship between the *teshuvah* of Yom Kippur and the *teshuvah* of the rest of the year. *Sefer ha-Hinukh* follows a similar course.[3] He too counts a single mitzvah of *teshuvah,* encompassing the whole calendar year and the entirety of one's personal lifespan, but he concludes his presentation by declaring that one who squanders the opportunity to do *teshuvah* on Yom Kippur actively violates the mitzvah of *teshuvah*:

> ועובר על זה ולא התודה על חטאיו ביום הכפורים שהוא יום קבוע מעולם לסליחה וכפרה ביטל עשה זה, ואוי לו לאדם אם ימות בלא וידוי ונשא עונו.

2. I address Rambam's broader approach to the mitzvah of *teshuvah* and *viduy* in the chapter "*Teshuvah* and *Viduy*: The Ambitious Method of Coming Closer to Hashem."
3. *Sefer ha-Hinukh,* mitzvah 364.

> One who transgresses this and does not confess his sins on Yom Kippur, which is the day set from time immemorial for forgiveness and atonement, has violated this positive commandment. And woe to a man if he dies without confession and carries his iniquity!

Sefer ha-Hinukh thus implies that there is a special dimension of *teshuvah* for Yom Kippur – but, again, one that is articulated in the larger context of *teshuvah, not* in the specific framework of the *mitzvot* of Yom Kippur!

These presentations stand in sharp contrast to what appears to be the more intuitive view of Rabbeinu Yonah, who delineates an independent mitzvah of *teshuvah* on Yom Kippur that is distinct from year-round repentance.[4] His source is the verse "*Lifnei Hashem tit'haru* – You shall be purified in front of Hashem" (*Vayikra* 16:30), which he boldly interprets as an imperative rather than as a promise. While Rabbeinu Yonah's source and conclusion are innovative, his position distinguishing the two *teshuvot* is unambiguous and compelling, whereas the more nuanced perspective of Rambam and *Sefer ha-Hinukh* is puzzling. What is the special character of repentance on Yom Kippur, and how does it relate to repentance during the rest of the year?

Nature of the Day of Yom Kippur

In truth, the question of *teshuvah* is a microcosm of a broader issue that must be investigated first: the general relationship between Yom Kippur and the rest of the year. Examining the broader halakhic character of Yom Kippur will provide a foundation that will not only illuminate the dilemma regarding the role of *teshuvah,* but also offer direction to its resolution.

At first glance, Yom Kippur appears to be an incomparable, inimitable, singular day, not only because of the stakes involved and the opportunities it provides, but in its halakhic structure and character. When the Torah twice describes Yom Kippur as "*ahat ba-shanah* – singular in the year" (*Shemot* 30:10; *Vayikra* 16:34), this is not merely a technical quantitative description, but rather a projection of Yom Kippur's

4. *Sha'arei Teshuvah* 2:14, 4:17.

uniqueness. This is understandable, given the ambition of "*be-zot yavo Aharon el ha-Kodesh* – with this Aharon shall enter the Holy" (*Vayikra* 16:3), on this day, as well as the broader significance of entry into the innermost sanctum for the *Kohen Gadol* and all of *Klal Yisrael*, whom he represents. The distinction of Yom Kippur is particularly acute given that entering the *Kodesh ha-Kodashim* is incompatible with the halakhic protocols that prevail year round.[5] This day not only tolerates that which typically is perceived as an egregious sacrilege and an intolerable trespass (*me'ilah*) – the entry into the most sacred and intimate precincts of *hashra'at ha-Shekhinah* (divine presence) – but is defined by it. This underscores how *sui generis* this day truly is.

The uniqueness of Yom Kippur is reflected in numerous other halakhic norms that characterize this day, most obviously in the rule-breaking *korbanot* (offerings) and *seder ha-avodah* (ritual service) that are its centerpiece. These include the pair of *se'irim* (goats), which achieve polar opposite destinies and which each are very different from a standard *korban hatat* (sin-offering), the need for the *Kohen Gadol*'s active participation in all phases, and the *Kohen Gadol*'s unique *bigdei lavan* (special white garments). Furthermore, it is even possible that each annual Yom Kippur is unique vis-à-vis future Yom Kippurs, as attested to by the *genizah* (abandonment) of each year's *bigdei lavan* and other manifestations.[6]

Importantly, many of the laws of *avodat Yom ha-Kippurim* are derived from the *milu'im* (dedication) process of the *Mishkan*. This is

5. See the chapter "The *Kohen Gadol*'s Role on Yom Kippur" regarding whether Aharon followed the same or a slightly different protocol for the *avodah* on Yom Kippur as a regular *Kohen Gadol* and whether he was personally granted year-round access by means of the proper halakhic protocols. See also my "Yom Kippur: The Day of the *Kohen Gadol*," in *Days of Awe, Days of Joy* (Torahweb, 2018), 183–186. I intend to further address this topic in the second volume of this series.
6. Yom Kippur's unique treatment is also reflected by the Torah's presentation of the *avodah* in *Parashat Aharei Mot*, disconnected from both the *parashat ha-mo'adim* in *Emor* and the *parashat ha-mussafim* in *Pinehas*. While this may be partially attributed to the context and contrast of the untimely and tragic deaths of Nadav and Avihu, it remains significant. Of course, as previously noted, the very requirement to enter the innermost precinct of the *Kodesh ha-Kodoshim* as a centerpiece of the *avodah*, particularly in light of the transgression of Aharon's sons, is extremely consequential.

surprising, because that process is characterized by its singular rules and designed for a one-time dedication, while the *avodat Yom ha-Kippurim* is performed annually.

Yom Kippur's distinctiveness is also exhibited in its Yom Tov-related *halakhot,* those distinct from the *avodat Yom ha-Kippurim.*[7] Yom Kippur does not blend perfectly with the other *mo'adim.* This is exemplified most obviously by the requirement to fast on Yom Kippur and the sweeping prohibition of *melakhah,* like that of Shabbat. These stand in stark contrast to the other *mo'adim,* with their essential motif of *simhah* and the *heter okhel nefesh* (permissibility of *melakhot* related to food preparation). Furthermore, each of the other *mo'adim* has a dual status – its specific themes and its generic Yom Tov identity – but it is unclear if Yom Kippur includes a general Yom Tov component at all.

Yom Kippur's special status is highlighted upon close examination of the text of *Parashat Emor,* where the *mo'adim* are discussed. On the one hand, the ubiquitous, generalizing designation of "*mikra kodesh*" is applied to Yom Kippur as well as to the other *mo'adim.* However, there is a subtle but crucial difference: "*Mikra kodesh*" normally signifies the generic identity of Yom Tov by linking each *mo'ed* with the standard *issur melakhah* (vs. its independent character). In contrast, the phrase is applied to Yom Kippur regarding its singular and highly symbolic mitzvah of *innuy*:

> **אך בעשור לחדש השביעי הזה יום הכפרים הוא מקרא קדש יהיה לכם ועניתם את נפשתיכם.**
>
> However, on the tenth day of this seventh month is Yom ha-Kippurim; it shall be a holy day to you, and you shall afflict your souls… (*Vayikra* 23:27)

The singular status and central role of the Yom Kippur *ketoret* ("*dakah min ha-dakah*") that is offered in this most sanctified venue (a topic to be addressed independently) is a further manifestation.

7. For an extensive discussion of this, see the chapter "Yom Kippur: The Quintessential Shabbat."

Thus, even when the Torah places Yom Kippur in the context of the other *mo'adim*, it takes care to emphasize Yom Kippur's *sui generis* character!

Rambam was clearly profoundly impressed by Yom Kippur's singular nature, as powerfully demonstrated by his organization of *Sefer Zemanim*. The laws of Yom Kippur, which are in *Hilkhot Shevitat Asor*, are placed right after *Hilkhot Shabbat* (and the complementary *Hilkhot Eiruvin*) and before *Hilkhot Yom Tov*.[8] This is surprising, but very symbolic and highly revealing about the relationship between Yom Kippur and the standard *mo'adim*. Reinforcing this, when Rambam begins *Hilkhot Yom Tov* with a list of "the *Yamim Tovim*," he omits Yom Kippur.

Not only does Yom Kippur deviate from the rest of the calendar and from the other *mo'adim*, but it is a day that defies the normal rules of time. The source for *tosefet kedushah* (temporal addition of sanctity) is Yom Kippur, which is basically a twenty-four-hour-plus day. Furthermore, Yom Kippur alone is a day with intrinsic powers; "*Itzumo shel yom mekhaper* – The day itself achieves atonement."[9] One of the reasons that there is no institution of *Yom Tov Sheni Shel Galuyot* on Yom Kippur may be that it is an inherently singular day and experience that would be undermined by replication.[10]

---

8. This stands in contrast to *Tur* and *Shulhan Arukh* (*Orah Hayim* 604), who place these laws between those of Rosh ha-Shanah and Sukkot.
9. According to R. Yehudah ha-Nasi (*Shevu'ot* 13a), the day achieves atonement even without *teshuvah*.
10. See *Rosh ha-Shanah* 21a and Yerushalmi *Hallah* 1:1. It is evident that when there was concrete doubt about the authentic date of Yom Kippur, *sefeika de-yoma* was applied in the absence of actual danger. This perspective also underpins the position of Tosafot (*Pesahim* 54b, s.v. *li-kevi'ah*) regarding a secluded wanderer ("*holekh ba-midbar*") who is confused about the date. Once the calendar was established, the factor of *piku'ah nefesh* was invoked by many authorities to justify a different policy for Yom Kippur, even as an elite cadre continued to practice a second day as a measure of *hasidut*. The *Rishonim*, particularly in Ashkenaz, vigorously debated the value of this stringency. See *Or Zaru'a*, Yom Kippur, end of 281; *Hagahot Maimoniyot*, end of *Hilkhot Shevitat Asor*, s.v. *terei*; *Tur*, *Orah Hayim* 624; Rema, *Orah Hayim* 624:5. It is conceivable that in addition to the consideration of *sakanah*, others refrained from this pietistic practice out of conviction that Yom Kippur is inherently singular, both in terms of its exclusion from the *minhag* of *Yom Tov Sheni* (*Beitzah* 4b) as well as with

Yom Kippur's Integration with the Rest of the Year

Despite its clear uniqueness, there is strong evidence that Yom Kippur is also integrated with other *mo'adim* and, even more strikingly, with the daily routine and rhythms of life. A variety of examples demonstrate this point.

The context of the *avodah* itself reflects the theme of integration and continuity. Rambam surprisingly begins *Hilkhot Avodat Yom ha-Kippurim* by noting that the standard *tamid* offerings are brought on Yom Kippur, just as they are offered every single day, a peculiar way to set the tone for a unique *seder avodah*. Furthermore, the structure of the *avodah* requires the *Kohen Gadol* to constantly switch between singular Yom Kippur *avodot* and routine *avodot*, thereby emphasizing the integration of the singular Yom Kippur with broader themes. This is demonstrated even more starkly by the obligation for the *Kohen Gadol* to repeatedly change from his standard *bigdei zahav* to unique *bigdei lavan* and back. Reinforcing this theme, the donning of each set of clothing (and discarding of the sanctified sets), including the routine *bigdei zahav,* demands independent *tevilah* (immersion) and *kiddush yadayim ve-raglayim* (sanctification of hands and feet).

The *korbanot* of Yom Kippur themselves reveal elements of integration. The Torah divides the discussion of the *korbanot* of Yom Kippur between two separate *parshiyot*. The unique *korbanot* of *avodat Yom ha-Kippurim* are detailed in *Parashat Aharei Mot,* the section that focuses exclusively on the *avodah,* whereas the more generic *korban mussaf* of the day is discussed together with all the other *mussaf* offerings in *Parashat*

---

respect to its status as an un-replicable day. Moreover, while the presumed exclusion may be attributed to the heightened concern for *sakanah,* it is also conceivable that it stems from the inimitable character of the day, "*itzumo shel yom.*"

It is noteworthy that among those authorities who embraced a second day, there is a dispute whether this practice included *tefillah,* and possibly other significant components of a typical Yom Kippur as well. A range of theories –*lo titgodedu, berakhah le-vatalah,* undermining of *erev* Yom Kippur, etc. – were formulated to justify the fragmentation of a second day (see *Tur, Beit Yosef, Bah,* and *Magen Avraham, Orah Hayim* 624). It is possible that the inherently unique stature of Yom Kippur is central to this complex position. See also the discussion in the Rosh, Mahari Weil, *Darkhei Moshe,* and others regarding the capacity to retract or condition one's commitment to observe a second day of Yom Kippur.

Pinehas. However, Rebbi contends that there is an overlap between the two passages: The ram that *Aharei Mot* requires the community to offer (*Vayikra* 16:5) is the same as the ram legislated as part of the *mussafin* in *Pinehas* (*Bamidbar* 29:8).[11]

The theme of integration and continuity is certainly evident with respect to the *mo'ed* character of Yom Kippur. First, notwithstanding the significant differences cited earlier, Yom Kippur remains firmly ensconced in *Parashat Emor* in the *parashah* of the *mo'adim*, located in the proper chronological order, between Rosh ha-Shanah and Sukkot. If one were not to notice the subtle difference in presentation, one could easily assume that Yom Kippur is a *mo'ed* like any other.

Second, there are points of connection between Yom Kippur and Sukkot that demonstrate that Yom Kippur, despite all its singularity, relates meaningfully to the other *mo'adim*. Rema rules that one should begin building the *sukkah* immediately upon the conclusion of Yom Kippur. Significantly, he includes this *halakhah* in the framework of *Hilkhot Yom Kippur.*[12] Indeed, it is conceivable that the omission of *Tahanun* in the period between Yom Kippur and Sukkot reflects a significant link between these two *mo'adim,* despite the fact that they are quite different, and even opposite, from one another.[13] This reinforces the conclusion that with all its singularity, Yom Kippur remains an integral part of the unit of the *mo'adim*.

Third, Maharsha notes that Moshe's enactment that one begin to review the *halakhot* of a particular festival one month prior was never articulated with respect to Rosh ha-Shanah and Yom Kippur. Maharsha explains that the theme of *teshuvah* that dominates this period belongs to the entire year, while Moshe's *takanah* applies only to themes that are unique to a particular festival.[14] This reflects that Yom Kippur, the most unique of the *mo'adim*, is actually the most pivotal, relevant, and

11. *Yoma* 3a, 70b. See also Rambam's presentation in *Hilkhot Avodat Yom ha-Kippurim* 1:1.
12. Rema, *Orah Hayim* 624:5.
13. See the chapter "Yom Kippur and Sukkot: Joy and Awe as Complementary Expressions of Avodat Hashem," which chronicles the special relationship between these two *mo'adim*.
14. Maharsha, *Megillah* 32a.

integrated of the *mo'adim* vis-à-vis daily routine – not despite, but *because* of its unique character!

Dual Sense of Yom Kippur's Integration

This tension between Yom Kippur's singularity and integration does not pose a problem. Rather, it attests to the remarkable stature of Yom Kippur, reflecting its ambition and opportunity. In order to understand how, we must recognize that this complex relationship between Yom Kippur and the rest of the year is itself dual and reciprocal.

On the one hand, Yom Kippur constitutes the inspiration, spiritual ambition, *raison d'etre,* and justification for the whole year. Maharam Schiff articulates this point explicitly:

> תכלית השנה ימים טובים תכלית ימים טובים יום כפור.
>
> The purpose of the year is festivals, and the purpose of festivals is Yom Kippur.[15]

The *ahat ba-shanah* on which *Klal Yisrael,* through the *Kohen Gadol,* physically enters *lifnai ve-lifnim,* sustains every Jew throughout the year. What occurs on this singular day reflects the intensity of the relationship with Hashem at all times and man's lofty spiritual potential every day of the year. In fact, there is evidence that the *Kohen Gadol* must be worthy all year round to serve on Yom Kippur; his qualifications as *Kohen Gadol* may be determined and even defined by the anticipation of his role on this special day.[16]

As noted, the *avodat Yom ha-Kippurim* includes standard, year-round elements, such as the *temidim* and *mussafim,* in addition to the unique *korbanot* for the day. But this is not simply a blending of standard

15. Maharam Schiff, *Bava Kama* 119b.
16. For example, Rambam (*Hilkhot Issurei Bi'ah* 17:13) argues that the *Kohen Gadol*'s requirement to be married applies throughout the year. Additionally, Rambam (*Hilkhot Klei ha-Mikdash* 4:13) implicitly argues that it is ideal for any newly anointed *Kohen Gadol* to abstain from serving for a seven-day waiting period, a requirement clearly derived from the Yom Kippur service. See the chapter "Yom Kippur: The Day of the *Kohen Gadol*."

korbanot with unique ones. The very integration of these *korbanot* transforms them into part of the unique *kedushat avodat Yom ha-Kippurim.*[17] This is clearly evidenced by the need for all the *korbanot* to be offered specifically by the *Kohen Gadol.* The fact that this unique day prominently integrates the standard *bigdei zahav* and the routine daily or *mo'ed korbanot* demonstrates that Yom Kippur's towering potential inheres all year round; it is merely expressed differently.

Yom Kippur thus impacts the rest of the year more than any other day. Far from being an isolated bubble, it is actually the most relevant day of the year.

On the other hand, Yom Kippur is also the most dependent and contingent experience of the year. If Yom Kippur remains isolated, detached from routine life, it becomes reduced to a hollow, frustrating, and haunting memory of potential unrealized, ambitions just beyond one's grasp, accenting the gaping chasm between one magical spiritual moment and a daily routine devoid of significant spiritual meaning. Yom Kippur's supremely aspirational *avodah* performed in *bigdei lavan* would be inconceivable without the introduction and integration of standard *korbanot.*

It is striking that Rema cites the link between Sukkot and Yom Kippur twice – at the end of *Hilkhot Yom ha-Kippurim* and at the beginning of *Hilkhot Sukkah.* This conveys that not only does Sukkot draw from the halakhic-spiritual attainments of Yom Kippur, but that it is equally important for Yom Kippur to be linked immediately to Sukkot and beyond.

Yom Kippur's Relevance

How does the uniqueness-relevance theme of Yom Kippur translate into the lives of individuals, particularly in an era in which the *avodat Yom Kippur,* which so centrally captures those themes, is unfortunately inaccessible? I would argue that Yom Kippur is even more relevant to the modern complex situation in which we find ourselves.

---

17. See *Zevahim* 91a. See also the discussion of the view of *Or Samei'ah* (*Avodat Yom ha-Kippurim* 1:2) in "Yom Kippur: The Day of The *Kohen Gadol,*" n. 417.

Yom Kippur, with its emphasis on *innuy* and intrinsic, expansive *issur melakhah,*[18] projects the radical theme of *kulo la-Hashem*, complete dedication to God. This sharply contrasts with the normative ideal of the other *mo'adim* – the balance of "*hetzyo la-Hashem ve-hetzyo lakhem* – half for *Hashem* and half for you."[19] Our customs on Yom Kippur reflect our aspiration to model the stature of the angels on high (standing, reciting "*Barukh shem kevod malkhuto le-olam va-ed*" out loud, etc.), a sharp contrast to the normally more desirable status and aspiration in which flawed humans strive to attain spirituality.[20]

Moreover, Yom Kippur is a day of simple stark choices. The two *se'irim* are a striking symbolic case in point. They constitute a pair, equal in every way, even in the circumstances of their acquisition:

> שני שעירי יום הכיפורים, מצוותן שיהיו שניהן שווין במראה ובקומה ובדמים ובלקיחתן כאחד.
>
> The mitzvah regarding the two Yom Kippur goats is that they be identical in appearance, height and price, and that they be acquired simultaneously.[21]

Nevertheless, they are subject to absolutely divergent, incompatible destinies, determined only by an arbitrary lottery (*goral*). Each is ceremoniously directed to an extreme fate – one ushered into the *Kodesh ha-Kodashim* to serve as a primary vehicle of collective purification, the other expelled to the wilderness to suffer an ignominious end, even as it plays an outsize role in collective *kapparah*. Both of these are unacceptable results for a *korban* on any other day of the year. The Torah's depiction and simultaneous tracking of these phenomena, each indispensable to the integrated and calibrated *avodat ha-yom*, emphasizes both the unity and dichotomy of this pair.

---

18. This is reflected in the possible inclusion of *hiluk melakhah*. See the chaper "Yom Kippur: The Quintessential Shabbat."
19. *Pesahim* 68b.
20. See *Shabbat* 88b.
21. *Yoma* 6:1.

The message is clear. Yom Kippur is a day that tests halakhic-spiritual loyalty and that provides only extreme choices – *lifnai ve-lifnim* or *la-azazel*. There is no room for the normal subtleties, nuances, and even the balance that typically characterizes halakhic life.

The purpose of this singular perspective is to unequivocally establish our primary loyalty, our real spiritual identity. That can become obscured when one is forced to deal with the vicissitudes and complexities of life, including the ubiquitous challenge of balancing competing halakhic considerations. For this reason, *hetzyo la-Hashem ve-hetzyo lakhem*, the quintessential formula of halakhic equilibrium and the normative policy regarding the *mo'adim*, is an inappropriate model for this unparalleled day. Yom Kippur reveals our true aspirations and embodies our spiritual potential. Its singular themes – showcasing our ability to spiritually compete with the angels if necessary, decisively choosing *lifnai ve-lifnim* while perceiving any alternative as the equivalent of *azazel*, and rejecting physical experiences in favor of an exclusively spiritual focus – all demonstrate and reinforce our ultimate priorities. The foundational Yom Kippur experience in turn recasts and thereby justifies the more balanced and nuanced way that we live daily. Having established our spiritual credentials and priorities, our daily physical interactions, replete with challenges and pressures, rise in significance and prominence to constitute the authentic ideal of halakhic life.

The Avraham Model and the *Akeidah* Paradigm

Avraham Avinu, the re-discoverer of monotheism and father of the nation, personified this approach. His simple faith, *yirat Hashem* (fear of God), and *ahavat Hashem* (love of God) are particularly exemplified in the epic episode of *akeidat Yitzhak*. For this reason, *akeidat Yitzhak* is a central theme on the *Yamim Nora'im*. We read the *akeidah* story on Rosh ha-Shanah, we mention it in the *Zikhronot* section of the Rosh ha-Shanah *Amidah*, and we refer to it throughout *Selihot* and on Yom Kippur as well.

Notwithstanding all of his immense contributions and formidable accomplishments, only in the aftermath of the *akeidah* is Avraham's character definitively appraised:

ויאמר אל תשלח ידך אל הנער ואל תעש לו מאומה כי עתה ידעתי כי ירא אלקים אתה ולא חשכת את בנך את יחידך ממני.

> And he said, "Do not extend your hand toward the lad, and do not do anything to him, for I now know that you are a man who fears God, since you did not withhold your son, your only one, from Me." (*Bereishit* 22:12)

Surely Avraham's whole career demonstrated his intense commitment and his maximal devotion to Hashem. The revelatory "*ata yadati* – I now know" seems incommensurate with Avraham's life of absolute dedication to disseminating Hashem's existence, His word, and His pervasive presence and relevance to earthly existence.

However, it is precisely the complex, challenging, and potentially confusing nature of Avraham's aspirational mission that resolves this conundrum. Avraham was consistently compelled to make difficult choices as he sought to apply transcendent values to pragmatic circumstances. He was continuously beset with the need to mediate diverse motifs in order to maximize halakhic-spiritual ends. His complicated relationships with Lot and Yishmael, his efforts to navigate precarious relationships with Pharaoh and Avimelekh, his apparently ambivalent posture on Sedom, his multifaceted intervention in the battle of the kings, and even his halakhic ruling assigning precedence to *hakhnassat orhim* (welcoming guests) over *kabbalat penei ha-Shekhinah* (greeting the divine presence) defy simple classification and could easily be misconstrued. Was he prioritizing pragmatism over idealism, *hesed* (human kindness) over spirituality, or did he perceive these and parallel factors as internal manifestations of a broader halakhic idealism? An outsider uninitiated in the wide-ranging and complex scope of Torah values might, in fact, question some of these choices and priorities.[22] The *akeidah*, the ultimate surrender to divine will and the most acute expression of divine faith and loyalty – *kulo la-Hashem* – provided absolute clarity and retrospectively put to rest any doubts. In light of the *akeidah*, there

22. *Hazal* in fact report that the *malakhim* on high did challenge Avraham's fidelity; see Bereshit Rabbah 55:4 and 56:7.

could be only increased appreciation for the greater magnitude and scope of Avraham's commitment, as reflected precisely in his balanced and complex decisions.

It is significant that the Torah introduces the *akeidah* matter-of-factly, with the phrase, "*Va-yehi ahar ha-devarim ha-eileh* – And it was after these matters" (*Bereishit* 22:1). This conveys that this event is simply another chapter in a life-long odyssey. Similarly, the Torah reports that after the dramatic events of the *akeidah*, Avraham returns to the routine of his broader duties, attending to the mundane needs of other members of his family, using the same words: "*Va-yehi ahar ha-devarim ha-eileh*" (ibid. 22:20). Unlike Yitzhak, whose very identity and persona is defined by the *akeidah* experience, Avraham reintegrates into his previous life.[23] In this subtle fashion, the Torah locates the true significance of this inimitable episode. It defines the unparalleled idealism of Avraham, serving as the touchstone for his consistent, comprehensive, complex, integrated *avodat Hashem*. In this respect, Yom Kippur is the *akeidah* of the *mo'adim*, of the entire yearly calendar.

The day of Yom Kippur serves as a yearly reinforcement of *Klal Yisrael*'s idealistic priorities, justifying or simply providing the necessary context to properly understand the more challenging nuanced and balanced ideal that prevails throughout the year.

This duality is captured by the Torah's insistence that *avodat Hashem* is accessible in the concrete, physical world:

> לא בשמים היא לאמר מי יעלה לנו השמימה ויקחה לנו וישמיענו אתה ונעשנה. ולא מעבר לים היא לאמר מי יעבר לנו אל עבר לים ויקחה לנו וישמיענו אתה ונעשנה. כי קרוב אליך הדבר מאד בפיך ובלבבך לעשותו.

23. In contrast to Avraham, Yitzhak's religious personality was deeply impacted and shaped by the *akeidah* experience. For an exposition of Yitzhak's character and particularly the *akeidah*'s effect on his life, see my "Who Is Yitzhak and What Is His Legacy?" available at torahweb.org. For more on the impact of the *akeidah* on Yitzhak's persona and destiny, see also my article, "Isaac's Enigmatic and Heroic Legacy," in *Letters to President Clinton: Biblical Lessons on Faith and Leadership*, ed. Menachem Genack (Sterling Publishing, 2013), 30–31.

> It is not in the heavens, such that you may say, "Who will ascend to the heavens and take it for us, and we will listen to it and do it!" And it is not across the sea, such that you may say, "Who will pass across the sea and take it for us, and we will listen to it and do it!" For this matter is very close to you; it is in your mouth and your heart, so that you can fulfill it. (*Devarim* 30:12–14)

Irrespective of whether these verses refer to Torah study[24] or to the obligation of *teshuvah*,[25] they reflect the reality of *avodat Hashem* more generally. The Torah emphatically affirms that we can serve God in the physical world. At the same time, *Hazal* note that the verse equally implies that one's success in attaining spiritual growth in this world requires a commitment that would entail the willingness to scale the heavens, were it necessary.[26]

In this sense, Yom Kippur is both the most singular and most relevant day of the year, atypical in conduct and emphasis, but fully normative in establishing our intensity of commitment and our core priorities. Like the test of the *akeidah*, the experience of Yom Kippur is both a crucial exercise in self-discovery[27] as well as a transforming, exhilarating, and inspirational growth experience of *kulo la-Hashem* that develops man's spiritual potential into something concrete, thereby building momentum for the future. Energized by the experience, Avraham Avinu returned to his normal routine after the *akeidah*. His posture is normative and ideal.

Responding to Yom Kippur

As with any transformative milestone or experience, there can be three responses to a Yom Kippur phenomenon or experience.

It can remain a singular isolated event, so overwhelming that it fails to integrate into the broader fabric of routine existence. Such a

24. *Eiruvin* 55a; Rashi, *Devarim*, ad loc.; Rambam, *Hilkhot Talmud Torah* 3:8.
25. Ramban *Devarim*, ad loc.
26. *Eiruvin* 55a. For a discussion of this conception of *teshuvah*, see the chapter "A Blueprint for *Teshuvah*."
27. See the commentaries of Ramban and Netziv on the *akeidah* episode (*Bereishit* 22:12).

response is typically spiritually counterproductive, a source of corrosive frustration and disappointment that may engender feelings of religious inadequacy that inhibit authentic halakhic aspirations.

Another possibility is the "Yitzhak response," in which the singular charismatic experience is completely transformative, to the point that it redefines one's religious persona and completely shapes one's spiritual agenda and destiny. This more ascetic and spiritually targeted perspective may be appropriate and even ideal for the *Kohen Gadol* and for an elite cadre of *hakhmei ha-mesorah* in every generation, but it is not attainable for most people. More significantly, this approach is not conducive to cultivating the equally compelling broader spiritual agenda that particularly characterizes halakhic life.

Finally, there is the normative "Avraham perspective" that we strive for, in which the event achieves its greatest impact precisely by being assimilated – though not diluted – into a broader and ultimately more ambitious and idealistic program of *avodat Hashem*. This way of experiencing Yom Kippur inspires and energizes the rest of the *mo'adim*, as well as every day of the year. Stripped of its impact and relevance to the rest of time and life, the Yom Kippur experience would be diminished.

Achieving this ideal experience of Yom Kippur requires several prerequisites. First is thoughtful preparation. If used properly, the seven days between Rosh ha-Shanah and Yom Kippur, comprising the *Aseret Yemei Teshuvah* – like the seven-day preparation period of the *Kohen Gadol* – provide that opportunity. Additionally, a successful Yom Kippur requires a sense of *zerizut* (alacrity), just like Avraham demonstrated at the *akeidah*.[28] We must face Yom Kippur suffused with the feeling that this constitutes a real opportunity. Experiencing the day with a spirit of burden, counting the hours until its conclusion, is inconsistent with this approach.[29] In the Torah, the mitzvah of "*ve-initem et nafshoteikhem*" is

28. Avraham's *zerizut* at the *akeidah* is exemplified most famously in his rising early and personally saddling his donkey; see *Bereishit* 22:3 and Rashi, ad loc. In several startling *midrashim*, *Hazal* state that Avraham was extremely reluctant to refrain from sacrificing Yitzhak even after receiving the initial command from the angel; see, for example, *Pesikta Rabbati* 40:6.

29. The theme of *tosefet Yom ha-Kippurim* hints at this point as well. See the chapter titled "*Tosefet Yom Kippur*: The Lasting Impact of a Singular Day."

formulated only as a positive command, not as an *issur*, and it is counted that way by R. Sa'adiah Gaon. The implication is clear: Fasting is not a burden, but an opportunity. One is punished severely for cavalierly squandering such an opportunity.

Teshuvah on Yom Kippur

Let us return to our point of origin. It is evident that Yom Kippur is unique, with its absolute spiritual focus and its emphasis on stark choices and spiritual loyalty. As such, it clearly constitutes a most propitious opportunity for *teshuvah*. As Rambam wrote, it is indeed the "*ketz mehilah u-selihah le-Yisrael.*" According to *Sefer ha-Hinukh*, squandering the opportunity of *teshuvah* in an environment that is so intensely conducive to introspection and spiritual advancement actually constitutes an act of commission, a *bitul aseh*. In this respect, the demand for *teshuvah* on Yom Kippur differs from all other times.

Rambam extends this perspective further when he formulates the proactive obligation of repentance (in contrast to the obligation of *viduy* that he speaks of elsewhere) only on this extraordinary day of intense spiritual focus. This is consistent with the unique, ambitious program of halakhic-spiritual self-definition that is the theme of Yom Kippur. At the same time, the decision of Rambam and *Sefer ha-Hinukh* to codify these Yom Kippur norms in the broader context of *teshuvah*, rather than in the framework of Yom Kippur itself, emerges as a truly profound testament to the relevance of this inimitable day. It highlights not only its enduring impact, but also the ultimate objective of the integration of *kulo la-Hashem* as the true foundation of a spiritually ambitious balanced life.

Chapter 17
The Custom of Immersion and the Theme of Purification on Yom ha-Kippurim

The Problematic Blessing of R. Sa'adiah Gaon

Shulhan Arukh codifies the prevalent custom to immerse in a *mikveh* on *erev* Yom Kippur.[1] The practice traces back to the *Ge'onim*; Rosh records that both R. Sa'adiah Gaon and R. Amram Gaon would purify themselves in a *mikveh* in preparation for the Day of Atonement.[2] Rosh further reports that R. Sa'adiah Gaon mandated a blessing upon emerging from the *mikveh*, a conclusion that troubled many of the *Rishonim* (including Rosh himself) and later the *Aharonim*:

ואמר רב עמרם טובל אדם בשבע שעות ומתפלל תפלת המנחה. ואמר רב סעדיה בעלייתו מלטבול מברך על הטבילה.

1. *Orah Hayim* 606:4.
2. Rosh, *Yoma* 8:24.

R. Amram said that one should immerse at the seventh hour and then pray the afternoon service. And R. Sa'adiah said that upon emerging from the *mikveh,* one should recite the blessing of "*al ha-tevilah*" (upon immersion).[3]

Rosh strongly objects to R. Sa'adiah Gaon's ruling, arguing that there is no support and not even a hint of this practice in the Talmud. Consequently it is equivalent to any other unsourced custom, which does not justify a blessing.[4]

Rosh precludes the possibility, evidently proposed by some, that the source for R. Sa'adiah Gaon's directive is R. Yitzhak's view that one is obligated to purify himself before a festival:

ואמר רבי יצחק: חייב אדם לטהר את עצמו ברגל, שנאמר "ובנבלתם לא תגעו".

R. Yitzhak said: One is obligated to purify himself at the time of the festival, as it is written, "You shall not touch their carcasses" (*Vayikra* 11:8; *Devarim* 14:8).[5]

Rosh argues that this law cannot justify R. Sa'adiah Gaon's position, because it is presently inapplicable. According to Rosh, one can fulfill

3. Generally speaking, one recites a blessing on a commandment before performing it; this is the well-known principle of "*kol ha-mitzvot mevarekh aleihen over la-asiyatan*" (see *Pesahim* 7b). However, the Talmud notes that immersion in a *mikveh* is an exception to the rule. Tosafot (ad loc., s.v. *al ha-tevilah*) record a dispute regarding whether the Talmud's exception refers specifically to the immersion of a convert, who cannot make the blessing before immersion because he is not yet Jewish, or to every immersion. This is a matter of dispute between *Shulhan Arukh* and Rema (*Yoreh Deah* 200:1).
4. The Talmud (*Sukkah* 44b) records that R. Elazar bar Tzadok would not recite a blessing when he would hit his *aravot* on the ground at the end of Sukkot, because he held the practice was only a *minhag nevi'im* (a custom of the prophets). Rosh argues that the unsourced custom of immersing in a *mikveh* on *erev* Yom Kippur would not even have the status of *minhag nevi'im,* let alone that of a full-fledged commandment.
5. *Rosh ha-Shanah* 16b.

R. Yitzhak's dictum only by accomplishing a comprehensive purification, but that would require ashes from the *parah adumah* (red heifer) to neutralize *tumat met* (ritual impurity conferred by exposure to a corpse). Since the current status quo is that of universal defilement without access to purifying ashes, R. Yitzhak's charge is presently unattainable. This *gemara* therefore cannot underpin R. Sa'adiah Gaon's *berakhah*.[6]

Rosh acknowledges that the custom to immerse on *erev* Yom Kippur is widespread and that its adherents claim a *semakh* (support) to this practice from a *midrash* that describes the Jews on Yom Kippur as being "*neki'im ke-malakhei ha-sharet* – pure like the ministering angels."[7] Nevertheless, Rosh firmly maintains that the practice is not obligatory, and hence does not warrant a blessing.

Sha'agat Aryeh confirms Rosh's rejection of R. Sa'adiah Gaon's blessing, but argues that it can be disputed on even more fundamental grounds.[8] He assumes that the reason for R. Yitzhak's obligation to purify oneself before the *regel* is to enable entering the Temple and discharging the unique *mitzvot* of the three *regalim* (Pesah, Shavu'ot, and Sukkot): *aliyah le-regel, hagigah,* and *simhah*.[9] Accordingly, the obligation to purify

---

6. Rosh briefly references and rejects another possible justification for R. Sa'adiah Gaon's position: immersing in a *mikveh* in order to remove *tumat keri* (defilement through seminal emission). Since nowadays we do not mandate immersion to purify from *keri* during the rest of the year, Rosh argues that there cannot be any obligation to immerse specifically before Yom Kippur, and a blessing therefore would still not be warranted.

   It should be noted that there are multiple reasons for a *ba'al keri* to immerse in a *mikveh*. The most basic is to purify himself from ritual impurity (*Vayikra* 15:16). Additionally, the Talmud (*Bava Kama* 82a) records that Ezra issued a decree that a *ba'al keri* must immerse before engaging in Torah study. However, elsewhere (*Berakhot* 22a), the Talmud quotes Zeiri's statement that Ezra's decree no longer applies. Regarding whether or not any remnant of Ezra's decree still applies, see Rambam, *Hilkhot Keri'at Shema* 4:8, and *Shulhan Arukh, Orah Hayim* 88:1.

7. The comparison to *malakhei ha-sharet* parallels the beginning of *siman* 24 in the Rosh, where he discusses a passage in *Pirkei de-Rabbi Eliezer* (45) that draws a more extensive comparison between the Jewish People on Yom Kippur and the ministering angels.

8. *Sha'agat Aryeh*, no. 67.

9. In the time of the *Mikdash*, every Jewish man had to perform these three special commandments on Pesah, Shavu'ot, and Sukkot. *Aliyah le-regel* is the obligation to

oneself should be inapplicable nowadays, since we cannot currently perform these obligations.[10] It should certainly be irrelevant to Yom Kippur, which mandates no such obligations whatsoever.

Sha'agat Aryeh writes that this understanding of R. Yitzhak's dictum emerges from Rambam's codification:

> כל ישראל מוזהרין להיות טהורים בכל רגל מפני שהם נכונים ליכנס במקדש ולאכול קדשים, וזה שנאמר בתורה ובנבלתם לא תגעו ברגל בלבד ואם נטמא אינו לוקה אבל בשאר ימות השנה אינו מוזהר.
>
> All Jews are obligated to be pure for each *regel*, because they should be ready to enter the Temple and eat from the sacrifices. And that which is written in the Torah, "And their carcasses you shall not touch" (*Vayikra* 11:8; *Devarim* 14:8), refers to the *regel* alone. If one became impure, he does not receive lashes. But on the other days of the year, he is not obligated [to be pure].[11]

Sha'agat Aryeh notes that Rambam clearly links this obligation to purify oneself with the special imperatives on the *regalim* to appear in the Temple and eat from the sacrifices. It appears to be exclusively a function of these commandments and should therefore be completely inapplicable to Yom Kippur.

Thus, Rosh and *Sha'agat Aryeh* together provide three reasons why the commandment to purify oneself before the *regel* should not apply in advance of Yom Kippur. First, Rosh argues that R. Yitzhak's requirement applies only if one can completely purify himself, which is

---

make a pilgrimage to the Temple, which must be accompanied by a special offering called the *olat re'iyah*. The *hagigah* is a special peace offering that was brought on these festivals. The commandment of *simhah* refers to rejoicing on the *regel*, which, in the times of the Temple, required the sacrifice of additional peace offerings commonly referred to as the *shalmei simhah*. See Rambam, *Hilkhot Hagigah* 1:1.

10. The obligation of *simhah* still applies today, although not in its original form of bringing sacrifices. There is a famous dispute between the *Rishonim* regarding whether the obligation nowadays is Biblical or Rabbinic; see Tosafot, *Mo'ed Katan* 14b, s.v. *aseh de-yahid*; Rambam, *Hilkhot Yom Tov* 6:17–18. However, this question does not affect the relevance of immersion to Yom Kippur nowadays.

11. *Hilkhot Tumat Okhlin* 16:10.

impossible nowadays. Second, *Sha'agat Aryeh* argues that it only applies on the three *regalim*, when one is mandated to appear in the *Mikdash*, not on Rosh ha-Shanah or Yom Kippur. Finally, *Sha'agat Aryeh* adds that the obligation to achieve ritual purity should apply only when the *Mikdash* is extant and we can actually enter and bring sacrifices.

Rambam's Approach to R. Yitzhak and Purity Year Round

In order to understand the perplexing position of R. Sa'adiah Gaon and address the challenges posed by Rosh and *Sha'agat Aryeh*, we must take a broader view of the halakhic significance of purity in general and its role on Yom Kippur in particular.

The optimal starting point for this analysis is Rambam's understanding of R. Yitzhak's charge to purify oneself before the *regel*. As we saw above, *Sha'agat Aryeh* asserts that this is a technical *halakhah* intended simply to enable the unique imperatives of the *regel* ("*hekhsher mitzvah*") inside the *Mikdash*. He marshals support from Rambam, who links this purification obligation to one's capacity to enter the *Mikdash* and bring the appropriate sacrifices. However, although *Sha'agat Aryeh*'s interpretation of Rambam is certainly plausible, it fails to explain several anomalies. A careful analysis of Rambam's codification of R. Yitzhak's ruling reveals a more fundamental conception of the role of purity.

First, if the obligation to be pure were truly entirely about preparation for the *regel*, we would expect Rambam to codify it in *Hilkhot Hagigah*, where he discusses those topics.[12] Instead, Rambam places it in *Hilkhot Tumat Okhlin*, where he organizes the laws of food-impurity.

It is particularly noteworthy that Rambam codifies this *halakhah* toward the end of *Hilkhot Tumat Okhlin*, where he discusses the religious value of ritual purity. While he generally dismisses the need to maintain a state of *taharah* except with respect to entering the *Mikdash* and partaking of the *korbanot*, *terumah*, and *ma'aser sheni*,[13] he formulates R. Yitzhak's requirement on the *regel* as an exception to this rule. Moreover,

12. Alternatively, we would expect to find it in *Hilkhot Yom Tov*, *Hilkhot Hametz u-Matzah*, or *Hilkhot Sukkah*.

13. *Hilkhot Tumat Okhlin* 16:8.

he concludes this section and the entire *Hilkhot Tumat Okhlin* by affirming and endorsing the spiritual benefits of purity practiced year round by *hasidim ha-rishonim*:

> אף על פי שמותר לאכול אוכלין טמאין ולשתות משקין טמאים, חסידים הראשונים היו אוכלין חולין בטהרה ונזהרין מן הטומאות כולן כל ימיהם, והן הנקראים 'פרושים'. ודבר זה קדושה יתירה היא ודרך חסידות שיהיה נבדל אדם ופורש משאר העם ולא יגע בהם ולא יאכל וישתה עמהם שהפרישות מביאה לידי טהרת הגוף ממעשים הרעים וטהרת הגוף מביאה לידי קדושת הנפש מן הדעות הרעות וקדושת הנפש גורמת להדמות בשכינה שנאמר: והתקדשתם והייתם קדושים כי קדוש אני ה' מקדשכם.
>
> Even though it is permissible to eat foods that are impure and drink liquids that are impure, the early pious ones (*hasidim ha-rishonim*) would eat all food in a state of purity and would avoid all impurities for all of their days. They are the ones called "Separated Ones" (*Perushim*). This practice is a matter of great sanctity, and it is the way of piety: to be separate from people at large, to hold oneself apart from them, not to touch them, nor eat and drink with them. For setting oneself apart leads to the purification of the body from wicked actions. Purifying one's body leads to sanctifying one's soul from wicked character traits. And the holiness of the soul causes one to resemble the divine presence, as it is stated, "And you shall make yourselves holy; and you shall be holy, because I, God, who makes you holy, am holy" (*Vayikra* 11:44).[14]

Rambam characterizes this spiritually rigorous lifestyle as a manifestation of both *kedushah yeteirah* and *derekh hasidut,* which ultimately produce the transcendent results of "*taharat ha-guf,*" "*kedushat ha-nefesh,*" and "*le-hidamot la-Shekhinah*" (*imitatio Dei*).

While there is certainly a strong pragmatic orientation in Rambam's initial presentation of *perishut* as insularity that protects from improper conduct and its ramifications, the general tone, and certainly

14. *Hilkhot Tumat Okhlin* 16:12.

the ultimate attainments, also convey an intrinsic value that transcends the effects facilitated by isolation. Furthermore, there are other indications throughout Rambam's writings that *taharah* is a valued and elevated status. Conceivably, it is not merely a technical requirement, but a core precondition for the aforementioned select group of halakhic experiences (i.e. entering *Mikdash,* partaking of *korbanot* etc.) precisely for this reason.[15]

Although Rambam's broader purview in this context does not preclude *Sha'agat Aryeh*'s practical view of R. Yitzhak's *halakhah,* it certainly may also suggest a more idealistic motif. Even in his record of that *halakhah,* Rambam eschews R. Yitzhak's formulation of an obligation to become ritually pure on the *regel* ("*hayav adam le-taher atzmo ba-*

15. See Rambam's peroration at the end of *Hilkhot Mikva'ot/Sefer Taharah,* where *tevilah* of *taharah* is depicted as analogous to *tevilah be-mei ha-da'at* and where the requirement of *kavanah,* proper intent, is associated with this lofty attainment as well. See my article "*Be-Inyan Mitzvat Tevilah ve-Taharah be-Mikveh u-Vema'ayan,*" *Kol Tzvi* 5 (2002), 11–39. See also *Hilkhot Mikva'ot* 1:8, where Rambam implies that *kavanah,* while it does not obstruct other *tevilot,* is a preferred or ideal adjunct even for *tevilat hullin.* See also the concluding paragraphs of Rambam's magisterial introduction to *Taharot* in his commentary on the Mishnah, where he depicts *taharah* as a ladder toward *ru'ah ha-kodesh* and invokes the same source ("*ha-perishah mevi'ah li-yedei…*") that he cites at the end of *Hilkhot Tumat Okhlin.*

At the same time, elsewhere in *Perush ha-Mishnayot* (*Taharot* 2:2), Rambam does articulate a fundamentally pragmatic explanation that focuses primarily on distancing from *amei ha-aretz.* R. Kapach notes that this formulation is unparalleled in Rambam's writings. Evidently, he did not perceive the passage in *Hilkhot Tumat Okhlin* in this purely instrumental way.

Moreover, we should note Rambam's double emphasis in *Hilkhot Tumat Okhlin,* referring to the attainment of "*kedushah yeteirah*" and "*derekh hasidut.*" It is conceivable that the pragmatic dimension and benefits of *perishut* – if that is what he truly intends – refer only to the latter. See also the usage of "*tovat ha-guf*" in *Hilkhot Teshuvah* 8:6 and elsewhere. Although Rambam in *Sefer ha-Mitzvot* (109) proclaims that there is no impetus or urgency to *taharah* absent *kodshim* and *kenisah la-Mikdash,* a view that reinforces a more pragmatic approach, see the contrast in *Sefer ha-Hinukh* (175), who takes issue with this and formulates the intrinsic stature and value of *taharah* in this context.

On the other hand, Rambam's own ruling on *tevilah bi-zeman ha-mitzvah,* a matter of controversy among commentators, may further support the idealistic approach. In any case, the absence of obligation or any explicit ideal or *kiyum* is not inconsistent with the conclusion that *taharah* constitutes a significant spiritual stature.

regel"). Instead, he curiously employs terminology that accentuates the urgency of being *tahor* at this time: "*muzharin le-heyot tehorim.*"[16] The more emphatic and negative term "*muzharin*" (warned) does not typically connote a *hekhsher mitzvah.*[17] Furthermore, the fact that Rambam conjoins the *kedushah yeteirah* and *derekh hasidut* value of consistently maintaining a state of purity with R. Yitzhak's view mandating purification during the *regel* may be instructive as to how Rambam perceives that *halakhah.*

Third, Rambam begins the *halakhah* noting that *all* Jews are advised to attain a pure status on the *regel.* This universal statement, an added emphasis of Rambam, seems to include even the many Jews who are exempt from the various *mitzvot* of the *regel.*[18] If they are not obligated to appear in the *Mikdash* and take part in the offerings, why are they obligated to be pure at this time?

Fourth, while even a cursory reading of Rambam reveals some connection between purity and the *Mikdash* obligations, a closer reading demonstrates that the connection is a subtle one. If, as *Sha'agat Aryeh*

---

16. Tosafot (*Hullin* 2b, s.v. *tamei be-hullin mai le-meimra*) famously take this a giant step further and argue that there is an actual prohibition to become impure through the ingestion of impure foods. Although Rambam clearly does not believe there is such a prohibition, he still asserts that there is spiritual value in avoiding this contamination.

17. It is significant that Rambam invokes the initial formulation that the *gemara* employed when it considered "*u-venivlatam lo tiga'u*" to be a year-round prohibition, a typical *lav*. The fact that Rambam retained this phraseology even as he codified the *gemara*'s far more restrictive conclusion regarding the *regalim*, which the *gemara* itself articulates simply as "*hayav adam le-taher atzmo ba-regel,*" supports our analysis. He placed this *regel* requirement at the culmination of *Hilkhot Tumat Okhlin* because it conceptually-legally constitutes an outlet for the aspiration of ritual purity as a personal standard of spirituality, somewhat of an echo of the original Talmudic thought.

    It is also noteworthy that although Rambam employs the language of "*muzharin*" and cites the verse upon which this law is based, he does not codify the requirement of ritual purity on the *regel* in his enumeration of the 613 *mitzvot* – not in *Sefer ha-Mizvot*, the *minyan ha-katzar*, or in the *koteret* to *Hilkhot Tumat Okhlin*. This supports either *Sha'agat Aryeh*'s view that this law is really a *hekhsher mitzvah* or the perspective that we will develop, according to which it is simply an application and outlet for the broader spiritual value of *taharah*.

18. See *Hilkhot Hagigah* 2:1, where Rambam lists all those exempt from the various commandments of the *regel*.

asserts, purification was indeed a mere preparatory step for appearing in the *Mikdash* and eating sacrifices, we would have expected Rambam to say:

> כל ישראל מוזהרין להיות טהורים בכל רגל כדי שיהיו נכונים ליכנס במקדש ולאכול קדשים...
>
> All Jews are obligated to be pure for each *regel in order to be* ready to enter the Temple and eat from the sacrifices...

Instead, Rambam uses the slightly different – but very significant – conjunction, "*mipnei she-heim,*" which focuses on the fact that they are in a state of purity in which it is appropriate to enter:

> כל ישראל מוזהרין להיות טהורים בכל רגל מפני שהם נכונים ליכנס במקדש ולאכול קדשים...
>
> All Jews are obligated to be pure for each *regel because they should be* ready to enter the Temple and eat from the sacrifices...[19]

Rambam's choice indicates that self-purification is not simply preparatory; rather, it is a state that defines one's spiritual persona on the *regel.* Being in a state of purity and readiness to appear in the *Mikdash* pertains not to *hekhsher mitzvah,* but rather to *kedushat ha-gavra* (sanctity of the individual). Rambam is not saying that one should purify himself merely in order to enter the *Mikdash* and eat sacrifices, but that achieving a state of purity – and concomitantly a state of readiness to enter the *Beit ha-Mikdash* and eat sacrifices – is in and of itself a great spiritual attainment, a higher level of *kedushat ha-gavra* that one must aspire to on the *regel.* Irrespective of whether or not one will, or is even obligated to, enter the *Mikdash,* there is intrinsic significance to achieving this state in which one is fit to enter the abode of God's divine presence.

---

19. "*Mipnei she-heim*" would literally translate as "because they are." Contextually, that does not make sense; I have therefore rendered it "because they should be."

This dimension of *kedushat ha-gavra* may be valuable all year round and is possibly an expression of "great sanctity" and "the way of piety." But during specific times of the year (i.e. the *regalim*), it rises from a mere value to an actual imperative.

This perspective toward purity resolves each of the anomalies in Rambam's presentation of this *halakhah*. The Rambam deliberately places this in *Hilkhot Tumat Okhlin* – and not in *Hilkhot Hagigah* or *Yom Tov* – because this law is not solely about preparing for the *regel*.[20]

Additionally, this explains why Rambam expands this advice to "*all* of Israel." If indeed there is spiritual value in attaining the *kedushat ha-gavra* expressed by the readiness to enter the Temple – even if one does not plan on actually entering – then it stands to reason that it should be sought by all, irrespective of the technical obligation to appear in the *Mikdash* on the *regel*.

Finally, we can now understand Rambam's strange formulation, "*mipnei she-heim nekhonim*," which conveys a necessary status of readiness, as opposed to a *hekhsher mitzvah*, which would have been conveyed by a more unambiguous "*kedei she-yiheyu*"[21]

---

20. This approach could also explain a perplexing comment of Meiri. In his commentary to *Rosh ha-Shanah* 16b (s.v. *ve-khen*), Meiri writes that one must purify himself "לאכול חוליו בטהרה," to eat his non-sanctified foods in a state of purity. At first glance, this appears to be the exact opposite of Rambam, who claims that the purpose of this requirement is specifically to eat sacrifices in a state of purity. Moreover, it is unclear why one would need to pursue a state of purity in order to eat non-sanctified food, which never requires a state of purity (according to most *Rishonim*; see n. 9 above). According to our approach, Meiri is actually in sync with Rambam's conceptual orientation, despite his different emphasis. Meiri, like Rambam in *Hilkhot Tumat Okhlin* 16:12, is conveying that there is general spiritual value in eating *hullin* in a state of purity; however, one is only obligated to do so on the *regel*.

21. One point still requires explanation: Why does Rambam rule there are no lashes for one who becomes impure before the *regel*, if this is indeed a full-fledged negative commandment derived from the verse "*u-venivlatam lo tiga'u*"? *Sha'agat Aryeh* marshals this as additional proof for his view that the entire imperative is merely a facilitation of the positive *Mikdash* obligations associated with the *regel*. According to our approach as well, this is not a stand-alone prohibition; as noted previously (n. ? above), it is not delineated in the 613 count. Attaining the state of purity, although it is couched negatively in the form of a warning to avoid defilement during this sanctified period, is in actuality a *kiyum*, a charge to elevate one's spiritual profile

Revisiting R. Yitzhak's Source

In truth, this approach toward purity coheres better with R. Yitzhak's original presentation. R. Yitzhak's source is the verse, "*u-venivlatam lo tiga'u* – you shall not touch their carcasses." Analyzing this verse, the Talmud proposes an expansive prohibition against defilement:

> תניא נמי הכי: "ובנבלתם לא תגעו", יכול יהו ישראל מוזהרין על מגע נבילה - תלמוד לומר (ויקרא כא) "אמר אל הכהנים בני אהרן" - בני אהרן מוזהרין, בני ישראל אין מוזהרין...אלא, מה תלמוד לומר "ובנבלתם לא תגעו"? ברגל.
>
> We have also learned this in a *beraita*: "You shall not touch their carcasses" – Perhaps all of Israel would be commanded not to touch the carcass of an animal? [This can't be so!] For the verse says, "Speak to the priests, the children of Aharon [and you shall tell them that they should not be defiled through contact with a human corpse.]" We see that the sons of Aharon are commanded, but not the rest of Israel.... What, then, does "You shall not touch their carcasses" teach? It must be referring to the *regel.*

R. Yitzhak's original source mandating purification before the *regel* is a verse that has nothing to do with the festivals; the verse of "*u-venivlatam lo tiga'u*" pertains to impurity in general. Indeed, the *beraita* initially suggests that all Jews should be forbidden from contacting animal carcasses and other defiling agents all year round. The *beraita* rejects this only because *Kohanim* are explicitly singled out in the commandment to avoid corpse-impurity, excluding the possibility that an even broader general prohibition applies to all Jews. However, the source itself clearly implies a general injunction, rather than one that merely facilitates proper observance of the *regel,* as the *beraita*'s radical suggestion clearly demonstrates.

---

on the *regel.* Because it is not essentially a *ma'aseh aveirah* or even a prohibition, notwithstanding Rambam's added emphasis of "*muzharin,*" but rather a spur to be in a state of purity, to rise to the spiritual demands and opportunities engendered by the *regel,* it does not incur lashes. Cf. Ramban, *Vayikra* 8:11, who proves from the lack of lashes that this entire law is Rabbinic and that the source attribution is merely an *asmakhta.*

It is compelling to conclude that R. Yitzhak understood that the broad spiritual value of maintaining a state of purity expressed in the unqualified "*u-venivlatam lo tiga'u*" is expressed specifically on the *regel*, a time in which we elevate our standards to a level that qualifies us to enter the *Mikdash* and partake of the sacrifices. While there is certainly no actual obligation to practice purity all year round – and, in fact, the rigor and demanding lifestyle required preclude this even as a recommended ideal for the masses – the theoretical ambition still resonates.

This perspective validates Rambam's choice of *Hilkhot Tumat Okhlin*, rather than *Hilkhot Hagigah* or *Yom Tov*, as the appropriate venue to codify R. Yitzhak's insight. His usage of the term "*muzharin*" further bolsters both the significance of the original language of the *gemara* and the *taharah*-centric nature of R. Yitzhak's conclusion. But regardless of whether this is the accurate reading of Rambam, it remains a valid explanation of the sources and is therefore a possible basis for R. Sa'adiah's practice.

Visiting One's Teacher on the *Regel*: A Similar Model

An analogous phenomenon, further reinforcing our analysis of Rambam, may be found in the immediately preceding statement of R. Yitzhak:

ואמר רבי יצחק: חייב אדם להקביל פני רבו ברגל.

R. Yitzhak says: One is obligated to greet his teacher on the *regel*.

There is a celebrated debate about the conceptual nature of this *halakhah*.[22] Once again, the central question is why this obligation, which seems general in nature, is confined to the *regel*. Significantly, Rambam does not place this imperative in *Hilkhot Yom Tov*, but rather in *Hilkhot Talmud Torah*, further exacerbating this enigma. Moreover, Rambam locates this obligation in a chapter that codifies the laws of honoring one's teacher, a ubiquitous charge, integrating it into a *halakhah* that includes general expressions of respect that apply at all times:

22. See, for example, *Noda bi-Yehudah Tinyana, Orah Hayim* 94; *Shu"t Divrei Yatziv, Orah Hayim* 248; *Tzitz Eliezer* 17:41:3; *Pahad Yitzhak, Iggerot u-Ketavim*, 20.

> וחייב לעמוד מפני רבו משיראנו מרחוק מלא עיניו עד שיתכסה ממנו ולא יראה קומתו ואח״כ ישב, וחייב אדם להקביל פני רבו ברגל.
>
> One is obligated to stand before his teacher from the moment he enters his sight until he can no longer be seen, and afterward he may sit. And one is obligated to greet his teacher on the *regel*.[23]

The equation between the constant requirement to stand in the presence of one's teacher, which certainly applies all year long, and the obligation to greet one's mentor specifically on the *regel* implies that the latter, while implemented restrictively in practice, also fulfills a broader mandate of *kevod rabbo* (honoring one's teacher). Although there is no strict halakhic requirement to interact with one's *rebbi* on a daily basis, any and every visit is a highly appropriate manifestation of *kevod rabbo*. Halakhah demands that we formally address this spiritual value on the *regalim,* a time of greater practical opportunity that also acutely accentuates the vital spiritual import of the *rebbi-talmid* relationship.[24] The ambience of the *mo'ed* promotes a sense of reflection that recalls the indispensable impact of the *rebbi* and his teachings upon one's general spiritual life, as well as his appreciation of the *mo'ed*.

R. Yitzhak's dictum to visit one's teacher on the *regel* thus conceptually mirrors his dictum to purify oneself before the *regel*. Each crystallizes a broader halakhic aspiration that rises to the level of obligation during the sanctified time of the festivals.[25]

---

23. *Hilkhot Talmud Torah* 5:7.
24. See *Penei Yehoshua, Rosh ha-Shanah* 16b, s.v. *ve-amar,* who suggests that this obligation is not a *mitzvat aseh she-hazeman grama* (time-bound positive mitzvah), and women should therefore be obligated as well: "על כרחך צ״ל דבכה״ג לא מיקרי מצות עשה שהזמן גרמא שמצד הסברא היה חייב להקביל פני רבו בכל שעה אלא א״א משום ביטול מלאכה – One must understand that this is not considered a positive time-bound commandment, because fundamentally, one is obligated to greet one's teacher all the time; it is simply impossible to do so, because doing so would impede one's livelihood."
25. An additional issue to evaluate in this context is the debate concerning *tevilah bizemanah mitzvah,* if there is a mitzvah to immerse to attain purity at the designated time, which is debated by the *Tanna'im* (see *Shabbat* 120b–121a; *Yoma* 8a; ibid. 88a; *Niddah* 30a). Rambam's view on this matter is disputed (see especially *Lehem*

Revisiting R. Sa'adiah's Ruling

Returning to the practice of purification prior to Yom Kippur, it is possible that R. Yitzhak held that the obligation to immerse is not exclusively reserved for the *regalim,* but applies to Yom Kippur as well. Indeed, if we conceptualize this obligation as the overt expression of the value of attaining purity as a form of *kedushat ha-gavra,* which generally lies dormant for practical reasons but finds normative expression during particularly sanctified moments of the year, Yom Kippur emerges as a most compelling candidate. After all, Yom Kippur itself provides an essential outlet for the value of *kulo la-Hashem* that generally permeates our lives in a more selective, balanced, and nuanced manner.[26] Achieving the rigorous criteria of ritual purity is certainly consistent with that motif.

It is noteworthy that many authorities expand R. Yitzhak's parallel mandate to visit one's teacher beyond the *regalim,* based on his prooftext, which implies that such interactions are anticipated also on Shabbat or Rosh Hodesh.[27] Although there is no statement of obligation, the Talmud, regarding the *issur* of *rehitzah* (washing) on Yom Kippur, refers matter-of-factly to such trips on Yom Kippur, which might affect the injunction against coming into contact with water on this day.[28] Likely, this phenomenon minimally establishes such excursions as a fulfillment of a mitzvah (*kiyum ha-mitzvah*), if not an absolute *hiyuv.*[29] Rambam

---

Mishneh, Hilkhot Yesodei ha-Torah 6:6). If Rambam adopts the position of *tevilah bi-zemanah mitzvah* at any level, that would indicate that there is internal value to entering a state of purity. Cf. *Sefer ha-Mitzvot, aseh* 109; *Sefer ha-Hinukh,* mitzvah 175.

26. See *Pesahim* 68b. Many of the essays in the Yom Kippur section of this volume elaborate on different dimensions of this theme. See, for example, the chapter "The Unique *Teshuvah* of Yom Kippur."

27. See, e.g., Rabbeinu Hananel, Ritva, *Turei Even, Rosh ha-Shanah* 16b.

28. *Yoma* 77b. This issue is also contingent on whether neutralizing the prohibition of *rehitzah* on Yom Kippur demands a formal mitzvah or simply requires that the contact is not gratuitous or *le-shem ta'anug* (for pleasure).

29. *Shulhan Arukh* describes it as a mitzvah in the context of *Hilkhot Shabbat* (*Orah Hayim* 301:4), but does not refer to it as such in the laws of Tishah be-Av (554:12). *Magen Avraham* (301:7) distinguishes between *regel,* when it is an obligation, and Shabbat, when there is no obligation but just a mitzvah. By extension, *Magen Avraham* likely treats Yom Kippur the same as Shabbat. *Bi'ur Halakhah* strongly disagrees with the *Magen Avraham.*

twice depicts the Yom Kippur journey to visit a *rebbi* as a "mitzvah," a formulation that is absent from the Talmudic passage, although he applies this classification broadly in this context, encompassing other laudable visitations as well – to a parent, scholar, or *beit midrash.*[30]

It is conceivable that R. Yitzhak's ruling concerning purification likewise extends beyond the *regalim* and includes Yom Kippur as well. The principle that a personal stature worthy of Temple entry is particularly appropriate on Yom Kippur may have been perceived as self-evident. R. Yitzhak required an independent source only to establish that this high bar of personal sanctity extends also to the *regalim,* which, relative to Yom Kippur, are less personally demanding and even less *Mikdash*-centric than the *avodah*-dominated *kedushat ha-yom* of Yom Kippur.

Indeed, it is noteworthy that Rosh, intensely critical of R. Sa'adiah's stance, did not object to the premise that R. Yitzhak's required state of purity extends to Yom Kippur. Unlike *Sha'agat Aryeh,* he rejected only the notion that R. Yitzhak's ruling could apply in a post-Temple era. At the same time, if R. Yitzhak's mandate is not the actual facilitation of *regalim* imperatives, but the aspiration to attain the personal spirit of purity appropriate to *kedushat ha-zeman,* Rosh's assumption that only absolute and comprehensive purity qualifies for R. Yitzhak's charge, and that is inaccessible in the absence of the *parah adumah,* is no longer absolutely compelling, providing a potential basis for R. Sa'adiah's blessing.

Purification as a Core Theme of Yom Kippur

With this analysis, we have sought to rehabilitate the suggestion that Rosh considers and subsequently rejects: that R. Yitzhak's dictum is the basis for the custom to immerse prior to Yom Kippur with a blessing. However, perhaps it is more likely that R. Sa'adiah's position stands independent of R. Yitzhak's statement, albeit based on the ideals we have examined. Even if this is exclusively a Yom Kippur phenomenon, it neither precludes nor is predicated upon our earlier analysis of R. Yitzhak. Perhaps the custom to immerse on *erev* Yom Kippur is an example of a

30. *Hilkhot Shevitat Asor* 3:6. *Maggid Mishneh,* in contrast to Rambam, restricts the *gemara*'s statement by employing the word "*ha-rotzeh,*" instead of "*ha-holekh,*" which may be a subtle way of indicating that it is not a *hiyuv.*

broader association between Yom Kippur and purity, which finds instantiations in many diverse aspects of Yom Kippur.

Yom Kippur's association with purification has strong roots in the Torah itself. First, in *Parashat Aharei Mot*, the Torah states that the special Yom Kippur goat that is offered inside the *Kodesh ha-Kodashim* purifies the Sanctuary and the incense altar:

> וכפר על הקדש מטמאת בני ישראל ומפשעיהם לכל חטאתם, וכן יעשה לאהל מועד השכן אתם בתוך טמאתם וכו׳ והזה עליו מן הדם באצבעו שבע פעמים, וטהרו וקדשו מטמאת בני ישראל.
>
> He shall bring atonement upon the Sanctuary for the impurities of the Israelites and for their transgressions, even all their sins; and so shall he do for the Tent of Meeting, which dwells with them amid their impurity.... He shall sprinkle from the blood upon [the altar] with his finger seven times, and he shall purify it and sanctify it from the impurities of the Israelites. (*Vayikra* 16:16, 19)

It is extraordinary that the focus of this offering – one of the most unique, elemental parts of the Yom Kippur service – is on the purification of the altar.

Second, toward the end of the passage, the Torah focuses on purity from our sins:

> כי ביום הזה יכפר עליכם לטהר אתכם; מכל חטאותיכם לפני ה׳ תטהרו.
>
> For on this day he shall provide atonement for you to purify you; from all your sins before God you shall be purified. (ibid. 16:30)

The cleansing-purging of our sins, the central purpose of Yom Kippur, is described as a purification. Moreover, purification is invoked twice in the verse, highlighting its centrality even more boldly. The Torah thus explicitly places purification at the very core of both the Yom Kippur service and the Yom Kippur atonement. Indeed, this verse assumed great significance as the embodiment of the *kedushat ha-yom* of Yom Kippur in the liturgy of this most crucial and remarkable day of the year.

In light of these Biblical sources, it is not surprising that we find themes of purity throughout the Yom Kippur liturgy. The prayers of Yom Kippur play a key role in our experience of the day, and its themes are thus particularly instructive about the nature of the day – and purity plays an outsized liturgical role.

In the *Amidah* of every Shabbat and festival, we request, "*Ve-taher libeinu le-ovdekha be-emet* – Purify our hearts to serve you in truth," but this theme enjoys unique importance on Rosh ha-Shanah and Yom Kippur. This prayer ordinarily appears in the middle of the preamble to the concluding blessing for the sanctity of the day. For example, on Shabbat, it is followed by "*ve-hanhileinu Hashem Elokeinu et yom ha-Shabbat ha-zeh.*" However, on Rosh ha-Shanah and Yom Kippur, there is no intervening thought; "*ve-taher libeinu*" transitions directly to the actual blessing, integrating it into the core expression of each day's main theme. On Rosh ha-Shanah, that theme is truth:

> וטהר לבנו לעבדך באמת כי אתה אלקים אמת ודברך אמת וקיים לעד. ברוך אתה ה'...
>
> Purify our hearts to serve You in truth. because You are the God of truth, and Your Word is true and everlasting. Blessed are You Hashem…

On Yom Kippur, that theme is forgiveness:

> וטהר לבנו לעבדך באמת כי אתה סלחן לישראל ומחלן לשבטי ישורון בכל דור ודור, ומבלעדיך אין לנו מלך מוחל וסולח אלא אתה. ברוך אתה ה' מלך מוחל וסולח...
>
> Purify our hearts to serve You in truth, because You are the Pardoner of Israel and the Forgiver of the tribes of Yeshurun in every generation, and we have no king, forgiver, and pardoner other than You. Blessed are you Hashem, King, forgiver, and pardoner...

Purity is thus elevated on Rosh ha-Shanah and Yom Kippur – each according to its unique focus – from a generic aspect of the liturgy to an expression of the essence of the day.

Purification and the Repentance of Yom Kippur

The idea that purification is a core theme of Yom Kippur finds striking expression in Rabbeinu Yonah's *Sha'arei Teshuvah*. In the second chapter, Rabbeinu Yonah surveys how various experiences – suffering, old age, Torah study, etc. – motivate repentance. In this context, he explores the impact of the Ten Days of Repentance between Rosh ha-Shanah and Yom Kippur and the prospect of the impending divine judgment as an effective catalyst for *teshuvah*. He then proceeds to assert that Yom Kippur is essentially different from other catalysts. It is not merely an auspicious opportunity for repentance, but constitutes a new and distinctive obligation as well, one that is anchored in the concept of *taharah*. Remarkably, his proof-text is the verse in *Aharei Mot* about purification:

> ומצות עשה מן התורה להעיר אדם את רוחו לחזור בתשובה ביום הכפורים, שנאמר "מכל חטאתיכם לפני ה' תטהרו".
>
> There is a positive Biblical commandment for man to arouse his spirit to return in repentance on Yom Kippur, as the verse states, "From all your sins before God you shall be purified."

According to Rabbeinu Yonah, the Torah's reference to purification on Yom Kippur actually reflects an independent commandment to repent on Yom Kippur, distinct from the general year-round commandment of *teshuvah*.

It is noteworthy that in Rabbeinu Yonah's creative exegesis, "*lifnei Hashem tit'haru*," typically rendered as a promise, is also perceived as an imperative. In any case, the fact that this distinct *teshuvah* obligation is formulated as "purification" dramatically highlights the extent to which purification is a defining theme of Yom Kippur, even as it likely refines the very character of this singular manifestation of *teshuvah*.

Importantly, the *mishnayot* of *Masekhet Yoma* conclude on a climactic note with the celebrated formulation of R. Akiva, who compares the repentance of Yom Kippur to purification by and in the presence of God:

> אמר רבי עקיבא אשריכם ישראל לפני מי אתם מיטהרין מי מטהר אתכם אביכם שבשמים שנאמר (יחזקאל לו:כה) וזרקתי עליכם מים טהורים וטהרתם ואומר (ירמיה יז:יג) מקוה ישראל ה׳ מה מקוה מטהר את הטמאים אף הקדוש ברוך הוא מטהר את ישראל.
>
> R. Akiva said: Praiseworthy are you Israel! Before whom have you become purified? Who purifies you? Your Father in heaven, as it is said, "I will sprinkle pure water upon you and you shall be purified" (*Yehezkel* 36:25), and it says, "The hope (*mikveh*) of Israel is God" (*Yirmiyahu* 17:13). Just as a *mikveh* purifies the impure, so too, the Holy One, blessed is He, purifies Israel.

The statement itself, as well as its strategic placement at the end of the tractate, strikingly exemplifies the importance of purification to the sanctity of Yom Kippur.

Furthermore, there is significance to R. Akiva's complex formulation. R. Akiva makes two statements – first that Israel is purified *before* God, and second that Israel is purified *by* God. However, the verses cited in the *mishnah* seem to address only the latter statement; there is no clear reference to Israel being purified "before God." Maharsha posits that the pivotal verse in *Aharei Mot* that culminates the *avodah* and crystallizes the essential character of Yom Kippur –"Before God you shall be purified" – is the source for R. Akiva's initial statement, "Before whom have you become purified?"

R. Akiva's double formulation is, in fact, unclear. What is gained by referring to God on Yom Kippur as both "Before whom have you become purified" and as "Who purifies you"? It may be that R. Akiva conveys the dialectical character of repentance-purity, which is later captured by the statement of Reish Lakish: "*Ha-ba l-taher misayin oto* – If one comes to purify himself, he is provided assistance."[31] The penitent must take the initiative, which, in turn, triggers divine assistance.

31. *Yoma* 38a; *Shabbat* 104a; *Avodah Zarah* 55a; *Menahot* 29b.

Rambam[32] and Ramban[33] disagree as to whether the "assistance" consists of the innate human capacity and proclivity to repent with which man has been endowed or if it refers to active divine intervention.[34] But in either case, the prominence of purity as a means of spiritual elevation and *teshuvah* on Yom Kippur is further reinforced. Thus, Yom Kippur's association with purity sheds light on the particular nature of the repentance that the day demands.[35]

---

32. *Hilkhot Teshuvah* 6:5.
33. Ramban, *Devarim* 30:6.
34. *Tosefot Yom Tov, Yoma,* ad loc., also links the two dimensions presented in the *mishnah* with Reish Lakish's formulation, albeit in a slightly different manner. With respect to the double formulation of R. Akiva, see *Tiferet Yisrael* and other commentators, who suggest alternative interpretations. Avudraham (*Seder Tefillot Yom Kippur*) also perceives an expanded role for the concept of "*Ha-ba l-taher misayin oto,*" commenting that the supplication, "יה"ר מלפניך ה' אלוקינו ואלוקי אבותינו שלא אחטא," is based on this principle.

    It is noteworthy that Rambam's concluding peroration of *Hilkhot Mikva'ot* and *Sefer Taharah* emphasizes "*tevilah be-mei ha-da'at,*" again accenting the attainment of ritual purity as a metaphor for spiritual transformation. In that context, Rambam employs language that evokes R. Akiva's insight and invokes the *pesukim* recorded in the *mishnah.*
35. Another intriguing example of the special status of *taharah* on Yom Kippur is found in the *halakhot* relating to the *se'ir la-azazel.* Even though the *azazel*-goat is flung off a cliff rather than slaughtered, the Talmud (*Yoma* 64a) rules that flinging it off the cliff on the same day that its mother is slaughtered would violate the Biblical injunction not to slaughter an animal and its mother on the same day. Although this injunction applies only to *shehitah* (slaughtering), the Talmud explains that concerning the *azazel*-goat, "*dehiyato la-tzuk zo hi shehitato*" – its being flung off the cliff constitutes its slaughter. Tosafot (ad loc., s.v. *dehiyato*) imply that being flung off the cliff serves as a form of *shehitah* for the purpose of preventing the carcass from receiving the impurity of *neveilah* (based on a similar Talmudic passage regarding the *eglah arufah, Zevahim* 70b). *Minhat Hinukh* (185:10) argues that the reason for this is that being flung off the cliff is, in this unique context, conceptualized as a form of *shehitah,* and it therefore takes on *shehitah*'s properties, including the circumvention of *neveilah* impurity. Following this line of reasoning to its conclusion, *Minhat Hinukh* even speculates if it would be permissible to eat the limbs of the dead goat.

    However, it is alternatively possible that the mysterious purification of the dead *azazel*-goat is another example of purity as a pervasive theme on Yom Kippur. Given the association between purification and atonement on Yom Kippur, it is possible that the atonement achieved by completing the process of flinging away the *azazel*-goat also purifies the goat itself.

In addition to R. Akiva's insight and Rabbeinu Yonah's seminal position, we can identify several facets of *taharah*-purity that parallel and are strongly associated with the repentance and atonement of Yom Kippur, setting it apart from repentance during the rest of the year.

First, *taharah* is a transformative process that demands meticulous preparation; it requires rigorous safeguards to ensure that the lofty goal is not subverted by a failure to neutralize obstacles or to sufficiently distance from the initial agents of impurity. A central idea in the laws of immersion is that "*tovel ve-sheretz be-yado*" (immersing while still clutching the impure item) impedes the attainment of *taharah*. One must first take care to confirm complete disassociation from the sources of impurity before immersing in the *mikveh*. Moreover, transition to a state of *taharah* requires the scrupulous elimination and avoidance of any *hatzitzah*. Any presence that significantly interposes between the *tamei* and the *mikveh* compromises or dilutes the comprehensive immersion experience.

Perhaps most important is the question of intent. The Talmud records a debate between R. Yohanan and Rav regarding whether or not ritual immersion requires active intent.[36] The majority of *Rishonim*, including Rambam,[37] rule like Rav, who maintains that intent is not required. However, Rav himself distinguishes between standard immersion and immersion that purifies one to partake in *kodshim*. For the purposes of that more ambitious form of purification, there is universal agreement that active intent is a necessary prerequisite for immersion.[38]

Each of the factors indispensable to *taharah* is symbolically essential to the experience of a Yom Kippur *taharah*-themed repentance as well. Like *taharah*, Yom Kippur demands meticulous preparation, scrupulous inspection and introspection, the rigorous neutralization of obstacles and distractions, and a thoughtful and focused approach.

---

36. *Hullin* 31a–31b. The relationship between this debate and the general question of whether *mitzvot* require intent is subject to dispute. See Ramban, ad loc., and *Milhamot Hashem, Rosh ha-Shanah* 28b in *dapei ha-Rif.*
37. *Hilkhot Mikva'ot* 1:8.
38. Interestingly, the commentary *Melekhet Shlomo* on the final *mishnah* in *Yoma* perceives the requirement of intent in the attainment of *taharah* as implicit in R. Akiva's double formulation.

The first three *mishnayot* in *Yoma* reflect both extraordinary precautions, beginning with the *Kohen Gadol*'s seven-day confinement, which aims to preclude contingencies that threaten to derail his qualification to preside over the *avodah*, as well as extensive preparation to facilitate this pivotal process. The inimitable repentance and atonement of Yom Kippur occur only in the aftermath of a dedicated Hodesh Elul, and especially within the framework of the *Aseret Yemei Teshuvah*. It is the culmination of an intricate progression that is deliberate and nuanced. Certainly the hallmark of Yom Kippur repentance is thoughtful introspection, an embrace of the motif of "*kulo la-Hashem*," and a commitment to consistent conduct and the unequivocal rejection of the agents of transgression. There is no tolerance for the equivalent of "*tovel ve-sheretz be-yado*" on this singular day of repentance-*taharah*.

The halakhic maximalism ("*kulo la-Hashem*") and exclusive spiritual orientation ("*ve-initem et nafshoteikhem*") that define this day of *taharah* preclude any metaphoric "*hatzitzah*" that would attenuate or disrupt the immersive "*tevilah be-mei ha-da'at* – immersion in an exclusive spiritual environment" experience.[39] Indeed, the concluding *mishnah* in *Yoma*, which underscores the *taharah* theme, also articulates the principle that repentance is denied those who fail to internalize its significance and who choose, instead, to cynically exploit the institutions of atonement to further their transgressions:

> האומר אחטא ואשוב אחטא ואשוב אין מספיקין בידו לעשות תשובה; אחטא ויום הכפורים מכפר אין יום הכפורים מכפר.
>
> One who says, "I will sin, and then repent, I will sin [again], and then repent," will not receive an opportunity to repent; [for one who says,] "I will sin, and Yom Kippur will atone," Yom Kippur will not atone.[40]

It is significant that the atonement of Yom Kippur is singled out, as its efficacy under circumstances of overt insincerity and flawed integrity

39. See Rambam, conclusion of *Sefer Taharah* (*Hilkhot Mikva'ot* 11:12).
40. *Yoma* 8:9.

is more emphatically and absolutely excluded ("*ein Yom ha-Kippurim mekhaper*") than in the case of typical *teshuvah* ("*ein maspikin be-yado la-asot teshuvah*"). It is likely that this, too, underscores the distinctive rigorous *taharah* dimension of Yom Kippur's *teshuvah*, which is fundamentally incompatible with inconsistency and compromised standards.[41]

The parallel between the concept of *taharah* and the repentance of Yom Kippur further extends to the comprehensive nature of both.

In sharp contrast to standard *teshuvah* obligations, which are triggered by specific transgressions and focused on neutralizing those infractions in order to repair one's spiritual record, the repentance imperative of Yom Kippur is dictated by the calendar, by the urgency of the impending divine judgment, by the aspiration to attain a pristine state of *taharah* in the presence of Hashem, and as a manifestation of "*kulo la-Hashem*." For this reason, it is conceivable that apart from also focusing on specific sins and failings, Yom Kippur holistically addresses all transgressions and, even more broadly, the comprehensive profile of the religious persona. This distinctive emphasis derives from and conforms to the *taharah* anchor of Yom Kippur atonement that we have analyzed.

A basic axiom of purification is that it must be all-encompassing. There is no such thing as partial purification; the individual must immerse completely. Moreover, one may not do so piecemeal, limb by limb, but rather must immerse all at once. It is unsurprising then that Yom Kippur similarly focuses on comprehensive repentance. The liturgical practice to enumerate an extensive, wide-ranging list of "*Al Het*" – many of which are broad value-flaws – is consistent with this emphasis. This formidable list of failings is typically incorporated into the confession (*viduy*) irrespective of one's personal culpability.

This more general orientation is further highlighted by the juxtaposition of two statements made by Rambam in *Hilkhot Teshuvah*. Rambam begins *Hilkhot Teshuvah* by introducing the obligation to confess one's sins when repenting. He presents a standard formulary

41. While the *mishnah* subtly distinguishes between Yom Kippur and standard *teshuvah*, as noted, many commentaries, including Rambam (*Hilkhot Teshuvah* 4:1), do equate them. See the chapter "The Relationship Between Yom Kippur and the Rest of the Year" for further analysis.

for that *viduy* that details the specific infraction that stimulates feelings of regret (*haratah*) and embarrassment (*bushah*) and that strengthens resolve to resist repeating the offense (*kabbalah le-haba*).[42] However, one chapter later, Rambam codifies the obligation to repent on Yom Kippur, and there he writes that a broad, generic confession suffices: "*Aval anahnu hatanu* – However, we have sinned."[43] The disparity itself is surprising; it is even more intriguing that Yom Kippur, the most pivotal day of repentance in the entire year, mandates only a minimalist confession.

The key to deciphering this mystery is appreciating that it is a derivative of Yom Kippur's comprehensive ambition. In the beginning of *Hilkhot Teshuvah,* addressing the standard theme of repentance, Rambam formulates a response to a particular sin that endangers one's relationship with Hashem. Yom Kippur's agenda, however, is not primarily focused on particular infractions, but on the attainment of purity, the transformation of the holistic religious persona. "However, we have sinned" is a general response, whose goal is not the piecemeal repair of a single sin or even a group of transgressions, but rather a broad indictment that demands a comprehensive reassessment of priorities and a rigorous spiritual immersion that will achieve purification.[44]

Appreciating the Custom of R. Sa'adiah Gaon

Given all the evidence we have surveyed, we can certainly appreciate why R. Sa'adiah Gaon deemed it appropriate and even compelling to recite a blessing upon immersing in a *mikveh* prior to Yom Kippur. Yom Kippur's association with purity is both deep and broad. While Rosh and *Sha'agat Aryeh* struggled to identify any source for R. Sa'adiah's position, focusing the discussion on R. Yitzhak's dictum in *Rosh ha-Shanah*

42. *Hilkhot Teshuvah* 1:1.

43. Ibid. 2:7–8.

44. In the chapter "*Teshuvah* and *Viduy*: The Ambitious Method of Coming Closer to Hashem" I suggest that the fact that Rambam formulates *teshuvah* (rather than *viduy* in context of *teshuvah*; see *Hilkhot Teshuvah* 1:1, 2:7) as an obligation only in conjunction with Yom Kippur is consistent with this perspective as well.

demanding purification before the *regalim*, it is conceivable that R. Sa'adiah perceived the need for *tevilah* with a blessing as implicit in the essential *kedushat ha-yom* of Yom Kippur, characterized by the Torah's assertion-promise (and, according to Rabbeinu Yonah, imperative) of "before God you shall be purified."

Chapter 18
Yom Kippur and Sukkot: Joy and Awe as Complementary Expressions of *Avodat Hashem*

The period of *teshuvah* and *yirah* (awe of God) that Rosh ha-Shanah ushers in appears to culminate dramatically with the blowing of the *shofar* at the conclusion of *Ne'ilah* on Yom Kippur. Sukkot, which follows, seems to constitute an entirely independent holiday with an orientation that contrasts sharply with that of the *Yamim Nora'im*. While Yom Kippur accentuates the imitation of angels (reflected in the custom to stand much of the day and to minimize sleep), self-abnegation (*innuy*), and other expressions of divine awe, Sukkot projects the theme of *simhah* (joy) and focuses on the physical dimension of divine service. Eating and sleeping in the *sukkah*, as well as the very principle of "*teshvu ke-ein taduru*" (dwelling in the *sukkah* similar to normal residence), which regulates much *sukkah*-related conduct, attest to this emphasis.[1]

The Parallel and Perplexing Biblical Treatments of Yom Kippur and Sukkot

However, a thorough analysis of the contrast between Yom Kippur and Sukkot reveals a surprising link between the two holidays, one that undoubtedly reflects a profound reciprocal relationship between them. There is an undeniable pattern of parallel expressions and anomalies that characterize the treatment of Yom Kippur and Sukkot, differentiating them from the other *hagim*. An examination of the verses in *Parashat Emor* that delineate all of the festivals illustrates this.

Both Yom Kippur (*Vayikra* 23:27) and Sukkot (*Vayikra* 23:39) are introduced with the word "*akh*," an exclusionary phrase:

> אך בעשור לחדש השביעי הזה יום הכיפורים הוא...אך בחמשה עשר יום לחדש השביעי באספכם את תבואת הארץ תחגו את חג ה׳ שבעת ימים.
>
> But (*akh*) on the tenth day of this seventh month, it shall be a day of atonemen.... But (*akh*) on the fifteenth day of the seventh month, when you are gathering the produce of the land, celebrate Hashem's holiday of seven days.

This usage of "*akh*" binds the two holidays together and establishes each as *sui generis* vis-à-vis the rest of the festivals. Although Rashi and Ramban minimize the specific significance of this expression by narrowing its application, Ibn Ezra and Sforno perceive it as being broadly emblematic of the unique character of these two holidays.

In addition, several commentators (particularly Netziv) note the Torah's emphasis of "*la-hodesh ha-shevi'i ha-zeh* – *this* seventh month" (23:27, 34) regarding both Yom Kippur and Sukkot. The extra word "*ha-zeh*" implies a connection – and probably a progression – between the three *mo'adim* of Tishrei.

1. See *Sukkah* 28b.

Although the term "*mikra kodesh*" is ubiquitous in *Parashat Emor* to signify the various *hagim*, the Torah applies it unusually only with respect to both Yom Kippur and Sukkot. Usually, "*mikra kodesh*" signifies a generic notion of Yom Tov as manifested by the *issur melakhah* (prohibition of labor) to which it is linked. However, in the context of Yom Kippur, "*mikra kodesh*" is disconnected from *issur melakhah* and is instead expressed by the singular features of "*ve-initem et nafshoteikhem*" (ibid. 23:27). In the second, more expansive, rendition of Sukkot in *Emor* (ibid. 23:39), the phrase "*mikra kodesh*" is omitted altogether. The pattern reinforces the impression that neither Yom Kippur nor Sukkot is a conventional *mo'ed*.

It is unusual for the Torah to explicate the reason for particular laws. The Torah does, however, elaborate on the background of two of Yom Kippur (ibid. 23:28) and Sukkot (ibid. 23:43):

> כל מלאכה לא תעשו בעצם היום הזה כי יום הכיפורים הוא לכפר עליכם לפני ה׳ אלוקיכם...למען ידעו דורותיכם כי בסוכות הושבתי את בני ישראל בהוציאי אותם מארץ מצרים אני ה׳ אלוקיכם.
>
> No work shall be done on that day, for it is a day of atonement to atone for you before Hashem your God.... So that the generations shall know that I placed *Bnei Yisrael* to dwell in booths when I took them out of Egypt; I am Hashem your God.

Furthermore, the Torah depicts both of these unique festivals as periods in which the Jewish People stand before the divine presence (ibid. 23:28, 40). Again, Yom Kippur and Sukkot are linked by their parallel anomalous treatment. The fact that these parallels also acknowledge the contrast between and the juxtaposition of the two holidays – Yom Kippur as a day of atonement and Sukkot as a day of joy – does not diminish the connection. However, it does deepen the mystery: What does the Torah intend to convey by its parallel-opposite presentation of these two *mo'adim*?

Simhah and *Yirah*: Compatible and Incongruous Methods of *Avodat Hashem*

We may better illuminate the intriguing relationship between Yom Kippur and Sukkot by examining the relationship of their underlying motifs: *simhah* and *yirah*.

In *Sefer Devarim*, we find references to both "*avodah be-yirah*" as well as "*avodah be-simhah u-vetuv levav.*" In *Tehillim*, we encounter contrasting formulations, with one verse (2:11) commanding, "Serve God with fear and rejoice with trembling," and another, "Serve God with joy, come before Him with song" (100:2). The *midrash* notes these dueling formulas of service:

> אם בשמחה איך ביראה; ואם ביראה איך בשמחה?...בשמחה יכול שלא ביראה ת"ל ביראה. אמר ר' אחא עבדו את ה' ביראה בעולם הזה, כדי שתגיע לעולם הבא בשמחה.
>
> If with happiness, how with fear? If with fear, how with happiness?... [Rather,] with joy – could it be meant without fear? It was taught: With fear. R. Aha said, serve God with fear in this world, to gain entry to the World to Come with happiness.[2]

One perspective articulated by this *midrash* perceives the relationship as one of short-term method (*yirah*) and long-term result (*simhah*). Another view depicts *yirah* and *simhah* as competing but equally valid approaches to *avodat Hashem*. However, there is a third integrative approach, which may also highlight the relationship between Yom Kippur and Sukkot: *Avodah be-yirah* and *be-simhah* are two sides of a single coin, each necessary for a comprehensive and holistic *avodat Hashem*. One absent the other would be deficient, possibly even destructive.

The integration of *ahavat* and *yirat Hashem* is rooted in the earliest paradigm in our history. Avraham Avinu embodies each of these qualities. He is described as "*Avraham ohavi* – Avraham who loves Me" (*Yeshayahu* 41:8),[3] but at the same time, the *akeidah* makes clear "*ki*

2. *Midrash Tehillim* 100:3.
3. This reading is based on Rambam, *Hilkhot Teshuvah* 10:3. Rashi and Radak (*Yeshayahu*

yerei Elokim atah – that you are a man who fears God" (*Bereishit* 22:12). Rambam integrates these themes as one, synthesizing the obligations to both love Hashem and serve Him out of fear.[4] For Rambam, who details the paths through which to attain both, the concepts of love and fear of Hashem are harmonized, not contradictory.

This complementary perspective of *avodat Hashem mei-ahavah* and *mi-yirah* is emphasized by *Hazal*. Thus, for example, the *gemara* resolves an apparent discrepancy in a *pasuk* by articulating this principle:

> וגילו ברעדה - במקום גילה שם תהא רעדה.
>
> "And rejoice with trembling" (*Tehillim* 2:11) – In the place of rejoicing there should be trembling.[5]

Elsewhere, King David's outlook is elaborated:

> אמר דוד המלך יראתי מתוך שמחתי. ושמחתי מתוך יראתי. ואהבתי על כולם.
>
> King David said: My fear is from my joy, and my joy is from my fear, and my love is above all.[6]

In connecting *avodah mei-ahavah* and *mi-yirah*, *Hazal* identify the two modes of worship as fused and inseparable, despite their differences.

The function of *yirah* is evident. *Yirah* is the prerequisite for wisdom and Torah study and provides the necessary humility and motivation that are absolutely necessary for spiritual growth: "The beginning of knowledge is fear of God" (*Tehillim* 111:10). It is unsurprising that the Torah emphatically projects the centrality of *yirah*:

41:8) read "*Avraham ohavi*" as Hashem describing His love for Avraham. See also Rambam, *Sefer ha-Mitzvot*, 3.

4. *Hilkhot Yesodei ha-Torah* 2:1–2.
5. *Berakhot* 30b.
6. *Tanna de-Vei Eliyahu Rabbah* 3.

ועתה ישראל מה ה׳ אלוקיך שאל מעמך כי אם ליראה את ה׳ אלקיך...

> And now, Yisrael, what does Hashem your God ask of you, but only to fear the Lord your God. (*Devarim* 10:12)

Although the role of *simhah* is less obvious, it is equally crucial, even indispensable, in religious observance and growth. Aside from *simhah*'s prominence on Yom Tov, it is also a prerequisite for prophecy:

אין שכינה שורה לא מתוך עצבות אלא מתוך דבר שמחה של מצוה.

> The *Shekhinah* cannot rest within sadness, but rather can only rest within the happiness of a mitzvah.[7]

Talmud Torah, the apex and foundation of religious development ("*keneged kulam*"), is particularly associated with a state of *simhah,* based on the verse "The statutes of Hashem are straight and gladden the heart" (*Tehillim* 19:9). R. Avraham min ha-Har posits that the principle that mitzvah performance is not deemed a personally pleasurable act ("*mitzvot lav le-he'enot nitnu*") that would, for example, violate the prohibition of *issurei hana'ah* does not apply to Torah study, as it is inherently suffused with spiritual pleasure.[8] R. Aharon ha-Kohen of Lunel relates the first of the *birkhot nissu'in* (blessings upon marriage), "*she-hakol bara li-khvodo,*" which focuses on the very purpose of creation, with the concluding *berakhah,* "*asher bara sasson ve-simhah,*" devoted to the creation of joy and happiness. He explains that the attainment of spiritual joy – *avodah* by means of *simhah* – constitutes a significant spiritual achievement, because genuine happiness builds a bridge to Hashem.[9]

Rambam concludes *Hilkhot Lulav* with a stirring peroration about the importance of *avodah be-simhah*:

7. *Shabbat* 30b.
8. R. Avraham min ha-Har, *Nedarim* 48a.
9. *Orhot Hayim, Hilkhot Nissu'in.*

השמחה שישמח אדם בעשיית המצוה ובאהבת הא-ל שצוה בהן עבודה גדולה היא. וכל המונע עצמו משמחה זו ראוי להפרע ממנו שנאמר תחת אשר לא עבדת את ה׳ אלוקיך בשמחה ובטוב לבב...ואין הגדולה והכבוד אלא לשמוח לפני ה׳ שנאמר והמלך דוד מפזז ומכרכר לפני ה׳.

> The happiness one should feel with the performance of a mitzvah and love of God who commanded us to perform service is a very great thing. Anyone who refrains from partaking in this happiness is liable to suffer for it, as the *pasuk* states, "For you did not serve Hashem your God with happiness and good heart."... And grandeur and honor is meant only to rejoice before Hashem, as the *pasuk* states, "King David danced vigorously before God."[10]

The demands of Yom Tov ordinarily represent a balance between different values and moods. We generally adopt the balanced approach of R. Yehoshua, "*hetzyo la-Hashem ve-hetzyo lakhem.*"[11] Occasionally, however, Halakhah demands that we accentuate one of the extreme manifestations of *avodat Hashem,* such as *simhah* or *yirah,* in order to address particular challenges. In this manner, it is possible to further cultivate and refine our dedication to each independent *avodah* value. The parallel-contrast of Yom Kippur-Sukkot facilitates greater commitment to each of the respective values of *yirah* and *simhah.* Both Yom Kippur and Sukkot transcend and transform the routine *mikra kodesh,* fostering a more intense expression of "*lifnei Hashem Elokeikhem.*"

Sukkot's Unique Expression of Mitzvah Observance

There appears to be a special emphasis on the role of *mitzvot* as the premium expression of *avodat Hashem* on Sukkot. In addition to the exceptional fact that there are two distinct *mitzvot* on this *hag,* it is noteworthy that each of these *mitzvot* – *lulav* and *sukkah* – particularly accentuates the concept of the special stature of *hekhsher mitzvah* (the steps needed to prepare for and enable a mitzvah), *heftza shel mitzvah* (an object used in *mitzvot*), and *hiddur mitzvah* (beautification of *mitzvot*).

---

10. *Hilkhot Lulav* 8:15.
11. *Pesahim* 68b.

Sefer ha-Hinukh formulates this emphasis without elaborating its foundation regarding Sukkot.[12] However, the halakhic perspective on the significance of building the *sukkah*[13] and regarding the integration of the diverse *minim* exemplifies this point. The concept of *huktzah le-mitzvato,* which determines that the *sukkah* materials can be utilized exclusively for the mitzvah, and the parallel concept with respect to the use of the four *minim,* project the prominence of mitzvah objects.[14] The special role of "*hadar,*" the esthetic quality of the *etrog* and other *minim,* and the status of *sukkah* decorations ("*noy sukkah*") constitute a definite motif of *hibuv ha-mitzvot* during Sukkot. Clearly, Sukkot's relationship with mitzvah observance is unique.

Yom Kippur, the embodiment of *avodah mi-yirah,* overrules many Yom Tov norms, while Sukkot, suffused with added *simhah,* intensifies those standard manifestations. Rambam explains that *Hallel* is omitted on Rosh ha-Shanah and Yom Kippur because of a mitigation of *simhah* in favor of *yirah.*[15] In fact, according to Rambam, one should even recite *Tahanun* on Yom Kippur.[16] On Sukkot, in contrast, we encounter more than the standard obligation of *Hallel* on Yom Tov. Unlike on Pesah, every day of Sukkot generates a full *Hallel* obligation,[17] and Ramban considers the possibility that recitation of *Hallel* on Sukkot may be a Biblical obligation.[18] The *gemara* links *Hallel* on Sukkot with the *lulav*

---

12. *Sefer ha-Hinukh,* mitzvah 325.
13. See *Ketubot* 86a; *Shevu'ot* 29a; *Sukkah* 46a; Tosafot, ad loc., s.v. *ha-oseh* and s.v. *nikhnas.* See also Netziv in *Ha'amek Davar,* and especially in his commentary on the *She'iltot.* I address this topic more extensively in my article "*Be-Inyan Mitzvat Sukkah,*" *Beit Yitzhak* 30 (1998), 285–297.
14. *Sukka* 9a.
15. *Hilkhot Hanukah* 3:6 and *Perush ha-Mishnayot, Rosh ha-Shanah* 4:7, based on *Arakhin* 10b.
16. End of *Hilkhot Tefillah.*
17. In *Arakhin* 10b, this is attributed to the differences in the configuration of the *korbanot.* The Netziv (*Ha'amek Davar* on *Emor, Pinehas,* and *Re'eh*) views this factor as representative of broader differences between the holidays, as does R. Soloveitchik. See also Yerushalmi *Sukkah* 5:1, where the factor of *lulav* in the *Mikdash* is cited.
18. *Sefer ha-Mitzvot, shoresh* 1, based on the formulation of "*u-semakhtem lifnei Hashem Elokeichem shivat yamim*" (*Vayikra* 23:40).

obligation,[19] and Rambam identifies *Hallel* as the appropriate time for *mitzvat* and *birkat lulav*.[20]

Indeed, while Rambam characterizes Rosh ha-Shanah and Yom Kippur as being deficient in *simhah*, "*ein bahem simhah yeteirah*,"[21] he depicts Sukkot as a festival of excessive *simhah*:

> אף על פי שכל המועדות מצוה לשמוח בהן בחג הסוכות היתה שם במקדש שמחה יתירה שנאמר ושמחתם לפני ה׳ אלוקיכם שבעת ימים.
>
> Even though on all the holidays there is a mitzvah to rejoice, on Sukkot there was an added joy in the *Beit ha-Mikdash*, as it says, "And you shall rejoice before the Lord your God seven days."[22]

Yom Kippur projects the centrality of the *innuyim* and a posture of *kulo la-Hashem*, completely for God, while the laws of Sukkot make allowances for human comfort to such an extent that *mitzta'er patur min ha-sukka* – one who is uncomfortable is exempt from sitting in the *sukkah*.

Simhah on Yom Kippur and Seriousness on Sukkot

The parallel-contrast between Yom Kippur and Sukkot establishes not only the common need to rigorously emphasize each of the independent values of *yirah* and *simhah*, but also highlights their subtle yet crucial interplay. Neither unbridled *innuy-yirah* nor unfocused *Hallel-simhah* constitute ideal expressions of *avodat Hashem*. Without precise halakhic structure, these principles can be easily abused and corrupted.

Thus, like other *mo'adim*, Yom Kippur conflicts with and cancels *aveilut* (mourning practices). Notwithstanding its *innuy-yirah* focus, Yom Kippur's life-affirming and optimistic underpinnings are inconsistent with extreme depression and categorical loss. Indeed, according to many halakhic sources, there are numerous expressions of joy and opportunity even on Yom Kippur, the most solemn of days. *Sefer*

19. *Pesahim* 117a.
20. *Hilkhot Lulav* 7:10.
21. *Hilkhot Hanukah* 3:6.
22. *Hilkhot Lulav* 8:12.

ha-Hinukh stresses this theme in his discussion of the mitzvah.[23] Rabbeinu Yehonatan explains that *simhah* is the basis for the recitation of *birkat ha-zeman* on Yom Kippur.[24]

In parallel, *simhat Yom Tov* and even *simhat Sukkot* require proper perspective. Rambam distinguishes between authentic *simhat Yom Tov,* on the one hand, and gluttony and frivolity, on the other; the latter would amount to a corruption of *simhah.*[25] At the conclusion of *Hilkhot Lulav,* Rambam reiterates that the primary participants in the joyous *simhat beit ha-sho'evah* celebration that reflects the "*simhah yeteirah*" theme of Sukkot should be the scholars and religious leaders, who are acutely sensitive to genuine, spiritually focused *simhah.*[26]

Another unique facet of Sukkot is that it magnificently embodies the necessary temporal transition from *kabbalat ol malkhut Shamayim* (acceptance of the yoke of Heaven) to *kabbalat ol mitzvot* (acceptance of the yoke of the *mitzvot*). The *Yamim Nora'im* – particularly Yom Kippur – reaffirm the indispensable principle of *kabbalat ol malkhut Shamayim* in many of its facets. Indeed, the *Ne'ilah* prayer concludes with a ringing articulation of the *Shema* and *yihud Hashem* (declaration of God's unity). But as the *mishnah* notes, this foundational but abstract commitment always demands the follow-up of *kabbalat ol mitzvot,* the ideal vehicle for *avodat Hashem.*[27] In this respect, Sukkot, with its dual *mitzvot,* each of which particularly embodies the broader perspective and parameters of *mitzvot* as the ideal avenue to *avodat Hashem,* perfectly follows, reinforces, and completes the singular holiday cycle of "*ha-hodesh ha-shevi'i ha-zeh,*" the foundation for Torah life year round.

A Singular Juxtaposition

In light of these considerations, we may better appreciate the special link between these two unusual *mo'adim.* Yom Kippur anticipates and paves the way for Sukkot, and Sukkot is partially defined by taking place in

23. *Sefer ha-Hinukh,* mitzvah 313.
24. Rabbeinu Yehonatan, *Eiruvin* 40a.
25. *Hilkhot Yom Tov* 6:17–18.
26. *Hilkhot Lulav* 8:14.
27. *Berakhot* 13a.

the aftermath of Yom Kippur. Is it a coincidence that the shortest time between any two *mo'adim* separates the extreme manifestations of *yirah* and *simhah*?

Beit Yosef records that *Tahanun* is not recited between Yom Kippur and Sukkot, attributing this to the fact that the *Beit ha-Mikdash* was established in this period.[28] However, *Arukh ha-Shulhan* suggests that *motza'ei* Yom Kippur initiates a period of "*yemei simhah,*" days of joy.[29] It is conceivable that this period, the bridge between *yirah* and *simhah,* was also a particularly propitious time to initiate the *Mikdash,* characterized by its own exceptional blend and integration of *yirah* and *simhah.*

The *Rishonim* speculate why Sukkot is not celebrated during Nissan, in the aftermath of *yetzi'at Mitzrayim,* which it commemorates. Ramban[30] and *Tur*[31] posit that climate conditions during Nissan would have obscured the obligatory and spiritual character of the mitzvah of *sukkah*. However, *Tzeror ha-Mor* and *Arukh ha-Shulhan* propose that the Torah intentionally delayed the holiday of Sukkot in order to integrate its celebration with that of Yom Kippur. They explain that having successfully confronted the challenges of *din* (justice) by attaining atonement, *Bnei Yisrael* achieved a level of completeness hitherto unattained, even at *yetzi'at Mitzrayim* and *matan Torah*. *Tzeror ha-Mor* argues that these achievements are symbolized by the *mitzvot* of *lulav* – an expression of victory and success – and *sukkah* – underscoring the transition from anxiety, even panic, to total self-confidence in God's *hashgahah*. These establish Sukkot as the premier *mo'ed,* worthy of a double treatment in *Parashat Emor* and of unprecedented daily *Hallel* throughout the entire *hag*.[32]

Further evidence of the interplay between Yom Kippur and Sukkot is the custom to continue certain practices of Elul and Yom Kippur on Sukkot. According to the Zohar and many *Rishonim,* we revisit the

---

28. *Beit Yosef, Orah Hayim* 131.
29. *Arukh ha-Shulhan* 624:7.
30. Ramban, *Vayikra* 23:43.
31. *Tur,* beginning of *Hilkhot Sukkah*.
32. *Tzeror ha-Mor, Vayikra* 23:24.

themes of Yom Kippur on the last day of Sukkot, *Hoshana Rabbah*. This accounts for many of the special practices and *tefillot* on this day. It further reinforces the notion that Sukkot and Yom Kippur – and by extension the respective themes of *simhah* and *yirah* that they embody – are intended to be mutually enhancing. Additionally, we continue to recite the chapter of "*Le-David Hashem ori ve-yishi*" (*Tehillim* 27) until the end of Sukkot.[33] The simple yet powerful themes of "*shivti be-veit Hashem*" and "*kaveh el Hashem*" stand at the core of both *avodah mei-ahavah* and *avodah mi-yirah*. Indeed, they articulate the spiritual goal that unites and unifies these seemingly disparate methods.

Shulhan Arukh formulates the obligation to begin the building of the *sukkah* on *motza'ei* Yom Kippur twice: once in the last *halakhah* in *Hilkhot Yom Kippur* and again in the very first *halakhah* of *Hilkhot Sukkah*, which immediately follows *Hilkhot Yom Kippur*. While the commentators labor to distinguish between these seemingly identical contiguous *halakhot*, it remains puzzling that this theme, even given its multiple nuances, was not codified in a single location. In light of our analysis of the intricate, mutually enhancing relationship between Yom Kippur and Sukkot, however, we may now appreciate the precision of this classification. *Shulhan Arukh* subtly conveys two interrelated perspectives. The building of the *sukkah*, crystallizing the ambition "*u-semahtem lifnei Hashem*," is a fitting climax to and transition from Yom Kippur's *avodah mi-yirah*, even as the afterglow of Yom Kippur's *yirah* and the charge and promise of "*lifnei Hashem tit'haru*" constitutes the perfect framework to initiate a period of intense *avodah be-simhah*.

With this understanding, illuminated through the many examples presented, the nuanced interplay between Yom Kippur and Sukkot can be understood in a clearer light. Highlighted by their idiosyncrasies and unique natures, both holidays present ideals necessary for successful *avodat Hashem*. The themes of *yirah* and *simhah* symbolize opportunities to serve Hashem with one's entire being, albeit in opposite yet parallel manners, and the obligations, *mitzvot*, and restrictions of Yom Kippur

33. For further explanation of this psalm, see the chapter "*Le-David* and *Teshuvah*: Achieving Clarity of Purpose."

and Sukkot emphasize their practical applications. The juxtaposition of these landmark *mo'adim* provides guidance in the most profound and impactful methods of *avodat Hashem*.

Source Index

Tanakh

Mishnah

Midrash Halakha

Other Writings of *Hazal*

Talmud Bavli

Rishonim

Works of Rabbi Joseph B. Soloveitchik

Works of Rabbi Michael Rosensweig

Other Works

Subject Index

The fonts used in this book are from the Arno family

Maggid Books
The best of contemporary Jewish thought from
Koren Publishers Jerusalem Ltd.